Shakespeare and Elizabeth

Shakespeare

and Elizabeth

THE MEETING OF TWO MYTHS

Helen Hackett

PRINCETON UNIVERSITY PRESS *Princeton and Oxford*

Published by Princeton University Press, 41 William Street, Princeton, New Jersey 08540
In the United Kingdom: Princeton University Press, 6 Oxford Street, Woodstock, Oxfordshire
OX20 1TW

Library of Congress Cataloging-in-Publication Data
Hackett, Helen.
Shakespeare and Elizabeth : the meeting of two myths / Helen Hackett.
p. cm.
Includes bibliographical references and index.
ISBN 978-0-691-12806-1 (cloth : alk. paper) 1. Shakespeare, William, 1564–1616—In literature. 2. Shakespeare, William, 1564–1616—Contemporaries. 3. Shakespeare, William, 1564–1616—Relations with literary patrons. 4. Shakespeare, William, 1564–1616—Influence. 5. Elizabeth I, Queen of England, 1533–1603—In literature. 6. Elizabeth I, Queen of England, 1533–1603—Contemporaries. 7. Elizabeth I, Queen of England, 1533–1603—Relations with authors. 8. Elizabeth I, Queen of England, 1533–1603—Influence. 9. English literature—History and criticism. 10. American literature—History and criticism. I. Title.
PR2911.H33 2009
822.3′3—dc22 2008018419

British Library Cataloging-in-Publication Data is available

This book has been composed in Centaur
Printed on acid-free paper. ∞

press.princeton.edu

Printed in the United States of America

10 9 8 7 6 5 4 3 2 1

For Eddie and Marina

with love

CONTENTS

ILLUSTRATIONS

ACKNOWLEDGMENTS

I am very grateful to Katherine Duncan-Jones and Henry Woudhuysen for many kinds of support and advice over many years.

At Princeton University Press, I would like to thank Hanne Winarsky, for her patience, sage guidance, and commitment to this book, and Ellen Foos for her common sense and cordiality. Victoria Wilson-Schwartz was an outstanding copy-editor.

Thanks are due to the anonymous publishers' readers for their insightful comments, from which the book benefited greatly. I am also grateful to audiences at the University College London English Department Staff-Graduate Seminar and the Shakespeare Institute in Stratford-upon-Avon.

The staff and students of UCL English Department are a constant source of intellectual companionship and stimulation. Thank you to everyone who has discussed this book with me and expressed interest in it. In particular, Kathryn Metzenthin and Anita Garfoot have helped the project in many ways. I am also grateful to the department for two periods of research leave.

I would like to thank the staff of the British Library, UCL Library (especially John Allen), the University of London Senate House Library, and the British Film Institute. UCL English Department, UCL Arts Faculty Dean's Research Fund, and Princeton University Press kindly helped with the costs of securing illustrations. Staff of the various archives where illustrations were housed, as detailed in the captions, were gracious and efficient in their assistance. Mary Hinkley of UCL Media Services helped with digital imaging.

Bob Armstrong, Gwynneth Knowles, Lillian Schwartz, and Lady Sally Vinelott made generous gifts and loans of illustrative and research materials. Rosemary Ashton and Annette Schäffler kindly helped with translation from German.

Rosalyn Alexander, Alison Light, John Morton, Kate Rumbold, and John Sutherland made timely and productive suggestions. A number of valued friends at the Cavendish School, Camden Town, and Westminster Cathedral Choir School showed generous interest in the book's progress and kept my spirits up.

Fortis Green Nursery, Fortis Green Kids' Club, Carole Donnelly, and many kind friends have given invaluable help with childcare, while Birute Gelumbauskiene has been indispensable in keeping the domestic side of life under control; I am profoundly aware that without all their hard work this book would never have come into being. Thank you too to Richard Feesey, Noelle Griffith, and their sons Ned and Huw for their hospitality in North Wales, where significant portions of the book were produced.

Paul Cobb and Jeri McIntosh generously provided computer equipment as well as much general encouragement. I have also been cheered on by the late Mrs. Hannah Rooke, Mrs. Kathleen Taylor, Tony and Mary Hackett, and more Hacketts too numerous to name but no less appreciated.

I am sincerely grateful to Eddie and Marina Hackett for putting up with this book for an unduly long time, and for their resourcefulness in finding other things to do when it kept me away from them. This book is for them. As for Steve Hackett, as ever I find it impossible to express in words my gratitude for everything he has done.

The book's remaining deficiencies are, of course, entirely my own responsibility.

A NOTE ON THE TEXT

I/j and *u/v* spellings have been modernized and contractions have been expanded, except for examples of their purposeful use in forged documents or as deliberate anachronisms. Dates are given "new style," that is, with the new year beginning on January 1, not March 25. All references to Shakespeare's works are to *The Norton Shakespeare,* general editor Stephen Greenblatt (New York and London: Norton, 1997), unless otherwise stated. Publishers of works prior to 1900 are not named.

Shakespeare and Elizabeth

INTRODUCTION

Many people who, like me, grew up in Britain in the 1960s and '70s, will have fond memories of Ladybird Books, a highly successful series of small, hardback, colorfully illustrated books for children which aimed to educate and entertain. They included, among a wide range of titles, the *Adventures from History* series. From *The Story of the First Queen Elizabeth* we learned that "The Queen liked Shakespeare's plays so much that he was frequently commanded to bring his company to the palace".[1] In the accompanying picture we saw the Bard gesturing flamboyantly as he declaimed lines from a freshly drafted manuscript (fig. 0.1). His puffed breeches showed off the fine lines of his hose-clad legs, while just a few feet away Elizabeth I, in a sumptuous, flowing gown, leaned forward attentively from her throne, a posture imitated by her ladies-in-waiting. The physical distance between monarch and author was respectful but small, and the Queen's inclination toward the playwright suggested warm appreciation, perhaps even attraction. It was an enchanting and inspiring scene: England's most celebrated ruler and most revered poet brought together in one glorious and romantic historical moment, jointly producing the birth of England's national literature and national greatness. Young readers like myself could not have guessed from this version of history that there is no evidence that any such scene ever took place. There are records of performances at court by Shakespeare's company, the Lord Chamberlain's Men, but no record of any face-to-face encounter between Shakespeare and Elizabeth.

Many years later, as an academic writing about *A Midsummer Night's Dream*, I became familiar with readings of "Oberon's vision," the passage where Oberon explains to Puck the provenance of the love charm, as a reference to Elizabeth I (2.1.148–64). Oberon describes how he saw Cupid take aim "at a fair vestal thronèd by the west." She was immune to Cupid's arrow, which was "quenched in the

FIGURE 0.1

John Kenney, Shakespeare Reading to Elizabeth I, from L. du Garde Peach, *The Story of the First Queen Elizabeth* (Loughborough: Wills and Hepworth, 1958), 45.

chaste beams of the wat'ry moon" and fell instead on a flower, turning it into the love charm. Meanwhile "the imperial vot'ress passèd on, / In maiden meditation, fancy-free." I found general agreement among critics that the terms applied to this figure—virginity, regal serenity, imperial power, and association with the moon, emblem of the virgin goddess Diana—match the terms extensively applied to Elizabeth in court poetry of the 1590s, and that therefore this must be a reference to her. The critics disagreed widely and prolifically, however, about what this reference to the Queen meant. Was it a compliment to Elizabeth, soliciting or perhaps reciprocating her gracious patronage of Shakespeare? Was it evidence that she must have been present at an early performance of the play to hear this compliment in person? Or was it a passage full of darkly critical subtexts, representing Elizabeth as aging and remote and her virginity as unnatural and sterile?[2]

As I looked into this further, I found that behind both the Ladybird *Story of the First Queen Elizabeth* and the critical debate about *A Midsummer Night's Dream* lies a long tradition, reaching back over centuries, of a desire to bring Shakespeare and Elizabeth together. Despite the lack of any evidence that they had contact—or indeed perhaps because of this—there has been a persistent impulse to assert their interest in one another. In the very first biography of Shakespeare, in 1709, Nicholas Rowe stated that "Queen *Elizabeth* had several of his Plays Acted before her, and without doubt gave him many gracious Marks of her Favour."[3] He was unable to say anything more specific about what these "gracious Marks" were, but his depiction of a warm patronage relationship had a far-reaching appeal and influence. A century later, in 1825, Richard Ryan declared that "It is well known that Queen Elizabeth was a great admirer of the immortal Shakespeare, and used frequently (as was the custom with persons of great rank in those days) to appear upon the stage before the audience, or to sit delighted behind the scenes, when the plays of our bard were performed."[4] He recounted an incident in which Elizabeth supposedly dropped a glove on stage to distract the Bard while he was acting, upon which he elegantly extemporized to pick it up without leaving his role, to the Queen's great delight. By this time Shakespeare's imaginary relationship with Elizabeth was developing beyond a warm mutual regard to become a flirtatious intimacy. In the next century, E. Brandram Jones's 1916 novel *In Burleigh's Days* depicted Elizabeth enjoying a performance of *Romeo and Juliet* at court, and enjoying even more her conversation with Shakespeare after the play: "The player had interested her; his refined, handsome and poetic face appealed to her as a woman, as much as the sonnets had appealed to her mind."[5] The pairing of Shakespeare and Elizabeth is in fact one of England's, and Britain's, most entrenched and persistent cultural myths. This imagined golden moment from the nation's history was replayed again and again as England increased in power and confidence and came to preside over the United Kingdom of Great Britain. It became even more prominent in national myth as the British Empire extended its power over vast territories. The double myth of Shakespeare and Elizabeth brought together a man claimed as the greatest writer of all time with a woman claimed as one of the greatest rulers of all time to create a potent and irresistible image of the preeminence of the British nation.

As the dominance of Britain as a world power declined, we might expect this double myth to have declined too. We might wish to see those 1709, 1825, and 1916 versions of the scene as imperialistic assertions of British superiority, and the Ladybird *Story of the First Queen Elizabeth* as a late and nostalgic survival of that imperialist ideology. We might regard it as an entertaining fairytale version of history for children which we have now discarded as we have learned better. Indeed, even as I was poring over my Ladybird book in the late 1960s, some Shakespeare scholars were turning their back on the double myth, preferring to keep the playwright as far apart from the Queen as possible in order to assert his populist and protosocialist credentials. Shakespeare as man of the people and "Shakespeare our contemporary" came to the fore, and versions of him as the Queen's pet poet or literary lackey were seen as conservative and outmoded.[6] Moreover, over the course of the twentieth century our myths of the past were multiply assailed by such movements as modernism, poststructuralism, and postmodernism. In 1998 audiences flocked to see *Shakespeare in Love*, a film widely acclaimed for its irreverent, ironic, and self-conscious treatment of the Bard. This, critics said, was postmodern costume drama. History, and cultural icons, looked different now, it seemed; we viewed them skeptically, askance, playfully. And yet—at the climax of the film, Elizabeth emerged from the shadowy gallery of the playhouse to express her enjoyment of *Romeo and Juliet* and to invite the playwright to come to her palace at Greenwich, where "we will speak some more."[7] This zeitgeist-conscious 1990s film culminated in a scene that would have been comfortably at home in a work from the 1890s or 1790s.

There is something about the imagined meeting between Shakespeare and Elizabeth that we want to cling to, something that we will not let go. It is so deeply ingrained, so frequently recurrent, that we seem to take it for granted. It is perhaps more fundamental to our sense of ourselves than we have consciously realized. But who are "we"? The double myth of Shakespeare and Elizabeth originated as an English myth, and then became a British myth. As time passed, its influence spread to those ruled by the British, and, crucially, it was adopted and adapted by Americans. Now that America dominates world culture, it is America's investment in the double myth that has ensured its survival. *Shakespeare in Love* had many of the characteristics of a British costume drama and had a number of British actors in its cast, but they mingled with Hollywood stars, and Miramax, a major Hollywood studio, financed the film. Its "Britishness" was all part of a commercial and artistic package designed to succeed in America. Its triumph was marked by distinctively American accolades: record-breaking U.S. box office takings combined with multiple awards at the Oscars ceremony.

It is perhaps precisely because we do not know whether Shakespeare and Elizabeth ever met that writers have been so eager to imagine this scene. As a gap in history, it has been a provocation and an inspiration to novelists, painters, and filmmakers. It has created inventiveness in biographers and critics too and deserves scrutiny as a topic that has often brought scholarship into closer proximity to fiction than scholars might have wished to acknowledge. Rowe was the first of many biographers to construct hypothetical connections between Shakespeare and Elizabeth. Enterprising forgers have sometimes provided the missing documentary evidence of contact between them. Literary scholars seeking a key to unlock baffling passages in Shakespeare's works, or looking for buried subtexts in his writings, have often claimed, sometimes persuasively, sometimes less so, that Elizabeth is lurking there. One of the most enduring of such readings concerns Oberon's aforementioned vision in *A Midsummer Night's Dream.* He introduces his description of the "imperial vot'ress" by recollecting how he saw and heard "a mermaid on a dolphin's back" singing sweet music, and how the "stars shot madly from their spheres" (2.1.150, 153). There is a theory that, combined with the references to Elizabeth later in the same speech, these passages allude to the water pageants and fireworks at the "Princely Pleasures" of 1575 at Kenilworth in Warwickshire, a series of lavish festivities laid on for the Queen by her favorite Robert Dudley, the Earl of Leicester. Young Shakespeare, it is suggested, as a Warwickshire boy, might well have been present at these pageants. This theory has been in circulation since the early nineteenth century and remains in favor with a number of respected Shakespeare scholars today. Yet, as we shall see in chapter 4, it has surprising origins in a literary critic's ill-informed reading of a historically inaccurate novel, a fact which illustrates the creative interplay between scholarship and fiction that can occur in the construction of cultural myth.

Although scholars and fictionalizers occasionally concur in this way, another striking feature of the double myth of Shakespeare and Elizabeth is the ingenuity and diversity of imaginings of their relationship. It has been suggested that they were lovers, or that Shakespeare was Elizabeth's secret son, or that Elizabeth was the true author of Shakespeare's works. They have not always been imagined enjoying a warm patronage relationship or flirtatious repartee: they have sometimes been depicted instead as bitter antagonists, with Elizabeth a vain and oppressive tyrant and Shakespeare a vigorous critic of her regime. Intriguingly, it has often been those writers who suggested that Shakespeare was Elizabeth's secret son who have imagined the most hostile relationship between them.

The purpose of this book is to explore why this legendary pairing has had such enduring appeal and what we can learn from the wide variations in the representation of that pairing in different periods, different genres, and different cultural contexts. It is subtitled *The Meeting of Two Myths* because it looks both at the recurrent scene of an imagined meeting between the icons Shakespeare and Elizabeth and at the ways in which their two myths have met and intertwined over the centuries. The persistent fascination with Shakespeare and Elizabeth, each in his/her own right, and the ways in which their images have mutated to suit different historical and cultural contexts, have been explored elsewhere—most notably, for Shakespeare, by Samuel Schoenbaum and Gary Taylor, and for Elizabeth, by Michael Dobson and Nicola Watson, and Julia M. Walker.[8] The work of all these scholars and others has touched upon the double myth of Shakespeare and Elizabeth; indeed, Dobson and Watson give several pages of their extremely informative and entertaining book, *England's Elizabeth,* to the Queen's relationship with the national poet. It is a pleasure to record my indebtedness to all these eminent predecessors in the field. However, the long and complex interrelationship of the cults of Shakespeare and Elizabeth has not as yet received the book-length analysis that is merited by the volume and richness of the material. The present study aspires to tell this combined story more fully than others, who have focused on either Shakespeare or Elizabeth separately, have been able to do.

In my previous research into the copious and complex literary images of Elizabeth from her own lifetime I have encountered the productive idea, developed by Louis Montrose, that by investigating such iconography we can gain insight into the "cultural unconscious" of the Elizabethan period.[9] By exploring, for instance, why the image of Elizabeth as virgin mother of the nation was so popular and successful in the sixteenth century, we might gain a better understanding of the drives and desires that shaped Elizabethan culture; in other words, we might fruitfully apply some of the tools of psychoanalysis to a whole culture. A similar approach may be extended to the question of how and why fictions and theories combining Shakespeare and Elizabeth have persistently recurred through the ages. In this case the subject of the psychoanalysis is not an individual, or even a particular culture, but a number of cultures, in different periods and different nations. Many of the materials considered in this book may be thought of as having been repressed, in the psychoanalytical sense of unacknowledged, unexamined, and unresolved. Materials like historical novels and films have been classified as popular culture and therefore disregarded as of no value or serious interest. Authorship theories linking Shakespeare (or "Shakespeare") and Elizabeth have been dismissed (often with some justice) as unscholarly. However, we should not ignore the cultural forces that have generated and perpetuated these materials and ideas. Some of the more inventive contributions to these genres seem, frankly, bizarre or even ludicrous, but precisely because of this they may be regarded as symptomatic of something in the culture that produced them.[10] On the other hand, works of Shakespeare biography and scholarship have sometimes traded in authoritative assertions about contact between Shakespeare and Elizabeth that have remained unquestioned because they rest upon assumptions so deep-rooted as to be almost invisible. Much may be learned by bringing such assumptions out into the light.

In 1876 Friedrich Nietzsche argued that historical truth was an illusion:

> [The past] is always in danger of being a little altered and touched up and brought nearer to fiction. Sometimes there is no possible distinction between a "monumental" past and a mythical romance . . . For the things of the past are never viewed in their true perspective or receive their just value; but value and perspective change with the individual or the nation that is looking back on its past.[11]

History, then, is always inevitably subjective, and shades into myth. Works of history, biography, or textual scholarship may aspire to objectivity but cannot avoid selective emphases, omissions, and interpretations which reflect the concerns and interests of their authors and readerships. Fiction, drama, the pictorial arts, and film deal in more visible and self-conscious adaptations, distortions, and elaborations of the archival record. Across all these genres, the construction of different versions of history forms its own metahistory, a history of ideology. Imagined meetings between Shakespeare and Elizabeth are of interest less for what they tell us about the time and place they depict than for what they tell us about the time and place when they were confected, the means by which they circulated, and the ways in which they were used. They might reveal much about the desires which they fulfilled, the fantasies which they enabled, and the ideological work that they did in constructing a present out of an imagined past. Homage to, or reaction against, a constructed heritage is necessary to the self-definition of any culture, and for Anglophone cultures the double myth of Shakespeare and Elizabeth has been at the heart of that heritage.

Could They Have Met? The Historical Evidence

The most likely occasion for any contact between Shakespeare and Elizabeth would have been a performance of a Shakespeare play at court. From the mid-1590s until the end of his career Shakespeare was a leading member and resident playwright of the Lord Chamberlain's Men; the first record of him in relation to any specific playing company and performance is for a play at court at Christmas 1594, when he was named as one of those who received payment on behalf of this company.[12] In that year the Lord Chamberlain's Men, along with the Lord Admiral's Men, had been granted a virtual duopoly over commercial theatrical performances in London, based in their own fixed playhouses. Both the Lord Chamberlain and the Lord Admiral were Privy Councillors, but the Lord Chamberlain's Men were especially well connected at court, since their patron was the official in charge of all court entertainments. This was further enhanced by the fact that until 1596 the Lord Chamberlain was Henry Carey, Lord Hunsdon, the Queen's cousin and possible half-brother, who was one of Elizabeth's most well-loved and trusted courtiers.[13] In 1597, after briefly passing outside the family, the position of Lord Chamberlain descended to his son, George Carey. Elizabeth, always cautious with money, avoided direct patronage in her own name, but the Lord Chamberlain's Men were in effect the official playing company of the court. It was they who most often enjoyed the accolade of being summoned to perform for the Queen: records can be found of thirty-three performances by them at court between their inception in 1594 and Elizabeth's death in 1603, compared with twenty by the Admiral's Men, and many fewer by other, less flourishing companies.[14] Their status as the royal players became official on Elizabeth's death, when James I adopted them as the King's Men. Even so, their status was no more than that of servants or retainers, and playing remained a relatively humble and disreputable profession.

The playing companies had frequent disputes with the authorities of the City of London, who were mainly of a Puritanical outlook and opposed playing as idle and likely to encourage vice. In these disputes the players were often able to invoke the protection of Elizabeth's Council, on the grounds that they needed to exercise their trade for commercial audiences in order to be in good practice to entertain the Queen when required. From the point of view of the court, the main purpose of the playing companies was to entertain Elizabeth and her entourage, and public performances were merely rehearsals for this and a means of meeting the companies' expenses.[15] The players were summoned to court on such occasions as visits by foreign dignitaries, holidays, and celebrations. Christmas was especially busy for them: sometimes as many as twelve plays were performed at court over the period of the festivities.[16] Performances were usually staged in the old Banqueting House at Whitehall, or in the Great Halls of Hampton Court, Greenwich, Richmond, or Windsor, and took place after supper, between around 10 PM and 1 AM.[17] The Queen sat on a "state" or throne in a prominent position directly in front of the stage and clearly visible to the rest of the audience, so that she was as much a part of the spectacle as was the drama itself.[18] There is strong evidence that she had a real enjoyment of drama, not least in the fact that she continued seeing plays right up to her final weeks of life.[19]

Although there were writers who produced plays especially for court performances, the plays brought by the commercial playing companies were not usually specially commissioned but were transfers of successes from the public playhouses. It is difficult to establish how many of Shakespeare's plays Elizabeth saw. We have fuller records for the reign of James I, when payments for some seventeen plays by "Shaxberd" were listed in the account book of the Revels Office.[20] Unfortunately, court performances of Shakespeare's plays are not recorded by name and date before 1603, but it must often have been his plays that the Chamberlain's Men presented to the Queen. Printers of his works sometimes used this as a selling point: the first surviving edition of *Love's Labour's Lost*, from 1598, asserted that it had been "presented before her Highnes this last Christmas," while the first edition of *The Merry Wives of Windsor* in 1602 asserted that it had been acted "before her Majestie."[21]

It is possible that at the end of one of his plays Shakespeare might have been presented to the Queen as the author; such presentations were not unusual. It is thought that John Lyly, who wrote a number of plays for court performance in the 1580s and early 1590s, was probably presented to the Queen early in his career by his patron, Edward de Vere, the Earl of Oxford. In 1595 and 1598 Lyly wrote two embittered petitions to Elizabeth complaining that he had been waiting fruitlessly for years for her to fulfil promises to him to give him a high position in the Revels Office, the court body in charge of entertainments. The terms of the petitions strongly imply both that he was personally known to the Queen and that she had held at least one conversation with him: "I was entertayned, your Majesties servant; by your owne gratious Favor strangthened with Condicions, that, I should ayme all my Courses, at the Revells; (I dare not saye, with a promise, butt a hopefull Item, of the Reversion) For the which, theis Tenn yeares, I have Attended, with an unwearyed patience."[22] Edmund Spenser, also, was presented to Elizabeth by his friend Sir Walter Raleigh in 1589, shortly before the publication of the first part of *The Faerie Queene*, his epic poem celebrating Elizabeth.[23] It is even more likely that Elizabeth would have seen Shakespeare perform; a recent biographer has argued convincingly that "the prominence and continuity of Shakespeare's career as a player have been consistently under-estimated."[24] The First Folio places Shakespeare himself first in the list of "The Names of the Principall Actors in all these Playes."[25] There are traditions that he played the parts of Adam in *As You Like It* and the Ghost in *Hamlet*; and we know that he acted in at least two plays by Ben Jonson, *Every Man in his Humour* (1598) and *Sejanus* (1603–4).[26] So, the Queen may have seen Shakespeare as one actor in the cast of a play, but this would be a significantly less personal encounter than most myth-makers of later centuries have liked to imagine. Even if he were presented to her as an author, any conversation would have been brief and formal.

Many mythologizers have loved to imagine Elizabeth attending a Shakespeare play at a playhouse, usually the Globe. The scenario has many attractions: it depicts Elizabeth mingling democratically with her subjects and sharing their pleasures; and it presents in one neatly encapsulated scene the essential ingredients of the so-called Elizabethan golden age: Gloriana, Shakespeare and his characters, and the vivacious and rumbustious people of Tudor England, all dressed in colorful and picturesque period costume. Yet this event is not only undocumented but also highly unlikely. If the Queen had deigned to grace a public playhouse with her presence, it would have been an exceptional and sensational occurrence and would undoubtedly have been recorded, but no such records exist. We do know that a later Queen of England attended a playhouse: Henrietta Maria, wife of Charles I, went several times to see plays at the Blackfriars theatre. However, bills for these performances were referred to the office of the Lord Chamberlain—whose responsibilities included overseeing plays and playhouses—suggesting that they were specially commissioned private performances, rather than that the Queen simply joined the paying audience at the usual kind of public performance.[27]

There is only one piece of evidence that Elizabeth might ever have gone to a playhouse. This is a letter of December 29, 1601, from the courtier Dudley Carleton to John Chamberlain, in which he reports that

> The Queen dined to-day privately at my Lord Chamberlain's. I have just come from the Blackfriars, where I saw her at the play with all her *candidae auditrices* [fair attendants]. Mrs Nevill, who played her prizes, and bore the belle away in the Prince de Amour's revels, is sworn maid of honour; Sir Robt. Sydney is in chase to make her foreswear both maid and honour.[28]

The reference here to "the Blackfriars" might possibly be to the Blackfriars playhouse. In 1601 this was a so-called "private" indoor playhouse, catering to more select audiences for a higher admission price than did the open-air playhouses, and all performances there were by a company of boy players. At the very most, this letter reveals Elizabeth attending a private, exclusive playhouse performance of a quite different nature from those open to the general public at the Globe and its neighboring playhouses for which Shakespeare principally wrote. However, the reference to "the Blackfriars" may not be to the playhouse at all but simply to the Blackfriars area, where the Lord Chamberlain's house was situated. In this case the play at which Carleton saw Elizabeth would have been even more private and exclusive, performed in the Lord Chamberlain's house after dinner, and the performers might have been the company that bore the host's name as their patron, the Lord Chamberlain's Men, Shakespeare's company. If so, Elizabeth did not visit the playhouse on this occasion, but she might have seen Shakespeare act, or he might have been present while she watched one of his plays. Alternatively, the play might have been a performance by Elizabeth's own ladies, as suggested by the slightly cryptic reference in the next sentence to the maid-of-honor Mrs. Nevill, who "bore the belle away in the Prince de Amour's revels";[29] or the "play" might have been not drama but gambling, another favorite court pastime.[30] Carleton's 1601 letter, then, is an ambiguous piece of evidence and at most describes a private occasion on which Shakespeare might have been one of the performers before the Queen.

It is of course much more likely that Shakespeare would have seen Elizabeth than that she would have knowingly seen him. London, although growing rapidly, was still a relatively small city by modern standards, with a population of around 200,000, and it was not unusual for the Queen to be seen by her metropolitan subjects.[31] Large crowds turned out to see her as she departed upon and returned from her summer progresses each year.[32] Shakespeare would almost certainly have seen Elizabeth making use of the Thames, London's principal thoroughfare, both for business and pleasure; indeed, the ornate royal barge was kept near to the playhouses.[33] After he officially became a gentleman, a holder of a family coat-of-arms, in 1596, he would have been entitled to enter any of the Queen's London palaces on a Sunday to see the royal procession to chapel and the ceremonial laying of the royal dinner that was enacted while the Queen was at prayer.[34] These and other occasions when Elizabeth made public appearances would have been marked by impressive spectacle and ritual, and Shakespeare may well have found himself in the audience of the living theatre of sixteenth-century monarchy. It is extremely unlikely, though, that anything that we might term a meeting with the Queen would have taken place on such an occasion.

Earlier in Shakespeare's life there were several times when Elizabeth's summer progresses took her near to his home town of Stratford-upon-Avon. In 1570, when William was just six years old, she stayed overnight at Charlecote Park, seat of Sir Thomas Lucy, four miles northeast of Stratford.[35] Four years later, the annual royal progress came to Warwick, only eight miles from Stratford; and in 1575, as mentioned above, Elizabeth visited Kenilworth Castle, seat of the Earl of Leicester, twelve miles from Stratford, for the celebrated entertainments known as the Princely Pleasures. On any of these occasions Shakespeare and his family may have joined the crowds who turned out to see the Queen. Of course, we do not know whether Shakespeare saw Elizabeth at any of these events, and if he did, it would only have been from a distance.

This comprises the generally accepted historical evidence for a meeting between Shakespeare and Elizabeth. It is scanty and inconclusive, leaving us with some rather tenuous possibilities but no proof either way. There have been various further hypotheses: Leslie Hotson, for instance, contended that *Twelfth Night* was commissioned for and performed at a court occasion, and James Shapiro believes that part of the published epilogue to *Henry IV Part 2* and another anonymous epilogue might be speeches Shakespeare wrote and delivered in person to the Queen.[36] However, these are individual interpretations of evidence and continuing subjects of debate, so the proper place to discuss them will be chapter 4, when we look at the role of Elizabeth in later readings of Shakespeare's works.

What Did Shakespeare Think of Elizabeth? The Literary Evidence

Many critics have turned to Shakespeare's works to seek evidence of his feelings toward Elizabeth. There are several places where we can be reasonably sure that he is referring directly to her. These include Oberon's vision in *A Midsummer Night's Dream*, as discussed above; a reference to the owner of Windsor Castle in *The Merry Wives of Windsor* (5.5.57); the mention in *Henry V* of "our gracious Empress" (5.0.30); and the "mortal moon" in Sonnet 107. Overall, the number of reasonably certain references to Elizabeth in Shakespeare's oeuvre is relatively small, in an age when many writers were competing with each other to celebrate their monarch in ever more extravagant terms as Gloriana, Cynthia, Diana, Astraea, and so on. John Lyly, for instance, as mentioned above, wrote plays for the court which centered on allegorical figures of Elizabeth. However, there are many more places in Shakespeare's writings where critics have detected supposed allusions to the Queen which are concealed or indirect. It has been proposed at various times that Cleopatra, or Gertrude, or the cross-dressing heroines in the comedies, or many other Shakespearean figures might reflect aspects of Elizabeth.

Critics have varied widely in the deductions that they make from these materials, and even from Shakespeare's more explicit references to Elizabeth, about the playwright's attitude to his monarch. Some have compiled evidence from his works to demonstrate that Shakespeare was a fervent admirer of the Queen; others have found evidence of dissent and subversion. One of the most contentious cases is *Richard II*: since the mid–nineteenth century, debate has raged as to whether it was the play performed to entertain the conspirators on the eve of the Essex Rebellion in 1601 and whether Shakespeare was involved in this apparently seditious performance. Moreover, at least one putative appearance by Elizabeth in Shakespeare's works—one which includes extensive comment upon the Queen and her reign—simply dissolves in our grasp when subjected to scholarly scrutiny. This is the climactic scene of *Henry VIII*, written in collaboration with John Fletcher in 1612–13, when the baby princess Elizabeth is being christened. Her godfather, Archbishop Cranmer, is seized by prophetic inspiration and eloquently sets forth a vision of the peace and plenty that will be brought to England by her rule (5.4.14–62). A. L. Rowse wrote in 1963 that "It is this that gave Shakespeare the opportunity to round off his life's work with that tribute to her he had not written when she died in 1603, and to sum up for us what he thought of the Elizabethan age now forever over."[37] Other critics have stressed the ambivalences and troubling undertones in the speech, but in any case, most textual scholars of the play believe this scene to be by John Fletcher.[38] Far from being Shakespeare's final celebration of Elizabeth, it was probably not even written by him. Overall, the kinds of evidence to be found in Shakespeare's plays and poems are tantalizingly mobile and elusive, and tend to reinforce whatever preconceptions about Shakespeare's relationship with Elizabeth were brought to the text by each reader as shaped by the ideological positions of these particular individuals and their particular cultural and historical contexts.

Two comments from Shakespeare's contemporaries on his relations with the Queen are worth mentioning. Shakespeare, as Rowse observes above, did not publish an elegy for Elizabeth on her death in 1603, and this was noticed at the time by the poet Henry Chettle. In *England's Mourning Garment* he summoned fellow authors to lament the Queen, and upbraided those who had failed to do so, including "Melicert":

> Nor doth the silver tonged *Melicert,*
> Drop from his honied muse one sable teare
> To mourne her death that graced his desert,
> And to his laies opend her Royall eare.
> Shepheard remember our *Elizabeth,*
> And sing her Rape, done by that *Tarquin,* Death.[39]

Melicert is clearly Shakespeare, as we can tell not only from the allusion to *The Rape of Lucrece* but also from the reference to Shakespeare's renowned honeyed sweetness of style; Francis Meres, for instance, had recently praised "mellifluous & honytongued *Shakespeare*" for his "sugred Sonnets."[40] Some later writers have emphasized Chettle's assertion that Elizabeth "graced his desert," regarding this as evidence that Shakespeare received public and personal favor from the Queen.[41] Others have drawn attention to Shakespeare's silence on this occasion, seeing this as a sign that he was no great admirer of Elizabeth and had no wish to express sorrow at her death.[42]

Seven years after Shakespeare's own death, Ben Jonson wrote in his prefatory verses for the 1623 First Folio of Shakespeare's works:

> Sweet Swan of *Avon*! what a sight it were
> To see thee in our waters yet appeare,
> And make those flights upon the bankes of *Thames*,
> That so did take *Eliza*, and our *James*![43]

Again this is open to diverse interpretations: Jonson may be merely referring to the fact that a number of Shakespeare's plays were performed before Elizabeth, corroborating the other evidence for this; or he may be implying that Elizabeth bestowed direct and knowing personal patronage upon Shakespeare; or he may be merely aggrandizing his dead friend.

I have only briefly indicated here the competing and contradictory interpretations of these passages from Shakespeare and contemporary observers; in chapter 4 I will explore in more detail the fascinating history of readings that find allusions to Elizabeth in Shakespeare's works. The main point to make here, as with the historical evidence for contact between Shakespeare and Elizabeth, is that the contemporary literary materials are brief, fragmentary, and ambiguous. Nevertheless, these scattered pieces have formed the foundation of a rich and enduring double myth. We need to investigate why this might be.

Why Do We Want Shakespeare and Elizabeth to Meet? Sexuality, Class, Nationhood

Shakespeare and Elizabeth, each an icon individually, have had even more power as a joint icon. The creation of Shakespeare's posthumous fame from the early eighteenth century onward was partly dependent upon the idea that he was patronized by the glamorous Good Queen Bess, redoubtable defender of the nation.

On the other side, the posthumous glory accruing to Elizabeth as one of the most notable of English monarchs was partly dependent upon the idea that she recognized and cultivated the genius of Shakespeare. Their notional mutual esteem has been instrumental in constructing an idealized Elizabethan golden age which later ages have viewed with nostalgic pleasure and have deployed to help construct myths of their own origin and identity.

The Shakespeare-and-Elizabeth scenario works for a variety of reasons. In the first place, it has piqued the curiosity of after-ages for the simple reason that she was a woman and he was a man. Some literary critics, especially since the advent of new historicism in the 1980s, have been interested in the nature of Shakespeare's patronage relations with James I once his company became the King's Men, and what this might imply about the relations between drama and power.[44] However, there has been far more effort to locate references to Elizabeth in Shakespeare's works, and beyond the academy there has been little interest in possible meetings between the playwright and James I, even though James was on the throne for nearly half of Shakespeare's career. An imagined encounter between Shakespeare and Elizabeth, in view of the reputation they have each enjoyed for a highly quotable way with words, offers far more opportunity for witty repartee, and also for flirtation. Elizabeth was nearly thirty years Shakespeare's senior, but, given that she is well known to have had a string of favorites, this has not deterred writers from depicting her as a coquette who views Shakespeare with the gaze of a connoisseur of virile young men. After all, her last favorite, Robert Devereux, Earl of Essex, was a year younger than Shakespeare. The presumed affair between Elizabeth and Essex was romanticized in scandalous "secret histories" of the late seventeenth century, and this tradition has persisted through Lytton Strachey's dual biography *Elizabeth and Essex* (1928) and on into recent historical fiction and screen dramas. Many versions of Shakespeare's relationship with his Queen place him in a similar role, as a witty and attractive young sparring partner who enflames the interest of the mature but passionate Queen.

Nevertheless, in eighteenth- and nineteenth-century versions of their encounter, warm interest and flirtatious repartee is as far as any sexual relationship goes. Desire is titillatingly implied while being contained within safe boundaries. Indeed, constructing Shakespeare and Elizabeth as a romantic but chaste couple was often a means of regularizing their sexuality, which in each case presented challenges to the respectable bourgeois morality that was increasingly promoted through the eighteenth and nineteenth centuries. Shakespeare's unfortunate sexual history included a hasty wedding at eighteen to a pregnant older woman, rumors of dalliances with female playgoers and innkeepers' wives, and a sequence of sonnets that expressed passion for both a fair young man and a promiscuous dark lady. Elizabeth as Virgin Queen was troublingly anomalous in relation to the Protestant middle-class celebration of matrimony and was surrounded from her own lifetime onward by murky rumors of her affairs with favorites or of her freakish hermaphroditism. Ben Jonson, for instance, gossiped that "she had a membrana on her, which made her uncapable of man, though for her delight she tried many," while her Principal Secretary Sir Robert Cecil remarked after her death that "she was more than a man, and in troth, sometimes less than a woman."[45] Bringing Shakespeare and Elizabeth together in a devoted but unconsummated pairing, a kind of Neoplatonic courtly love, cleaned up and straightened out both their public images.

Studies of nationalism have placed increasing emphasis upon iconographies of sexuality.[46] Normative icons of patriarchal masculinity and maternal femininity, radiant with virtue and stripped of sexuality, have often been deployed in various periods and cultures as symbols of national identity. Many eighteenth- and nineteenth-century versions of Shakespeare and Elizabeth conformed to this model. Michael Dobson has found that although Shakespeare and his works were invoked to stir up the virility of British manhood, the representation of the Bard himself was often paradoxically sexless and even disembodied. Meanwhile, the chastely affectionate patronage that he supposedly received from Elizabeth was used to certify his sexual virtue.[47]

Since the early twentieth century, however, there has been increasing attraction to the different kinds of queerness which both Shakespeare and Elizabeth personify—he because of the strong indications of homoerotic feelings in his writings, she because of her position as a woman in a man's role. Modern fictions have responded to this double ambiguity to depict Shakespeare and Elizabeth as involved in complex merry-go-rounds of unorthodox sexual couplings involving other partners as well as each other. Both of them are sexual enigmas who may be imagined as indulging in secret and scandalous passions behind their public masks, and this has become a large part of their fascination. They can be deployed, then, as subversive rather than normative figures.

The erotic charge of the imagined encounter between Shakespeare and Elizabeth is intensified by the transgression of the invisible boundary between monarch and commoner. Shakespeare was a tradesman's son from rural Stratford-upon-Avon, plying his trade among the brothels and bear pits of Bankside. A large part of his continuing appeal is founded on the idea that he may have been a genius but he was also "one of us," a man of the people, writing for groundlings and speaking timeless truths to us across the centuries. It has been felt that he shares and understands our common humanity. By contrast, a large part of Elizabeth's glamor is her regality, those bejeweled farthingales and headdresses, her position at the apex of a glittering and adoring court. Yet part of the historical myth of each has also been a certain class mobility. From his humble origins, Shakespeare ascended to see his plays performed at court and posthumously achieved a kind of literary divinity: Schoenbaum wrote of him, "Thus did the grammar-school product in whose veins no blue blood coursed stray into the vestibule of power."[48] Elizabeth, meanwhile, spent much of her youth as an outcast, branded a bastard by her father and imprisoned for treason by her sister, and this enabled her to enhance her queenship with protestations of her affection for and kinship with the common people of her realm. She asserted more than once that she would rather be a milkmaid than a queen and said, "I am indeed endued with such qualities that if I were turned out of the realm in my petticoat, I were able to live in any place of Christendom."[49] Thus the Queen and the playwright have each, in their different ways, personified democratic values, of a kind which came to be associated with Englishness, then Britishness, then with American national ideals. We may see the imagined encounters between them as dramatizing these democratic values: to make them meet in legend, either Shakespeare must be taken to court or Elizabeth must descend to the stage of the commercial playhouse, as in *Shakespeare in Love* and numerous earlier fictions. The scene is a fantasy of the temporary dissolution of class boundaries, and for class-conscious cultures this has given it a magical resonance and intensity.

In fact, the history of such class-defying iconography reaches back to Shakespeare's and Elizabeth's own time and beyond. The Elizabethans loved stories which fantasized meetings between kings or queens and commoners. Themes of their history plays and ballads included, for instance, Richard Lionheart in disguise feasting on venison with Robin Hood and his merry men, then pardoning them, thus foxing the wicked Sheriff of Nottingham, or Henry II rewarding a miller for his rustic hospitality by knighting him.[50] The pleasure of such tales seems to have lain in the belief that, if monarch and subject could meet directly, bypassing self-interested aristocrats and corrupt officers of the law, they would find mutual goodwill, good humor, affection, and understanding. The king was shown to be simply a man at heart; the commoner was allowed to feel special and individual enough to converse with a king. Imagined meetings between Shakespeare and Elizabeth may be seen as a persistence of this kind of folklore. The meeting of their two myths involves the meeting of two different social and cultural worlds, both of which are thereby shown to be founded on shared values of wit, improvisation, and generosity of spirit.

This set of values has often been claimed as the essence of Britishness. Nation formation has clearly been another crucial factor in the developing iconography of

Shakespeare and Elizabeth, and this process frequently depends upon an idealized and even fabricated vision of the past: as Ernest Renan wrote in 1882, "getting its history wrong is part of being a nation."[51] Inventing a meeting or relationship between Shakespeare and Elizabeth has been one significant form in which Britain and other Anglophone nations have purposefully got history wrong in the pursuit of national identity. For the English, from the eighteenth century onward, the depiction of Shakespeare and Elizabeth presiding harmoniously over a nostalgically recalled "merrie England" was instrumental in the self-definition of the nation as democratic, divinely sanctioned, and innately civilized. Following the Act of Union in 1707, which joined Scotland with England and Wales in a United Kingdom of Great Britain ruled from London, the idea of "Englishness" came to be frequently elided with the idea of "Britishness," and the values represented by the double myth of Shakespeare and Elizabeth became symbolic of a British identity disseminated not only throughout the United Kingdom, by authors like Sir Walter Scott (a Scot who enthusiastically enhanced the Shakespeare and Elizabeth myth in his 1821 novel *Kenilworth*), but also throughout the burgeoning British Empire.

Adrian Hastings, a historian of nationalism, writes that in the development of nationhood "by far the most important and widely present factor is that of an extensively used vernacular literature." In short, a nation is "normally identified by a literature of its own."[52] Shakespeare's works, as unquestionably the most "extensively used" in the English language, have played a crucial role in the construction of not only English and British national identity but that of other Anglophone nations too. In America, Shakespeare grew in prominence through the nineteenth century as an English-speaking cultural elite strove to impose a unified national identity upon the polyglot diversity created by immigration.[53] Moreover, the Shakespeare-and-Elizabeth pairing was increasingly appropriated for myths of the origins of the American nation. One American, John S. Jenkins, writing in 1851, voiced an enthusiastic admiration for the British imperial success of which Shakespeare and Elizabeth had become personifications: "In her reign, the great stars of literature shone, and England, from a second-rate kingdom, began the splendid career by which, at this hour, she boasts an eighth of the habitable globe, forty colonies, and a seventh of the world's population, or one hundred and eighty million subjects."[54] Such admiration turned to appropriation and transcendence as Americans began to lay claim to Shakespeare and Elizabeth as progenitors of their own national ideals and aspirations. Peter Markoe, an American poet, wrote as early as 1787 that the Bard was no longer the exclusive property of Britain: "Shakspeare's bold spirit seeks our western shore."[55] The age of Shakespeare and Elizabeth, after all, was the age of exploration and colonization, when bold adventurers whose spirit they supposedly shared eagerly set sail for the west to found a new nation. Charles William Wallace enunciated this view of history in a lecture of 1914: "England in the days of good Queen Bess was only young America in the buoyant heedlessness and lawlessness of childhood in chasing over all obstacles after the purse at the end of the rainbow." Men looked west for "infinite possibilities" of wealth, idealism, and self-fulfilment, and "into this age and of it were Shakespeare and America born."[56] Metaphorically, then, Shakespeare and America were twins born to their mother Elizabeth; or, to configure the metaphorical family slightly differently, Shakespeare and Elizabeth were the proud parents of the American Dream.

The myth of a meeting between Shakespeare and Elizabeth may be compared with another mythical encounter from the Tudor period, the supposed meeting between Elizabeth and Mary Queen of Scots. This encounter, too, though frequently depicted by creative writers and visual artists, is unrecorded in documentary history. Jayne Elizabeth Lewis has written of how versions of the imagined meeting between Elizabeth and Mary supplement history to give us something that we yearn to think might have happened, a scenario that satisfies complex desires: they "tear the veil that customarily divides fact from fantasy, wish from fulfilment."[57] Imagined meetings between Shakespeare and Elizabeth may likewise be thought of as a wish-fulfilling fantasy and as giving us access to the dream life of the cultures which produced them. The Elizabeth-and-Mary encounter has produced an enduring iconographical tradition because the reputations of the two queens lend themselves to the personification of intellect versus romance, Machiavellian calculation versus reckless adventurousness, androgyny versus femininity: in essence, head versus heart.[58] The pairing of Shakespeare and Elizabeth may appear to differ in that they often personify complementary rather than opposing values: masculinity and femininity; a man who loves men and a woman with male qualities; a kingly commoner and a queen with the common touch; a writer who understands human nature and a ruler who understands her people. However, they have been used to represent antagonisms too. In some versions of their encounter, stress is laid upon their age difference. In such works Elizabeth is characterized as decaying, capricious, and tyrannical, the personification of a defunct feudal past, whereas Shakespeare, humble and underappreciated in his own age, awaits the recognition of posterity. He is imagined as a progressive thinker, a man of the people and of the future. In American works in this vein, it is Shakespeare alone who inspires those looking to the west and founds the American Dream, overcoming restrictions and obstacles imposed by the backward-looking Elizabeth. In recent Shakespeare criticism, their relationship has been reconfigured again, with

Shakespeare pictured as a Catholic or at least a Catholic sympathizer, siding with those who sought to preserve the old faith and its traditions in the face of Elizabeth's cruel persecutions. Shakespeare and Elizabeth, then, can personify either complementary or opposing values of many different kinds, and this adaptability to the iconographical needs of different periods and national cultures is surely a significant ingredient in the persistence of their double myth.

Meetings of the two myths of Shakespeare and Elizabeth have been numerous and multifarious. Not all could be included here for reasons of space, but my aim has been to give a broad sample of their range and variety, while tracing significant trends and pointing out influential interventions. The ensuing chapters are organized partly by chronology and partly by thematic and generic concerns. Chapter 1 charts the presence of Elizabeth in Shakespearean materials of eighteenth-century Britain, from Rowe's biography in 1709 to the Ireland forgeries in 1795, and the shifting roles which she plays in these materials. Chapter 2 surveys the development of the double myth in nineteenth-century Britain, through more Shakespeare biographies and forgeries but also in the burgeoning genres of historical fiction, drama, and painting, where the encounter between Shakespeare and Elizabeth takes on new meanings as the British Empire expands and in the context of comparisons between Elizabeth and Queen Victoria. Chapters 3, 4, and 5 then deal with particular trends in the double myth from the nineteenth century to the present. Chapter 3 is a short bridging chapter which brings American appropriations and adaptations of the double myth into the story; from this point on, American as well as British materials are treated. Chapter 4 examines the many and various invocations of Elizabeth in literary-critical interpretation of Shakespeare's works. Chapter 5 considers Elizabeth's role in the Shakespeare authorship controversy, where she has featured as Shakespeare's mother or lover, or has even merged with him to be proposed as the true author of his works. Chapter 6 concentrates on twentieth-century fictions, charting the emergence of many different Shakespeares and Elizabeths in novels, plays, television dramas, and films, and seeking to place these in context. To conclude, the epilogue considers the continuing and creative evolution of the double myth since the year 2000 and asks what kinds of encounters Shakespeare and Elizabeth might enjoy in years to come.

We will almost certainly never know whether Shakespeare and Elizabeth met in real life. However, we can be sure that they have met many times, across the centuries, in books, pictures, plays, and films, and in the minds of the makers and audiences of these artefacts. This book aims to convey a sense of the richness and creative diversity of those encounters, and to investigate why it is that Shakespeare and Elizabeth keep on meeting, again and again.

1

Lives and Legends in the Eighteenth Century

The story of Shakespeare's posthumous relationship with Elizabeth I begins in England in the early eighteenth century, as far as printed evidence is concerned. At this point, Shakespeare and Elizabeth each separately occupied a distinctive but also mobile cultural position. Elizabeth, of course, had become firmly established in her own lifetime as a national icon, an embodiment of heroic Protestant England. Through the seventeenth century, as John Watkins has shown, she persisted in the forefront of the national consciousness and at the center of political debate, as both defenders of absolutist monarchy and proponents of the rights of Parliament claimed her for their causes.[1] By the end of that century, however, her public image was shifting significantly as "secret histories" appeared, scandal fictions translated from French which claimed to reveal the private, sensational doings of historical figures behind closed doors. Several of these, from 1678 onward, narrated Elizabeth's supposed affairs with the Earl of Essex and others, presenting an Elizabeth who was passionate and self-divided, tragically torn between love and duty.[2] She appeared in a similar guise on stage, in John Banks's she-tragedies *The Unhappy Favourite* (1682) and *The Island Queens* (1684), the latter being the first of many works to imagine a face-to-face meeting between Elizabeth and Mary Queen of Scots.[3] Elizabeth's role modulated: although she continued to be a political and religious symbol, she also became a more romantic figure, more akin to a historical personality or celebrity, with a corresponding fascination and glamor. She entered the eighteenth century as a figure at the center of a growing body of fable and anecdote.

Shakespeare too, over the course of the seventeenth century, had acquired a rather colorful and racy reputation. Since 1602, when it was first recorded in a law student's diary, the story had circulated that Shakespeare had wittily supplanted his colleague Richard Burbage in the bed of a female playgoer.[4] In the 1680s the gossipy biographer John Aubrey recorded the rumor that Sir William Davenant, the author and theatre manager, was the child of Shakespeare's affair with an Oxford tavernkeeper's wife.[5] Aubrey also claimed to have heard from Shakespeare's Stratford neighbors that as a boy he worked in a butcher's shop, and "when he killed a calf, he would do it in a *high style*, and make a speech."[6] Such anecdotes give us some sense of the oral traditions that were circulating about Shakespeare, probably being elaborated and exaggerated as they passed around and suggesting a Shakespeare who was promiscuous, witty, a little wild, and given to extravagant gestures.

Parallel to the circulation of these biographical traditions, Shakespeare's fame and reputation as a dramatist were in the ascendant. Following the reopening of the London theatres at the Restoration, his plays were revived and became a mainstay of the repertoire, albeit often in adapted form.[7] As Michael Dobson has shown, the processes of adaptation and canonization were mutually dependent, as revisers strove to construct Shakespeare as a father figure for Augustan literature.[8] As early as 1667, John Dryden wrote that "*Shakespear*'s pow'r is sacred as a King's."[9] From 1679 onward, the "ghost" of Shakespeare appeared on stage with increasing frequency in dramatic prologues and epilogues, urging his countrymen to strive for excellence in both dramatic and national endeavor.[10] By the early 1700s he was rapidly moving toward his position as the most acclaimed of English authors.[11]

As we have seen, Shakespeare had been associated with royalty in Ben Jonson's prefatory verses for the 1623 First Folio, which asserted that his plays "so did take *Eliza*, and our *James*!"[12] Thomas Otway took up the theme in a prologue of 1680, claiming that "A gracious Prince's Favour chear'd his Muse, / A constant Favour, he ne'r fear'd to lose."[13] It is unclear whether Otway meant James or Elizabeth by the "gracious Prince"; indeed, there seems to have been an oral tradition, first recorded in print in an early eighteenth-century edition of Shakespeare's poems, that "That most learn'd Prince, and great Patron of Learning, King *James* the First, was pleas'd with his own Hand to write an amicable Letter to Mr. *Shakespeare*; which Letter, tho now lost, remain'd long in the Hands of *Sir William D'avenant*, as a credible Person now living can testify."[14] Since Davenant was reputed to be Shakespeare's illegitimate son, the authority of a direct link back over the years to the living Shakespeare was being claimed here—even though the letter was unfortunately lost. The personal approbation of the monarch was invoked to verify the worth of Shakespeare's writings; the King's letter was described as "very much to his Honour, and very remarkable." Shakespeare's association with royalty in this case rests upon James, but as Elizabeth's image became increasingly glamorous and intriguing, it was predictable that she would come to play a more prominent role than her less charismatic successor in Shakespeare's cultural ascent. Moreover, in 1688 James I's grandson James II was ousted from his throne, amid opposition to his Catholicism and his attempts to assert monarchical power over Parliament. After this, invocation of James I risked association with James II, whereas nostalgia for Elizabeth—a Protestant defender of England against Spain, who repeatedly spoke of how she valued the love of her people—was more in keeping with the Whig domination of politics and culture in the late seventeenth and early eighteenth centuries.

The Merry Wives of Windsor and Royal Patronage

Many of the early efforts to link Shakespeare and Elizabeth revolved around *The Merry Wives of Windsor*. In 1702 John Dennis revised the play as *The Comical Gallant: or, The Amours of Sir John Falstaffe*. He explained that some people thought *The Merry Wives* too admirable to be adapted, others, too despicable. However,

> That this Comedy was not despicable, I guess'd for several Reasons: First, I knew very well, that it had pleas'd one of the greatest Queens that ever was in the World, great not only for her Wisdom in the Arts of Government, but for her knowledge of Polite Learning, and her nice taste of the Drama, for such a taste we may be sure she had, by the relish which she had of the Ancients. This Comedy was written at her Command, and by her direction, and she was so eager to see it Acted, that she commanded it to be finished in fourteen days; and was afterwards, as Tradition tells us, very well pleas'd at the Representation.[15]

This is a complex and ambivalent passage, at once praising and dispraising both Shakespeare's original play and Elizabeth's taste. Dennis appears to invoke Elizabeth as a custodian of learning and culture in order to defend *The Merry Wives*: she is here a wise ruler, a scholar, and a connoisseur of drama. Her interest and patronage guarantee the literary value of the play, functioning in much the same way as the story of James's letter to Shakespeare. Yet at the same time Dennis acknowledges that some think *The Merry Wives* "despicable," and that it stood in need of rescuing and polishing. Shakespeare and Elizabeth are simultaneously revered and implicitly denigrated as representatives of a relatively backward age. Dennis deployed the idea of speedy composition to meet a royal demand to explain the deficiencies of the play and justify his rewriting: "I knew very well, that in so short a time as this Play was writ, nothing could be done that is perfect" (ibid., A2r–v). Within this statement lay an assumption that "raw" Shakespeare would not do for modern times; and within this again lay an implicit acknowledgment that the works of Shakespeare and the myth of Elizabeth were being combined, adapted, and plundered for the needs of the eighteenth century.

There is, in fact, documentary evidence of a connection between Elizabeth and this particular play, though not necessarily of the kind Dennis claims. *The Merry Wives* was advertised on the title page of the 1602 Quarto edition as having been "divers times Acted by the right Honorable my Lord Chamberlaines servants [i.e., the Lord Chamberlain's Men, Shakespeare's company]. Both before her Majestie, and else-where."[16] The play's setting, in Windsor, implies some association with the Queen, and specifically with the Order of the Garter, whose knights were ceremonially installed at an annual ceremony at St George's Chapel in the castle. This association is confirmed by the speech made by Mistress Quickly in the role of the Fairy Queen, which includes a conceit of fairy rings as Garter badges, quoting the motto of the Order: " *'Honi soit qui mal y pense'* write / In emerald tufts, flowers purple, blue, and white." She invokes a fairy blessing on the castle's owner, unnamed but self-evidently Elizabeth (5.5.52–70). Many modern scholars agree that the play, or part of it, is likely to have been designed for performance at the Garter Feast of April 23, 1597. The Garter Feast was an annual celebration held at one of the London royal palaces—in this case, Whitehall—a month before the installation of the new knights at Windsor.[17] In this year one of the five newly elected knights was George Carey, who had recently succeeded his father, Henry Carey, as Baron Hunsdon, then as Lord Chamberlain, and therefore patron of Shakespeare's company.[18] It seems likely that he commissioned the play from the leading playwright of his company as his own contribution to the Garter Feast, probably to be performed in the evening after supper. The appearance by the Fairy Queen and the fairy blessing upon a ruler's house both suggest an intention of recalling *A Midsummer Night's Dream,* a play which had associations not only with Elizabeth but also possibly with the Carey family.[19]

Various internal details of the history plays from which *The Merry Wives* is an offshoot strongly indicate that it was written after *Henry IV Part 1* and around the same time as *Henry IV Part 2.* The Lord Chamberlain's Men had acted at court on several dates not long before the 1597 Garter Feast; it is not impossible, then, that the Queen saw *1 Henry IV* on one of these occasions and then asked to see Falstaff in love.[20] There is also another view that only the masque at the end of *The Merry Wives,* with its specific references to the Order of the Garter, was written for the 1597 Garter Feast, and that the rest of the play was added later, after *Henry V* in

1599. Falstaff's death is described in that play, and the full version of *The Merry Wives* may have been produced in response to audience disappointment, including perhaps royal disappointment, at the demise of this very popular character.[21] But all of this must remain no more than conjectural.

Dennis seems to assume that his readers will be familiar with the story of the Queen's commission and the rapid composition of the play, an assumption which implies that he is drawing upon an oral tradition. This is of course impossible to verify, but the fact that this story was deployed by Dennis to present his adaptation to the public, and that it was subsequently frequently repeated in print, demonstrates that early eighteenth-century readers and writers found it appealing. Its folkloric qualities were accentuated by the fact that, two years after he first published it, Dennis compressed Shakespeare's feat of a fortnight's composition into an even shorter period: Elizabeth, he wrote, "commanded *Shakespear* to write the Comedy of the *Merry Wives,* and to write it in ten Days time."[22] The reduction in the timescale to make a taller and taller tale illustrates how the story belongs to a popular tradition which readers found entertaining and historically satisfying regardless of its unreliability.

The tale is next found in Nicholas Rowe's 1709 life of Shakespeare, the first biography of the playwright and the basis of all successive biographies until Edmond Malone's in 1821. Rowe amplified Elizabeth's motivation: "She was so well pleas'd with that admirable Character of *Falstaff,* in the two Parts of *Henry* the Fourth, that she commanded him to continue it for one Play more, and to shew him in Love. This is said to be the Occasion of his writing *The Merry Wives of* Windsor. How well she was obey'd, the Play it self is an admirable Proof."[23] Dennis in 1702, although somewhat equivocal about the artistic merit of the play, had defended it on the grounds that it pleased Elizabeth. Rowe went further: for him, the combination of Elizabeth's originating idea and Shakespeare's dramatic gifts produced an "admirable" dramatic success. Elizabeth provided the occasion, Shakespeare the execution, making Elizabeth almost a collaborator in the production of the play, or a sort of midwife to its delivery.

Writers of the late seventeenth and early eighteenth centuries had a particular incentive for disseminating in print the oral legends which associated Shakespeare with his monarchs: their own sense of grievance at their lack of royal patronage. When Otway in 1680 claimed that Shakespeare's muse was cheered by "a gracious Prince's Favour," his point was that Shakespeare lived in a "blest" age. Because Shakespeare never feared to lose the "constant Favour" of his monarch, "he wrote with Fancy unconfined, / And Thoughts that were Immortal as his Mind."[24] When Dennis in 1704 used the story of Elizabeth's commission for *The Merry*

Wives to expound upon that Queen's encouragement of and pleasure in drama, he was making a polemical point about the contemporary neglect of playwrights by the Crown. Similarly, when Rowe conflated the *Merry Wives* story with Shakespeare's "Compliment" to Elizabeth as the "fair vestal" in *A Midsummer Night's Dream* to assert that "Queen *Elizabeth* had several of his Plays Acted before her, and without doubt gave him many gracious marks of her Favour," he was not only enhancing Shakespeare's cultural status but also promoting the entitlement of writers to royal recognition and support.[25] Gary Taylor paraphrases him thus: "Shakespeare's Queen Elizabeth, unlike Rowe's Queen Anne, had actually commissioned plays, as it were . . . (Those were the good old days! People knew a genius when they saw one! But now . . .)."[26] Authors who repeated and embroidered the stories of royal patronage of Shakespeare were expressing a specific authorial nostalgia for a time when they believed, or at least rhetorically claimed, that their profession was more appreciated.

Rowe's biography firmly established the idea that Elizabeth had been Shakespeare's chief protector and benefactor. Charles Gildon repeated the *Merry Wives* story in 1710, with the play gaining yet more in stature through its royal association: "The *Fairys* in the fifth Act makes [*sic*] a Handsome Complement to the Queen, in her Palace of *Windsor,* who had oblig'd him to write a play of Sir *John Falstaff* in Love, and which I am very well assured he perform'd in a Fortnight: a prodigious Thing, when all is so well contriv'd, and carried on without the least Confusion."[27] The *Biographia Britannica* (1747–66), an important early biographical dictionary, reiterated the assocation of Elizabeth with the *Merry Wives* and *A Midsummer Night's Dream,* and closely echoed Rowe in asserting that "Queen Elizabeth . . . shewed Shakespeare many marks of her favour," without, again, indicating precisely what these marks of favor might have been. Similar statements appeared in the entries on Shakespeare in other biographical dictionaries, such as the *Bibliotheca Biographica* of 1760 and the *Biographia Literaria* of 1777.[28]

This anecdote thus became an unquestioned belief for eighteenth-century British readers. It constructed the play as the outcome of a fortunate conjunction of Shakespeare's abundant creativity and Elizabeth's controlling hand, and it demonstrated Shakespeare's remarkable facility as a writer, composing fluently at high speed. It depicted Elizabeth simultaneously as regal—her presiding influence elevates the play—and as engagingly human and populist, appreciating both rumbustious humor and romantic comedy. The tale of the inception of *The Merry Wives* thus functioned as a nostalgic fable of social cohesion. The play is notable as the only one of Shakespeare's comedies to have an English and Elizabethan setting, and especially lends itself to celebration of "merrie England," a rustic, provincial place of pranks and sport, love games and folk rituals, plump knights and scheming wives; indeed, its title alone is enough to associate it with this set of ideas. To posit the play as the joint production of Shakespeare and Elizabeth was to set them up as the presiding figures of a good-humored, harmonious nation where Queens and commoners laughed together at the same jokes. Leah Marcus invokes such ideas in her account of the textual history of the play, which attempts to rescue the 1602 edition from its usual status as a "bad Quarto." This text lacks most of the royal and courtly references found in the 1623 First Folio version, and Marcus argues that the scholarly preference for the Folio text rests in no small part upon the golden image of Elizabethan England that it can be used to support: "a timeless vision of court and countryside in harmonious alliance, of simple rural folk and their superiors, nay even the queen herself, as working reciprocally for mutual prosperity and betterment."[29] Though Marcus locates this textual preference in the late nineteenth and early twentieth centuries, we can trace it back to its origins in the eighteenth-century desire to believe that the Queen commissioned the play.

Early biographers related another anecdote apparently grounded in the oral traditions of Stratford: the story that the young Shakespeare had poached the deer of Sir Thomas Lucy of Charlecote Park. According to Rowe, Shakespeare resented his severe punishment by Sir Thomas and took revenge by composing a satirical ballad which only increased Sir Thomas's vindictiveness, forcing the young poet to leave Stratford for London.[30] Most modern scholars dismiss this story as unfounded,[31] but we can trace its appeal to its mingling of Shakespeare's image with that of another national icon, Robin Hood, with Sir Thomas Lucy cast as the draconian Sheriff of Nottingham. It also offered an opportunity to connect Shakespeare's works with his life: Rowe claimed that Shakespeare made Falstaff a deer stealer in *The Merry Wives* in order to mock Sir Thomas in the character of the pompous but ineffectual Justice Shallow.[32] Douglas Lanier has shown how the story may also be linked to the characterization of Prince Hal in the *Henry IV* plays: "The deer-poaching incident . . . gives Shakespeare's life a redemptive trajectory, from youthful roguery to a successful theatrical career and middle-class respectability, a trajectory mirrored by Prince Hal in his passage from tavern to throne."[33]

As this story too took hold, means were quickly found to involve Elizabeth. The *Biographia Britannica* volume of 1763 asserted that, having been incarcerated for his crime of deer poaching, "it is certain that Shakespeare owed his release at last to the Queen's kindness." The evidence adduced for this was a legal treatise of 1581, *A Compendious or Briefe Examination of certayne ordinary Complaints of diverse of our*

Countrymen. The author of this legal treatise wrote in his dedication of "your Majestie's late and singular clemency, in pardoning certayne my undutifull misdemeanours," and "your gracious goodness and bounty towards me," and gave his initials as "W.S."[34] A 1751 reprint confidently identified him as "the most extensive and fertile Genius that ever any Age or Nation produced, the inimitable Shakespeare," whose dedication offered his homage to "the Most Illustrious Potentate then in the world, the great *Elizabeth*."[35] In fact it is highly unlikely that this was a work by Shakespeare: it would be his only publication on legal matters, and a very precocious one given that in 1581 he was only seventeen years old. He would not begin to be known as a writer in London for another decade, and it seems highly improbable that the Queen would have intervened in the prosecution for petty theft of an unknown youth from rural Warwickshire. By the time the *Compendious or Briefe Examination* was next republished, in 1876, the author W. S. had been convincingly identified as one William Stafford, and the editor conclusively dismissed any association with Shakespeare and deer poaching as "This absurd notion."[36]

Once again, what is significant is the desire of eighteenth-century readers to believe in Shakespeare as a reckless young deer poacher saved by the intervention of his magnanimous monarch. The *Biographia Britannica* dextrously wove this tale together with other materials: the story about the royal commission for *The Merry Wives* was augmented by the assertion that "his address to her upon this occasion is admirable, in making this favourite a deer-stealer," turning Rowe's claim that Shakespeare made Falstaff a deer poacher in order to satirize Sir Thomas Lucy into a knowing private joke between playwright and Queen. Meanwhile, Oberon's vision of the "fair vestal" in *A Midsummer Night's Dream* was supposedly how Shakespeare "expressed his gratitude to Queen Elizabeth, in his own way."[37] Thus the *Biographia* ingeniously integrated all of these materials into apparent evidence of the close patronage relationship between Shakespeare and Elizabeth, all grounded upon the fabricated story that the Queen stepped in to pardon the young poacher. Since this story depended upon Shakespeare's youth, it also implied that Elizabeth somehow recognized his qualities and potential even before he had achieved fame in London. This in turn implied that the lives of the Queen and the poet were fated to converge, by inevitable forces of destiny and providence.

Rowe's seminal biography drew extensively upon oral sources, including Davenant, an elderly actor named William Beeston (whose reminiscences were also used by Aubrey), and reports gathered in Stratford by the actor Thomas Betterton.[38] Margreta de Grazia has argued that the oral traditions—of poaching, of fathering Davenant, of killing calves in high style, and so on—cohere with the prefatory materials of the 1623 First Folio to produce a consistent characterization of the playwright as "short on education, original rather than imitative, natural rather than artful, spontaneous rather than industrious."[39] This Shakespeare was a witty trickster, given to outlandish feats and subversive pranks, and, in de Grazia's words, an "extravagant and vagrant genius." However, the oral traditions also asserted his contact with those in authority: the commendatory letter from King James, Elizabeth's commissioning of the *Merry Wives*, and a story from Davenant via Rowe of a lavish gift of a thousand pounds from the Earl of Southampton.[40] As de Grazia observes, in these three anecdotes "Shakespeare, rather than spurning societal norms and laws, is patronised, commended, and solicited by the ruling establishment."[41] Yet they remain tales of prodigious wonders: the gift from Southampton was, as Rowe remarked, "a Bounty very great, and very rare at any time."[42] It was called forth by Shakespeare's genius, just as the amazingly rapid composition of *The Merry Wives* proved his exceptional brilliance. The stories bespeak a fruitful collaboration between Shakespeare's extraordinary natural talents and the guiding and controlling hand of those in positions of worldly power.

In the particular case of *The Merry Wives*, the channeling and regulation of Shakespeare's gifts by the Queen is paralleled by the dramatic scenario which she requested: Falstaff in love, Falstaff domesticated and tamed by women.[43] The transgressiveness and excessiveness of Falstaff are contained—and this includes the containment of his excessive lust. This too is paralleled in the metaplot of the Queen's commission. As we have seen, both Shakespeare and Elizabeth entered the eighteenth century with somewhat murky sexual reputations, but Dennis and Rowe chose not to dwell upon this. Instead, their accounts of Elizabeth's commission emphasized her "Wisdom in the Arts of Government . . . knowledge of Polite Learning, nice taste of the Drama, . . . [and] the relish which she had of the Ancients," as Dennis put it.[44] In Rowe she is a "gracious" patron and a "Maiden Princess."[45] This encounter between the Queen and the poet is entirely asexual, as they combine to produce a work of intellect and art. Elizabeth's regal serenity and Shakespeare's dutiful service to her have a mutually chastening effect upon their reputations. It is part of a process that Michael Dobson has noted whereby the elevation of Shakespeare to the status of national icon was accompanied by a tendency to make him respectable and to represent him as serenely transcending sexuality or even as a disembodied spirit.[46]

The case of *The Merry Wives* shows us Shakespeare's reputation at a turning point in the early to mid eighteenth century. There is a growing desire to record details of his life in print, but at this stage these print accounts are dependent upon oral traditions which represent him as somewhat roguish and wayward, rather like the younger sons and other free-spirited youths of fairy tales who take chances, use their wits, and win the hands of princesses. In Shakespeare's case, instead of a princess's hand he wins the approval and patronage of the Queen. In the process, the public images of both Elizabeth and Shakespeare are made purer and more virtuous, and the mischievous, freewheeling Shakespeare begins to be assimilated to a more official and institutional kind of national myth making.

Shakespeare and Elizabeth in the Formation of British National Identity

The idea that Shakespeare's art benefited from Elizabeth's appreciation and guidance was complemented by the idea that Elizabeth could not have been the mighty Gloriana without inspiration from Shakespeare. The Elizabethan period inspired nostalgia in the eighteenth century not only as a "merrie England" of social harmony but also as an age of great naval success, chiefly exemplified by the 1588 victory over the Spanish Armada. Representations of this event figured the Protestant English nation as indomitable and impenetrable, gloriously preeminent over the nations of doubtful religion and morality that surrounded her—a nation, in short, chosen and protected by God. Elizabeth, of course, presided over this patriotic vision, and Shakespeare increasingly shared the role of national guiding spirit.

In 1707 Dennis, again, in a prologue spoken by "Shakespeare" at a subscription performance of *Julius Caesar*, claimed that it was the playwright who had emboldened Elizabeth to defy and conquer the Armada:

SHAKESPEARE: This tragedy in great Eliza's reign,
Was writ, when Philip plagu'd both land and main

. . . .

My noble scenes Eliza's soul inspir'd,
And Britain with a just disdain was fir'd,
That we who scorn'd great Caesar here should reign,
Should take an universal king from Spain.

In the very year of the Act that created the United Kingdom of Great Britain, Dennis's lines silently elided England with Britain, a symptom of English hegemony over the new nation. Elizabeth had never, in fact, been Queen of Britain; it was England, not Britain, which had gone to war against Spain; and the "we . . . here" for whom Shakespeare wrote were English, not British, audiences. Here, though, the age of their martial and artistic triumphs was invoked in order to draw all of Britain together in a new kind of patriotism. There were other historical details too that Dennis either did not know or did not care about: in 1588 Shakespeare had scarcely embarked upon his career as a dramatist, and *Julius Caesar* lay many years ahead. Dennis ignored this in order to merge the inception of British naval power with the birth of English literature. If Britons continued to value Shakespeare, he asserted, they would continue to be blessed with the fortitude and military success of Elizabeth:

SHAKESPEARE: Oh, may my scenes be still your chief delight!
So may ye long be fortunate in fight!
So may your glory, like my genius, soar,
And tow'r to heights ye never knew before.[47]

Writings from the first half of the eighteenth century laid an emphasis upon Britishness that was partly inward-looking, attempting to forge a coherent and united identity for the new nation, and partly outward-looking, promoting the cause of Britain against her enemies and celebrating the global advance of British power and trade as the Empire began to grow and flourish. As Shakespeare was increasingly accorded the status of greatest British author, the publication and performance of his plays became a significant part of the fashioning and assertion of a British national identity. As in Dennis's prologue, they were deployed as works that would inspire national pride and martial valor. In the early decades of the century they were promoted as a patriotic alternative to Italian opera, notably by the Shakespeare Ladies' Club, who in 1736–37 mounted a campaign to increase performances of his plays, with the effect that by the 1740–41 season a quarter of all theatrical performances in London were of Shakespeare.[48] An epilogue of 1738 praised the ladies' efforts and claimed that keeping Shakespeare's plays alive would advance "your country's cause" and restore "The manly genius of *Eliza*'s days."[49] A mid-eighteenth-century song urged Britons to "bow at Shakespear's shrine"; like him, they should be "unconfin'd / And rule the World as he the mind."[50]

Over the middle decades of the eighteenth century Shakespeare's reputation and status soared, as he was converted from mischievous deer poacher into the British Bard.[51] The first half of the century saw no fewer than five editions of his plays: Rowe's in 1709 was followed by those of Alexander Pope (1725), Lewis Theobald (1733), Sir Thomas Hanmer (1744), and William Warburton (1747).[52] In 1741 Peter Scheemakers' statue of Shakespeare was erected in Westminster Abbey, showing him as a noble and pensive figure, musing on high thoughts (fig. 1.1). This Shakespeare was a marble monument surrounded by a classical portico, very

FIGURE 1.1

Peter Scheemakers, memorial statue of William Shakespeare, Westminster Abbey, 1740. © Dean and Chapter of Westminster.

unlike the wayward Warwickshire lad derived from oral traditions. By the 1760s, as Michael Dobson relates, readers could consult "dictionaries of Shakespearean quotations, essays on Shakespeare, biographies of Shakespeare, poems on Shakespeare, even a Shakespearean novel."[53] Quotations from or allusions to Shakespeare became ever more frequent in literature, as cultivated readers were assumed to have a thorough acquaintance with his writings. Knowing and recognizing Shakespeare was a mark of education and social status. Shakespeare became, in Jean I. Marsden's phrase, "the hero of English culture."[54]

Theophilus Cibber complained in the 1750s of recent cuts and distortions made to Shakespeare's plays in performance. For him the purity of Shakespeare must be defended as a patriotic duty: "Rouse *Britons*, rouse, for shame! . . . Think you see *Shakespear's Injur'd* Shade, with Patriot-Anguish, sighing over your implicit Belief, and Passive Obedience; your Non-Resistance to this Profanation of his Memory."[55] The terms of his call to cultural arms reflect an increasing contemporary concern with national identity and national confidence. Linda Colley has written of how "the two decades that followed the Battle of Culloden [1746] were an intensely creative period in terms of patriotic initiatives and discussion of national identities . . . the British Museum was founded and so was the *Encyclopaedia Britannica*."[56] The successive editions of Shakespeare's collected works were part of this effort to define and assert a national culture, and more continued to appear, from Samuel Johnson (1765), Edward Capell (1767–68), George Steevens (1773), and John Bell (1773–74). In his dedication Capell made clear his nationalistic purpose, writing explicitly of Shakespeare's works as Britain's cultural capital—"a part of the kingdom's riches" which "are talk'd of wherever the name of *Britain* is talk'd of"—and of his editorial task as a patriotic duty.[57]

Biographical dictionaries like the *Biographia Britannica* (1747–66), the *Bibliotheca Biographica* (1760), and the *Biographia Literaria* (1777) were yet further manifestations of this endeavor of national self-definition and self-commemoration. As we have seen, some of these works perpetuated and elaborated upon the legends which linked Shakespeare to Elizabeth. For Warburton in his 1747 edition of Shakespeare, Oberon's vision in *A Midsummer Night's Dream* showed Shakespeare inspired by the Queen to give of his best: "on these occasions *Shakespear* always excels himself. He is born away by the magic of his enthusiasm, and hurries his reader along with him into these ancient regions of Poetry."[58] Elizabeth here was the author's regal muse, elevating his ideas and imagination. The *Biographia Britannica* in 1763 concurred: in these lines Shakespeare was not only inspired above all other poets, but "even raised above himself." It concluded that "Queen Elizabeth could not but be pleased with our author's address on this occasion," once again taking the lines to be evidence of some kind of reciprocal relationship between monarch and poet.[59]

In fact the *Biographia* went even further than this in attributing a large measure of Shakespeare's dramatic accomplishment to the influence of the Queen. It maintained that when Shakespeare arrived in London and began to write plays they were rough-hewn, crude, and grubbily commercial, designed to please the ignorant groundlings:

> the whole view of this first attempt in stage-poetry being to procure a subsistence, he directed his endeavours solely to hit the taste and humour that then prevailed amongst the meaner sort of people, of whom the audience was generally composed; and therefore his images of life were drawn from those of that rank. These had no notions of the rules of writing, or the model of the ancients. Shakespeare also set out without the advantage of education, and without the advice or assistance of the learned; equally without the patronage of the better sort, as without any acquaintance among them. (ibid.)

Emphasis upon Shakespeare's provincial and relatively humble background eventually provoked questions about how he could have written works of such brilliance and produced rival claimants to their authorship, as we shall see in chapter 5. In 1763, however, the *Biographia Britannica* did not yet look for an alternative Shakespeare but found the solution to the apparently baffling discrepancy between background and achievement in royal influence: "But when his performances had merited the protection of his Prince, and the encouragement of the Court had succeeded to that of the Town, the works of his riper years are manifestly raised above those of his former" (6:3629–31). As we have seen, the *Biographia Britannica* lays great emphasis upon Elizabeth's patronage of Shakespeare, in relation to both the *Merry Wives* and *A Midsummer Night's Dream,* so the prince meant here is clearly Elizabeth and not James. Again Elizabeth serves as Shakespeare's muse, or even a kind of collaborator, raising the tone and standard of his works.

However, as Shakespeare was elevated to increasingly heroic and symbolic status, his reputation became less dependent upon stories of royal approval. In 1735 both Shakespeare and Elizabeth were included in the Temple of British Worthies erected at Stowe by Richard Temple, Viscount Cobham, and designed by William Kent. This was a hall of fame of national icons, and yet more evidence of the interest in defining and promoting British national identity. It contained sixteen busts, eight (including Shakespeare) representing the contemplative life and eight (including Elizabeth) representing the active life; thus Shakespeare and Elizabeth were here regarded as equally meriting commemoration and enshrinement as national "Worthies."[60] However, when Scheemakers' statue of Shakespeare was unveiled at Westminster Abbey in 1741, the pedestal was decorated with portraits of Henry V and Richard III, regal characters from Shakespeare's plays, and of Elizabeth, his presumed patron (fig. 1.1).[61] Shakespeare now had monarchs placed beneath him, supporting the pedestal on which he leaned. They are represented as disembodied heads, masklike, characterless, and merely decorative, whereas the full-length figure of Shakespeare that towers above them is graceful, magisterial, and soulful. Here Elizabeth has no different status from other monarchs fictionalized by Shakespeare: like them she is subordinate to him, simply an inspiration to his genius, and another of his poetic creations (presumably with Oberon's vision and the christening scene of *Henry VIII* in mind).

By the time of the Shakespeare Jubilee at Stratford-upon-Avon, organized in 1769 by David Garrick, Shakespeare was being hailed as "the Bard of all bards" and "the god of our idolatry."[62] He was almost a national messiah: Garrick described his birthplace as "the humble shed, in which the immortal bard first drew that breath which gladdened all the isle," and his admirers were urged to "rush thither to behold it, as pilgrim would to the shrine of some loved saint."[63] Shakespeare hardly needed any more stories of Elizabeth's patronage and approval. These began to recede from prominence, and not only because of Shakespeare's remarkable cultural ascent, but also because Elizabeth's reputation and posthumous identity were extremely complex and unstable. Even during her lifetime, Elizabeth had presented a problem to iconographers. Edmund Spenser had written in *The Faerie Queene* of the need to reflect her "In mirrours more then one" in order to celebrate her problematic combination of the supposedly masculine qualities of a ruler (such as warlike courage, authority, and judgment) with the qualities of the ideal woman (beauty, pity, mercifulness, and so on).[64] To her Protestant supporters she was the Virgin Queen and God's agent on earth, but to her Catholic enemies she was a Jezebel or the Whore of Babylon, the promiscuous offspring of an adulterous and incestuous liaison.[65] Her image had always been multifaceted and riven by ambiguities and contradictions, and this continued not only through the seventeenth century, as John Watkins has shown, but through the eighteenth too.[66]

Some eighteenth-century writers, such as David Hume in his 1759 *History of Great Britain*, continued to celebrate Elizabeth's reign as a golden age when England led the world in religious reform, military success, commerce, and intellectual progress. A song of the 1730s that enjoyed long popularity acclaimed Elizabeth as the epitome of robust Englishness:

> When good Queen Elizabeth sate on the throne,
> Ere Coffee and Tea and such slip-slops were known,
> The world was in terror if e'er she did frown.
> *Oh! The Roast Beef of old England, and old English Roast Beef.*[67]

However, the terms which this song used to praise Elizabeth also illustrate one of the reasons why she was a problematic figure for the eighteenth century. A Queen who, it is implied, dines upon copious quantities of roast beef sounds hearty, indelicate, unfeminine, and perhaps even rather comical. In the Stowe Temple of British Worthies, there was something anomalous about the fact that Elizabeth, the only woman among the sixteen busts, appeared on the side representing the active life, alongside politicians and soldiers. That epilogue of 1738 which asserted that staging Shakespeare's plays would restore "The manly genius of *Eliza*'s days" sounded acceptable insofar as Elizabeth presided over the manliness of her male subjects, but also revealed how far the image of the Queen herself was tinged unsettlingly with masculinity.[68]

Meanwhile works which accentuated Elizabeth's womanliness brought her reputation into another kind of difficulty. Some fictions and dramas perpetuated and expanded upon the scandals found in the secret histories and she-tragedies about the Queen written in the late seventeenth century. Continuing interest in Elizabeth's supposedly scandalous private life was directly related to the contemporary British monarchy's decline in power and charisma.[69] The Glorious Revolution of 1688 had installed a new kind of monarchy that was obliged to observe the will of the people and the forces of political pragmatism. In 1714, the accession of George Lewis of Hanover, after more than fifty candidates with closer blood ties to Queen Anne had been passed over on grounds of their Catholicism, weakened even further the already fragile mystique of the monarchy. George I and his successors did little to foster any cult of personality and seemed on the whole rather dull and stolid, at once too ordinary and too remote to inspire much excitement.[70] By contrast Elizabeth commanded nostalgic appeal, epitomizing an age when royalty was more glamorous and more racy. Works such as James Ralph's *The Fall of the Earl of Essex* (1731), Henry Jones's *The Earl of Essex* (1753), and Henry Brooke's *Earl of Essex* (1761) showed an Elizabeth in love who was tragically divided between head and heart.[71] Other authors showed a Queen who had sacrificed her femininity to become bitter, cruel, and warped. Novels like Sophia Lee's *The Recess* (1785), which told the story of the secret twin daughters of Mary Queen of

Scots and their romantic tribulations at Elizabeth's court, and *The Statue Room* (1790), published under the pseudonym "Rosetta Ballin," depicted Elizabeth as a gothic villainess, jealous of female rivals, whose hopes of true love she vindictively destroyed.[72]

Thus Elizabeth was variously depicted as a woman of unnaturally thwarted sexuality, or a woman disreputably dominated by her sexuality, or a woman who was disturbingly like a man. In each of these guises her image was increasingly out of harmony with eighteenth-century constructions of femininity. With the rise of the cult of sensibility from the 1740s onward, women were expected to be tender-hearted and emotionally sensitive, while at the same time strictly observing sexual propriety and social decorum. Elizabeth's position as lone ruler and as an unmarried woman surrounded by dashing male courtiers rendered her deeply anomalous and problematic. Her private life tended to be depicted as scandalous and troubled, while even those who celebrated her public success did so in terms that rendered her inescapably unfeminine. A 1775 life of George Lillo complained that in adapting Shakespeare's *Pericles* into his own *Marina,* Lillo had not sufficiently purified it, and blamed Elizabeth for its vulgarity: "words which might have been spoken without censure in the drawing room of Elizabeth, a swearing and masculine queen . . . would scarce be permitted now in some houses devoted to pleasure. A modern audience rejects with disgust the companions and language of a brothel."[73] This Elizabeth is both a mannish, thigh-slapping beef-eater and a woman who is too frank and knowing about matters of sex. The writer goes on to acclaim Shakespeare as "sweet Fancy's child," adapting Milton's phrase and thereby associating Shakespeare with the transcendent powers of the imagination and with the innocence of nature.[74] Elizabeth now occupied an opposite position to that accorded her in earlier works: rather than being Shakespeare's muse or elevating patron, offering inspiration and necessary artistic guidance, according to this account she was a coarsening influence who debased and defiled his natural gifts.

The shift in the relative status of Shakespeare and Elizabeth is further exemplified by a 1774 introduction to *The Merry Wives of Windsor.* The play was now found defective, and these deficiencies were attributed to Elizabeth's imposition of a subject not of his own choosing upon Shakespeare and to the enforced haste of composition. Above all, Elizabeth's reputed enthusiasm for Falstaff was seen as profoundly improper and unfeminine:

> If, as we are told, Queen *Elizabeth* relished the former parts of *Falstaff* so much, as to express a wish of seeing him produced in love, it was a great compliment to the Author, and such a one as not a tythe of female

spectators, from that time to this, would pay the Knight. Rhodomontades, lies, and jollity, have but an awkward relish with the softer sex.[75]

"The softer sex": Elizabeth's perceived lack of "softness" became increasingly problematic. Again here her tastes were represented as excessively masculine, crude, and sexual. The *Biographia Literaria* of 1777 also introduced striking variations to the conventional tale of Elizabeth's patronage of Shakespeare. The author dutifully repeated the traditions concerning the *Merry Wives* and the *Dream* and the familiar contention that "Queen Elizabeth, we are told, was much delighted with Shakespeare's dramatic genius, and shewed him many marks of her favour," citing Rowe as source. However, more than customary weight was applied to that phrase "we are told," and the author expressed a new skepticism: "What these many marks of her majesty's favour were, we are not informed; nor indeed can I find proof of his having received any favours at all."[76]

Thus as Shakespeare was elevated to ever higher levels of admiration and veneration, Elizabeth's relative status diminished. In the early part of the eighteenth century, she was represented as a gracious, imperial lady, whose patronage refined Shakespeare's art and cast luster upon it. He was a humble provincial and a mischievous young prankster, endowed with natural but wayward gifts which were given direction by the benign influence of the Queen. As the century proceeded, however, Shakespeare was converted into a national monument and a secular god, with little need of stories of royal patronage to verify the value of his works. Meanwhile Elizabeth's troublingly androgynous sexuality was increasingly out of keeping with eighteenth-century feminine ideals of sensibility, modesty, and politeness. For some she was a coarse, indecorous virago, a representative of a less civilized age, whose influence on Shakespeare had been detrimental and debasing. According to this version of literary history, Elizabeth was not an inspiration to Shakespeare but an impediment. Yet because Elizabeth's image was always multifaceted, complicated, and adaptable, other versions of her persisted as well, and she and Shakespeare continued to be paired as joint progenitors of British greatness.

Elizabeth in the Ireland Shakespeare Forgeries

In 1789 John Boydell opened his Shakespeare Gallery, featuring painted scenes from the plays; and in the following year, Edmond Malone published his magisterial edition of *The Plays and Poems of William Shakspeare*, the result of unprecedentedly thorough and scrupulous research. This magnum opus claimed Shakespeare as the property of a learned elite and sought to inculcate new standards of scholarly accuracy, rejecting the unreliable oral traditions drawn upon by Rowe and his contemporaries. At the same time, however, Shakespeare's influence was spreading ever more widely into popular culture: songs and topical caricatures deployed Shakespearean quotations and allusions, sayings from Shakespeare passed into the language and became proverbial, and recognition of references to Shakespeare could be assumed in audiences and readers across a range of social strata.[77]

This was the pervasive cultural presence of Shakespeare when in 1795 Samuel Ireland, an avid collector of Shakespeare memorabilia, announced the discovery of a collection of papers in Shakespeare's own hand, including legal documents and personal letters. Samuel's nineteen-year-old son, William-Henry, claimed to have obtained the papers from the country seat of an aristocrat, a mysterious Mr. H. They were placed on display in the Irelands' London home, where crowds flocked to see them. Luminaries such as James Boswell and Francis Webb, the secretary of the College of Heralds, pronounced them authentic, and Samuel Ireland was summoned to an audience with the Prince of Wales, who likewise declared that the papers looked genuine to him. A number of Shakespeare scholars were skeptical but largely held their fire until Samuel Ireland's publication in December 1795 of *Miscellaneous Papers and Legal Instruments Under the Hand and Seal of William Shakespeare.* Criticism now became more vocal, and a decisive blow was struck in late March 1796 by Malone's publication of an authoritative 424-page study of the papers, declaring them to be forgeries.[78] William-Henry Ireland confessed that he was the perpetrator, but Samuel went to his grave in 1800 persisting in his belief that the papers were genuine and that his son was incapable of such elaborate and skillful deceptions.[79]

Many of the Ireland papers were legal and financial documents, but the more sensational items included a love letter to Anne Hathaway and a letter from Elizabeth to Shakespeare (fig. 1.2). Even after the impressive scholarly endeavors of Malone's 1790 edition of Shakespeare, the man behind the works remained elusive, with numerous enigmatic gaps persisting in his biography, including, of course, the absence of solid evidence of contact with the Queen. William-Henry Ireland responded to the cravings of his father and the general public for more Shakespeare materials by obligingly filling in those gaps. Given the previous century of Shakespearean traditions, it was unsurprising that these inventions included a letter to the playwright from his Queen. What was more remarkable was its intimate tone:

> WEE didde receive youre prettye Verses goode Masterre William
> through the hands off oure Lorde Chambelayne ande wee doe

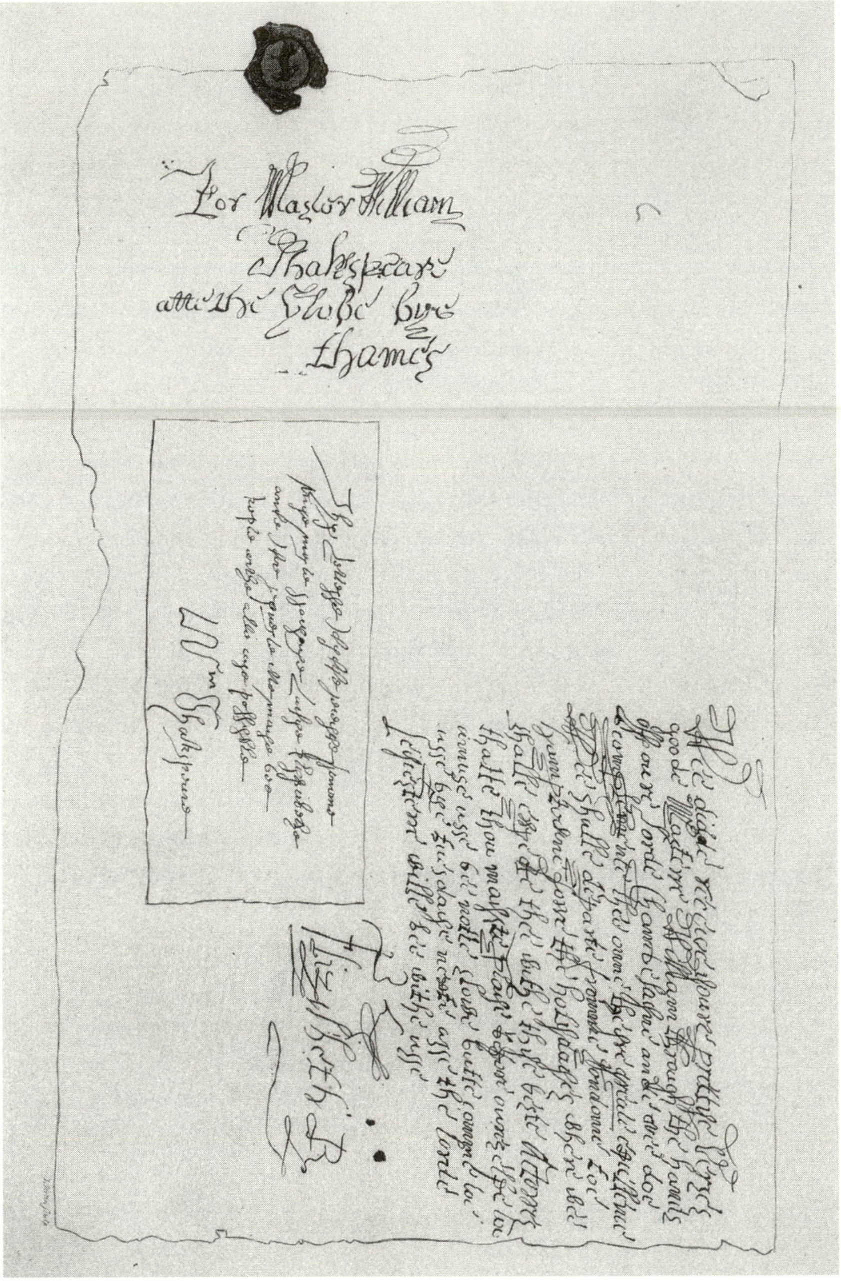

FIGURE 1.2

William-Henry Ireland, forged letter from Elizabeth I to William Shakespeare, published in *Miscellaneous Papers . . . Under the Hand and Seal of William Shakespeare,* ed. Samuel Ireland (London, 1796), 22. Reproduced by permission of the British Library.

complemente thee onne theyre greate excellence Wee shalle departe fromme Londonne toe Hamptowne forre the holydayes where wee Shalle expecte thee withe thye beste Actorres thatte thou mayste playe before oureselfe toe amuse usse bee notte slowe butte comme toe usse bye tuesdaye nexte asse the lorde Leiscesterre wille bee withe usse

Elizabeth R

The letter bore the following address:

For Master William Shakespeare
atte the Globe bye thames

It also bore an inscription:

Thys Letterre I dydde receyve fromme mye moste gracyouse Ladye Elyzabethe ande I doe requeste itte maye bee kepte withe alle care possyble

Wm Shakspeare[80]

This conveniently supplied the evidence of the "many gracious marks of her favour" that Rowe and his successors had been unable to specify. William-Henry's Elizabeth is in keeping with other eighteenth-century characterizations of her as both loftily imperious and a participant in "merrie England"–type holiday pleasures, but he adds a new note in extending Elizabeth's reputation as a promiscuous flirt to include Shakespeare. The mention of Leicester invokes the secret-history tradition of Elizabeth as surrounding herself with handsome favorites, but the emphasis of the letter is upon how delighted she has been with Shakespeare's "prettye Verses," presumably the Sonnets, poems of love. For Shakespeare's part, his careful preservation of the letter suggests both a deferential subject saving a potential heirloom for posterity and a lover saving a keepsake of the lady who inspired his amorous poetry. Overall, the implied relationship between Elizabeth and Shakespeare is one of unprecedented warmth and intimacy.

The fact that anyone believed in the rather unconvincing Ireland forgeries attests to the intense public hunger for more knowledge of Shakespeare's life and personality. It is especially surprising that anyone was persuaded by the letter from Elizabeth, given its obvious flaws, including its peculiar script and spelling, which are unlike any Elizabethan examples. Moreover, the Earl of Leicester died in 1588, some years before the opening of the Globe playhouse, as was pointed out by James Boaden, a playwright, biographer, and Shakespeare scholar who was at first a believer in the Shakespeare papers but then a convert to skepticism.[81] Francis Waldron, an actor and playwright, observed the absurdity of the address on the letter, which was "as carefully worded, as if it were to have been sent by the penny-post; had the office so named been then established."[82] Boaden and Waldron also questioned whether Elizabeth would have written to Shakespeare in such friendly terms: Boaden doubted whether "the haughtiest of monarchs" would have condescended to write a personal letter to "a young adventurer," thus characterizing the Queen as aloof, proud, status-bound and the young playwright as enterprising and imaginative, and thereby participating in the growing tendency to denigrate Elizabeth while enhancing Shakespeare's mystique.[83] He had fun devising his own "discovered" letter from Elizabeth to Shakespeare:

> Wee werre mightylye tickledde at the per fourmaunce offe thye pleasaunte Commedie offe the MERYE WYFFES. Thye wytte couthe welle Maisterre William . . . We give thee nottice thatte wee shalle *drinke Tea* withe thee bye Thames Tomorrowe, thou Monarche offe the *Globe* . . .
>
> P.S. More offe oure virgin beautye.
>
> Thynne everre toe commaunde,
>
> ELIZABETH, R.
>
> *Greenwyche,*
> *Julye Ninethe,* 1580.[84]

Boaden mocks not only Ireland's eccentric orthography, but also, in the invitation to tea, his anachronisms and his construction of an improbably cosy relationship between monarch and poet.

Yet in spite of all these forceful objections, the tradition that Elizabeth personally favored Shakespeare had sufficient enduring allure for significant numbers of supporters to give credence to Ireland's forgery. In his confession, he explained, "I wrote Queen *Elzabeth*'s [*sic*] letter from her signature only, which I copied from an original in my father's possession, this letter was produced to make our *Bard* appear noticed noticed [*sic*] by the greatest personage of his time, and thereby add, if possible, fresh lustre to his name."[85] His "if possible" admits that by now it seemed difficult to augment any further the lofty claims made for Shakespeare's genius. Yet even so, Elizabeth's stature as "the greatest personage of his time" created an irresistible desire to assert proximity and contact between them. H. R. Woudhuysen has described how in Elizabeth's own lifetime documents in her hand were treasured and even venerated, being felt to convey a sense of Elizabeth's presence and of the private selfhood of a powerful public figure.[86] Ireland's forgeries were motivated by a comparable desire to simulate presence and intimate contact: to produce for readers the real Shakespeare and the real Elizabeth.

Before his forgeries were exposed, William-Henry Ireland was emboldened to create a whole "newly discovered" Shakespearean work, *Vortigern*, which was staged, disastrously, two days after the publication of Malone's *Inquiry*. He also planted in one of his "Shakespeare" manuscripts a reference to "mye chosen Interlude neverr yett Impryntedd & wrottenn for & bye desyre of oure late gracyouse & belovedd Quene Elizabethe called ye Virginn Quene & playde 3 tymes before herreselfe att the Revells."[87] He explained in his confession that he had intended to compose both *The Virgin Queen* and another play, *Henry VII*, and present them as Shakespeare's.[88] A play by Shakespeare about Elizabeth would clearly have been a sensational event, and Ireland's tantalizing notion was taken up by Waldron in his critique of the Ireland papers, published anonymously in 1796, which offered extracts from a play called *The Virgin Queen*. However, it disappointed expectations: Waldron acknowledged that the title might lead readers to anticipate a drama "related to the history of our Virgin Queen, Elizabeth, herself," but explained that as a woman of "masculine mind" Elizabeth "could not have endured to see herself pageanted in a Stage-play, or Interlude." Instead, the play was a sequel to *The Tempest*, in which Claribel, Queen of Tunis, was the Virgin Queen. Waldron teasingly prolonged the mystery of its authorship: "that it was written by Shakspeare I will not take upon me to assert; yet, it is not likely that any other person should attempt a Sequel to . . . the Tempest."[89] The following year, 1797, *The Virgin Queen, A Drama in Five Acts*, was published in full, but by now Malone had conclusively discredited the Ireland forgeries and the debate was over, so Waldron simply published under his own name, representing it as a self-confessedly "weak essay at an imitation of our immortal SHAKSPEARE,"[90] and claiming that he composed it as a contribution to the exposure of the Ireland forgeries, to show how easily imitations of Shakespeare could be foisted on the public.[91] A recent biographer of Waldron describes it as "one of the worst pieces of drama inspired by Shakespeare."[92] Thus *The Virgin Queen* emerged as neither about Elizabeth nor by Shakespeare, and the episode ended in a bathetic non-event.

It is not coincidental that William-Henry Ireland's transgression of the boundary between scholarly research and invention occurred just when others, led by Malone, were policing that boundary with unprecedented rigor. For Margreta de Grazia, Malone's 1790 edition of Shakespeare, followed by his life of Shakespeare, published posthumously in 1821, marked a watershed in attitudes toward Shakespeare: "Malone's overwhelming preoccupation with objectivity marks a significant shift in the focus of Shakespeare studies away from what might be termed the discursively acceptable to the factually verifiable, from accounts whose validity was assured by continued circulation to information whose accuracy was tested by documents and records."[93] Until this point all biographies of Shakespeare derived from Rowe, who in turn relied upon oral testimony, but Malone scorned and rejected "traditionary tales" as unreliable (ibid., 72–76). His high standards of verification made him the nemesis of the Ireland forgeries, yet the new era of documentary scholarship that he helped to inaugurate was also the context for their production. His 1790 Shakespeare edition contributed to the public desire for more Shakespearean documents and for a sense of contact with the real Shakespeare. William-Henry Ireland responded to these desires and, despite his incompetence, sought to trade in the commodities of authenticity and veracity which Malone had raised to a new value.

In the particular case of the letter from the Queen, Ireland's flouting of the line between scholarship and fabrication was also motivated by the persistent desire to bring Elizabeth and Shakespeare into ever closer proximity. Malone's rejection of the traditions representing Shakespeare as a somewhat wayward, deer-poaching youth had sanitized the playwright's image and left it rather lifeless. Ireland's invention of a flirtatious letter from Elizabeth thanking Shakespeare for his poems was an ingenious response to this: it attributed to both Elizabeth and Shakespeare a romantic interest in the opposite sex which was intriguing yet also normal and natural, protecting her from a reputation as Amazonian or mannish and distracting attention from the fact that many of the Sonnets were addressed to a lovely youth. In creating personal voices for Shakespeare and Elizabeth, Ireland also gave a new directness and immediacy to representation of their personalities and their relationship, anticipating techniques which would shortly flourish in historical fiction. He was a resounding failure as a forger, but it is appealing to speculate that if he had been born a generation or two later he might have enjoyed some success as a novelist.

Indeed, the exposure of the Ireland forgeries not only reflected the growing aspiration among scholars to enforce a rigid separation between fact and invention but also laid the groundwork for the new genre of historical fiction. Any versions of history that could not be fully authenticated were now increasingly excluded from the realm of the biographer and the editor, but they did not disappear: rather, they found a new home in the novel. Scholars were no longer supposed to imagine the past or to report hearsay, but novelists were subject to no such restrictions and could therefore make powerful claims to take the reader back into history as lived experience. At the beginning of the next century, fiction writers, led by Sir Walter Scott, began to develop a genre in which historical and biographical research, making a claim to factual truthfulness, were combined with and even altered by licensed invention, making a claim to psychological truthfulness. As the desire to connect Shakespeare and Elizabeth became more difficult to satisfy in biographical scholarship, it could thus be amply indulged in historical fiction, as we shall see in the next chapter.

2

Facts and Fictions in Nineteenth-Century Britain

By the beginning of the nineteenth century, Shakespeare's cultural status depended less upon stories of Elizabeth's favor, yet the Ireland forgeries illustrate a persistent desire to connect the two figures. Both Shakespeare and Elizabeth were by now historical celebrities, each of them generating anecdote and myth; and since they were contemporaries, it was inevitable that their two growing bodies of legend would interconnect. Moreover, while Shakespeare was increasingly revered as a timeless genius, Elizabeth conveniently personified the age that bore her name. This meant that depiction of her as an admirer of Shakespeare supported modern Bardolatry by implying that it had deep and venerable origins.

Shakespeare and Elizabeth also continued to function as a powerful double emblem of British greatness. A somewhat tongue-in-cheek prologue of 1792 described Elizabeth as a queen who "Defied each foreign threat" and "gen'rous, open, hearty and sincere, / Eat good old English beef, and drank strong beer."[1] By 1814, in Jane Austen's *Mansfield Park*, Henry Crawford could declare Shakespeare to be "part of an Englishman's constitution."[2] Shakespeare and Elizabeth as separate entities were each established and potent symbols of Englishness and Britishness, and they could perform this role even more effectively when brought together to epitomize a golden age in which the nation's greatness was founded. In Thomas Dibdin's two-volume *Metrical History of England* (1813), a section on the glorious reign of Elizabeth ran through the executions of Essex and Mary Queen of Scots, the Armada victory, and the personal gifts of the Queen and her courtiers, but culminated in her highest achievement of all—to have watched Shakespeare's plays: "And, climax of a wondrous age! / Who first saw SHAKESPEARE's genuine page, / Give truth and nature to the stage? / ELIZA."[3] As here, Shakespeare increasingly stood center stage, with Elizabeth called upon as merely a witness to his genius, yet that witness remained essential. A life of the playwright from 1826 by Charles Symmons related that

> Elizabeth, as it is confidently said, honoured our illustrious dramatist with her especial notice and regard. She was unquestionably fond of theatric exhibitions; and, with her literary mind and her discriminating eye, it is impossible that she should overlook; and that, not overlooking, she should not appreciate the man, whose genius formed the prime glory of her reign.[4]

For such writers the "prime glory" of Elizabeth's reign was, not Gloriana herself, but Shakespeare. Even so, her discernment and appreciation of his exceptional gifts had become an integral and indisposable part of his myth.

Elizabeth in Nineteenth-Century Shakespeare Biography

In 1821 Edmond Malone's long-awaited life of Shakespeare was posthumously published by James Boswell the younger. The rigorous Malone was scathing about Nicholas Rowe's "meagre and imperfect narrative"; he opined that its status as Shakespeare's official biography for eighty years after its first publication "cannot be contemplated without astonishment."[5] He rejected traditions such as the deer-poaching anecdote and inveighed against "the deviation from truth which the inquiries I have made have enabled me to detect, in several received accounts concerning our poet and his family, which, for a century, have been considered as authentick" (119). It is surprising, therefore, that he continued to describe *The Merry Wives of Windsor* as "being, it is said, composed at the desire of Queen Elizabeth, in order to exhibit Falstaff in love" (373–74). That phrase "it is said" carefully signals that he has not personally verified this theory, but also opens a question as to why Malone was not stirred to investigate this particular myth when he challenged a number of others. The answer may lie in later parts of the *Life*, in discussions of other plays. Malone follows Rowe again in surmising that *Henry VIII* was written out of regard for Elizabeth[6] and finds plausible a suggestion that *The Winter's Tale* was written to please her, as an exoneration of Anne Boleyn (388–94, 460–62). Later still, in the final parts of the *Life*, which were completed by Boswell from Malone's notes, there is reiteration of the tradition that Elizabeth commissioned *The Merry Wives* and an assertion that Shakespeare "appears to have enjoyed the approbation and favour of two successive monarchs. Queen Elizabeth, who was at all times attached to theatrical entertainments, had the good taste to appreciate the talents of that great poet whose genius has shed so much lustre on her reign" (478).

Malone did not imagine that Elizabeth visited the playhouses; in his 1790 "Historical Account of the English Stage," often reprinted, he had given a succinct and authoritative history of royal playgoing: "Neither Queen Elizabeth, nor King James the First, nor Charles the First, I believe, ever went to the public theatre; but they frequently ordered plays to be performed at court . . . Queen Henrietta Maria, however, went sometimes to the publick theatre at Blackfriars."[7] Even so, and even while assiduously testing many of the other biographical anecdotes about Shakespeare, Malone clung to the idea that the playwright enjoyed the personal patronage and approbation of his Queen. Because of Malone's authority and influence, this was a significant contribution to the reiteration and perpetuation of this belief. It is also strong testimony to the ideological potency of the double myth of Shakespeare and Elizabeth, functioning to affirm the "genius" of Shakespeare and the "lustre" of Elizabeth's reign, in Malone's words, and thereby on this particular issue blurring the vision of an otherwise stringent Shakespeare scholar.

However, Malone did not dignify with any attention a particular Shakespeare-and-Elizabeth anecdote which had first appeared in the popular press in 1796, when the furor surrounding the Ireland forgeries was at its height. This story had even less authority than Rowe's traditionary tales. Elizabeth, it was said, was watching Shakespeare perform the role of a king when she dropped a handkerchief onto the stage. Shakespeare, without for a moment stepping out of role, returned it to her with the effortlessly ad-libbed lines, "But, ere this be done, / Take up our SISTER's handkerchief."[8] The story was retold and elaborated in 1825 by Richard Ryan, an Irish biographer:

> It is well known that Queen Elizabeth was a great admirer of the immortal Shakespeare, and used frequently (as was the custom with persons of great rank in those days) to appear upon the stage before the audience, or sit delighted behind the scenes, when the plays of our bard were performed. One evening, when Shakspeare himself was personating the part of a King, the audience knew of her Majesty being in the house. She crossed the stage when he was performing, and, on receiving the accustomed greeting from the audience, moved politely to the poet, but he did not notice it! When behind the scenes, she caught his eye, but still he would not throw off his character, to notice her: this made her Majesty think of some means by which she might know, whether he would depart, or not, from the dignity of his character, while on the stage. Accordingly, as he was about to make his exit, she stepped before him, dropped her glove, and recrossed the stage, which Shakspeare noticing, took up, with these words,

immediately after finishing his speech, and so aptly were they delivered, that they seemed to belong to it:

> "And now though bent on this high embassy,
> Yet *stoop* we to take up our *Cousin's* glove!"
>
> He then walked off the stage, and presented the glove to the Queen, who was greatly pleased with his behaviour, and complimented him upon the propriety of it.[9]

Dryden in 1667 had written that "*Shakespear*'s pow'r is sacred as a King's," and Boaden's spurious letter from Elizabeth in 1796 saluted Shakespeare as "thou Monarche offe the *Globe*."[10] Similarly, in the glove anecdote, Shakespeare's kingly stage role emphasized his intellectual and artistic supremacy, with increasingly meritocratic and democratic implications, here raising him to sibling- or cousin-like parity with the Queen. Ryan's version of the tale also amplified Ireland's and Boaden's suggestions in their fabricated letters of Elizabeth's amorous interest in Shakespeare: the dropped glove is at once an imperious and a flirtatious gesture, seeking to command Shakespeare's service as both a subordinate and a courtly lover. Shakespeare, meanwhile, in his response, is caught between two competing mistresses, his dramatic art and his queen. He succeeds graciously in asserting his dedication to his professional vocation—Elizabeth cannot deflect him from his performance—while satisfying the vanity of his royal spectator. The very aristocratic ease with which he does this implies his innate superiority over the haughtily attention-seeking Queen.

The way in which Ryan writes about the audience and Elizabeth's interaction with them seems to assume a performance at the public playhouse where Elizabeth has dropped in unannounced, rather than a performance at court. Indeed, for the byplay between Shakespeare and Elizabeth—the meeting of glances, the slipping on and off stage—he seems to imagine a nineteenth-century–style theatre with a proscenium arch and wings, not the apron stage of the Elizabethan amphitheatre playhouse. Ryan either had not read Malone on Elizabeth's absence from public playhouses or chose to ignore him. Yet the historical implausibility of the glove anecdote did not prevent it from enjoying wide circulation throughout the nineteenth century. Indeed, a biography of Shakespeare published in the same year as Ryan's anecdote, 1825, simply melded self-contradictory materials: it duplicated Ryan's story and at the same time followed Malone in stating that Elizabeth never attended the public theatre.[11]

The glove story appeared again in the *New Monthly Magazine* of 1837,[12] and in James Orchard Halliwell's Shakespeare biography of 1848. Halliwell felt some skepticism: "I cannot say who invented this story, but there is no good authority for it, however possible it may be that it is founded on an earlier and less circumstantial tradition."[13] Nevertheless, he still mentioned it in support of his belief that "Shakespeare was certainly fortunate enough to attract the notice and commendation of royalty early in his career" (151). Halliwell took some pains to substantiate this, citing Jonson's elegy, the *Merry Wives* anecdote, Oberon's vision, and Chettle's *England's Mourning Garment* and taking less notice of Shakespeare's silence at Elizabeth's death than of Chettle's assertion that Elizabeth "graced his desert, / And to his laies opend her Royall eare" (152–53).[14] He also adduced Otway's 1680 claim of Shakespeare that "A gracious Prince's Favour chear'd his Muse," though as we saw in chapter 1 this might have referred to James I rather than Elizabeth.[15] Halliwell combined the glove anecdote, despite his doubts about it, with these other pieces of evidence to give a cumulative sense that Shakespeare enjoyed Elizabeth's encouragement and patronage.

All the same items of evidence were cited by Samuel Neil, a Scottish Shakespearean, in 1861, though he looked more favorably upon the glove tale as "a well-known, and not an improbable story." Indeed, he added detail to it: he identified the play being performed as *Henry IV*.[16] He pursued the discussion in a further Shakespeare biography in 1869, where he attributed the glove-dropping incident to Elizabeth's annoyance at Shakespeare's reticence in praising her:

> "The Great Elizabeth," who had delighted in the creations of our Bard, and who being accustomed to poetic flattery, was perhaps touched with jealousy because he did not directly praise her, is reported to have showed him a special courtesy as she passed along the stage to her seat, by letting her glove drop where he must needs stoop to pick it up, and so receive her personal thanks.[17]

Neil here presents a kind of contest for preeminence; after all, casting down a glove may be not only a flirtatious gesture but also a challenge to a duel. Shakespeare is at first aloof from Elizabeth, and Elizabeth is stung into forcing him to acknowledge her presence and her supremacy: giving him her personal thanks is a way of making him bow before her. Elizabeth triumphs in the immediate event, but Shakespeare triumphs in the more appealing impression which he makes on posterity.

The glove story continued to be retold through the later decades of the nineteenth century, though sometimes relocated at court and thereby rendered marginally more credible.[18] It appears as late as a novel of 1919 (see chapter 6). There was evidently enduring appeal in the episode's direct yet inexplicit interaction between Shakespeare and Elizabeth, with its loaded gestures and Shakespeare's wittily ambiguous speech, behind which the scene is fraught with cross-currents of class rivalry and erotic tension.

Meanwhile, John Payne Collier, who had emerged in the 1830s as a leading Shakespeare scholar, turned out to be a successor to the Irelands rather than Malone.[19] In *New Facts Regarding the Life of Shakespeare* (1835), he explained that he had found significant manuscripts relating to Shakespeare, hitherto unexplored and some indeed previously unopened, in the collection of Lord Francis Egerton, Earl of Ellesmere, at Bridgewater House. Egerton's ancestor was Sir Thomas Egerton, later Lord Ellesmere, Keeper of the Great Seal to Elizabeth I. One of Collier's "discoveries" was a letter signed "H.S." introducing Shakespeare and Burbage to Egerton. Collier identified "H.S." as Henry Southampton, that is, Henry Wriothesley, Earl of Southampton, Shakespeare's early patron. The letter describes Shakespeare as "my especiall friende, till of late an actor of good account in the cumpanie, now a sharer in the same, and writer of some of our best English playes, which as your Lordship knoweth were most singularly liked of Quene Elizabeth, when the cumpanie was called vppon to performe before her Matie at Court at Christmas and Shrovetide."[20] The following year, in *New Particulars Regarding the Works of Shakespeare,* Collier announced another exciting "find": "within the last few weeks I have found proof that Othello was written, not in 1604, according to Malone's Chronology . . . but certainly as early as 1602 . . . This important fact I learn from the detailed accounts preserved at Bridgewater House . . . of the expenses incurred by Sir Thomas Egerton, afterwards Lord Ellesmere, in entertaining Queen Elizabeth and her Court for three days at Harefield."[21] He provided a transcription of these accounts:

> 31°. July et 1°. et 2° Augusti 1602, the Queenes Matie beeing at Harefield iij nights . . .
> 6 Aug. 1602. Rewardes to the Vaulters Players and Dauncers. Of this £10 to Burbidge's players for Othello.

Collier concluded, "It is indisputable, from this evidence, that *Othello* was acted at Harefield in 1602."[22] His "Life of William Shakespeare" in an 1844 edition of the works included among much respectable scholarly discussion a fuller account of this performance for the Queen. The occasion was

> the latest visit [Elizabeth] paid to any of her nobility in the country . . . only nine or ten months before her death . . . Whether [Shakespeare] was or was not one of the "players" in "Othello," in August 1602, there can be little doubt that as an actor, and moreover as one "excellent in his quality," he must have been often seen and applauded by Elizabeth.[23]

The community of Shakespeare scholars at first saw little reason to challenge Collier's apparent discoveries, or perhaps had too much investment in mutual gentlemanly support to wish to do so. Although J. W. Croker was suspicious of the "H.S." letter as early as 1841,[24] many scholars shared Alexander Dyce's view in 1844 that "Mr. Collier's *Life of Shakespeare* exhibits the most praiseworthy research, a careful examination of all the particulars which have been discovered concerning the great dramatist, and the most intimate acquaintance with the history of the early stage."[25] By 1848 James Orchard Halliwell was aware of an error in another supposed transcription by Collier but nevertheless wrote confidently in his *Life of William Shakespeare* of that year that "Mr. Collier discovered that Othello was acted at Harefield Place . . . before Queen Elizabeth in July 1602, when she was entertained by Lord Keeper Egerton."[26]

However, as other scholars came to consult the manuscripts in Bridgewater House, doubts grew, and by 1853 Halliwell had dramatically altered his view and denounced all the documents supposedly found there by Collier as modern forgeries.[27] In 1859, manuscript annotations on a volume dubbed the "Perkins Folio" of Shakespeare, which according to Collier dated to the early seventeenth century and were based on Shakespeare manuscripts or early performances, were scrutinized and found to be modern and written in a hand similar to Collier's own.[28] With C. M. Ingleby's publication in 1861 of *A Complete View of the Shakspere Controversy*, Collier was utterly discredited: many of his supposed documents, wrote Ingleby, "are not known to have had any existence, except from the statements of Mr. Collier: the fact being that they are not in the depositaries where he professes to have found them."[29] The terms of Ingleby's attack on Collier illustrate the godlike status to which Shakespeare had by now ascended: "Shame to the perpetrator of that foul libel on the pure genius of Shakspere. The texts of Shakspere and of the English Bible have been justly regarded as the two river-heads of our vernacular English . . . Yet it is one of these texts that a tasteless and incompetent peddler has attempted to corrupt."[30]

Collier's forgeries were of a very different order from Ireland's in their professionalism and credibility. Collier had a substantial reputation as an authoritative Shakespeare scholar—indeed, alongside his fabrications he made significant contributions to the field—and drew upon his expertise to render his forgeries convincing. Like Ireland, however, in inventing Shakespearean materials he found it irresistible to compensate for the absence of evidence recording direct contact between Shakespeare and Elizabeth.

In 1861, the year that Ingleby published his denunciation of Collier, Samuel Neil's biography of Shakespeare reported that "At Harefield (Middlesex), the seat of Sir Thomas Egerton, the sum of £10 was paid to 'Burbidge's players' for performing 'Othello' before Queen Elizabeth, 6th August, 1602."[31] We might think that the exposure of Collier's unreliability was too recent to have reached Neil, but eight years later he reiterated that in 1602 "'Othello' was presented before Queen Elizabeth at Harefield in Middlesex at the residence of Sir Thomas Egerton by 'Burbage's players.'"[32] The Collier forgeries show us not only how strong was the continuing desire to find evidence linking Shakespeare and Elizabeth but also, through their persistent influence, just how resistant writers could be to give up such beguiling evidence, even when it had been publicly discredited.[33]

The year 1821, when Malone's life of Shakespeare came out, also saw the publication of Sir Walter Scott's *Kenilworth*, a seminal historical novel featuring Elizabeth and Shakespeare. It can be plausibly argued that Malone's influence caused scholarship and fiction to be more rigidly demarcated: scholarship confined itself now to verifiable fact and relegated more creative imaginings about Shakespeare and Elizabeth to fiction. There is some truth in this, yet the boundary between scholarship and fiction remained permeable. As we have seen, Malone himself could not resist the myth of Shakespeare and Elizabeth. His successors as Shakespeare biographers continued to merge documentary and traditionary evidence, including one tradition, the glove anecdote, which was of recent and dubious origin. Collier went further and blurred scholarship and fabrication to a point where they were indistinguishable to all but the most expert eye, ironically deploying a Malone-like scholarly professionalism to render his invented materials all the more convincing, and thereby achieving a persistent influence on other biographers. What all these materials indicate is that nineteenth-century Shakespeare biographers, for all their new dedication to truth and evidence, remained committed to telling a good story, and therefore continued to reproduce enthusiastically any available materials which connected Shakespeare with Elizabeth. They were also committed to the celebration of Shakespeare and of the British cultural excellence that he personified, and Elizabeth's contribution as royal worshiper at his shrine therefore continued to be essential.

Kenilworth (1821) and the Development of Historical Fiction

Shakespeare and Elizabeth had featured in various kinds of historical fiction before the nineteenth century. Elizabeth's supposed torrid love affairs were depicted in the secret histories of the late seventeenth century, while Sophia Lee's *The Recess* (1785) had taken her into Gothic romance. Shakespeare had featured in *Memoirs of the Shakespear's-Head in Covent-Garden* (anon., 1755), in which his ghost lamented his own youthful errors (reiterating traditionary tales such as that of the deer poaching) and then narrated and deplored scenes of folly and vice which he had witnessed in the Shakespear's Head tavern.[34]

Such works drew upon history fairly loosely as a source for plots and characters, but the publication of Sir Walter Scott's novels, beginning with *Waverley* in 1814, introduced a new level of authenticity to historical fiction. Scott was assiduous in his archival research and in his attempts to recreate the dialects of particular eras and regional locations. Just as Malone sought to bring a new empiricism and probity to literary scholarship, so Scott's novels evinced a post-Enlightenment concern with truth, probability, and realism. They were simultaneously innovative and nostalgic: products of an age of industrialization and revolution, they gave Scott's readers a consoling escape to a world before such turmoils but also found parallels to those turmoils, and indeed their origins, in the historic past. They were also distinctively of their own time in their concern with national identity: with relations between England and Scotland, with the concept and origins of "Britishness," and with the role of the monarchy.[35] Scott thus imbued historical fiction with a new topicality and a new seriousness and stature. He recognized that sentimentality and Gothic sensationalism were effective in engaging readers, but he deployed these in novels which aspired to a closer knowledge and understanding of the past. By grounding his narratives upon figures and events from history, but also exercising artistic invention, Scott aimed to recreate the experience of the past for his readers, drawing them into the thoughts and feelings of his characters to simulate how it felt to live in the midst of famous and momentous events.

In 1820 Scott published *The Abbot,* a novel set in Scotland in 1567–68 which featured Mary Queen of Scots as a character, and which led him for his next project toward the subject of Elizabethan England.[36] *Kenilworth* centers upon the Princely Pleasures offered by Elizabeth's favorite Robert Dudley, the Earl of Leicester, to entertain her at Kenilworth Castle on her summer progress of 1575. Historians have often regarded these sumptuous festivities, which included pageants asserting the pleasures and virtues of matrimony, as a final attempt by Leicester to woo Elizabeth, despite his furtive marital entanglements with Lady Douglas Sheffield and Lettice Knollys, Countess of Essex. Scott, however, ignored the scandals involving these ladies, and, despite the new authenticity which he had brought into historical fiction, exercised artistic license to represent Leicester's first wife, Amy Robsart, as a tragic secret bride in 1575. In fact, she died in suspicious circumstances in 1560, fifteen years before the Princely Pleasures. Scott further distorted history by incorporating Shakespeare in his narrative as an adult and established author, despite the fact that in 1575 he was only eleven years old.

These distortions of history were nevertheless underpinned by extensive archival research.[37] Scott had edited several sixteenth- and seventeenth-century texts, including Robert Carey's *Memoirs* and Robert Naunton's *Fragmenta Regalia,* and had read widely in Elizabethan materials.[38] For particular details of the Princely Pleasures, he consulted two Elizabethan eyewitness accounts, Robert Laneham's letter and George Gascoigne's *The Princely Pleasures at the Courte at Kenelworth* (1576), both reproduced in the first volume of John Nichols's *Progresses and Public Processions of Queen Elizabeth* (1788), of which Scott owned a copy.[39] It is a mark of his scholarly concern that after *Kenilworth*'s publication, when an antiquarian friend sent him a newly discovered inventory of the household effects of Kenilworth Castle, he insisted on revising later editions accordingly.[40] His archival sources included Thomas Percy's *Reliques of English Poetry* (1794), which he first read as a boy.[41] Percy had noticed that Kenilworth Castle was only twelve miles from Stratford, and that it was therefore possible that Shakespeare as a boy was among an audience of local people admitted to watch the Princely Pleasures. Percy mentioned the traditional Coventry play presented before the Queen and observed,

> Whatever this old play, or "storial show" was at the time it was exhibited to Q[ueen] Elizabeth, it had probably our young Shakespeare for a spectator, who was then in his twelfth year, and doubtless attended with all the inhabitants of the surrounding country at these "Princely pleasures of Kenelworth," whence Stratford is only a few miles distant.[42]

Percy imagined that "our young bard" would have been highly entertained by both the Coventry play and all the pageants and shows put on during the festivities: "we may imagine what an impression was made on his infant mind." The spectacles "must have had a great effect on a young imagination, whose dramatic powers were hereafter to astonish the world" (ibid.). This gave new force and specificity to the idea of Elizabeth as Shakespeare's muse. According to this model, the Queen and the entertainments devoted to her were an early catalyst of Shakespeare's dramatic gifts and furnished material to inspire him in his later career. Percy's hypothesis was widely accepted; it was endorsed by Malone in 1796 and repeated in subsequent lives of Shakespeare. As we shall see in chapter 4, from 1832 onward it became significant in readings of *A Midsummer Night's Dream.*

Scott followed Percy in centering his novel on the Princely Pleasures and in trying to connect Shakespeare and Elizabeth, but departed from him in depicting Shakespeare not as a boy but as an adult, already established as a notable writer. One reason for this was that it enabled Scott to mobilize what one modern editor has called his "encyclopaedic knowledge of Elizabethan dramatic literature," which is evident in *Kenilworth* in several forms.[43] The novel draws upon *Macbeth* and *Othello* as templates for some specific scenes[44] and is permeated throughout by many echoes of and allusions to Shakespeare and other Elizabethan dramatists. These are most obvious in the chapter epigraphs but are also present in the endeavor to forge a dialogue style which is at once comprehensible to the early-nineteenth-century reader but also marked as Elizabethan. Pseudo-Shakespeare was a literary language which Scott's readers could be assumed to recognize and share. As Edmund Bertram had remarked in Jane Austen's *Mansfield Park* in 1814, "No doubt one is familiar with Shakespeare in a degree . . . from one's earliest years. His celebrated passages are quoted by everybody; they are in half the books we open, and we all talk Shakespeare, use his similies [*sic*], and describe with his descriptions."[45] Scott draws upon his own close personal knowledge of Shakespeare's works to fill *Kenilworth* with Shakespeareana, thus giving the novel an aura of period authenticity even if its factual detail is not strictly accurate.

There is therefore aesthetic, if not historical, decorum in the fact that, not long after we first encounter Elizabeth in the novel, she starts quoting Shakespeare. She is dispensing advice on love to the fictional hero of the novel, Amy Robsart's true love, Edmund Tressilian:

> Think of what that arch-knave Shakespeare says—a plague on him, his toys come into my head when I should think of other matter—Stay, how goes it?—
>
> > Cressid was your's, tied with the bonds of heaven;
> > These bonds of heaven are slipt, dissolved, and loosed,
> > And with another knot five fingers tied,
> > The fragments of her faith are bound to Diomed.
>
> You smile, my Lord of Southampton—perchance I make your player's verse halt through my bad memory—but let it suffice.[46]

Elizabeth's tone suggests that she has an established and easy familiarity with both the "arch-knave" Shakespeare and his works by 1575, the year in which the novel is set, although the lines she quotes are from *Troilus and Cressida*, probably composed around twenty-five years later.[47]

A few pages on, the playwright himself makes an appearance, spotted by the Earl of Leicester in a crowd of petitioners:

> "Ha, Will Shakespeare—wild Will!—thou hast given my nephew, Philip Sidney, love-powder—he cannot sleep without thy Venus and Adonis

under his pillow!—we will have thee hanged for the veriest wizard in Europe. Heark thee, mad wag, I have not forgotten thy matter of the patent, and of the bears."

The Player bowed, and the Earl nodded and passed on—so that age would have told the tale—in ours, perhaps, we might say the immortal had done homage to the mortal. (168)

Here Scott blithely abandons historical sequence: it is supposed to be 1575, but Leicester refers to *Venus and Adonis,* which was not published until 1593, some years after his own death in 1588 and that of Sidney in 1586. It is striking, though, that Scott's embroidering of history does not extend to giving Shakespeare dialogue, as if to imagine the speech and inhabit the mind of the inimitable Bard would be unthinkably presumptuous. This would not inhibit later historical novelists, as we shall see; Scott, however, wisely prefers to leave Shakespeare silent and ineffable. At the same time, Leicester's jocularity is carefully pitched by Scott in order to combine a sense of Shakespeare's unmistakable genius with a sense of historical distance. Leicester cannot help noticing the quality of Shakespeare's works but is too obtuse to recognize their full greatness. The irony of a view from posterity is accentuated in the image of the immortal bowing to the mortal, where Scott momentarily steps out of period to allow himself and his readers a brief satisfaction in the superior knowledge and discernment of their own time.

In his appearance in *Kenilworth,* then, Shakespeare is a figure at once shadowy and marked with significance, a strongly felt presence even as he lurks in the margins of the narrative. Although he does not appear again in person in the novel, this is not the last we hear of him, and again, he is introduced by means of Elizabeth. As she passes along the Thames in her barge with her courtiers, they debate a petition from the keeper of the royal bears. Elizabeth explains: "He complains, that amidst the extreme delight with which men haunt the play-houses, and in especial their eager desire for seeing the exhibitions of one Will Shakespeare, (whom I think, my lords, we have all heard something of,) the manly amusement of bear-baiting is falling into comparative neglect" (173). Various courtiers debate the value of plays and playing, until Elizabeth reveals herself as Shakespeare's most perceptive and far-sighted critic: "touching this Shakespeare, we think there is that in his plays that is worth twenty Bear-gardens; and that this new undertaking of his Chronicles, as he calls them, may entertain, with honest mirth, mingled with useful instruction, not only our subjects, but even the generation which may succeed to us" (175). She alone has some sense, if a limited one, of Shakespeare's significance to posterity.

Scott incorporates the deer-poaching anecdote: the Earl of Sussex relates that Shakespeare "stood, they say, a tough fight with the rangers of old Sir Thomas Lucy of Charlecot, when he broke his deer-park and kissed his keeper's daughter" (174). This romantic elaboration of the myth continues the tradition of reading Falstaff's deer stealing in *The Merry Wives of Windsor* as autobiographical. In the play Justice Shallow, who since Rowe had been assumed to stand for Lucy, accuses Falstaff as follows:

> SHALLOW: Knight, you have beaten my men, killed my deer, and broke open my lodge.
>
> FALSTAFF: But not kissed your keeper's daughter?
>
> SHALLOW: Tut, a pin. This shall be answered.
>
> FALSTAFF: I will answer it straight: I have done all this. That is now answered.
>
> (*Merry Wives of Windsor*, 1.1.93–98)

In *Kenilworth* the identification of Shakespeare with Falstaff, and especially the addition of the stolen kiss to the stolen deer, enhances Shakespeare's personality, making him sound bold, dashing, and virile. Scott also enhances the myth that Elizabeth intervened personally to commute Shakespeare's sentence: "'I cry you mercy, my Lord of Sussex', said Queen Elizabeth, interrupting him; 'that matter was heard in council, and we will not have this fellow's offence exaggerated—there was no kissing in the matter, and the defendant hath put the denial on record'" (174). Elizabeth is clearly jealous, with an interest in the playwright and his works which is romantic as well as aesthetic: Scott here takes up the developing idea that the Virgin Queen's feelings toward the Bard might have been a little warmer than merely the favor of a gracious patron. It is notable that the first Shakespeare works to be mentioned by Scott's characters were *Troilus and Cressida* and *Venus and Adonis*; Shakespeare is introduced as primarily a poet of love, who whould naturally arouse the interest of the passionate Queen.

The case in favor of the playhouses is clinched when Sir Walter Raleigh, presented as a rising and dashing young favorite, recites "the celebrated vision of Oberon." Scott comments:

> The verses were not probably new to the Queen, for when was ever such elegant flattery so long in reaching the royal ear to which it was addressed? But it was not the less welcome when recited by such a speaker as Raleigh. Alike delighted with the matter, the manner, and the graceful form and

animated countenance of the gallant young reciter, Elizabeth kept time to every cadence, with look and with finger. When the speaker had ceased, she murmured over the last lines as if scarce conscious that she was overheard, and as she uttered the words,

> "In maiden meditation, fancy-free,"

she dropt into the Thames the supplication of Orson Pinnit, keeper of the royal bears. (176–77)

Shakespeare woos Elizabeth by proxy through the royal favorite Raleigh, an ingenious device by Scott to create a delicate and displaced erotic *frisson* between Queen and playwright without suggesting any scandalous or ahistorical encounter. As Elizabeth echoes the closing lines, she at once takes pleasure in them, relishing her iconic status as maiden Queen, and strikes an elegiac note, as if wistfully regretting her maidenhood. The moment also mimes her collusion with and even her dependence upon Shakespeare and the other poets of her reign to create her mythologized image and to make it endure. She seems to have some unarticulated sense of how her place in posterity and Shakespeare's are inextricably bound together. Fiction enables Scott to take his readers back into the past, and from there to look forward prophetically to the posthumous celebration of Shakespeare and Elizabeth in Scott's own day. In so doing he implies that he is to some degree ironically self-conscious about his own participation in that process of mythologization.

We have seen that Scott's treatment of the encounter between Shakespeare and Elizabeth is full of anachronisms. A novelist who was also a scholar, and who has been acclaimed for making historical fiction more authentic, in this work flagrantly and knowingly mingled several discrete episodes in Elizabethan history. As a modern historical novelist has explained, "I'm a storyteller, not a historian. Of course you try to get the history right, but in the end you sacrifice the history for the story."[48] The Scott scholar Harry E. Shaw goes further and argues that "a work can become more historical, not less historical, if it rearranges individual aspects of the historical record for the sake of demonstrating a larger pattern."[49] According to this line of thought, Scott's refashioning of events gives us a version of Elizabethan England which is authentic in essence if inaccurate as to facts. It is notable that his idea of the essence of Elizabethanism includes the association of Elizabeth and Shakespeare.

Shakespeare himself, of course, practiced selection and compression in his conversion of chronicle materials into drama. Scott's contemporaries recognized this, describing him as "the Shakespeare of novelists."[50] This encompassed not only his flexible treatment of history but qualities of scope and scale in his works which were also identified as Shakespearean: a democratic social range embracing both low and high characters; a generic hybridity combining the tragic and comic; and a general plenitude, inventiveness, and humanity.[51] In around 1830 Scott was pictured bowing his head in reverence before Shakespeare's tomb, both acknowledging his master's greatness and receiving a kind of benediction from him as his natural successor (fig. 2.1). In *Kenilworth* itself Scott described Shakespeare as "a halting fellow," that is, a man with a limp, following a tradition derived from literal readings of line 3 of Sonnet 37 ("So I, made lame by fortune's dearest spite"). This was a detail which assisted the identification of novelist and poet, since Scott himself had been lame in one leg since infancy.[52] Accordingly, his portrait at Shakespeare's tomb gives prominence to the walking stick on which Scott leans. Thus the incorporation of Shakespeare and Shakespeare-related materials in *Kenilworth* advanced Scott's own literary stature; and even though Elizabeth features more prominently in the plot of the novel than Shakespeare does, it has an overall pseudo-Shakespearean manner which would have a far-reaching influence.

The supposedly "Shakespearean" qualities of Scott's fiction, such as inclusiveness, expansiveness, and generosity of spirit, contributed to developing ideas about what it meant to be British. *Kenilworth* was only the second of Scott's novels to have an entirely English setting; the first was *Ivanhoe,* in 1819. There are several ways in which we can understand why a famous Scottish author should have turned to English subject matter, and specifically, to the celebration of the "merrie England" of Shakespeare and Elizabeth. *Ivanhoe* may be read as a fictional compliment to the Prince Regent, whom Scott revered, and who would reward him with a knighthood; *Kenilworth* similarly expresses Scott's veneration of the monarchy. A political conservative, he was an enthusiastic supporter of the Union of Scotland and England and a believer in British imperialism, which he saw as rooted in the energy and enterprise of the Elizabethans. He was also well aware of the demands of the literary market; he was anxious not to "wear out the public favour" by endlessly rehearsing Scottish themes, and at the same time wanted to enhance his appeal to an English readership. This he very successfully did with *Kenilworth,* which helped to establish him as a British rather than merely Scottish writer.[53]

Kenilworth was highly esteemed through the nineteenth century, inspiring a whole genre of pseudo-Elizabethan fiction, sometimes described as "tushery" or "gadzookery."[54] It generated numerous stage adaptations and burlesques, at least eleven operas, popular redactions, and even a scene in a set of dioramas for home display.[55] In 1865 Arthur Sullivan composed *Kenilworth: A Masque of the Days of Queen Elizabeth,* with words by Henry Chorley, who apologized in his introduction for

FIGURE 2.1
Attrib. Sir William Allan, *Sir Walter Scott at Shakespeare's Tomb*, c.1830.

using the "summer night" scene from *The Merchant of Venice* in his depiction of the Princely Pleasures but pointed to Scott's own precedent in anachronistically using *Troilus and Cressida* and *A Midsummer Night's Dream* in a novel set in 1575.[56] Both Chorley and Scott knowingly distorted history in the cause of art; and, for both of them, an important motivation in this was the urge to bring Shakespeare and Elizabeth together.

Victoria and Shakespeare and Elizabeth

As we have seen, toward the end of the eighteenth century Elizabeth's image became increasingly complex and self-contradictory. She never ceased to be praised for presiding majestically over a golden age and as a personification of national greatness, yet at the same time she was increasingly vilified in personal terms as coarse and unfeminine. Mary Deverell, in the Prologue to her 1792 historical tragedy *Mary Queen of Scots,* apologized for her temerity in criticizing a national icon but added, "ELIZA blame! who, high in estimation, / Was (till of late) rever'd throughout the nation . . . ?."[57] That phrase "till of late" is telling; Elizabeth's reputation was evidently perceived to be at a watershed. Within the play, Mary's appealing beauty and femininity were set against Elizabeth's "masculine" mind. (ibid., 28). Malone, in his life of Shakespeare, while sustaining the idea of Elizabeth's regal patronage of the playwright, also disparaged her in passing, writing that Cranmer's prophecy in *Henry VIII* was designed to flatter a Queen who "became very solicitous about the reputation of virginity, when her title to it was at least equivocal."[58]

A new failing for which Elizabeth was criticized was meanness. According to an 1825 life of Shakespeare, Elizabeth's parsimony drove Shakespeare into sycophancy in pursuit of financial rewards that never came, "notwithstanding all the elegant flattery which the poet offered on the shrine of her vanity" (although as we saw in the Introduction above, Shakespeare's writings in praise of Elizabeth in fact were rather few and not particularly flattering).[59] Charles Symmons in 1826 made the same point:

> Favoured, however, as our Poet seems to have been by Elizabeth, and notwithstanding the fine incense which he offered to her vanity, it does not appear that he profited in any degree by her bounty. She could distinguish and could smile upon genius: but unless it were immediately serviceable to her personal or her political interests, she had not the soul to reward it.[60]

Unappreciated, undervalued, and uncomplaining, Shakespeare emerges much better from these accounts than the egotistical and unappreciative Queen. An 1843 biographer restated that Elizabeth did not reward Shakespeare "with anything more solid than her smiles; a cheap mode of remunerating genius."[61] This account appeared again in an 1857 edition of Shakespeare's works, where the *Merry Wives* tradition was repeated in an irreverent tone of jocular mock-chivalry toward Elizabeth: "if we are really indebted for so admirable a play to the stately old damsel's desire to see Falstaff in love, we are more than ever her maiden majesty's devoted servants."[62] This version of Elizabeth is a petulant and demanding old lady, an antiquated and somewhat absurd relic of a past age. In such accounts of Elizabeth's relations with Shakespeare, he rose above her autocratic and time-bound demands: more and more, she personified history whereas he personified the transcendence of history by timeless genius.

This idea of Elizabeth's mean-mindedness was linked to her reputed unfemininity. According to Anna Jameson in 1831, Shakespeare was patronized by Essex and Southampton, just as Spenser was patronized by Raleigh and Sidney, but "whatever countenance the Queen bestowed on the two greatest men of her time, was through the influence of these favourites."[63] She was "a woman whose avarice and jealousy, whose envious, relentless, and malignant spirit, whose coarse manners and violent temper, render her detestable; whose pedantry and meanness, whose childish vanity and intense selfishness, render her contemptible" (284). She was narrow-minded and narcissistic: "One more destitute of what is called *heart*, that is, of the capacity for all the gentle, generous, and kindly affections proper to her sex, cannot be imagined in the female form" (322). This supposed lack of womanly sensibility was deplored even more after the accession of Queen Victoria in 1837, and especially after her marriage to Prince Albert in 1840 and the birth of their first child the same year. As a female monarch who was a devoted wife and a prolific mother, Victoria presented a stark contrast to the Virgin Queen. Louisa Stuart Costello wrote in 1844 that Elizabeth's character "can never be popular with her sex," and that her qualities were all "manly", with the sole exception of her vanity: "Tenderness, softness, pity, and forgiveness, were unknown to her mind, and, but for her vanity, she would have been scarcely woman or human."[64] She was, in short, the antithesis of Victorian femininity, as was made clear when *The Victoria Magazine* compared the current sovereign:

> Two queens, belonging to two different types of womanhood . . . yet both stamping their own individuality . . . on the whole era through which they move . . . Elizabeth, with her masculine intellect, her iron will, . . . her

stately court . . . and the utter blank of her domestic life . . . ; Victoria, gifted with moderate not commanding talent, who if not born a Queen might have been much like an ordinary gentlewoman; refined, accomplished, wise, and good: in everything essentially womanly, and carrying through life a woman's best amulet, the power of loving nobly, deeply, and faithfully.[65]

When set against Victoria and the kind of femininity that was promoted in her reign, Elizabeth looked profoundly unnatural and unappealing.

Yet Elizabeth continued to have a very different symbolic role as the presiding monarch of a national golden age, an era of English naval success, colonialism, and cultural achievement. Reconstructions of that golden age took on increasing interest and importance as nineteenth-century Britain strove to assert its national identity and its imperial authority, and to anchor these in its past. Elizabeth frequently brought with her a large and attractive retinue of courtiers, poets, and adventurers, personifying the splendors, talents, and burgeoning global power of Elizabethan England. Even Jameson, for all her vilification of Elizabeth's unfeminine selfishness, celebrated her reign as "an age, in some respects, resembling our own; a period not only fertile in great events, but in great men; it was the age of heroism and genius, of wonderful mental activity, extraordinary changes, and daring enterprises, of fierce struggles for religious or political freedom. It produced a Shakespeare, the first of poets." It also produced Bacon, Hooker, Drake, Gresham, Sidney, Spenser, Raleigh, and Essex, "names renowned in history and song."[66] Charles Kingsley, writing in 1859, rhapsodized similarly:

> There was, in plain palpable fact, something about the Queen, her history, her policy, the times, the glorious part which England, and she as the incarnation of the then English spirit, were playing upon earth, which raised imaginative and heroical souls into a permanent exaltation—a "fairyland" as they called it themselves . . . There can be no doubt that a number of as noble men as ever stood together on the earth did worship that woman, fight for her, toil for her, risk all for her, with a pure chivalrous affection which has furnished one of the most beautiful pages in all the book of history . . . let us look at the fair vision as a whole, and thank God that such a thing has for once existed even imperfectly on this sinful earth.[67]

Iconographers of Britain's burgeoning imperial might sought to recreate this "fairyland" with Victoria presiding as a reincarnation of Gloriana. A children's book of 1848, *Peter Parley's Tales about Kings and Queens,* ended with Cranmer's prophecy from *Henry VIII* adapted and transferred to Victoria. References to virginity were excised, but the climactic prophecy of world empire was emphatically restated: "Wherever the bright sun of Heav'n shall shine, / Her name shall sound like sweetest music."[68] As Velma Bourgeois Richmond has commented, "Thus Victoria completes the role for England that Elizabeth began."[69]

Shakespeare too was an important foundation stone of the Victorian imperial project. Paul Franssen has written of how Empire builders took with them to their far-flung outposts both the King James Bible and their Complete Works of Shakespeare as instruments of civilization.[70] In a lecture of 1840, Thomas Carlyle spoke of how other nations were more and more compelled to acknowledge the cultural supremacy of Shakespeare: "I think the best judgment not of this country only, but of Europe at large, is slowly pointing to the conclusion, That Shakspeare is the chief of all Poets hitherto."[71] Part of what Carlyle valued in Shakespeare was national sentiment: he said of *Henry V* that "there is a noble Patriotism in it . . . a true English heart breathes, calm and strong, through the whole business" (178). He declared that "Shakspeare is the greatest of Intellects" (174), almost a new messiah bestowed upon England (Carlyle's emphasis is upon Englishness rather than Britishness): "I feel that there is actually a kind of sacredness in the fact of such a man being sent into this Earth. Is he not an eye to us all; a blessed heaven-sent bringer of light?" (181). This implicitly designated England as a new Israel, a new chosen nation of God. The climax of Carlyle's lecture was a vision of Shakespeare's works as unifying a global and millennial English-speaking empire:

> England, before long, this Island of ours, will hold but a small fraction of the English: in America, in New Holland [i.e., Australia], east and west to the very Antipodes, there will be a Saxondom covering great spaces of the Globe. And now, what is it that can keep all of these together into virtually one Nation, so that they do not fall out and fight, but live at peace, in brotherlike intercourse, helping one another? . . . Here, I say, is an English King, whom no time or chance, Parliament or combination of Parliaments, can dethrone! This King Shakspeare, does he not shine, in crowned sovereignty, over us all, as the noblest, gentlest, yet strongest of rallying-signs . . . ? We can fancy him as radiant aloft over all the Nations of Englishmen, a thousand years hence. (183–84)

Shakespeare's domain, he predicted, would extend from Paramatta (in New South Wales, Australia) to New York and beyond. This is a vision of a humanist, universal Shakespeare who transcends national boundaries, yet it is simultaneously a vision of English culture, as personified by Shakespeare, conquering the world.

To worship Shakespeare is to be fully English; to be fully English is to be fully human, a profoundly colonialist assumption.

India, the jewel in the crown of the Empire, presents a clear example of how Shakespeare was used to promote British culture and power. From the early 1800s the governing East India Company set up schools and colleges to train Indians as English-speaking administrators and clerks. Unsurprisingly, Shakespeare featured prominently on the syllabus, and students would often participate in amateur performances or recitation competitions. The English Education Act of 1835, which made English the official language of government-funded educational institutions, cemented the role of Shakespeare in what Jyotsna G. Singh has called the "civilising mission" of the ruling British. Knowledge of Shakespeare's works became an important form of cultural capital for Indians ambitious to gain positions in the imperial administration and to elevate themselves socially.[72]

The identification of Shakespeare with British national identity and increasingly with British imperial supremacy made it vital that Queen Victoria should be seen to support and enjoy the performance of Shakespeare's works. The Queen often attended London theatres in the first two decades of her reign, but her preference was for French and Italian operas and plays or burlesques and other kinds of rather low-brow entertainment. This provoked criticism that she was neglecting her duty to patronize and promote the native dramatic tradition.[73] In response, in 1844 Charles Kemble, one of the leading actor-managers of the day, was invited to Buckingham Palace to read from an abbreviated version of *Henry VIII*, but this did little to silence the critics, who observed that the royal family seemed only able to cope with Shakespeare in compressed form. The satirical magazine *Punch* published a letter, purportedly from Victoria to King Louis-Philippe of France, enthusing about Shakespeare and declaring "All I envy Elizabeth is her Shakespear," a barbed irony designed to ridicule the real Queen's apparent lack of interest in, and perhaps even aversion to, the works of the Bard.[74] In relation to theatrical patronage, comparisons between Victoria and Elizabeth were unfavorable to the later Queen: instead of surpassing Elizabeth in womanliness or completing the imperial project begun by Elizabeth, in this context Victoria was seen as failing to emulate her predecessor and letting British culture down. For the polemical purpose of exhorting Victoria to bestow more enthusiastic patronage on native British drama, Elizabeth was represented not as mean and parsimonious but as a generous, nurturing patron to Shakespeare.

The royal family attracted more opprobrium in 1847 when the government failed to buy Shakespeare's birthplace for the nation, and the royal party failed to attend a fund-raising gala performance of Shakespearean scenes at Covent Garden.

Prince Albert urged remedial action, so in the summer of 1848 the royal couple attended performances of English plays at Drury Lane and the Haymarket Theatre, including that of William Charles Macready, an established Shakespearean star, as Cardinal Wolsey in *Henry VIII.* They also revived the Elizabethan office of Master of the Revels, and announced the commissioning of private theatricals, to include Shakespeare, at Windsor Castle over the next Christmas season.[75] The organization of these performances was placed in the hands of Charles Kean, son of Edmund Kean and one of the leading Shakespearean actor-managers of the day. The Queen and Prince Albert selected the repertoire themselves, which included *The Merchant of Venice* and *Hamlet.*[76]

Both at home and abroad, 1848 was a year of political turmoil. The Chartists caused significant political agitation, though this fizzled out in April with the failure of a poorly organized petition and mass demonstration in London.[77] In Ireland there was radical activity by Young Ireland, a nationalist organization, but this too petered out as the Famine came to an end.[78] In the rest of Europe, it was the Year of Revolution, which saw governments overthrown in France, Austria, Prussia, Hungary, and Italy.[79] The fact that Britain, despite outbreaks of dissent, had escaped complete political upheaval seems to have created a national mood of relief and self-congratulation. A writer in the *Annual Register* for 1848 declared, "While almost every throne on the Continent was emptied or shaken by revolution, England stood firm, and even appeared to derive increased stability from the events which convulsed foreign kingdoms."[80] The 1840s had also seen a growing cultural nostalgia: as architects revived native Gothic forms and medievalism became a dominant strain in Victorian taste, the past became an important resource for the definition of British identity and pride.[81]

It was in keeping with all these aspects of the national state of mind that Queen Victoria and Prince Albert sat down at Windsor Castle at Christmas 1848 to watch performances of Shakespeare. The *Times* reported this as a revival of Shakespeare's golden age, when his gracious monarch requested "a series of English theatrical performances as a recreation in her own palace": "Fancy has wandered back to the days of Elizabeth and the first James, when such means of amusement were not uncommon; and perhaps, wandering forward, has augured that a new stock of dramatists worthy to compete with those of the Elizabethan era may spring into existence from the effect of the Windsor Theatricals."[82] The sense of historical precedent for the Windsor performances also inspired the publication in 1849 of John Kemble Chapman's *Complete History of Theatrical Entertainments, Dramas, Masques, and Triumphs, at the English Court.* Chapman, a theatrical publisher and theatre manager, directly compared Victoria with Elizabeth as patrons of drama: "In the present advanced state of our civilisation we look back in pleasure to the fostering care bestowed by Elizabeth on the theatre of her age, and it is, therefore, reasonable to expect that future generations will revert with equal gratification to the patronage extended by QUEEN VICTORIA to the stage."[83] That phrase "fostering care" signals that here Elizabeth is being figured as metaphorical mother to England and its theatre, and promotes the same role for Victoria.

Chapman related how Victoria, like her predecessor, sat in state to view the plays, herself as much of a spectacle as the on-stage performances: "In the front of the centre of the stage, upon a dais approached by three steps, and closed in on either side by a gorgeous screen of purple velvet, fringed with gold, sat QUEEN VICTORIA." She was surrounded by an entourage who personified the greatness of her age and her realm, "a brilliant circle of statesmen and warriors, nobles and ladies," recalling the glorious retinue of heroes and courtiers often imagined surrounding Elizabeth and personifying her imperial regime. Chapman described Victoria's attendants "listening with the deepest attention, and evidently deriving the highest intellectual gratification from the representation of those ever-enduring works of genius that have charmed in ages past, and must continue, through time to come, to delight every lover of truth and nature, from the monarch to the peasant" (38–39). Thus Shakespeare supposedly binds all classes together into one deep-thinking and civilized nation. Victoria recreates Elizabeth's age, and even betters it, not least in that she has "her Royal Consort by her side, and her beauteous group of children at her feet." The Virgin Queen may have been a metaphorical mother to the nation and its drama, but Victoria's physical fecundity enables her to pose more convincingly as an icon of feminine propriety and matriarchal abundance.

Richard W. Schoch has described Chapman's account of the Windsor theatricals as "embarrassingly sycophantic."[84] However, it had an admonitory edge: Chapman urged Victoria to go further in her emulation of Elizabeth's supposedly magnanimous theatrical patronage: "To the favour bestowed by Royalty upon the drama may in a great measure be attributed the flourishing state to which it attained during Elizabeth's reign. She not only encouraged the youthful dramatist, Shakspere, whose productions were represented at the Court of the Sovereign, but extended her protection to the theatrical profession generally" (13). Chapman deployed Shakespearean scholarship in support of this cause. While he knew that Elizabeth did not, like Henrietta Maria, visit the public theatres, he repeated the story of the commissioning of *The Merry Wives* and Collier's recent contention that *Othello* was performed for Elizabeth at Harefield in 1602. He added, "It was about the year 1588 that one of Shakspere's plays ('Love's Labour Lost,' it is believed) was performed at Court before Elizabeth" (13, 14, 25). In fact the quarto edition of

Love's Labour's Lost, which bore the title-page inscription "presented before her Highnes this last Christmas" dated from 1598, not 1588.[85] By placing the performance ten years earlier, in the year renowned for the Armada victory, Chapman associated Elizabeth's supposed patronage of Shakespeare with the birth of British naval and imperial power. Taken altogether, this was history polemically invoked in a contemporary cause: if Victoria "extended her protection" as generously as Elizabeth had, it was suggested, she too might nurture another Shakespeare to celebrate her rule and commemorate it for posterity.

The Windsor theatricals continued over every Christmas season until the death of Prince Albert in 1861 and often included Shakespeare plays. Victoria also continued to attend Shakespeare performances at the public theatres, including Charles Kean's *King John* (1852) and *Winter's Tale* (1856).[86] Kean's production style was characterized by attempts at historical accuracy in settings and costumes, ushering in a new antiquarianism in the Victorian theatre which chimed with the desire for Victoria to preside over a recreated Elizabethan age of great native drama. Despite her efforts to demonstrate a willingness to embrace this role, any signs of insufficient enthusiasm for Shakespeare on her part were keenly watched and invariably provoked unfavorable comparisons with Elizabeth. In 1853 she did not attend Samuel Phelps's notable production of *A Midsummer Night's Dream* because it was at the Sadler's Wells Theatre, which was thought to be too far north from central London and too unfashionable. *Punch* duly lamented that "our Elizabeth has not visited our Burridge" (i.e., Burbage, Shakespeare's leading actor).[87] However, Victoria and her family were delighted with Kean's medievally authentic production of *Richard II* in 1857, performed first privately for them in St. George's Hall at Windsor Castle and then in public at the Princess's Theatre, where the Queen saw it no fewer than five times. Ironically, the Shakespeare play which may have been used in an attempt to destabilize Elizabeth's rule on the eve of the Essex Rebellion (see chapter 4) in this instance became an affirmation of the ancient origins from which Victoria claimed her monarchical authority. She wrote, "It was curious that a Play, in which all my ancestors figured, should just have been performed in St. George's Hall." Shakespeare was now definitively the Bard of the British monarchy. The Princess Royal made a painting of the performance as a birthday present for her mother, and at Christmas Prince Albert gave Victoria a set of photographs of it which took pride of place under the royal Christmas tree.[88]

It was important for the self-image of Victorian Britain that their Queen should be seen to enjoy and patronize the works of the national poet as much as her sixteenth-century predecessor was supposed to have done. In practice Victoria satisfied this public desire only intermittently. She was sometimes praised for resembling Elizabeth as a patron of Shakespeare and sometimes criticized for not matching up to her; but in both cases the myth of Elizabeth's direct favor toward Shakespeare was amplified and reinforced for polemical and political purposes. This inevitably changed after Prince Albert's death in 1861: in Victoria's grief-stricken widowhood, at least in its early years, she could not be expected to attend plays even in private. However, she now took particular comfort in Tennyson's *In Memoriam*: the poet laureate had an audience with her at Osborne in April 1862 and others thereafter.[89] These occasions helped to fix in the public mind the idea of the preeminent poet of the day receiving royal favor and being regularly summoned to court, and contributed to the burgeoning genre of visual and literary images of Shakespeare reading or performing for Elizabeth.

Historical Fiction, Drama, and Painting

The success of *Kenilworth* created a flood of historical novels, plays, and paintings through the nineteenth century, in which encounters between Shakespeare and Elizabeth were, predictably, a recurrent theme. Three years after Scott's novel, Nathan Drake published *Noontide Leisure*, a fiction in which an older Shakespeare reminisced about his attendance at the 1575 Princely Pleasures. In a Shakespeare biography of 1817, Drake had enthusiastically taken up Percy's idea of the boy William's presence at Kenilworth:

> To the ardent and opening mind of our youthful Bard what exquisite delight must this grand festival have imparted . . . the dramatic cast of the whole pageantry, whether classical or Gothic, was such, as probably to impress his glowing imagination with that bias for theatrical amusements, which afterwards proved the basis of his own glory, and of his country's poetic fame.[90]

Now, in his novel, he made Shakespeare recall his experience of the Princely Pleasures, which he attended as the page of an old Stratford harper: "the pomp and splendour of the pageantry, and, above all, the dramatic cast of the greater part of the entertainments, absolutely fascinated, and, I may say, absorbed my imagination." He attracted the attention of the Queen herself, "probably struck with the tenderness of my years, and the fanciful dress which I had assumed." Later, Elizabeth's own recollection of their first encounter helped to advance him in his London career: "when in after life I had acquired some little publicity as a dramatic writer," this "brought the name of Will Shakspeare to her ear, with associations which, inducing her to ascertain if the page and the poet were the same, more readily disposed her to patronise the interests of the latter."[91] According to Drake, then, Elizabeth's Kenilworth visit was crucial to the creation of Shakespeare the dramatist, for it served not only as an early catalyst but also as the basis for her later patronage.

An early biographical drama about Shakespeare was Charles A. Somerset's *Shakspeare's Early Days* of 1829. The Queen has just heard of the Armada victory when the Earl of Southampton presents young Shakespeare to her, fresh from poaching deer in Warwickshire. The newcomer from Stratford hands Elizabeth a copy of *Hamlet,* which she reads "with evident delight." Much as Scott compressed and distorted chronology, so Somerset gives us a remarkably accelerated version of events: *Hamlet* is written before Shakespeare even arrives in London, and Elizabeth becomes his patron before he has even set foot in a playhouse. His rapid sequence of events presents a distinctively post-Romantic version of Shakespeare as a born genius, divinely inspired, with no need to spend time learning his craft. Moreover, by locating Shakespeare's introduction to Elizabeth immediately after the Armada victory, Somerset merges the inception of British naval and imperial power with the birth of English literature, jointly created by Shakespeare as author and Elizabeth as patron, to produce a single and mythically potent historical moment. Elizabeth, as in Scott, has exceptional discernment of Shakespeare's brilliance, and her role is largely to give it public and official certification: "in his eye there glows intelligence; / Which heaven alone, and not scholastic lore, / Could have inspired," she declares.[92] Accordingly, she pardons his poaching: "Sdeath! Shall we chastise / For a mere venal fault, where heaven, approving, / Hath showered down choicest gifts [?]" (46–47). She will be a surrogate mother to him—"He shall not lack a fostering hand to rear him"—and she rewards his resounding victory in a poetry contest with the pedantic Doctor Orthodox by hanging her picture on a gold chain round his neck, partly as a token of intimacy and affection, partly as a kind of chain of office for her effectual poet laureate. The play ends with a grand chorus praising Shakespeare, of which the final line is, "Shakspeare is his nation's pride!" (47–48). The public acclaim of his queen is central to the ritual confirming him as natural genius and national hero.[93]

Scott's influence on Drake's novel and Somerset's play is clear. It extended also to historical painting, which rose and flourished in the early nineteenth century. Like the historical novel, this medium licensed artists to use imagination as well as research to reconstruct the past and transport the spectator back into the emotional and psychological reality of the moment.[94] Notable historical events were depicted with color and emotion, frequently with much detail of costume and setting, and often on an epic scale. Sir Roy Strong dates the beginnings of historical painting to 1760, the year of the first annual exhibition by the Society of Artists, which in 1768 would become the Royal Academy. However, he celebrates the nineteenth century as its golden age, and shows how Scott's influence brought about both a new concern for historical accuracy and a desire to give personal, domestic glimpses of earlier ages.[95]

Historical painting was related not only to the historical novel but also to the genre of paintings based on literary works. Predictably, Shakespearean subjects had been especially popular since the eighteenth century. John Boydell's Shakespeare Gallery on Pall Mall, for which artists were commissioned to paint scenes from the plays, opened in 1789, with the professed intention of inaugurating "an English School of Historical Painting."[96] Meanwhile, from 1769 until 1830 there were around five to ten Shakespeare-based paintings shown each year in the Royal Academy exhibition. In the 1830s this figure jumped to around fifteen per year, and in the 1840s and 1850s it increased again, to an average of twenty per year.[97] Linking literary and historical painting, artists began to depict scenes from Shakespeare's life. These sometimes concerned his domestic life in Stratford; but artists were also inspired by scenes of either Shakespeare reading his works to Elizabeth or Elizabeth watching a Shakespeare play. Indeed, Julia M. Walker has justly commented that "There are so many pictures of Shakespeare reading to Queen Elizabeth that they almost constitute a genre in Victorian painting."[98]

One early example is Thomas Stothard's engraving *Shakespeare's Interview with Queen Elizabeth* (1827, fig. 2.2). Here the figures are imagined neither at court nor at the playhouse but in an intimate and romantic location, a leafy bower of a royal palace whose ornate turret can be glimpsed in the distance. In this shady and pastoral setting, Shakespeare reads from a manuscript to the Queen and an unnamed male courtier, presumably one of her favorites. Shakespeare, dressed in plain dark clothes and seen only in profile, his eyes lowered to his writing, cuts a serious and rather stiff figure. However, the words he is reading are evidently arousing warm feelings in the Queen and her favorite, who smile and lean toward one another. The Shakespeare imagined here is a court retainer, seated in a subordinate position, slightly below the Queen and her favorite. He furnishes his elevated patrons with poems of love, setting the mood for their amorous courtly pastimes, and in return they smile down on him benignly. Shakespeare is here associated with the court and with Elizabeth's love games but is not himself a participant.[99]

It became more usual to depict Shakespeare performing for Elizabeth in a public setting. An anonymous engraving dating from the late eighteenth or early nineteenth century shows him on a makeshift indoor stage, presumably in a royal palace

FIGURE 2.2
Thomas Stothard, *Shakespeare's Interview with Queen Elizabeth*, 1827.
Reproduced by permission of the Folger Shakespeare Library.

(fig. 2.3). Some of the audience of courtiers are distracted or chatting among themselves, but Elizabeth sits upright in her throne, directly facing the stage, apparently riveted by Shakespeare's performance. He seems to be addressing his speech solely to her, his head inclined toward her, his leg extended toward her, and his hands clasped to his heart. The picture appears to assert a special emotional

FIGURE 2.3
Anon., *Shakspeare Performing before Queen Elizabeth and Her Court*, c.1780–1850.
From the collection of the Library of Congress.

and intellectual connection between Shakespeare and Elizabeth; or, it may be that while appearing to address beguiling speeches to the Queen, he is really directing them to the lady standing behind her throne, who is also intently watching his performance, unseen by Elizabeth. Secret histories of Elizabeth and Leicester or Elizabeth and Essex often involved another lady of the court who was the male favorite's secret mistress and the Queen's rival in love; this picture seems to place Shakespeare in a similar scenario.

Historical novelists were turning increasingly to Shakespeare's life story. As we have seen, he had featured in various ways in *Memoirs of the Shakespear's-Head* (1755), *Kenilworth* (1821), and Nathan Drake's *Noontide Leisure* (1824), but Robert Folkestone Williams was the first to attempt a comprehensive fictional treatment of Shakespeare's life, in a series of novels beginning with *Shakspeare and his Friends* in 1838. Like the engraving just discussed, and like Scott's depiction of Elizabeth's rather too warm interest in whether or not Shakespeare had kissed the keeper's daughter, Williams discreetly explored possibilities for romantic feeling between the Queen and the poet. *The Youth of Shakspeare* (1839) develops Percy's theory that the boy Shakespeare was present at the 1575 Princely Pleasures. He is depicted as enraptured by the various dramatic entertainments, but frustrated when several days have passed and he still has not seen the Queen, because of the crowd of courtiers that constantly surround her. He becomes separated from his party and gets lost in the castle gardens, where he stumbles upon a "gorgeously apparelled" gentleman and lady in a secluded bower, recalling Stothard's engraving. The lady toys with young William by concealing her identity, but he guesses it anyway:

> "An't please you," said William Shakspeare respectfully, "it seemeth to me you must needs be the Queen yourself."
>
> "Ha, young sir! and why dost fancy that?" exclaimed Queen Elizabeth, for, as the reader may readily believe, it was no other.
>
> "Because you have so brave an appearance with you," answered he, "and look so gracious withal. Indeed, an' you are not her in truth, I should be well pleased an' you were, for never saw I so excellent sweet a lady."[100]

She is enchanted by his precocious charm: "'Indeed! But thou playest the courtier betimes, my pretty master!' cried her majesty in an admirable good humour." Then, just as he perceives her innate greatness, so she foresees that he will go on to high achievement and renown, and their encounter becomes a moment of mutual recognition and appreciation. Williams went on to depict a mature Shakespeare and Elizabeth in his third and last Shakespearean novel, *The Secret Passion* (1844), in which Warwickshire gossip claims that Shakespeare was driven to London by the shrewishness of his wife, and that his charms and talents again aroused Elizabeth's desires, now represented as somewhat predatory:

> his marvellous skill and learning so wrought upon the Queen's Highness, it was said she would have had him right willingly to have been her husband, had he not had already a wife of his own. Nevertheless, this stood so little in the way of his advancement that his fortune was made presently by her Highness, who would scarce let him out of her sight, and it was with much ado he could escape from her to attend to the wants of his young family.[101]

Williams characterized Elizabeth as a regular and enthusiastic visitor to the theatre. In *Shakspeare and his Friends* she declares, "We take great delight in the productions of this Shakspeare as exhibited at the playhouse . . . and do intend this afternoon to partake of the same amusement."[102] The players are equally delighted to receive her patronage; when Fletcher brings word to Shakespeare and Burbage that they are to receive a visit from the Queen, Burbage responds, "Hurrah! . . . we must to the playhouse" (1:17). The episode is presented very much in the "merrie England" vein; the play performed is *Henry IV Part 2*, and Elizabeth laughs at Falstaff "till her crown tottered again" (1:179). Shakespeare asks the actor playing King Henry how the performance is going: "'Never went anything better,' said he, very cheerfully" (ibid.). As in the eighteenth-century traditions surrounding *The Merry Wives*, Shakespeare and Elizabeth combine to represent a harmonious nation in which Queens and commoners join together in merriment, and the corpulent Falstaff personifies a culture of ease and good humor.

This particular scene from *Shakspeare and his Friends* appears to have influenced an artist named David Scott, who had painted a number of subjects from Shakespeare's plays. He now turned to an epic undertaking: a painting six feet high and nine feet wide of *Queen Elizabeth Viewing the Performance of "The Merry Wives of Windsor" in the Globe Theatre* (fig. 2.4), which he exhibited at the Royal Academy in 1840.[103] The painting gave visual form to Williams's literary description and may have participated in the campaign to encourage Queen Victoria to emulate Elizabeth's patronage of Shakespearean drama.[104] This colorful and densely populated canvas is the first known serious attempt to depict the inside of the Globe theatre, reflecting the antiquarian influence of Sir Walter Scott. It shows it accurately as a galleried amphitheatre, but with an anachronistic royal box. Falstaff and the merry wives (apparently played by women, not boys—another anachronism) are on stage at the right, while Elizabeth watches from the center back of the scene and Shakespeare looks on from among the audience to the left. They are surrounded by an Elizabethan hall of fame: a description supplied with the painting identified Leicester, Essex, Walsingham, Raleigh, Spenser, Southampton, Fletcher, Beaumont, Jonson, John Dee, Burghley, Sidney, Bacon, Drake, Massinger, Harington, and other notables among the spectators.

According to William Bell Scott, the artist's brother, intensive research went into the painting, as is evident in details of costume, though they range from styles of around 1580 to those of around 1610, and in the attempt to get the shape of the Globe right. However, as in Sir Walter Scott's *Kenilworth*, chronology is flagrantly violated in various details, such as the presence of Sidney, dead in 1586, and Leicester, dead in 1588, at a play of the late 1590s, and of course the historical solecism of bringing Elizabeth to the playhouse. David Scott seems to have used the playhouse scene in *Shakspeare and his Friends*, but with a significant difference: whereas Williams's Elizabeth laughed at Falstaff's antics "till her crown tottered,"

FIGURE 2.4
David Scott, *Queen Elizabeth Viewing the Performance of "The Merry Wives of Windsor" at the Globe Theatre*, 1840. Reproduced by permission of V & A Images / Victoria and Albert Museum.

the painter was criticized for making the Queen's expression too solemn and unappreciative, especially given that *The Merry Wives* was supposedly written specifically for her pleasure. He replied,

> Doubtless among equals, or indeed in any society, politeness and indulgence would mark the reception of any effort to please, but in the case of a queenly command, this would not necessarily be seen—in a proud-tempered queen certainly not; and, after all, the right thing to be done was to give the general and true character of Queen Elizabeth, in which I hope I have in some measure succeeded.[105]

David Scott himself was known for his melancholy disposition and his usual choice of somber and difficult themes.[106] Critics have noted the presence of disturbing elements which trouble the superficially festive mood, such as the knife held by Ford and the clenched fist of Ben Jonson.[107] Indeed, no one in the audience seems at all amused by the humiliation of Falstaff.

Despite its darker idiosyncrasies, this is a distinctively Victorian vision, cramming together all the individuals associated with the Elizabethan golden age—the majestic Queen and her entourage of flamboyant courtiers, sage ministers of state, colonialists, early practitioners of science, playwrights, poets, and wits—into a collective personification of the confidence and cultural preeminence of Britain. In turn, this illustrious crowd is gathered within the wooden O presided over by Shakespeare, the individual personification of this cultural preeminence. It is a scene which is historically impossible but ideologically potent, a resounding self-affirmation for a British nation seeking to define and justify its ascendancy over much of the world. This is the kind of scene that John Kemble Chapman was invoking nine years later when he described Queen Victoria watching Shakespeare performances at Windsor Castle attended by "a brilliant circle of statesmen and warriors, nobles and ladies" (see above). David Scott, like his novelist namesake Sir Walter, was Scottish, and like him he brings to the evocation of "merrie England" the slightly detached eye of one who belongs to a different nation, while at the same time incorporating that evocation into the newer, larger national identity of Great Britain. Equally, just as Sir Walter Scott turned to English subject matter in *Ivanhoe* and *Kenilworth* in order to establish himself in the English literary marketplace, so David Scott, an artist who had achieved a limited recognition in Scotland but felt underappreciated, appears to have sought a breakthrough to wider fame in choosing a "merrie England" subject and exhibiting it at the Royal Academy in London, rather than the Scottish Academy of which he had been a member since 1829.[108]

Paintings of Elizabeth beyond the playhouse were also influenced by Shakespeare's plays, such as Augustus Leopold Egg's *Queen Elizabeth Discovers She Is No Longer Young*, shown at the Royal Academy in 1848 (fig. 2.5).[109] Egg had previously produced a number of paintings on Shakespearean themes. This painting is based on the legend, dating back to Jonson's gossip, that in old age Elizabeth banned mirrors as she could not bear to see her face.[110] In Egg's imaginary scene, the Queen, seated on the floor at the foot of her bed, finally asks for a looking-glass. Confronted with the truth, she is gaunt and grim-faced, diminished and despairing. The picture conflates her with Shakespeare's Richard II, who after the loss of his crown also asks for a mirror, "That it may show me what a face I have, / Since it is bankrupt of his majesty," and laments, "For God's sake, let us sit upon the ground, / And tell sad stories of the death of kings" (4.1.256–57, 3.2.151–52). Both are monarchs confronted with their own human failings and with their mortality. Egg's Elizabeth may easily be imagined saying, as she reputedly did to William Lambarde, "I am Richard II. Know ye not that?"[111] Egg was not known for radical views, but nevertheless this visual allusion to Shakespeare's deposed monarch

FIGURE 2.5
Augustus Leopold Egg, *Queen Elizabeth Discovers She Is No Longer Young*, 1848. © Christie's Images Ltd., 2006.

must have carried considerable force in 1848, the Year of Revolution, when it was first exhibited. It was well received and perhaps fitted the fleetingly uncertain mood of that year. But just as the year seemed to end with confidence in British institutions renewed, so the effect of the potentially disturbing painting was to secure for Egg in November an associate membership of the Royal Academy.[112]

After Robert Folkestone Williams, the next noteworthy author of biographical Shakespeare novels was Henry Curling (1802/3–64), whose first such work was *Shakspere: The Poet, The Lover, The Actor, The Man.* This was published in 1848, not only the Year of Revolution but also, perhaps not uncoincidentally, a remarkably prolific year for contributions to the double myth of Shakespeare and Elizabeth.[113] Curling's novels in some ways exemplify Victorian attitudes to Shakespeare and Elizabeth but are also atypical in that they emphasize Shakespeare's dependence upon Elizabeth and her golden age for inspiration and material and do not relegate her to the role of admiring audience of the literary genius. Curling brought the poet to Tilbury in 1588 as troops were being mustered to meet the Armada, thus making him a witness to an iconic scene in the legend of Elizabeth:

> He saw that lion-hearted woman, and who had then borne the sceptre for thirty years; her body cleped in steel; her high pale forehead furrowed

with care; her bright and piercing eye, and her majestic form unbent by the pressure of years. He saw her thus, mounted upon her magnificent steed, like a true daughter of the Plantaganet, vindicating the honour of her kingdom. He saw her thus, undismayed by the tremendous armament threatening her coast, pass from rank to rank, "With cheerful semblance and sweet majesty"; and as she rode—

> "A largess universal like the sun,
> Her liberal eye did give to every one."[114]

Surprisingly there is no mention of the Tilbury speech ("I know I have the body but of a weak and feeble woman, but I have the heart and stomach of a king").[115] By quoting instead from *Henry V* (4.0.40, 43–44), Curling, like Scott, authenticates his narrative prose with echoes of Shakespeare's verse and at the same time attributes to Elizabeth inspiration for another Shakespeare text. In particular, he aligns Elizabeth with the democratic magnanimity which Shakespeare's Chorus claims for Henry on the eve of Agincourt, emphasizing how she communicates and connects with her people.

Shakespeare's role is that of a bystander and witness: "He saw her thus." This is Shakespeare watching Elizabeth, not Elizabeth watching Shakespeare. His function here is as an Everyman figure, and this is emphasized as Curling seeks to unite through Shakespeare the common soldiers of different centuries: "Those who have stood in the ranks of an English battalion can perhaps best imagine the proud feeling which must have animated Shakspere at this moment . . . he felt that no power which the invader could bring would be likely to subdue such a host" (2:67). Curling had served as an infantry officer, and many of his other works were on military themes. His Shakespeare is used both to gratify and to inflame nationalistic and martial sentiment in the Victorian reader, but by means of his likeness to, and fellow feeling with, the reader, not his exceptional genius. It is Elizabeth here who is the exceptional and inspiring figure. When Shakespeare reaches her court, he finds a golden age at its height, described by Curling in a rapturous manner which would be unusual, unless with tongue in cheek, a century later:

> And now a new epoch seems to have arrived, and England (for the time being) may indeed be called "*merrie England.*" The good old days of good Queen Bess are now in full force . . . Fully did the English at this moment appreciate the merits of their Queen. She was extolled, glorified, and almost deified in the exuberance of their joy and loyalty. (3:93)

In this perspective, Shakespeare's genius mainly results from his being in the right place at the right time: "The world around him . . . at the period in which he lived and wrote, presented much that was grand and exciting. He had but to note what he observed in the vicinity of Elizabeth's Court, in order to pourtray [*sic*] some of his scenes" (3:126).

Shakespeare becomes familiar and popular with all the leading courtiers and well acquainted with the Queen, who singles "good William" out from the throng at court to praise *The Rape of Lucrece* and to accept his invitation to the first performance of *Romeo and Juliet* (3:234–35). Curling's description of the interior of the playhouse appears to be influenced by David Scott's painting. "The boxes were a sort of gallery, along which stood and leant the gallants and ladies of the Court. The Queen and her own especial party being enthroned in a sort of canopy in the centre" (3:133–34). Also as in the painting, Elizabeth's attendants include some who were in fact dead by the time the scene in question took place, such as Leicester and Sidney. As the performance begins, the Queen keeps up an animated literary-critical commentary, in which, as so often, she is the onlooker who is most receptive to Shakespeare's art: she pronounces his poetry "most exquisite and unmatchable," and observes of the prologue to the play, "Marked you how much was contained in those few lines?" (3:141, 145). Yet at the same time Shakespeare's democratic appeal is demonstrated: "The audience, from the Queen down to the meanest person there, seemed held in a state of enchantment as the piece proceeded" (3:148).

We learn that Elizabeth takes more than a merely intellectual pleasure in the performance: "As the play proceeded, and the progress of Romeo's sudden passion developed itself, the thoughts of that stately Queen returned to her early youth, ere the sterner feeling of pride and power had obliterated all gentler sensations. She thought upon the days when she loved the handsome Dudley[116] with all the violence of a first passion" (3:153–54). Although Curling often represents Shakespeare as rather passively recording the glories of Elizabeth and her court, here his dramatic writing has an active effect, rejuvenating and humanizing the Queen. It also seems that some of the warmth she once felt toward Leicester is now in its revival redirected toward Shakespeare. Once Mercutio, played by Shakespeare, has been killed, he is summoned to the royal box to give a private commentary on the rest of the play. Elizabeth "ordered back whoever came so close as to inconvenience the poet, and seemed altogether delighted at having him so near her" (3:158–59). Later, his Sonnets too are implied to have stirred the Queen: "Sonnets, . . . innumerable, had fallen amongst the fair dames of the palace, like the perfumed flowers blown from the sweet south. Nay, William Shakspere was said to be a favourite with the Queen herself" (3:236–37).

In 1854 Curling adapted his *Shakspere* into a play, *The Merry Wags of Warwickshire; or, The Early Days of Shakspere,* which would be recycled again as a 1914 British silent film, *The Life of Shakespeare.*[117] He wrote numerous historical novels on other themes but returned to Shakespeare for his last work, published posthumously, *Geraldine Maynard* (1864). This deals with the closing years of Elizabeth's reign and is in some ways a darker work, perhaps reflecting Queen Victoria's withdrawal into mourning. Elizabeth suffers from a world-weariness which enhances her appreciation of *Hamlet,* and from a toothache which forces the performance to be cut short.[118] She and Shakespeare, alone among the Elizabethan throng, understand each other's melancholy state of mind; as the playwright again observes her on various public occasions, he reflects that "'tis better to be lowly born . . . Than to be perked up in a glistering grief" (2:169), quoting from *Henry VIII* (2.3.19–22). Curling still enthuses, "Oh, there was fun, rare sport, rare life, in rare old England in the palmy days of rare old Queen Bess," but perhaps in this excess and repetition there is a note of slightly hysterical self-parody and irony (3:3). His depiction of the Elizabethan age becomes increasingly inventive and bizarre: Elizabeth retires for her customary bedtime bath in wine while Shakespeare gives agony-uncle advice to Sidney on his troubles with Penelope Devereux, and Dr John Dee prophesies steamships and the London-to-Richmond steam railway, to the incredulity of Elizabeth and her attendants (1:155, 161–75, 192–95). Curling is consistent, however, in his contention that Shakespeare had only to write down what he saw around him: "It is a question whether Shakspere, had he lived in any other age or reign, and fallen amongst other and lesser men than he was associated with, could have penned the drama he has given to the world" (3:55–56n). This is a distinctive divergence from the conventional view of Shakespeare as timeless, universal genius. According to Curling's model, Shakespeare was little more than a journalist, simply recording faithfully the extraordinary dramas being enacted in the daily life around him. Shakespeare, Curling insists, could not have done it without Elizabeth and the glorious age which she, not he, created. His novels illustrate how diverse and even contradictory versions of the myth of Shakespeare and Elizabeth have often coexisted.

Though Curling, unusually, positioned Shakespeare as a spectator of Elizabeth, in the visual arts scenes of Elizabeth listening to the Bard became increasingly popular. A seminal painting in this genre of monarch-and-poet was Ford Madox Brown's 1847–51 picture of Chaucer reading to Edward III, an image intended to depict the birth of English literature (fig. 2.6). Other painters eagerly

FIGURE 2.6
Ford Madox Brown, *Chaucer at the Court of Edward III*, 1847–51. Oil on canvas, 372.0 x 296.0 cm. Purchased 1876. Collection: Art Gallery of New South Wales.

took up the scenario but transposed it onto the more famous and charismatic figures of Shakespeare and Elizabeth. Sometime around 1860 Charles Cattermole received a commission for a series of paintings of the life of the playwright, which were fairly widely reproduced as prints and postcards and were bequeathed to the Shakespeare Memorial Theatre.[119] They included both *Shakespeare Acting before*

FIGURE 2.7
Charles Cattermole, *Shakespeare Reading "The Merry Wives of Windsor" to Queen Elizabeth*, c.1860. © Royal Shakespeare Company.

Queen Elizabeth, which took Elizabeth to the playhouse,[120] and *Shakespeare Reading "The Merry Wives of Windsor" to Queen Elizabeth* (fig. 2.7), which brought the playwright to court, though Cattermole inventively set this latter scene not in a palace chamber but on Elizabeth's barge on the Thames. Dobson and Watson note the erotic implications in this, as the waterborne setting identifies Shakespeare and Elizabeth with Antony and Cleopatra and alludes to Elizabeth's reported public flirtations with Robert Dudley on her barge in the early years of her reign.[121] It also recalls the barge scene in Scott's *Kenilworth*, where Shakespeare does not actually join Elizabeth on her barge in person but is extensively discussed by the Queen and her courtiers in this picturesque setting (indeed, it is on her barge that we hear her rather too eager denial that Shakespeare kissed the gamekeeper's daughter). Erotic undertones are therefore present in Cattermole's choice of location, yet at the same time this is a distinctly public and nationalistic scene rather than an intimate one. Elizabeth, surrounded by oarsmen and the usual retinue of courtiers, sits straight-backed and dignified under her canopy, not dallying with Shakespeare, who stands upright at a respectful distance, nor with any other favorite. She is in effect enthroned upon the barge, with her royal standard flying from the stern,

FIGURE 2.8
After Eduard Ender, *Shakespeare before the Court of Elizabeth Reciting "Macbeth."* *The Century of Queens* (New York, 1872), facing 168. Author's collection.

and the expansiveness of the stretch of water on which the boat travels perhaps alludes to Britain's imperial aspirations. This is Elizabeth as Britannia, ruling the waves, with her court around her and with her Bard in attendance to declare her greatness to the elements and to posterity.

In the late 1860s the Viennese artist Eduard Ender painted *Shakespeare Reading "Macbeth" before Queen Elizabeth,* widely reproduced as an engraving (fig. 2.8). The setting is quite different from Cattermole's; it is a claustrophobic, Gothic interior, in keeping with the darker work which the playwright is reading. Ender depicted Elizabeth, not James I, listening to *Macbeth,* even though this play was written after the Queen's death and had several elements clearly designed to appeal to James;[122] this demonstrates how firmly established was the mythology of Elizabeth as Shakespeare's chief patron. For Julia M. Walker the picture "is much more about Shakespeare than it is about Queen Elizabeth," and it continues the practice, also by now well established, of making Elizabeth subsidiary to Shakespeare and primarily a witness to his genius.[123] There is much truth in this; Ender places the poet at the center of the scene, looking and speaking out of the picture directly at us, his future admirers. Nevertheless, Elizabeth was still an essential part of the composition, as were the crowd of glamorous young adventurers and aristocrats thronging her court, all gathered to hear Shakespeare. In fact, this work formed one of a series of historical paintings by Ender of great artists or scientists with their royal patrons: these included Tycho Brahe and Emperor Rudolf II at the imperial residence in Prague, François I in the workshop of Benvenuto Cellini, and the young Mozart playing for Empress Maria Theresa.[124] It is true that all these images to some extent sidelined the monarchs depicted and reduced them to the role of audience; moreover, they represented them as primarily cultural figureheads rather than war leaders or politicians in councils of state. Even so, Ender's paintings idealized bygone eras in which brilliant innovators and their rulers supposedly collaborated in human progress. His paintings simultaneously circumscribed and celebrated the powers of royalty in a way which reflects the intense nineteenth-century preoccupation with monarchy, produced by the turbulent shifts and redefinitions that were taking place in the status of ruling dynasties throughout much of Europe. Ender's Shakespeare-and-Elizabeth picture also illustrates the fame and stature which this pairing now possessed beyond Britain: not only was the painter himself Austrian, but the engraver who gave it wide circulation was a Frenchman, Pierre Cottin,[125] and it would go on to enjoy significant success in America, as we shall discover in chapter 3.[126]

Soon after Ender painted *Shakespeare Reading "Macbeth" before Queen Elizabeth,* there appeared a strikingly polemical version of the Shakespeare and Elizabeth myth from nineteenth-century Ireland: *Queen Elizabeth; or, The Origin of Shakespeare* (1872), a play by Tresham Gregg, a Protestant chaplain from Dublin. It was published three years after the extremely controversial disestablishment of the Church of Ireland by Gladstone's government and is framed by dedications to the Emperor of Germany and to General Ulysses S. Grant, the President of the United States, urging them to protect the true Christian religion, as the British government, it is implied, has failed to do. It is stridently anti-Catholic: Mary Queen of Scots, for instance, is an agent of Antichrist. Once again we see the young Shakespeare at Kenilworth in 1575, where he engages in a contest of wits, presided over by the Queen, against the young Francis Bacon. Shakespeare, as usual, is characterized as a natural and poetical genius, whereas Bacon is of a more scientific and academic bent. Over the course of the contest they develop a mutual appreciation and agree not to compete but to be friends and allies in the service of Elizabeth.

Gregg asserts that such great men are gifts from God to pious nations with pious rulers. Elizabeth herself voices this theory:

> It is my deep conviction that the Crown
> Is the true parent of those souls inspired
> Which to an age give immortality
> . . . a state disloyal to the skies
> Is curs'd with mediocrity in its subjects.
> It breeds or dolts, or simpletons, or knaves.[127]

Paul Franssen has suggested that Gregg's characterization of Elizabeth as a godly ruler who defies Catholic enemies and is rewarded with brilliant subjects is directed at Victoria, who had been unhappy about Gladstone's disestablishment policy.[128] However, the epilogue, spoken by Shakespeare, fiercely implies that Victoria falls very short indeed of Elizabeth's example, and that perhaps even a change of ruler is needed:

> Elizabeth, that peerless Queen,
> God grant her counterpart may soon be seen!
> Then will our country flourish like a tree,
> It will not know what's meant by poverty.
> We shan't have pharisees in crinoline,
> Telling the ragged with a snuffling whine,
> "Rags are thy lot, 'tis worldly to be fine." (128)

For Gregg, Shakespeare and Elizabeth form a joint emblem of a lost England which was God's own nation. For him, Victorian England was evidently failing to be that nation, and in the process was failing in its imperial responsibility toward Ireland.[129]

Gregg continues the tradition of flirtatiousness between Shakespeare and Elizabeth, even though, as in Williams's *The Youth of Shakspeare,* his Shakespeare is only an eleven-year-old boy. These scenes are likely to arouse queasiness in a modern reader, but they are typically Victorian in their sentimentalization and eroticization of a child. Elizabeth is enchanted by Shakespeare's flattering (if not artistically impressive) verses in praise of her:

> She's the wise and the beautiful,
> Queen of the realm;
> She's the mistress whose love doth
> Our hearts overwhelm. (118)

She confesses that "This mirthful boy bewitches all of us. / We can't resist his spell. Tell me now, Shakespeare, / What is a kiss?" (ibid.). And what, she asks, is love? Shakespeare's lengthy reply concludes "'Tis indescribable—'tis thou, the Queen"; and the stage erupts into general acclamation (119–25).

A strong vein of eroticism runs through most of the nineteenth-century images of Shakespeare and Elizabeth, whether they show young William catching the eye of Elizabeth at Kenilworth or an adult Shakespeare charming the Queen. We saw that Curling depicted Shakespeare as reviving Elizabeth's passion for Leicester; many such scenes also implicitly conflate Shakespeare with Robert Devereux, Earl of Essex, Elizabeth's younger favorite and reputed lover in her latter years. Elizabeth and Essex had been represented as star-crossed lovers since the 1678 secret history of their doomed affair.[130] Shakespeare, whose age difference from Elizabeth was very nearly the same as Essex's, could be readily assimilated to this established role of a younger object of desire in order to add glamor and passion to his imagined relationship with Elizabeth. The Virgin Queen, who might otherwise appear rather cold-hearted and masculine, could thereby be rendered more feeling and feminine, or, in more negative characterizations, sexual rapacity could be added to her list of failings. Meanwhile Shakespeare, always an elusive figure, who had been stripped of his deer-poaching and other, more mischievous exploits by Malone and other scholars and was in danger of seeming rather dull, could be converted into a more dashing and alluring character through his flirtatious encounters with the Queen. British nationalism and imperialism thus mingled with romance and eroticism in Victorian depictions of Shakespeare and Elizabeth to produce a potent and beguiling myth.

From Worship to Laughter

As we have seen, both Elizabeth and Victoria were at different times and in different contexts criticized for not showing sufficient appreciation of the incomparable Bard. Their status and popularity were variable, but Shakespeare's seemed unassailable:[131] by 1856 his birthplace in Stratford was attracting three thousand visitors a year, and these numbers grew after the arrival of the railway from London a few years later.[132] During the tercentenary celebrations in 1864, the Sunday nearest to his birthday was designated "Shakespeare Sunday," and sermons were preached by eminent churchmen eulogizing his exemplary morality and God-given genius, a practice which continued annually.[133] The first instance of the term "Shakspearolatry" is recorded in this same year by the *Oxford English Dictionary*. Shakespeare's works now enjoyed quasi-biblical status as sacred texts, and allusions to them were endemic in literature.[134] Shakespeare invaded popular culture too: Adrian Poole has found that he surrounded the Victorians, "on stage and on posters, in paintings and print and cartoons, in the air they breathed, on the china they ate off."[135]

After Prince Albert's death and Queen Victoria's withdrawal into mourning in 1861, depictions of Elizabeth as the leading member of Shakespeare's audience were perhaps partly seeking to coax the living Queen back into patronage of the theatre. In 1881 she attended her first play since becoming a widow, a private performance at the Prince of Wales's castle near Balmoral.[136] This was gradually followed by more performances at royal residences, including some Shakespeare, but Victoria never again visited a public theatre. After 1861 imaginary scenes of Elizabeth watching Shakespeare and of harmonious cooperation between Crown and stage had a double nostalgia: they evoked not only a lost England of the sixteenth century but also a lost early-Victorian Britain when the Queen frequently went to the playhouse and Shakespeare plays came frequently to court.

Nevertheless, Shakespeare was firmly entrenched as a national institution and was associated with royalty at every opportunity. For instance, Mary, Lady Monkswell, recorded in her diary how much she enjoyed an 1897 performance of *Twelfth Night* by the Shakespeare Society at the Hall of the Middle Temple. They tried "to give it exactly as it was given the first time it was acted (in the same Hall), before Queen Elizabeth in 1601."[137] There is indeed a record of a performance of *Twelfth Night* in the Middle Temple Hall in 1602,[138] but there is no evidence that this was the first performance of the play or that Elizabeth was present on the occasion.[139] Once again either Lady Monkswell or the play's organizers, or both, could not resist inserting Elizabeth into their imaginings of a Shakespeare performance in his own time. Lady Monkswell applauded the authenticity of the production:

> The same music, the same Elizabethan costumes; 3 ladies instead of 3 boys for Olivia, Viola & Maria, & the Prince of Wales instead of Queen Elizabeth. The Hall was crammed, it was quite a brilliant scene. In the front row sat the Prince of Wales & Princess Louise & the Duke of Teck, Lord Esher (Master of the Rolls), the Lord Chancellor, the Lord Chief Justice—Lord Russell,—the new Bishop of London . . .[140]

The list of distinguished names goes on for some length. The passage shows how the combination of Shakespeare and royalty was central to Britain's cultural, social, and political establishment.

However, the nineteenth century also saw reactions against this deification and monumentalization. As Shakespeare's position on the highest cultural pedestal became more and more secure, as his lines and characters became familiar and indeed perhaps over-familiar to large portions of the population, and as scenes combining him with Elizabeth became increasingly conventional set pieces, a countercurrent developed. Burlesques—comic plays which parodied high-cultural materials such as classical myth, opera, English history, and Shakespeare—were extremely popular in the Victorian period. They deployed doggerel verse and absurd puns to puncture the pomposity of their subject matter and combined these with topical jokes, song and dance, and slapstick. Scott's *Kenilworth* inspired a number of burlesques, including a "Comic Operatic Extravaganza" first performed in 1858 featuring Elizabeth as "A *Virgin* Queen, *verging* on Fifty, the original strong minded Woman, quite a *rough* character—at any rate a character in a ruff."[141] Elizabeth by now had such a presence in British culture that she could be sketched by means of a few instantly recognizable traits: her virginity, her aging female body, her domineering character, her stiff and elaborate costume. Meanwhile, Shakespearean burlesque was a flourishing and extensive subgenre and included such productions as *Macbeth Somewhat Removed from the Text of Shakespeare* (1853) and *A Thin Slice of Ham let!* (1863).

Richard W. Schoch has argued that such plays primarily mocked the excesses of the lavish and earnest Shakespeare productions of the great nineteenth-century actor-managers, J. P. Kemble, Macready, Kean, Phelps, and Henry Irving. Burlesque positioned itself not as ridiculing Shakespeare but as protecting him from "self-righteous Bardolaters, pedantic literary critics, mediocre performers, and sensationalising actor-managers," who were its chief targets.[142] To this extent, burlesque may be seen as recuperating and reinforcing Shakespeare's cultural supremacy. Yet at the same time it made Shakespeare's cultural meaning an object of contestation. What was signified by "Shakespeare"? If, as burlesque implied, nineteenth-century Bardolatry was distorting and ossifying Shakespeare, what would a pure or true Shakespeare be like? Moreover, to whom did Shakespeare belong? Burlesque assumed extensive knowledge of Shakespeare's works in its audiences and thereby laid claim to him for popular culture. As we have seen, Elizabeth's cultural meanings had always been multiple and conflicting; now Shakespeare's cultural meanings seemed to be fissuring and proliferating too.

In 1895 *Punch* printed a cartoon by E. T. Reed entitled "Unrecorded History.—V. Queen Elizabeth just runs through a little thing of her own composition to William Shakespeare" (fig. 2.9). The conventional and by now rather worn-out image of Shakespeare reading to Elizabeth is here reversed, in burlesque fashion. Elizabeth, smiling with satisfaction, reads to a glumly resigned Shakespeare from an inordinately long scroll which hangs down the steps of her throne. Shakespeare's own scrolls—labelled "Macbeth," "Merry Wives of Windsor," and so

UNRECORDED HISTORY.—V.

Queen Elizabeth just runs through a little thing of her own composition to William Shakespeare.

FIGURE 2.9
E. T. Reed, "Unrecorded History V: Queen Elizabeth just runs through a little thing of her own composition to William Shakespeare." *Punch,* Nov. 1895. Reproduced with the permission of *Punch,* Ltd., www.punch.co.uk.

on—lie firmly tied and ignored on a side table.[143] The numerous guards and courtiers in attendance yawn and nod. One of them stands behind Shakespeare's chair dutifully prodding him to keep him awake.

Reed's cartoon is funny partly because it simply inverts a by now over-familiar image. There is some satisfaction in interpreting it as Elizabeth's revenge for all those pictures where she was made to hang attentively on Shakespeare's every word. This is underscored by the political content of the image. Elizabeth is surrounded by the trappings of power: all those guards and courtiers, her enthroned and raised position on her dais, the massive presence of her father, Henry VIII, in the Holbein portrait behind her, her own physical bulk in her huge farthingale and ruff. Shakespeare, by contrast, is a timid and cowed figure, with his hands primly and childishly clasping his knees. The image cuts incisively through the romantic conventions of Bardolatrous myth: Elizabeth's court was an arena for the display of her power, not for a proto-Victorian adulation of the Bard. Those images where Elizabeth listens submissively while Shakespeare stands center stage are revealed as idealized fantasies. The diminution of the Bard thus has an element of realism, but it was also in its time a powerfully iconoclastic gesture, which must have provoked self-consciously mischievous and liberating laughter. It illustrates the shifting roles of Shakespeare and Elizabeth at the end of the nineteenth century, and the shifting dynamics of interactions between them.

The *Punch* cartoon, and all the prior images of Shakespeare reading to Elizabeth, may well have influenced a popular and well-known caricature of 1904 by Max Beerbohm, "Mr. Tennyson, Reading 'In Memoriam' to His Sovereign" (fig. 2.10).[144] Public knowledge of the solace which Victoria found in *In Memoriam,* and of Tennyson's several audiences with the Queen, probably contributed to the myth of Shakespeare as a regular visitor to court and as Elizabeth's personal adviser and entertainer. Beerbohm's picture reflects back upon the long tradition of pictures of poets reading to monarchs. Here Tennyson and Victoria sit alone in a vast room which is at once palatial in scale, dwarfing the poet and the monarch, and domestic in its trappings, dominated by the patterned wallpaper and carpet and other furnishings. Apart from these oversized furnishings and the two small human figures, the room is strikingly empty; the entourage of courtiers and heroes, personifying national and imperial glory, have departed. The poet sits at front left, with flowing hair and beard but a domed bald head; this and his black clothing make him very similar to conventional figures of Shakespeare. He leans back in his chair with legs splayed, raising one arm as he declaims enthusiastically from a manuscript. The Queen, on the right, is a tiny, huddled figure, sitting demurely in her customary widow's garb on an ordinary chair, with her feet on a red footstool. The center rear of the room is dominated by a large fireplace where we might expect a throne to be, surmounted by a portrait of Albert in profile, also looking toward Tennyson as if listening to him. Tennyson is a comical version of the poet as inspired bard, gesturing exuberantly and indecorously as his own poetry carries him away, and Beerbohm further punctures his dignity by calling him "Mr.," not "Lord" Tennyson. Victoria is an image of monarchy absurdly diminished and domesticated, a little old lady in a vast sitting room. At the beginning of a new reign, a new century, and a new, modern sensibility, this picture dispels the vestigial mystique of the long Victorian era. It also satirizes the iconic image of intellectual and aesthetic communion between a queen and her poet, an image fundamentally shaped by the myth of the divine Shakespeare reading to the glorious Elizabeth.

FIGURE 2.10
Max Beerbohm, *Mr. Tennyson, Reading "In Memoriam" to His Sovereign*, 1904. Private ownership. Reproduced by kind permission of the owner.

Nineteenth-century fictions, then, give us divergent representations of Elizabeth's relationship with Shakespeare. For many writers and artists she is an admiring accessory to the Bard; for some she is the inspiring muse without whom Shakespeare's works would not have been possible. In some depictions she offers a maternal nurturing hand to the fledgling author, while in others her interest in him is to some degree amorous. The supposed relationship between Shakespeare and Elizabeth is invariably put to ideological use: topically, to argue for contemporary royal sponsorship of the stage; and on a grander scale, to construct a resplendent image of the Elizabethan golden age which could underpin the claims of Victorian Britain to cultural and political preeminence in the world. However, the more firmly established this glorifying vision became, the more it provoked iconoclastic pastiche and parody. By the end of the nineteenth century, the double myth of Shakespeare and Elizabeth was more mutable and complex than ever, and its meanings were open to contestation and appropriation.

It is striking how many of the writers and artists discussed in this chapter were not English. Sir Walter Scott, Thomas Carlyle, and David Scott were Scottish; Edmond Malone, Richard Ryan, and Tresham Gregg were Irish; Charles Symmons was Welsh. The double myth of Shakespeare and Elizabeth was not merely imposed upon the further-flung parts of the British Isles by an English elite; it was embraced by the British beyond England and increasingly deployed by them as a myth which united Britons in a common imperial cause. Its reach now extended beyond Britain too: as we have seen, Eduard Ender, an Austrian, and Pierre Cottin, a Frenchman, produced one of the most striking and influential images of Shakespeare and Elizabeth. Other continental European participants in Shakespeare-and-Elizabeth iconography included Ambroise Thomas, also French, who showed Elizabeth as Shakespeare's muse in his opera *Le Songe d'une Nuit d'Été* (1850), and the Italian Donizetti, who used Scott's historical novel as the source for his opera *Elisabetta al Castello di Kenilworth* (c. 1854).[145] Most significantly, the combined myth of Shakespeare and Elizabeth became increasingly popular over the course of the nineteenth century in America. The reasons for this, and the forms which the myth took in the United States, will be discussed in the next chapter.

3

Shakespeare and Elizabeth Arrive in America

While the double myth of Shakespeare and Elizabeth was becoming firmly established in Britain in the eighteenth and nineteenth centuries, it was also taking hold in the United States. Its development there was caught up in complex processes of national identity formation, as Americans asserted their political distance from contemporary Britain yet simultaneously laid claim to cultural origins in Elizabethan England. This short chapter will trace this development in order to bring America into the story of the double myth and to serve as a bridge to subsequent chapters, in which American materials will feature as well as British ones.

1750 to 1900: Shakespeare as an American, Americans as Elizabethans

There is little evidence of interest in Shakespeare in the early American settlements, but from 1750 onward his works were extensively read, performed, quoted, and alluded to.[1] This seems to have been partly in emulation of theatrical and literary fashion in London, but other conflicting ideological currents were also involved, especially in the period of the Revolution (1775–83). Shakespeare plays were staged to entertain British troops and inspire them with patriotic zeal, and pro-British Americans flaunted their love of Shakespeare; but at the same time writers on the rebel side increasingly cited Shakespeare's works as a critique of tyranny and a manifesto for liberty.[2] In 1795 the first American-produced edition of Shakespeare's works was published in Philadelphia, with an emphasis on accessibility to the reader rather than textual notes.[3] By the early nineteenth century, many Americans were claiming Shakespeare as their own, asserting that as lovers of freedom they had a natural affinity with him and a deeper understanding of his works than the decadent and class-bound British. Shakespeare was read for pleasure and was not confined to a social or intellectual elite: Alexis de Tocqueville, who toured America in 1831, remarked, "There is hardly a pioneer's hut which does not contain a few odd volumes of Shakespeare."[4] In 1882 a German traveler, Karl Knortz, confirmed that even dwellers in the "backwoods" of the "far west" own "the Bible and in most cases a cheap edition of the works of Shakespeare." He declared that "there is no land in the whole earth in which Shakespeare and the Bible are held in such high esteem."[5]

Thus from the late 1700s onward, while the British were vaunting Shakespeare as a founding patron of their global empire, the Americans were simultaneously claiming him as their own. As early as 1787 the American poet Peter Markoe asserted that the ascendant nation of America was Shakespeare's true home:

> Monopolizing Britain! boast no more
> His genius to your narrow bounds confin'd;
> Shakspeare's bold spirit seeks our western shore,
> A gen'ral blessing for the world design'd,
> And, emulous to form the rising age,
> The noblest Bard demands the noblest Stage.[6]

British writers since Dryden had acclaimed Shakespeare as a king in the spheres of the arts and the intellect; in 1823 a Boston banker, Charles Sprague, gave this idea more political thrust, asserting that Shakespeare exceeded the defeated bearers of the British crown in the global reach of his power:

> Realms yet unborn, in accents now unknown,
> Thy song shall learn, and bless it for their own . . .
> Once more in thee shall Albion's sceptre wave,
> And what her Monarch lost her Monarch-Bard shall save.[7]

James Fenimore Cooper wrote in 1828 that

> The authors, previously to the revolution, are common property, and it is quite idle to say that the American has not just as good a right to claim Milton, and Shakspeare, and all the old masters of the language, for his countrymen, as an Englishman . . . Shakspeare is, of course, the great author of America, as he is of England, and I think he is quite as well relished here as there.[8]

American journalism, oratory, and song defined the new nation in opposition to Britain, which was perceived as arrogant and as bound by social structures which were hierarchical, archaic, restrictive, and iniquitous. Shakespeare was increasingly appropriated to this cause: according to Richard Grant White, a distinguished mid-nineteenth-century Shakespeare scholar, the poet originated "those principles of liberty, that intelligent respect for law, and that capacity for self-government" upon which the American nation was founded.[9]

By the mid-nineteenth century, Shakespeare's plays were performed frequently all over the United States, and numerous editions of his works were being published, purchased, and read.[10] Prominent Americans made the pilgrimage to Shakespeare's birthplace in Stratford-upon-Avon, including John Adams and Thomas Jefferson (in 1786), Washington Irving (in 1815, 1821, and 1831), Nathaniel Hawthorne (in 1855), and Herman Melville (in 1857). Several of them expressed dismay at the neglect of the building by the British.[11] The American showman and entrepreneur P. T. Barnum boasted that it was only his professed intention in 1847 to buy the birthplace and ship it to America that galvanized a group of British worthies into purchasing it.[12] A number of nineteenth-century American writers emphasized the "Anglo-Saxon" roots of American culture and celebrated "our Shakespeare" as a figurehead behind which a nation made increasingly diverse by immigration could unite.[13] In particular, American English was claimed to be purer and closer to the English of Shakespeare's time than was the language spoken in Victorian Britain. White picked out several phrases from Shakespeare as evidence that "like most of those words and phrases which it pleases John Bull to call Americanisms, they are English of the purest and best, which have lived here while they have died out in the mother country."[14] An 1895 article on "Shakespeare's Americanisms" expanded on this theme:

> The English speech was planted in this country by English emigrants, who settled Virginia and New England at the beginning of the seventeenth century. To Virginia came many educated men, who became the planters, land-owners, and leaders of the infant State . . . They would have been the last men to corrupt or abuse the mother-tongue, which they cherished more than ever in the new and distant land . . . The language which these people brought with them to Virginia and Massachusetts . . . was . . . the language of Shakespeare . . . it is passing strange that words not only used in Shakespeare's time, but used by Shakespeare himself, should have lived to be disdainfully called "Americanisms" by people now living in Shakespeare's own country.[15]

Such claims identified America as Shakespeare's true home while promoting a unifying Anglophone cultural and educational agenda. The English cultural heritage and its representative, Shakespeare, were appropriated not from motives of Anglophilia, but from motives of uniting a disparate nation while repudiating and outdoing the former colonial oppressor.

For William Cullen Bryant in 1870, Shakespeare was "a poet of the Americans . . . The blood that now warms American hearts and gushes through American arteries was once—nearly three hundred years ago, when it ran in the veins of our ancestors in the Old World, and while Shakespeare was yet alive—made to tingle by his potent words."[16] By 1927 Ashley Thorndike could state that "Washington, Lincoln, Shakespeare, they are the three whom Americans universally worship."[17] Shakespeare had in effect become an American. Americans embraced the idea of "our Shakespeare",[18] and began to regard his works and any available memorials and relics as their rightful property. Book collectors, including Horace Howard Furness (1833–1912) and Henry Clay Folger (1857–1930), amassed vast collections of Shakespearean materials. Furness's was bequeathed by his son to the University of Pennsylvania, while Folger's has been housed since 1932 in the Folger Memorial Library in Washington, D.C. Its site, near to the Capitol, at the heart of the American state, expressed Folger's belief that Shakespeare "is one of our best sources, one of the wells from which we Americans draw our national thought, our faith and our hope."[19] Today the Folger can claim to be the most significant Shakespeare collection in the world and is a global center for Shakespeare study.

Meanwhile representations of Elizabeth in nineteenth-century America echoed much of the hostility expressed toward her in Britain, but with an added intensity as the younger nation defined itself in opposition to monarchical government. Joseph Hopkinson, in his prefatory material to the first American-produced edition of Shakespeare's works in 1795, claimed that Elizabeth failed to appreciate Shakespeare, and that this was typical of the philistinism and decadence of the English:

> How wretched must have been the state of English literature in the days of Shakspeare, when six years elapsed after his decease, before his friends found it worth their trouble to print his plays! This did not arise from the poverty, but the total want of taste in the English nation, for Queen Elizabeth alone, during her "golden age," as it has been called, bestowed three hundred thousand pounds sterling upon a single paramour.

He added a stingingly sarcastic footnote: "British historians, with their wonted discernment, have celebrated the *magnanimity* and *chastity* of this accomplished princess."[20] John S. Jenkins in 1851 developed the familiar theme that, as a woman,

Elizabeth should not have ruled and should have married, but added a distinctively American bite to the idea that monarchy had been her personal tragedy:

> Had her destiny been the private, domestic circle, she might have been generally beloved through life, and perhaps have left a name in the annals of intellect. But, as she grew older, her proud station changed her stability to wilfulness, her high spirit to violent temper, her ambition to vanity; and her maiden life made the vinous fermentation of youth turn to the acetous vinegar of malign envy and jealousy.

Her leading characteristics, according to Jenkins, were "cunning," "coquetry," and an "extreme love of power."[21] The tyranny, irrationality, and unnaturalness of monarchy could be made to look even worse when personified by a woman. Yet it was Queen Elizabeth who had presided over the golden age which produced both Shakespeare and, apparently, the American nation. Jenkins accounted for this as mere historical luck, mingling republicanism with misogyny:

> She was fortunate in ascending the throne when the invention of Printing, the discovery of America, and the Reformation, had just aroused human intellect to new life, and produced great men in every department of human enterprise. Bacon, Shakspeare, Spenser, Raleigh, Sydney and Drake, and other names of like lustre, made the Elizabethan age glorious, not the selfish woman from whom it borrows its title. (ibid., 272–73)

Richard Grant White took a rather complex line on the relationship between Shakespeare and Elizabeth. On the one hand, he accepted the tradition that Elizabeth was mean toward Shakespeare:

> Empty compliment and his share of payment to the company for services rendered seem to have been all the benefit that Shakespeare obtained from royal favor. There is not the least reason for believing that either the strong-minded woman or the weak-minded man in whose reigns he flourished recognized his superiority by special distinction or substantial reward.[22]

He went further, characterizing both Elizabeth and James in terms which implied that Shakespeare was better off without their favor: Elizabeth's death, he said, "gave our fathers, instead of a royal family that tyrannized firmly and sagaciously, one that was at once despotic, feeble, and vacillating, and whose monstrous outrages upon the rights of Englishmen contributed mainly to the founding of an English nation upon this continent" (135). According to White, then, Shakespeare and the founding fathers of America were alike in being scorned and oppressed by Elizabeth and James. Shakespeare, again, was more deserving than these hereditary monarchs of the title of king, habitually taking kingly roles in his own plays (138).

Yet White enjoyed and reiterated the traditions that Shakespeare's "exquisite compliment" to Elizabeth in *A Midsummer Night's Dream* had pleased her, and that he had written *The Merry Wives of Windsor* to her commission, depicting in it "the manners, the costume, and the humors of the little town that nestles under the royal towers of Windsor as William Shakespeare saw them in the days of Good Queen Bess."[23] American hostility to Elizabeth as a tyrannical autocrat was here paradoxically combined with "Anglo-Saxon" nostalgia for "merrie England." According to White, it was in "the glorious reign of Queen Elizabeth" that the English nation cast off civil wars, feudalism, and the yoke of Rome, so that "we"—a significant pronoun—"attained to the full maturity of our English-hood." From this invigorated people

> there sprang an array of men glorious in arts and arms, in learning and in literature, in commerce and in statesmanship. It was this period, celebrated under the name of the princess whose reign filled the greater part of it, and which extended from about 1575 to 1625, which produced the men who changed the position of the English people before the world; and chief among them, though not then reckoned of them, was William Shakespeare.[24]

The Elizabethan age was hailed as both the age of Shakespeare and the cradle of the American republic. While the British invoked the double myth of Shakespeare and Elizabeth to support their imperial ambitions, Americans like White invoked it in the service of an American expansionist rhetoric. The true spirit of the age of Shakespeare and Elizabeth had been exported to the New World and was flourishing there as America grew in its aspiration to be the leading nation on the global stage.

There is evidence of the popularity of the Shakespeare-and-Elizabeth myth in the American sales of Eduard Ender's *Shakespeare Reading "Macbeth" before Queen Elizabeth* (fig. 2.8). This was one of the numerous European artworks imported to New York in the 1870s by Knoedler, a company dealing in fine art reproductions. There was a hungry appetite for European art on the New York market, and the customers were not only the wealthy and fashionable but also those of limited means. Knoedler offered engravings, lithographs, and photographs of paintings, and, at a higher price, painted copies. In 1873 *Shakespeare Reading "Macbeth" before Queen Elizabeth* was their nineteenth most popular picture; fifty-nine copies were sold. John Markriter, a paper hanger of Washington, D.C., bought no fewer than six painted copies.[25] Numerous copies were also sold of the engraved reproduction by Pierre Cottin. Perhaps American admirers of the picture enjoyed the way in which Shakespeare might be seen as triumphing over Elizabeth and her court, as he takes center stage and enthralls her with his words. Or perhaps they simply appreciated it as a conversation piece, in the genre of historical painting: an engaging composition, with numerous figures, some movement, and decorative costumes to attract the eye. The success of the picture indicates that the double myth of Shakespeare and Elizabeth had accrued value as cultural capital in nineteenth-century America: to own and display this picture was presumably to make a statement of one's literary and historical knowledge and to present oneself as a cultivated individual. Shakespeare was a cultural commodity, and Elizabeth was traveling with him to America as part of the package.

Ender's picture was reproduced in *The Century of Queens*, an anonymously edited miscellany published in New York in 1872.[26] Like White's writings, this volume contained mixed and unreconciled views of Elizabeth. On the one hand it offered an extremely vitriolic characterization: in her "all the ferocity, pride, and cruelty of the Tudors were concentrated"; she was "so imperious of will, so violent in her demonstrations of anger, in all things so true a daughter of Henry VIII"; she was endowed with "strong passions" and a fiery temper, which "displayed themselves in a manner alike domineering, selfish, and insatiable" (98–99). Some of the line illustrations interspersed in the text showed her as a wizened crone in fanciful costumes, often dancing absurdly (146, 153, 163). Yet it was also felt necessary and appropriate that the volume should include a chapter entitled "Queen Elizabeth and Shakspeare," which explained how Shakespeare's plays were frequently performed at court and asserted that both *A Midsummer Night's Dream* and *The Merry Wives of Windsor* were composed to amuse Elizabeth when she and the players were exiled from London because of the plague (167–71). In relation to Shakespeare, Elizabeth was required to be not a temperamental and vain old hag but the gracious and appreciative patron shown in Ender's picture, and this produced two very different Elizabeths within this one volume.

As the book went on, however, Elizabeth was supplanted by a more fitting female admirer for the Bard. The chapter entitled "Queen Elizabeth and Shakspeare" was immediately followed by a chapter paying tribute to the English author Mrs. Mary Cowden Clarke (1809–98) for her twelve years' labor in compiling her concordance to Shakespeare, published in 1844–45. Her other publications included *The Girlhood of Shakespeare's Heroines* (1850–52) and *World-Noted Women: or, Types of Womanly Attributes of All Lands and Ages* (1858); she was also the first female editor of Shakespeare's complete works (1860).[27] *The Century of Queens* contained a portrait of Mrs. Clarke, bowing her ringleted head demurely, and verses which praised her as a "Fair Vot'ress at great Shakespeare's shrine." It also included a picture of a gift presented to her by grateful American subscribers: "the Shakespeare Chair," a substantial piece of furniture adorned with rosewood carvings and gold brocade, at once a throne, not unlike the throne in which Elizabeth sits in Ender's picture, and a surrogate professorial chair (172–77). The modest and feminine Mrs. Clarke, a "gracious lady fair" (177), called forth more fervent admiration from 1870s America as a votaress of Shakespeare than did the problematic "imperial votaress" Elizabeth.

We have seen how in Britain the solemn public veneration of Shakespeare, and the appropriation of his works by high culture and academia, provoked a popular reaction in the form of burlesques. The same turn to parody occurred in America too, with productions like *Julius Sneezer, Hamlet and Egglet,* and *Much Ado about a Merchant of Venice.*[28] Indeed, Shakespeare travesties took on a distinctively American form in the repertoire of minstrel shows, in which black performers were obliged to perform foolish and humiliating roles.[29] Meanwhile, a privately circulated work by an emerging major American author punctured the romance and mystique of the Shakespeare-and-Elizabeth myth. In 1876, while working on *Huckleberry Finn,* Mark Twain diverted himself by writing *1601: or, Conversation as It Was by the Social Fireside in the Time of the Tudors.* It was confined at first to his closest friends, then was printed in a small private edition in 1882. The scene is supposedly extracted from the diary of "the Pepys of that day," an elderly nobleman who is Queen Elizabeth's cupbearer.[30] He is affronted to have to attend while the Queen and her ladies-in-waiting entertain "certaine th*a*t doe write playes, bookes, & svch like," including Bacon, Raleigh, Jonson, Beaumont, and "the famous Shaxpur" (i).[31] One satirical target, then, is the rigidity of British class boundaries, but the principal object of attack is the dignity and earnestness with which this period of history, and the famous figures who populate it, are usually treated. Somebody breaks wind, "yielding an exceding mighty & distressfull stink, whereat all did laffe full sore," and the Queen interrogates each of them to identify the guilty party. When it comes to Shakespeare's turn he declaims:

> In the grete ha*n*d of God I stand, & so proclaim my innocence. Tho'gh the sinless hosts of Heav'n hadde foretolde the comyng of th*i*s most desolating breath, proclaiming it a werke of uninspired ma*n*, its quaking thunders, its firmame*n*t-clogging rottennesse his owne achievement in due course of nature, yet hadde not I believed it; but hadde sayd the pit itself

hath furnished forth the stink, & Heav'n's artillery hath shook the globe in admiration of it. (iv)

Twain parodies *Hamlet* and *Lear* to imply that Shakespeare, or at least the aspect of his works which is conventionally applauded and reproduced, is typified by lofty philosophizing, cosmic imagery, and rhetorical excess. This "Shakespeare" is a purveyor of hollow bombast which is taken far too seriously.

Once Raleigh has confessed to the fart, Twain's Shakespeare adopts a lower tone, regaling the company with ribald tales from Montaigne. For instance, he recounts "the coustom of widows of Perigord to wear vppon the hedde-dress, in sign of widowhood, a jewel in the similitude of a man's member wilted & limber, whereat the queene did laffe & say, widows in England doe wear prickes too, but 'twixt the thighs, & not wilted neither, till coition hath done that office for them" (v–vi). The humor here is about as low as it can get; it relies simply upon making supposedly great figures from history say rude things. The sketch as a whole, however, offers relief from the general nineteenth-century veneration of Shakespeare and decorously flirtatious imagined encounters with Elizabeth. After some more obscene dialogue, the company listen to Shakespeare reading from *Henry IV* and *Venus and Adonis*, which they receive with "prodigious admiration" but which Twain's disgruntled narrator bathetically dismisses as "not of the ualve [i.e., value] of an arsefvl of ashes" (viii–ix).

The puerility of its scatological humor gives *1601* an exhilarating spirit of iconoclasm. Twain originally sent it in a letter to his pastor and close friend Joseph Twichell, and they took weekend walks in the woods in the course of which they read it aloud to each other and rolled on the ground laughing. Even when its circulation widened, it was only among male friends, and Twain never revealed it to his wife and daughters, treating it as a secret and guilty pleasure.[32] It can be read in diverse ways: perhaps Twain believed that the Elizabethans were franker about bodily matters than his own society and enjoyed the license this gave him; or perhaps he saw this more as an exercise in burlesque, bringing high and mighty figures down to an absurdly low level. Either way, it has a liberating and taboo-breaking effect amid all the solemnity and high-mindedness usually surrounding Shakespeare and Elizabeth.

Twain expressed his skepticism about Shakespeare, or at least what "Shakespeare" meant in American culture, in other places too. In *Huckleberry Finn*, the Duke and the Dauphin hilariously mangle Shakespeare's lines and exploit him as part of their conmanship, while in 1909, entering the authorship controversy, Twain published *Is Shakespeare Dead?* In which he gave some support to the anti-Stratfordian argument. Twain accepted as fact that in 1594 Shakespeare "played before the queen," but dismissed this as "A detail of no consequence: other obscurities did it every year of the forty-five of her reign. And remained obscure."[33] Running through all these works one can detect Twain's anxieties about how authors are treated by posterity and his own need to dethrone Shakespeare in order to define and assert himself as a great and authentically American author.

1900 to the Present: Shakespeare and Elizabeth as Icons and Commodities

Twain's is an idiosyncratic response to the double myth of Shakespeare and Elizabeth. In general Americans continued to idealize the Elizabethan period, and to seek their own origins within it. In 1916 Frederick Henry Koch, Professor of English at the University of North Dakota, presided over a remarkable dramatic endeavor to mark the tercentenary of Shakespeare's death. He supervised the group composition by twenty students of a community pageant, *Shakespeare, the Playmaker,* performed in an open-air theatre at Grand Forks. This Midwestern tribute to the Bard received wide acclaim and national press attention.[34] It has two sections: in the first, Shakespeare, as yet unknown, puts on his own community play to entertain Elizabeth, who enters the rural setting majestically on a barge. The play is supposed to be the tragedy of *Pyramus and Thisbe,* but the rustic performers mangle Shakespeare's lines to produce unintentional farce. He is concerned that "The Queen will think me but a scribbling knave,"[35] but he need not worry; when he is presented to Elizabeth as the author of the piece, she quickly recognizes his merits and understands what has happened. Their brief dialogue is a meeting of minds in which Elizabeth's comments on the comic possibilities of the play give Shakespeare an idea: "as 'tis a mirthful tragedy, 'twould fit well in a comedy, which might perchance succeed on London's stage" (33). The inspiration for *A Midsummer Night's Dream* thus arises from a combination of the jolly ineptness of the common people of England and the critical acumen of their Queen. Elizabeth completes part 1 of the pageant by rebuffing the impertinent Spanish ambassador and coolly departing to pass some time hunting, despite knowing that the Armada is on its way. The second part is set twenty years later, when Shakespeare is the leading dramatist of the age. From William Strachey and other travelers he hears tales of the New World and is amazed by the Native Americans that they have brought back with them. These encounters inspire him to write *The Tempest.*

Both halves of *Shakespeare, the Playmaker* begin with busy crowd scenes, the first with preparations for the village pageant and the second with a May Fair, complete with a maypole, morris dancers, and a procession including not only milkmaids, chimney sweeps, and gypsies but also Robin Hood and Friar Tuck (41–45). As an advertisement for the show put it, it presents "a colorful pageant of the middle-class folk in the merry England of Shakespeare."[36] One character enthuses that these are "great days . . . with the merry-makings at court, the banquets and the balls. And, thanks to good Queen Bess, on the Bankside are many theaters where plays are enacted, and all London is merry over the plays of Master Shakespeare" (40). At such moments the students of North Dakota seem seized by a remarkable nostalgia for "merrie England." It is striking that the double myth of Shakespeare and Elizabeth had such a grip even in these reaches of the American Midwest, very far from the sixteenth-century banks of the Thames. The English Department of the University of North Dakota deploys it to establish its academic status as a custodian and purveyor of traditional high culture. Yet at the same time, the movement of the drama gradually but firmly leaves "merrie England" behind. In part 1, Shakespeare takes inspiration from the ordinary people who bungle his play and from Elizabeth. The Queen and commons of England provide the origins of his dramatic career. In part 2, however, they are left behind. The mature Shakespeare is captivated by the travelers' tales of America, and it is these that elevate him into a poetic rapture in which he creates *The Tempest*. This is described as "Shakespeare's interpretation of the New World" (10) and is presented in abridged form as both the climax of *Shakespeare, the Playmaker* and the consummation of Shakespeare's dramatic genius.[37]

The Tempest as a play of the New World was central to Charles Mills Gayley's argument the following year in *Shakespeare and the Founders of Liberty in America*. Gayley traced Shakespeare's connections with some of the individuals involved in the Virginia Council, which was set up in London in 1606 to pursue the colonial project, and he demonstrated that some details of *The Tempest* derived from an unpublished letter from William Strachey written in 1610 to senior members of the Council. For Gayley this was evidence that Shakespeare was part of the inner circle that planned the Virginia project and developed its philosophy.[38] Shakespeare the colonialist appeared again in Frederick Henry Koch's next dramatic venture, *Raleigh, the Shepherd of the Ocean*, performed in 1920 at Raleigh in North Carolina, where Koch was now Professor of Dramatic Literature. Sir Walter Raleigh understandably became an increasingly important figure in the American celebration of English origins; but Shakespeare and Elizabeth also play large roles in this pageant. This time it is Raleigh's reports of the wondrous New World which inspire Shakespeare to write *The Tempest,* and once again there are lavish Elizabethan crowd scenes, in which Shakespeare's phrase "O brave new world!" is enthusiastically taken up as a rapturous westward-looking choral chant.[39] Before this, Elizabeth makes her appearance to rout the Armada, and also becomes a mouthpiece for Shakespeare as her famous Tilbury speech is replaced by the lines of Henry V before Agincourt (40).[40] Even this moment of distinctively English patriotic rhetoric is converted to the American cause: Koch's commentary explains that the Spanish had to be defeated so that the oceans were clear for English settlers to sail across the Atlantic. The pageant carries a foreword by Koch's colleague Edwin Greenlaw which declares that "the sources of that which now seems most truly American" are "in Shakespeare's England":

> It is in the sense of adventure in modern life, in the romance of the conquest of far-flung prairies and of mountains made to yield their treasure, in the building of giant industries, in the color brought by emigrants from every corner of the Old World, in the irrepressible confidence of youth finding it an easy leap to pluck honor from the pale-faced moon,[41] that we find our thought of America today. And the first-beginnings of this multifarious life we find in the adventure, the romance, the daring accomplishment, the color, and the youth of Elizabethan England. (15)

Modern America, according to Greenlaw, is Elizabethan England transplanted across the Atlantic.

Shakespeare and Elizabeth featured in another drama about Raleigh staged in North Carolina, Paul Green's *The Lost Colony.* This play tells the story of the failed settlement at Roanoke which Raleigh sponsored; it was first performed in 1937 at the open-air Waterside Theater on Roanoke Island, and has been performed there annually ever since, apart from a short break during the Second World War. Shakespeare appears as an unknown young poet, who begs Raleigh to let him travel with the Roanoke expedition: "No-one likes my poor verse here," he complains; "Give me an axe, I can cut trees."[42] In a later revised version, he has even more pioneer spirit: "In the wilderness there I'd do my part with any man."[43] Raleigh, however, recognizes his gift with words, and with the same foresight which motivates his colonial project, perceives its future importance to the world. He persuades Shakespeare that the New World is not for him, because "I fear you'd find no time for poetry there."[44] The narrator sums up: "And so through Raleigh's aid Shakespeare did not go to Roanoke Island, but that his imagination traveled to that new land is shown in some of his plays of later years [i.e., *The Tempest*]. Thus it was that the young adventurous spirits of England were fired to Raleigh's dream."[45]

Shakespeare may not have physically joined the colonists, but according to Green he was their kindred spirit. Like them he was unappreciated in his homeland and his own time, but posterity would acclaim his achievements.

While Green's Shakespeare is a fervent enthusiast for the American project, Elizabeth takes the opposite view. Her appearances give lavish opportunities for pageantry and spectacle, but she repeatedly expresses doubts about the colonial expedition. Her persistent concern is with England's national security and the threat from Spain. After some debate, Raleigh challenges her with the question, "Shall England be an empire or an island?" She reluctantly replies, "You may send your colony to Roanoke," but insists that Raleigh himself stay behind to fight the Spanish.[46] Toward the end of the play, as Raleigh begs her to let him send ships bearing aid to the starving and disease-afflicted settlers, she receives word of the coming Armada and refuses him.[47] The valiant colonists, including a brave heroine, Eleanor Dare, and her daughter, Virginia, the first child of English parents to be born on American soil, are abandoned to the wilderness.

The emotional and political tensions of the play are subtly orchestrated. It is hard to criticize Elizabeth for giving first place to the defense of her realm against an imminent threat; and yet she is also shown as cautious and lacking in vision. Her isolationism may be read in the 1937 context of increasing tension in Europe and anxiety about what this might mean for transatlantic relations, including the irony that it was now Britain that was likely to be looking to America for aid. The abandoned settlers are bold in adventure and noble in suffering. Shakespeare, by contrast with Elizabeth, shares their American dream, and despite the brevity of his appearance in person is present pervasively in the play in many echoes of his works (the beggar Old Tom is like Poor Tom in *King Lear*; the feast in act 1, scene 3, is like the sheep-shearing feast in *The Winter's Tale*; and so on). Thus the founding of America is rendered as a pseudo-Shakespearean drama.

Green wrote of his play as drawing upon medieval and Elizabethan traditions in its use of music, song, dance, and pantomime, and of his hopes that it would be emulated across America, creating "a real people's theatre, other than the movies."[48] In the play itself it is stated that the purpose of commemorating the Roanoke settlers was to "keep faith with them, . . . with ourselves and with future generations who demand of us that a nation of liberty and free men shall continue on the earth."[49] According to Green's recent editor, Laurence G. Avery, Green's purpose was "to rekindle a feeling for equality, a feeling for its social importance, in contemporary audiences. The play works to that end by showing how frontier conditions in America broke down European class distinctions between serf, peasant, yeoman, and noblemen . . . and placed all citizens on a level playing field in the game of life."[50] Green's Shakespeare, introduced as a shabby and anonymous young man, personifies this classless ethos.[51] However, the settlers are tragically *not* on a level playing field in the game of life: they are at the mercy of the old English order in the form of Elizabeth's autocratic will, and this in the end destroys them.

Elizabeth, then, seems to be the villain of the piece, yet over the decades she has become its star. The annual performance of Green's play attracts tourists eager to see her impersonated, with many spin-off events including Tea with the Queen, *Bloody Mary and the Virgin Queen* (a musical comedy), and *Elizabeth R* (a one-woman show); Elizabeth even presides over the Lost Colony Annual Golf Classic.[52] This is all symptomatic of Elizabeth's rise in popularity and cultural status in America over the course of the twentieth century. There will be more to say about this in chapter 6, but a few examples may be mentioned here. Hollywood took up Elizabeth as a feisty but conflicted romantic heroine in the Bette Davis films *The Private Lives of Elizabeth and Essex* (1939) and *The Virgin Queen* (1955).[53] After the U.S. screening in 1972 of *Elizabeth R,* the acclaimed BBC television series starring Glenda Jackson, the Queen began to look more and more like a feminist icon.[54] Moreover, as Elizabeth became an increasingly potent and glamorous figure in American popular culture, she became ever more prominent in representations of Shakespeare. In 1979 the Folger Shakespeare Library held a major exhibition entitled *Shakespeare: The Globe and The World.* The British artist David Hockney, who has enjoyed great transatlantic success, was commissioned to produce a drawing for the occasion (fig. 3.1).[55] It depicts two figures: Shakespeare and Elizabeth. Elizabeth thus stands as symbol of "the world" of Shakespeare's time, the personification of the whole Elizabethan age. Shakespeare is sketched in by means of just a few black lines, with many gaps. He is barely there, and yet instantly recognizable: a domed head, a beard, a ruff, legs clad in hose. Hockney vividly expresses the way in which we all feel we know Shakespeare, and yet he remains enigmatic and elusive. Elizabeth, on the other side, is in a posture based on the Ditchley portrait (fig. 4.1), with a huge ruff and farthingale, all embellished with bright colors, pattern, and detail. Hockney shows how we recognize her largely through her curled red hair and magnificent costumes. This, combined with the orb and scepter that she holds, suggests that she stands not only for the world but for worldliness, in the sense both of material goods and political power. She is a solid physical presence, while the few light and apparently hasty lines which make up Shakespeare indicate a more spiritual and intellectual entity. The composition opposes these two contrasting figures, yet also presents them as a pair, inclining toward each other while looking out of the picture at posterity. Shakespeare and the world, then, is Shakespeare and Elizabeth.

FIGURE 3.1
David Hockney, *Queen Elizabeth and Shakespeare,* 1979. Crayon on paper, 17 x 21 in.

By 1998 it seemed natural for a book by the American academic Barbara Hodgdon on the commodification of Shakespeare, *The Shakespeare Trade,* to include a chapter on representations of Elizabeth I.[56] Hodgdon also contributed to the catalogue of another Folger Shakespeare Library exhibition, *Elizabeth I Then and Now* (2003), which commemorated the four-hundredth anniversary of Elizabeth's death. It is not perhaps surprising that this occasion was marked by events in Britain, such as the self-styled "blockbuster" exhibition at the National Maritime Museum in Greenwich, which drew large crowds, exceeding visitor targets.[57] It is worthy of remark, however, that Elizabeth was now felt to deserve a major exhibition of her own at America's leading center for Shakespeare studies. Georgianna Ziegler, curator of the exhibition, explained in the glossy accompanying book that "the Folger Library has the largest collection of Elizabeth-related material in the United States."[58] This volume was notably unable to offer much material directly linking Elizabeth and Shakespeare, though it did briefly and judiciously review the evidence for court performances of his plays (85–88). Gail Kern Paster, in a foreword, set out the assumptions on which the exhibition was based: that Elizabeth "completely personifies sixteenth-century England," and "remains a figure of charismatic power in British and American culture" (10). Paster thanked the corporate sponsors of the exhibition, who had supported such events as "a reception for [Elizabeth's] political descendants in America—the women members of Congress" (11). Shakespeare may have served to represent American values since the early nineteenth century, but Elizabeth was clearly an emblem of values important to America at the dawn of the twenty-first century. "Our exhibit," concluded Paster, "seeks to convey the wonder of Elizabeth I" (11).

During this celebration Elizabeth seemed almost to eclipse Shakespeare. It would be truer to say, however, that their cults have become inseparable and mutually enhancing, and that they are now equal in their remarkable popularity in modern America. Elizabeth may have become a Hollywood star in the twentieth century, but Shakespeare has been one of the chief sources for American films, including musicals like *Kiss Me, Kate* (1953) and high-school comedies like *10 Things I Hate about You* (1999), as well as more or less "straightforward" adaptations of his plays.[59] Elizabeth may be a central attraction of the annual *Lost Colony* performances and events at Roanoke, but there are more than two hundred annual Shakespeare festivals in the United States, a figure which has doubled in the last decade alone and which dwarfs the fifteen Shakespeare festivals in the United Kingdom.[60] Elizabeth's 2003 exhibition at the Folger was succeeded in 2007 by *Shakespeare in American Life*, an exhibition richly illustrating "Shakespeare's deep involvement with American history from the nation's inception . . . his deep influence on all American popular art forms to the present day . . . [and] Shakespeare's central place in the rich canvas of the American cultural landscape."[61]

Thus for at least two centuries Shakespeare and Elizabeth have converged in America as well as in Britain. To a large extent the elaboration of the double myth has become something shared between the two nations, and yet each nation looks at it from a significantly different point of view. The British are the custodians of the geographical sites associated with Shakespeare and Elizabeth—Stratford-upon-Avon, the Globe reconstruction on Bankside, the Tower of London, Hatfield House, and so on—and perhaps rather unthinkingly assume Shakespeare and Elizabeth to be indisputably theirs, however much we might welcome American interest in them. Yet for Americans, for a long time, Shakespeare has been deeply felt to belong to them, ideologically and emotionally, and their national identity has been founded on a sense of themselves as the true successors of the Elizabethans.

Shakespeare is intensively and vigorously studied in British schools and universities and at various academic institutions in Stratford-upon-Avon, London, and elsewhere, but Shakespeare is also central to American education, and the Folger Shakespeare Library can make a just claim to be the world center for Shakespeare scholarship. The annual conference of the Shakespeare Association of America, held in a different American location each year, is the leading global gathering of Shakespeare scholars, to which many British academics travel. The British must now get on aeroplanes—or rather, airplanes—to keep in touch with Shakespeare and Elizabeth.

For more than two hundred years the British have made money out of American pilgrims to Shakespearean and Elizabethan sites; but perhaps more than we British realize or care to acknowledge, many versions of the double myth of Shakespeare and Elizabeth which we enjoy have been reflected back to us—and indeed sold back to us—by the Americans. The relation of the two nations to the double myth is a complex mixture of commerce, collaboration, and competition. We pass it back and forth between us, constantly adapting and embellishing it as we do so. The rest of this book will deal with American materials alongside British ones, as it discusses the development of the double myth in literary criticism, in the Shakespeare authorship controversy, and in fiction and film from 1900 to the present.

4

Criticism and Interpretation: Elizabeth as the Key to Shakespeare

Although there is little explicit reference to Elizabeth in Shakespeare's works, over a long period scholars have sought her there in veiled or encoded forms. This is partly because Shakespeare's plays and poems have come to seem increasingly difficult. His style is often dense and allusive, and sometimes rendered even more obscure by apparent errors of transcription or printing; and his language and cultural context have inevitably become more and more remote from readers as time passed. Alongside this process, since the early nineteenth century knowledge has become increasingly professionalized and institutionalized, the preserve of a trained elite of experts and specialists. Gary Taylor describes this movement and the attitudes and impulses behind it: "The past speaks in code; in order to understand it you must decipher its language. The fossils in the rocks, the hieroglyphics in Egyptian monuments, the manuscripts Pepys had bequeathed to Magdalene College, Cambridge—the messages had been there all along, but no one knew their meaning until the code was cracked."[1] Shakespeare's works also became regarded as encoded messages and cryptic puzzles. Solutions were often sought in topical allusions to political events or prominent personages which purported to fix the elusive meaning of the text, to anchor it to historical materials which were factual and indisputable. Such readings also enhanced the authority of the critic as he (rarely she) flaunted his scholarly credentials and arcane knowledge. Indeed, some readings proposed that Shakespeare, because of the dangerous political circumstances of his time, wrote in a secret language of allegory intended to be understood only by a few cognoscenti, so that in both past and present his true meaning was accessible only to an especially perceptive and well-informed coterie.

It was inevitable that historical readings would frequently center on Elizabeth, since her public life was the most fully documented of her time, she had an established public image as the most charismatic of Shakespeare's contemporaries, and she was an intriguing puzzle in her own right, as a Virgin Queen with a mysterious private life and feelings. Because of her powers of censorship and the severe punishments which she could inflict, it could also be argued that Shakespeare could only comment on her in his works in discreetly encoded terms. Even so, the allusions to Elizabeth which nineteenth-century scholars found in Shakespeare's works were mostly complimentary ones, supporting the myth of their close patron-client relationship. Sometimes more amorous feelings between Shakespeare and Elizabeth were detected, and in these instances literary criticism veered close to historical fiction. Interpretations which emphasized Shakespeare's attractiveness to the Queen, or his own romantic inclinations toward her, contributed to an image of the playwright as virile but respectable and were used to overcome difficulties like the affection for a young man expressed in the Sonnets. The identification of loyal tributes to Elizabeth in Shakespeare's works also served to refute rumors of his Catholic leanings. These rumors arose from a seventeenth-century report that "he died a papist" and the emergence in 1794 of a Catholic spiritual testament apparently belonging to his father[2] and were distinctly problematic for the ongoing promotion of Shakespeare as a pillar of the British establishment.

In the early to mid twentieth century formalist movements such as New Criticism in the United States and Practical Criticism in the United Kingdom turned away from historical readings, but others continued to find Elizabeth in Shakespeare's supposed participation in the "Tudor myth," the idea that the Tudors were a divinely ordained dynasty who had brought unprecedented peace and prosperity after decades of civil war. E.M.W. Tillyard claimed that this myth was part of an "Elizabethan world picture": the cosmos was regarded as a "Great Chain of Being" in which the political order was analogous with the divine order and the natural order, and political rebellion unleashed chaos and divine retribution.[3] According to this account, Shakespeare placed Elizabeth at the pinnacle of creation as a symbol of order and as an idealized ruler subject only to God. This characterization of Shakespeare as a loyal servant of the state and its attempts to enforce fixed hierarchies was vigorously challenged in the 1980s by new-historicist and cultural-materialist critics, yet their interest in finding political and subversive energies in Shakespeare's works itself gave a new impetus to the quest for concealed or encoded comment on Elizabeth in his works.

Over the long history of Shakespeare scholarship there have been considerable shifts in attitudes toward Elizabeth and in critical methodologies, reflecting larger shifts in culture and ideology. Nevertheless, some readings which have recently been presented and received as fresh and radical can be traced back to venerable origins, and literary criticism as much as historical fiction has been affected by the persistent desire to bring Shakespeare and Elizabeth together.

Oberon's Vision and the Princely Pleasures at Kenilworth

The clearest reference to Elizabeth in Shakespeare's works is arguably Oberon's vision in act 2, scene 1, of *A Midsummer Night's Dream*, already described in 1895 as "the subject of more voluminous speculation than any other twenty-five lines in Shakespeare":[4]

OBERON: Thou remembr'rest
Since once I sat upon a promontory
And heard a mermaid on a dolphin's back
Uttering such dulcet and harmonious breath
That the rude sea grew civil at her song
And certain stars shot madly from their spheres
To hear the sea-maid's music?

ROBIN: I remember.

OBERON: That very time I saw, but thou couldst not,
Flying between the cold moon and the earth
Cupid, all armed. A certain aim he took
At a fair vestal thronèd by the west,
And loosed his love-shaft smartly from his bow
As it should pierce a hundred thousand hearts.
But I might see young Cupid's fiery shaft
Quenched in the chaste beams of the wat'ry moon,
And the imperial vot'ress passèd on,
In maiden meditation, fancy-free.
Yet marked I where the bolt of Cupid fell.
It fell upon a little western flower—
Before, milk-white; now, purple with love's wound.

(*A Midsummer Night's Dream*, 2.1.148–67)

In 1709 Rowe identified the "fair vestal" as Elizabeth, and this has never been seriously challenged: her virginity, imperial power, and association with the moon, symbol of the virgin goddess Diana, a favorite image in 1590s royal panegyric, all suggest a persona of Elizabeth.

William Warburton wrote in his 1747 edition of Shakespeare that "By the *Vestal* every one knows is meant Queen *Elizabeth*." He also identified the mermaid as Mary Queen of Scots, arguing that the dolphin was her first husband, the Dauphin of France, and the stars that "shot madly from their spheres" were the English noblemen led to treason and destruction by their devotion to her. This reading, though topical, was less political than personal: Shakespeare had to write of these matters under the veil of allegory because the jealous Elizabeth "could not bear to hear [Mary] commended."[5] Warburton's interpretation was accepted and repeated for forty years before it fell out of favor, although it has been revived recently in the search for Catholic allusions in Shakespeare.[6]

Most critics have been more interested in possible connections between Oberon's vision and the 1575 Princely Pleasures at Kenilworth. As we saw in the discussion of Sir Walter Scott's *Kenilworth* in chapter 2, Thomas Percy in 1794 speculated that Shakespeare might have seen these as a boy, and that both the pageants and Elizabeth's presence as public spectacle might have inspired his dramatic career. Also in 1794, Walter Whiter suggested that Oberon's vision might refer to some actual Elizabethan masque or pageant, and three years later, James Plumptre proposed that "Cupid's attack upon the vestal" represented "the accomplishments of the Earl of Leicester."[7] Finally, in 1832, these various associations between Shakespeare's boyhood, Kenilworth, and Oberon's vision were drawn together by the same James Boaden who had participated in the exposure of William-Henry Ireland. Boaden agreed that Shakespeare was probably at the Princely Pleasures and "might perhaps have even discharged some youthful part in the pageant."[8] The spectacle must have made an impression upon "one of 'imagination all compact,' a youth of singular precocity, with a strong devotion to the Muses." This impression was recorded in Oberon's speech to Puck, and Boaden gleefully summoned to the passage "the critical attention which the reader is now, for the first time, called upon to give it, as a *record* of the 'Princely pleasures of Kenilworth'" (8–9).

Boaden quoted as evidence contemporary descriptions of the 1575 festivities, including that of George Gascoigne:

> "Triton in the likenesse of a MERMAID came towarde the Queene's Majestie as she passed over the bridge . . . Then Protheus appeared *sitting on a dolphin's back*," (the identical words of Oberon [*sic*],) "and the dolphin was conveyed upon a boate, so that the oars seemed to be his fynnes. Within the which dolphyn a consort of musicke was secretly placed." (13)[9]

The stars which Oberon says "shot madly from their spheres" were, believed Boaden, the spectacular fireworks of the Princely Pleasures, which astonished eyewitnesses.[10] He acknowledged some discrepancies between Oberon's vision and the Kenilworth reports but contended that Shakespeare's "description is exactly such as, after seventeen years had elapsed, a reminiscence would suggest to a mind highly poetical" (14).[11] He went further: Shakespeare was not just expressing personal nostalgia but representing, in the immunity of the "fair vestal" to Cupid's arrow, the conclusive failure, at Kenilworth, of Leicester's courtship of Elizabeth. "Then or never did the magnificent Leicester expect to carry his romantic prize," but she glided imperturbably on, "in maiden meditation, fancy-free . . . the happiest of all compliments to her virgin obduracy" (14–15).

This interpretation of Oberon's vision as a reference to Kenilworth and Elizabeth's resistance to Leicester's marriage campaign was to become one of the most influential and enduring topical readings of Shakespeare's works. Yet the looseness of Boaden's scholarship became evident in his identification of the "little western flower" which received Cupid's deflected arrow, or Leicester's deflected ardor: "Why, alas! Can we not ask the kindred spirit, Sir Walter Scott, whether he can conceive his own Amy Robsart more beautifully and touchingly figured than she appears to be in this exquisite metaphor?" (15). As mentioned in chapter 2, Leicester's first wife died fifteen years before the Princely Pleasures—around thirty-five years before the composition of *A Midsummer Night's Dream*. Boaden only connected her with the Princely Pleasures because Scott had done so in *Kenilworth*, and was seemingly unaware of the novel's flagrant distortion of chronology. Scott may have set a trend for novelists and artists to use archival sources, but in this instance he himself was set up, unwarrantably, as a historical authority, and the line of influence ran not from scholarship to fiction but from fiction to scholarship. Yet Boaden's general idea—Oberon's vision as a reminiscence of Kenilworth—took hold and continues to be reiterated today. It is one of the stranger episodes in the history of Shakespeare scholarship that an idea which has been found convincing by so many experts had such dubious origins.

In 1843 the Reverend N. J. Halpin, an Irish journalist and literary critic, published a study of Oberon's vision. He claimed to have arrived independently, through his own archival reading, at the conclusion that the passage was a recollection of the Princely Pleasures, and he criticized Boaden's dependence upon Scott's "charming but inaccurate Historical Romance of Kenilworth."[12] Halpin asserted his own superior understanding of both art and history: Scott had exercised "the poet's prerogative" to connect the Princely Pleasures with both Amy Robsart and an adult Shakespeare (29). However, he himself adhered to the idea that the young Shakespeare would have watched the festivities "as a capable and gratified spectator" (24), and he offered a reading of the "little western flower" essentially like Boaden's in proposing that the bloom represented a rival for Elizabeth in Leicester's affections. In this case, however, she was not Amy Robsart but Lettice Knollys, the widowed Countess of Essex, whom Leicester married in 1575 (29–30). It was "indisputable," therefore, that Oberon's vision related "to some romantic adventure, some affair of the heart, in which that coy Princess, Queen Elizabeth, was deeply and personally interested" (107). Once again, he assumed that Shakespeare's writings held secrets to be unlocked, and as a result, for all his impressive scholarship, he produced a reading of *A Midsummer Night's Dream* as a roman à clef or secret history. Although he distanced himself from Scott's distortion of events, in its outcome his reading of Oberon's vision was not far removed from the narrative pleasures and behind-closed-doors titillations of historical fiction.

Historical novelists after Scott assumed that the boy Shakespeare was at Kenilworth in 1575: the episode was used in both Robert Folkestone Williams's *The Youth of Shakspeare* (1839) and Henry Curling's *Shakspere* (1848), and the latter also connected the occasion with *A Midsummer Night's Dream.* As a young man, Curling's Shakespeare passes Kenilworth on his journey from Stratford to a new life in London. He remembers how he saw the pageants there, including "Arion, on a dolphin's back," and Oberon's vision is simply quoted, in slightly adapted form, as a description of the Princely Pleasures. Curling also adapts Theseus's account of his gracious demeanor toward unskilled performers as a description of Elizabeth's kindly manner toward local rustic actors at Kenilworth: "Her sport, to take what they mistook" (5.1.90–103). For Curling, Oberon's vision is simply a fragment of Shakespeare's autobiography.[13]

Identification of the "fair vestal" as Elizabeth has fueled the persistent belief that Shakespeare and the Queen enjoyed a warm patronage relationship. For Rowe in 1709 it was evidence that "Queen *Elizabeth* had several of his Plays Acted before her, and without doubt gave him many gracious Marks of her Favour";[14] for Scott in 1821, as can be seen in *Kenilworth,* Oberon's vision was unquestionably a royal panegyric; and for Boaden in 1832 it was "the happiest of all compliments to her virgin obduracy." The trend continued into the twentieth century: E. K. Chambers in 1930 read the passage as "obvious flattery of Queen Elizabeth"; and for Harold Brooks too, in his Arden edition of 1979, it was a compliment to the Queen.[15] For centuries, then, it was read as deferential praise, but this interpretation was overturned in 1983 by Louis Montrose's influential essay "Shaping Fantasies." As a new-historicist critic, Montrose was interested in the subjectivity and unreliability of historical sources and in the ideological effects of literary texts. He was interested too in how literary texts could express complex interdependencies between forces of subversion and forces of authority.[16] "Shaping Fantasies" applied this approach to *A Midsummer Night's Dream* and explored the play's relation to Elizabeth in ways which were crucial to the development of new-historicist thinking.[17]

Montrose set out by arguing that Elizabeth's "pervasive *cultural presence* was a condition of the play's imaginative possibility," and that at the same time "in the sense that the royal presence was itself *re*-presented within the play, it may be said that the play henceforth conditioned the imaginative possibility of the Queen."[18] Historical context, then, was not a fixed set of facts to be invoked to decode the play: it was mobile and could itself be reshaped by the play. Nevertheless, Montrose's methodology still relied upon using materials traditionally classified as nonliterary—an ambassador's report of an audience with Elizabeth, a diary entry recording a dream about Elizabeth—to elucidate the text. Laying these generically diverse materials alongside *A Midsummer Night's Dream,* Montrose argued that the Queen was a figure who combined political, maternal, and erotic qualities, and as such inspired a complex mixture of desires and anxieties in her subjects. Thus Bottom fulfils a fantasy of making love to the Fairy Queen, while Oberon intervenes as a higher male authority to put that unruly Queen firmly back into her place. Titania is not a direct allegorical representation of Elizabeth but a figure by means of which troubling feelings about her and about female rule may be explored. In Montrose's words, "a fantasy of male dependency upon woman is expressed and contained within a fantasy of male control over woman; the social reality of the player's dependency upon a Queen is inscribed within the imaginative reality of the dramatist's control over a Queen" (107). For Montrose, then, the play is full of ambivalence toward Elizabeth.

According to this reading, the ethereal and moonlike "fair vestal" of Oberon's vision is cold and sterile. Although her resistance to Cupid's arrow creates the love charm and thereby brings about the erotic confusions of the midnight wood, she herself is removed from and opposed to the chaotic but vibrant energies of youth, desire, and fertility which the play as a whole celebrates. Montrose argued that "Shakespeare's play is neither focused upon the Queen nor structurally dependent upon her presence or her intervention in the action. On the contrary, it might be said to depend upon her absence, her exclusion" (126). The imperial votaress's immunity to fleshly desires merely enables a male monarch, Oberon, to subject others to fleshly desires, and as a result "Shakespeare's royal compliment remythologises the cult of the Virgin Queen in such a way as to sanction a relationship of gender and power that is personally and politically inimical to Elizabeth" (127). In short, Oberon's vision is not a compliment but a reconfiguration of the Queen as icon which curtails and neutralizes her disturbing female authority and allure.

Montrose's reading of *A Midsummer Night's Dream* as expressing dark and turbulent feelings about Elizabeth has had an extensive influence in readings of other works by Shakespeare, as will be discussed below. Meanwhile the much older reading of Oberon's vision as a reference to the Princely Pleasures, to their inspirational effect upon the young Shakespeare, and to Leicester's failed wooing has remained popular and enduring. Its reach extended to the commercial tourist attractions of Stratford-upon-Avon, which in the 1990s included a "dark ride" entitled "The World of Shakespeare," in fact almost wholly devoted to the presence of Elizabeth and young Shakespeare at Kenilworth in 1575.[19] It is a reading which continues to be explored by highly respected scholars, including Katherine Duncan-Jones in her 2001 biographical study of Shakespeare[20] and Stephen Greenblatt in his best-selling *Will in the World* (2004). In the 1980s Greenblatt was in the vanguard of new historicism, but in this recent book he offered a distinctly "old historicist" reading of *A Midsummer Night's Dream*: like Boaden in 1832, he holds that "the playwright's imagination drew on the scene at Kenilworth in crafting a gorgeous compliment to Elizabeth," and that the "fair vestal" passage "clearly alludes to Leicester's attempt, some twenty years earlier, to charm the queen."[21] And like Percy in 1794, Greenblatt finds Shakespeare's first dramatic inspiration at the Princely Pleasures:

> If a wide-eyed young boy from Stratford did see her [i.e., Elizabeth], arrayed in one of her famously elaborate dresses, carried in a litter on the shoulders of guards specially picked for their good looks, accompanied by her gorgeously arrayed courtiers, he would in effect have witnessed the greatest theatrical spectacle of the age . . . Shakespeare's sense of the transforming power of theatrical illusions may be traced back to what he heard about or saw for himself in 1575 at Kenilworth. (ibid., 45–50)

The blurb on the jacket of *Will in the World* laid claim to new and exciting theories: "Bringing together little-known historical facts and little-noticed elements of Shakespeare's plays, Greenblatt makes inspired connections between an entertainment presented to Queen Elizabeth on a visit to the countryside during Shakespeare's boyhood and passages in *A Midsummer Night's Dream*." In fact, as we have seen, this was hardly news. Back in the 1980s, Leeds Barroll had cautioned that "many of the narratives presented by new historicists are disturbingly unselfconscious and static, constricted by old narratives that tell a traditional story of the drama in a special relationship to the state or to the person of the monarch." In other words, their new theories were sometimes built upon old anecdotes and legends.[22] The reading of Oberon's vision in *Will in the World* seems to confirm Barroll's implication that new historicists, for all their political awareness, have sometimes been dazzled by Elizabeth's glamor, and by the desire to assert the power of drama by associating it with the Crown. In this case, to use Barroll's words, we certainly return to an "old narrative that tells a traditional story."

The possible connection between Oberon's vision and Elizabeth at Kenilworth has thus been one of the most enduring and important elements of the double myth of Shakespeare and Elizabeth. Its history illustrates how that myth has crossed boundaries between academic scholarship, fiction, and popular culture, as many different kinds of readers and writers, and custodians and customers in the heritage industry, have taken a shared pleasure and satisfaction in the idea that Shakespeare's first inspiration came from the magnificent, spectacular figure of Elizabeth and the pageants in her honor.

A Midsummer Night's Dream: A Wedding Play?

Elizabeth has also been involved in theories that *A Midsummer Night's Dream* was written for a court wedding. These have been largely based on the play's emphatic bridal theme and the nuptial blessing by the fairies in the final act. In 1830 Ludwig Tieck suggested that the occasion was the wedding of Shakespeare's patron Henry Wriothesley, the Earl of Southampton, to Elizabeth Vernon in 1598:

> Vielleicht war der Kern oder die erste Skizze des Drama ein Glückwunsch für die Neuvermählten, in Form einer sogenannten Maske, in der Oberon, Titania und ihre Feen dem Brautpaar Glück und Heil wünschten und weissagten.[23]
>
> [Perhaps the germ, or the first sketch, of the drama was a felicitation to the newly married couple, in the form of a so-called masque, in which Oberon, Titania and their fairies wished and foretold good fortune and good health for the bridal pair.][24]

However, Tieck knew that the Queen opposed this wedding and would not have attended it:

> Auch Southampton vermählte sich gegen den Willen der Königin mit seiner Braut. Elisabeth scheint um die Heirath anfangs nicht gewusst zu haben; denn sie behandelte sie wie eine heimliche.[25]
>
> [Southampton also got married against the Queen's wishes. Elizabeth appears at first not to have known about the marriage, for she treated it as a secret one.]

A number of other critics through the later nineteenth century and early twentieth proposed various aristocratic weddings as possible occasions for the play but did not involve Elizabeth.[26] However, interpretation of Oberon's vision as a compliment to the Queen made it increasingly irresistible for critics to draw her into this scenario. Richard Grant White wrote in 1857, "Shakespeare never worked for nothing, and, besides, could he, could any man, have the heart to waste so exquisite a compliment as that is, and to such a woman as Queen Elizabeth, by uttering it behind her back?"[27] Gerald Massey suggested in 1866 that the *Dream* "was written with the view of celebrating the marriage of Southampton and Elizabeth Vernon," but that "the play was probably composed some time before the marriage took place, at a period when it may have been thought the Queen's consent could be obtained."[28] From the 1870s onward Elizabeth's presence at a nuptial performance of the play was increasingly asserted.[29]

Horace Howard Furness, the distinguished American Shakespearean, produced Variorum editions of Shakespeare's plays including, in 1895, *A Midsummer Night's Dream.* He was level-headed about most critical debates around the play: for instance, the "little western flower" of Oberon's vision was, he sensibly reasoned, neither Amy Robsart nor Lettice Knollys nor any other lady; it was simply a flower. After all, its juice had to be squeezed onto sleeping lovers' eyelids.[30] He objected to the Kenilworth reading of Oberon's vision because, he argued, the Princely Pleasures were simply too far in the past—twenty years—when the *Dream* was written (91). Yet on the wedding-play theory he contradicted himself. In the early pages of the volume he argued vehemently that Shakespeare was no client to the aristocracy but a popular, commercial artist who "wrote to fill the theatre and earn money for himself and his fellows." Beyond this, Furness scorned all topical readings; he believed it denigrated Shakespeare "to suppose that he could not, without a basis of fact, write a play with wooing and wedding for its theme, which should charm and fascinate till wooing and wedding cease to be." Shakespeare was "fixedly . . . grounded on the 'eternal verities'" and not interested in "trifling, local, and temporary allusions"; in the decoding method of criticism "the same denial of SHAKESPEARE's dramatic power is everywhere thrust forward" (xix–xx). Yet despite all this, later in the volume Furness stated placidly "it is not improbable, from the final scene of the play, that this *Dream* was composed for the festivities of some marriage in high life, at which possibly the Queen herself was present" (259).

The theory that *A Midsummer Night's Dream* was a wedding play and seen by Elizabeth gained weight from E. K. Chambers's magisterial 1923 study of the Elizabethan stage, in which he favored the idea that the occasion was the 1596 marriage of Thomas Berkeley and Elizabeth Carey and considered it "likely enough" that the Queen was present.[31] Many subsequent critics accepted this version of events, including Harold F. Brooks in his 1979 Arden edition of the *Dream*.[32] However, from the 1960s on others recoiled from this theory. Stanley Wells, in his 1967 Penguin edition, pointed out that there is no evidence for it beyond the nuptial concerns within the text and that when Elizabethan weddings were celebrated with dramatic entertainments, these were masques, not plays. Like Furness, he worried that the wedding-play theory diminished Shakespeare's artistry: "Some of those who hold this theory patronize the play as an 'occasional' piece, commissioned for an audience of specialized taste."[33] Wells reiterated these concerns in "*A Midsummer Night's Dream* Revisited" in 1991[34] and was supported by Peter Holland, who implied in his 1994 Oxford edition that adherents of the wedding theory were both childish and snobbish: "The wedding play theory appeals to critics who like the concept of a site-specific play, with fairies running through the noble house to bless the real wedding of members of the audience, and to those who wish to rescue the play from the clutches of the popular theatre audience. I fail to see the need to want either."[35]

The wedding-play debate, then, became a debate about ownership of Shakespeare: was he a writer for the people or a writer for a courtly elite? Gary Jay Williams wrote the most thorough history of the wedding-play theory, identifying no fewer than eleven weddings which had been proposed as occasions.[36] He contended that the theory "silently creates a picture of Shakespeare and his company as court dependent and tends to discount his public playhouse audience" (2). He pastiched it: "In most versions, England's greatest queen is surrounded by her court and the young newlyweds, virgin mother to all, watching the play by England's greatest poet in an oak-beamed Tudor great hall where the fairies dance by firelight" (1). He traced this vision back to Ludwig Tieck in 1830, who believed, according to Williams, "that Shakespeare's play was originally created for a court wedding at which Elizabeth I was present" (108). This is not strictly accurate; as we have seen, Tieck recognized the Southampton-Vernon wedding as a furtive event of which the hostile Queen was ignorant. It is true, as Williams writes, that in 1843 Tieck rejoiced in the patronage of his production of the *Dream* by Friedrich Wilhelm IV, King of Prussia, but it is not quite correct to claim that "this production conferred upon its patron the status of a modern Theseus/Elizabeth" (4);[37] Tieck had not posited Elizabeth as patron of the *Dream*. Williams's reading of Tieck, then, was affected by his own desire to detach Shakespeare from the world of the court.

Even so, there is much to agree with in Williams's assertion that the wedding-play theory flourished for a long period because it was "compatible with those idealizing visions of a homogeneous Tudor England under Elizabeth that have served the construction of German and British national identities and served the notion of Shakespeare as the loyal, national poet" (18). It was certainly widely used to attach Shakespeare to a nostalgic and hierarchical vision of Elizabethan culture. Late-twentieth-century opponents like Wells, Holland, and Williams voiced a refreshingly democratic reaction against this conservative and elitist appropriation of the playwright. Yet their resistance to locating the play in relation to a particular occasion, although characterizing Shakespeare as primarily a populist writer, was also grounded in a kind of literary-critical conservatism. Shakespeare as a writer for the people, for all of us, is essentially the same Shakespeare who has long been praised for his broad and inclusive humanity and his timeless insight into human nature.

By contrast, since the 1980s critics influenced by Marxist theory—including new historicists in the United States and, in Britain, cultural materialists like Jonathan Dollimore, Terence Hawkes, and Alan Sinfield[38]—have argued that all art (and indeed all literary criticism) is a product of political forces and material circumstances. For them, to claim that art is removed from specificities of time and history is to support conservative ideologies which view human nature as essentially unchanging. Viewed in this light, resistance to the wedding-play theory may be seen as based on an older, fundamentally Romantic kind of critical thinking, which regards any link between the play and a particular occasion and commission as a denigration of the author's mystical creative powers. Like Furness's assertion of Shakespeare's adherence to the "eternal verities," it implicitly celebrates him as a great individual expressing universal truths, detached from specific times and places, and from economic constraints and political contexts. Acknowledging the recent shift in critical climate, in 1991 Wells, in "*A Midsummer Night's Dream* Revisited," self-consciously assessed his own position in the wake of new historicism and cultural materialism: although he remained unconvinced by the wedding-play theory, because of the lack of firm evidence, he was also "prepared to admit that my scepticism was provoked by a somewhat romantic attitude to the relationship between the author and his work."[39]

In the wake of new historicism, especially Montrose's "Shaping Fantasies" essay, it is possible to see *A Midsummer Night's Dream* as sophisticatedly combining the conventional imagery of Elizabethan royal panegyric with darker critical undertones. Shakespeare could write about the Queen, perhaps even for performance in her presence, in a way which was far more complicated than mere toadying flattery. To suggest that she might have been present, or expected to be present, at the play is not necessarily to reduce Shakespeare to a demeaning position of royal flunkey: it is possible to go through the motions of compliment while conveying a good deal of implicit criticism. To situate the *Dream* in relation to the Elizabethan court and its patronage system, as well as the playhouse, is not necessarily to espouse a nostalgic vision of a hierarchical yet unified culture: it can involve critical analysis of the play's relation to the Queen and the court.

The wedding-play theory has been reassessed in this altered context, and some scholars have looked again at the considerable body of circumstantial evidence supporting association of *A Midsummer Night's Dream* with the Carey-Berkeley wedding. In 1993 David Wiles published *Shakespeare's Almanac,* which traced how references to time and astrology in the play corresponded to this wedding and explored the play in the context of Elizabethan epithalamia and court entertainments. Other corroborative evidence includes the fact that the bride was the granddaughter of the Lord Chamberlain, the patron of Shakespeare's company; if an entertainment were to be commissioned for the occasion, it is highly likely that he would have turned to his players and their chief writer. Both the bride and groom were the Queen's godchildren, and the Careys were Elizabeth's closest living relatives; the apparent compliment to the Queen in Oberon's vision may mark the fact that she was present, or expected to be present, at the wedding, or may simply be a flattering acknowledgment of the Careys' royal connection. *The Merry Wives of Windsor,* as we have seen, was almost certainly commissioned for a specific Carey family occasion—one which definitely did involve Elizabeth—and purposefully refers back to the *Dream* in its fairy scenes.[40] The recollection of Kenilworth may be explained not only as compliment to Elizabeth but also as a nostalgic evocation of their glory days for all the older generation of courtiers in the audience, including Henry Carey, the Lord Chamberlain. Moreover, it was while Elizabeth was at Kenilworth in 1575 that the bridegroom, Thomas Berkeley, was born at nearby Caludon, enabling her (albeit by proxy) to act as his godmother.[41] Meanwhile, as Duncan-Jones has pointed out, the bride, Elizabeth Carey, had a known interest in dreams, as shown by family letters and by the dedication to her of Thomas Nashe's *The Terrors of the Night* (1594), a text much echoed by Shakespeare in the *Dream.*[42]

This is quite a body of circumstantial evidence, but there is still no conclusive proof that *A Midsummer Night's Dream* was performed at the Carey-Berkeley wedding or that Elizabeth was present, and such proof is unlikely ever to emerge. The wedding-play theory will always provoke debate, in which different positions will continue to be symptomatic of diverse and conflicting critical methodologies and ideologies. Overall, the history of readings of *A Midsummer Night's Dream*—which first involve Elizabeth, then avoid her, then invoke her again—constitutes a brief history of different critical trends in reading Shakespeare in general.

Richard II and the Essex Rebellion

Until the 1980s many scholars found in *A Midsummer Night's Dream* a compliment to Elizabeth, but others were fascinated by records of a performance at the Globe playhouse which may indicate a more critical attitude toward the Queen. On February 8, 1601, Robert Devereux, Earl of Essex, Elizabeth's favorite through the 1590s but also an increasingly outspoken political rival, led an abortive uprising, on the eve of which some of his friends watched a play. According to later testimony by Augustine Phillips, a colleague of Shakespeare's in the Lord Chamberlain's Men, a group of Essex's confederates had come to speak to the players,

> to have the play of the deposyng and kyllyng of Kyng Richard the second to be played the Saterday next promysyng to gete them xl*s*. [forty shillings] more then their ordynary to play yt. Wher thys Examinate and hys fellowes were determyned to have played some other play, holdyng that play of Kyng Richard to be so old & so long out of use as that they shold have small or no Company at yt. But at their request this Examinate and his fellowes were Content to play yt the Saterday and had their xl*s*. more then their ordynary for yt and so played yt accordyngly.[43]

Was this play Shakespeare's *Richard II*? If so, was Shakespeare involved in this seditious performance? The three quarto editions which appeared during Elizabeth's lifetime did not include the deposition scene in which Richard publicly resigns his crown to Bolingbroke (4.1.145–308), perhaps suggesting that the play was regarded as subversive.

After the failure of his uprising, Essex was executed on February 25, 1601. A few months later, on August 4, William Lambarde, custodian of the archives in the Tower of London, came to the Queen's private chamber at Greenwich to present her with a descriptive account of the documents in his charge. According to a Lambarde family manuscript, the following dialogue ensued:

> her Majestie fell upon the reign of King Richard II. saying, "I am Richard II. know ye not that?"
>
> > *W[illiam] L[ambarde].* "Such a wicked imagination was determined and attempted by a most unkind Gent[leman] the most adorned creature that ever your Majestie made."
> >
> > *Her Majestie.* "He that will forget God, will also forget his benefactors; this tragedy was played 40^{tie} times in open streets and houses."[44]

Was she referring to Shakespeare's *Richard II*? If so, this would be the only recorded reference to a Shakespeare play by Elizabeth I.

By 1849 this cluster of tantalizing evidence was known to some, including a German, Georg Gottfried Gervinus, who pondered whether the deposition scene occurred in early performances of the play and argued that the play on the eve of Essex's rebellion was probably not Shakespeare's *Richard II*, since this play "demands such hearty sympathy for the dethroned king."[45] Other critics diverged; indeed, F. G. Fleay in 1881 believed not only that Shakespeare's *Richard II* was the play in question but that Shakespeare himself took the role of Richard, again manifesting his own innate kingly qualities.[46] The debate received a new impetus in 1927 from a long and learned article by Evelyn May Albright, who compiled evidence that Elizabeth was associated, pejoratively, with Richard II.[47] Albright believed that the February 7 play was Shakespeare's and expressed dismay at her contemporaries' resistance to topical and political readings of his work.

However, while making the case for the association of *Richard II* with the Essex Rebellion, Albright also drew attention to another candidate for the February 7 performance. In February 1599 Sir John Hayward published *The First Part of the Life and Raigne of King Henrie the Fourth*, which gave a detailed account of Richard II's deposition and death and was perceived by the government as drawing provocative topical parallels that warranted its suppression. Hayward's book was dedicated to Essex, and when the Earl was on trial in July 1600, after his disastrous return from his Irish campaign, he was charged with patronizing Hayward's book and "himself being so often present at the playing thereof, and with great applause giving countenance to it."[48] Albright argued that Shakespeare might have drawn upon Hayward's *Henry IV*, in manuscript, when writing *Richard II* in around 1595, and that Shakespeare's play was in fact regarded as a dramatization of Hayward's book (706). Others, including Ray Heffner in 1930, contended that Elizabeth's remark to Lambarde must refer to some other kind of dramatic performances based on Hayward, and that "There is no evidence to connect Shakespeare's *Richard II* with either Hayward or Essex."[49] Those who wished to distance Shakespeare from the February 7 performance, or at least from any seditious intent when he wrote *Richard II* some five or six years earlier, pointed out that the Lord Chamberlain's Men were not punished, and indeed performed at court again soon afterward, including on the eve of Essex's execution.

Also in 1930, E. K. Chambers helpfully set out all the documentary evidence potentially associating *Richard II* with the Essex uprising.[50] The battle lines were now drawn between critics who asserted Shakespeare's involvement in the rebellion and thereby characterized the playwright as politically engaged and oppositional, and critics who distanced him from these turbulent events and argued either that the play performed was not his, or that it was his play but used in a way that he had not intended. Predictably, the debate took on new energy in the 1980s in the hands of new historicists and cultural materialists, not only because of the potential of the episode for constructing a dissident Shakespeare, but also because of the apparent recognition of the subversive power of popular drama in Elizabeth's comments to Lambarde. Greenblatt wrote in 1982 that the February 7 play was "almost certainly Shakespeare's," and that "someone on the eve of a rebellion thought the play sufficiently seditious to warrant squandering two pounds on the players, and the Queen understood the performance as a threat."[51] Jonathan Dollimore in *Political Shakespeare* (1985) concurred: "A famous attempt to use the theatre to subvert authority was of course the staging of a play called *Richard II* (probably Shakespeare's) just before the Essex rising in 1601; Queen Elizabeth afterwards anxiously acknowledged the implied identification between her and Richard II."[52]

As we have seen, Leeds Barroll in 1988 warned new historicists against building new theories and interpretations upon old historical narratives. He accepted that the play performed before the rebellion was probably Shakespeare's but argued that it had by then accrued subversive associations unanticipated by Shakespeare because of the intervening appearance of Hayward's book. Undermining arguments that the authorities recognized the power of drama to provoke sedition, he contended that they were far more concerned about the inflammatory potential of Hayward's book than of Shakespeare's play, and that it may have been only the small group of Essex conspirators, not Shakespeare or Elizabeth or her government, who considered *Richard II* subversive. In its nineteenth-century origins, Barroll saw the story as a characterization of Shakespeare less as an insurrectionary than as a confidant of the aristocracy.[53] Blair Worden in 2003 then argued from his reading of the evidence that the commissioned play was probably not Shakespeare's but a dramatized version of Hayward's *Henry IV*, and once again a vigorous debate ensued.[54]

Beyond the core documents in the case, there is evidence that Shakespeare was associated with the disaffected and politically frustrated young men who gathered around Essex in the 1590s. The dedicatee of *Venus and Adonis* (1593) and *The Rape of Lucrece* (1594) was the Earl of Southampton, and the *Lucrece* dedication suggests intimate friendship beyond a mere patron-client relationship: "The love I dedicate to your lordship is without end . . . What I have done is yours; what I have to do is yours, being part in all I have, devoted yours."[55] Southampton was also one of Essex's closest confederates; he rode through London with him in the 1601 rebellion and was afterward committed to the Tower. Shakespeare also voiced admiration for

Essex not long before the uprising. In 1599 Essex, partly reconciled to Elizabeth, was dispatched to Ireland with an army to suppress rebellion, and it was during his absence that Shakespeare wrote *Henry V.* This play can be interpreted as drawing nationalistic parallels which celebrate both Henry and Elizabeth, he as victor at Agincourt, she as victor over the Spanish Armada in 1588. Alternatively, it can be read as differentiating between Henry, the virile young warrior personally leading his troops into battle, and Elizabeth, prohibited by her sex and now her age from leading the charge on the battlefield. The Essex faction criticized Elizabeth for an insufficiently warlike foreign policy and tended to attribute this to feminine timidity and vacillation. Shakespeare seems to share this view when he names Essex, not Elizabeth, as a topical counterpart for Henry. The Chorus asks us to imagine the popular acclaim on Henry's triumphal return to London,

> As, by a lower but high-loving likelihood,
> Were now the General of our gracious Empress—
> As in good time he may—from Ireland coming,
> Bringing rebellion broachèd on his sword,
> How many would the peaceful city quit
> To welcome him!
>
> (5.0.29–34)

Essex is presented as a glorious, virile commander, surrounded by cheering throngs; his "gracious Empress" is the source of his authority, but is accorded dutiful respect rather than enthusiasm, and is placed decidedly in the background of the scene. James Shapiro notes the ambiguity of the line "Bringing rebellion broachèd on his sword"—has Essex quelled rebellion, or has he brought it back with him, threateningly, right to the seat of power?[56]

Shakespeare probably wrote *Richard II* in 1595,[57] and even this early its subject matter was controversial. A Jesuit pamphlet of 1593–94, *A Conference about the Next Succession to the Crown of England,* drew direct parallels between Elizabeth and Richard II, declared Richard's deposition lawful, and was provocatively dedicated to the Earl of Essex.[58] Through the mid-1590s bad harvests led to food shortages and inflation, trade monopolies granted to favored courtiers caused hardship and resentment, and there was religious dissent from both Catholics and Puritans. Elizabeth was criticized both for negligence in her support of beleaguered Protestants abroad and for the costs of conflicts in the Netherlands, France, and Ireland in which she was reluctantly embroiled. Sir John Harington wrote that it was "a tyme, when malcontentes so abound in citie and countrie," and that their chief grievances were "that a few favorites gett all, that the nobilitie is depressed, the Clergy pilled and contemned, forraine invasions expected, the treasure at home exhausted, the coyne in Ireland imbased, the gold of England transported, exactions doubled and trebled."[59] Bishop Goodman later recalled that "the Court was very much neglected, and in effect the people were very generally weary of an old woman's government."[60] The last decade of Elizabeth's reign was fraught with rumors of her death and with mingled anticipation and insecurity as her subjects, many of whom had never known any other ruler, waited in suspense for the great changes that her demise would bring.

In this tense climate it was obviously provocative to present on stage an English king deposed, killed, and replaced by a rival who could command more popular support. The deposition scene was absent from the first quarto of 1597 and the two quartos of 1598; it was finally published in the fourth quarto of 1608, five years after Elizabeth's death:

> RICHARD: I give this heavy weight from off my head,
> [*Bolingbroke accepts the crown*]
> And this unwieldy sceptre from my hand,
> [*Bolingbroke accepts the sceptre*]
> The pride of kingly sway from out my heart.
> With mine own tears I wash away my balm,
> With mine own hands I give away my crown,
> With mine own tongue deny my sacred state,
> With mine own breath release all duteous oaths.
> All pomp and majesty I do forswear . . .
> "God save King Henry," unkinged Richard says.
>
> (4.1.194–210)

We cannot be sure whether this scene was omitted from versions printed in Elizabeth's lifetime because of censorship by government authorities, or self-censorship by the author, playing company or printers, or because it was written later.[61] However, the prevailing consensus among scholars, based on close examination of the passage and its place in the scene, is that, in the words of the recent Arden editor, "it was almost certainly present in the original copy but marked for deletion from the printed version for reasons of censorship."[62] We cannot know whether it formed part of the performance on the eve of the Essex rebellion, though Phillips, tellingly, referred to that performance as "the play of the deposyng and kyllyng of Kyng Richard the second," and Francis Bacon likewise, in a "*Declaration*" of Essex's "*Treasons*," called it "the play of deposing King Richard the second."[63] We can state with confidence, however, that the story of Richard II, even without this scene, was sensational subject matter amid the disillusionment and turbulence of the closing years of Elizabeth's reign. Moreover, as Albright perceptively comments, Shakespeare's characterization of Bolingbroke as a popular hero owes more to the public image of Essex in the 1590s than it does to the playwright's chief chronicle source in Holinshed, and indeed is not sustained—is even contradicted—in the characterization of the King in Shakespeare's *Henry IV* plays which follow, a fact which suggest a topical and polemical slant in *Richard II*.[64]

To sum up, it is irresolvable whether it was Shakespeare's play, with Shakespeare's participation, which was performed for the Essex conspirators, but the fact that Shakespeare wrote about Richard II in 1595 implies a critical stance toward Elizabeth I, and there is circumstantial evidence to connect him with the dissident Essex faction. Another question remains: are Elizabeth's reported remarks to Lambarde evidence that she viewed popular drama as a troublingly subversive medium? In the first place, the reliability of the source is open to doubt: it is a third-person account in an unattributed Lambarde family manuscript, and William Lambarde, on whose report it is presumably based, died only fifteen days after the interview with the Queen which it describes.[65] Secondly, although Elizabeth's reported remarks connect a play of Richard II with the Essex Rebellion, once again there is no specific attribution to Shakespeare. Moreover, the Queen's reported description of "this tragedy" as "played 40^{tie} times in open streets and houses" is perplexing. If the term "open" applies only to the streets but not the houses, the latter may be aristocratic houses like that of Essex, where private performances may well have taken place, either of a dramatized version of Hayward or of Shakespeare's play, which Elizabeth may have regarded as more or less the same. Or, the phrase "open streets and houses" may express the Queen's vague sense of the nature of performances at the commercial playhouses, which from the distance of the court must have seemed perturbingly public, urban, and open to all classes of people. The Richard II play performed the day before the rebellion was staged not at Essex House, but at the open air Globe playhouse, despite the fact that in February the weather was likely to be adverse and daylight would fail early.[66] Phillips's remarks indicate that a paying public audience was expected as well as Essex's followers. The clear intention was to involve and inflame the citizens of London.[67] Thus Elizabeth's remark about performances in "open streets and houses" may indicate not a general anxiety about the inflammatory potential of popular drama but a specific sense of outrage at this attempt by an aristocrat with delusions of kingly grandeur to use drama to stir up her common subjects against her.

This may help to explain why, despite Essex's execution and the other sentences meted out to his supporters, no punishment was inflicted on the Lord Chamberlain's Men. Their performance of *Richard II* for the conspirators was on February 7, 1601; on the twenty-fourth of that month, the eve of Essex's execution, they played at court; and the following Christmas they played a leading part in the court festivities, as usual.[68] This suggests, in contradiction of the Lambarde anecdote, that the government regarded playing as inconsequential and as having little bearing on matters of state; or, at least, that the players were regarded as merely the hired pawns of the Essex conspirators and not as insurrectionaries in their own right.[69] It may be that Elizabeth simply enjoyed the performances of the Lord Chamberlain's Men so much that she was loath to give them up.[70] After all, performances in the safely regulated venue of the court were quite a different matter from threatening stagings in "open streets and houses," and one of the most effective ways of controlling drama was to keep it close to and dependent upon the Crown, as recognized in James I's redesignation of Shakespeare's company as the King's Men a mere two years later. It is clear from Elizabeth's own highly effective deployment of dramatic spectacle that she had a Machiavellian understanding of its value in the enforcement of power. Her reported remarks to Lambarde, then, may indicate a shrewd awareness of the dangerous potential of drama, not as staged by and for the people, but as staged outside the authority of the Crown by an aristocratic faction attempting to win popular support. The outcome was reaffirmation of the court as the proper place for drama.

Overall, the case of *Richard II* and the Essex Rebellion illustrates how the survival of some contemporary documentary evidence of the circumstances of a performance can give us a little more indication of Shakespeare's position in relation to Elizabeth. But even here the many gaps in the record mainly give rise to further speculation and debate. Some of those who believe that Shakespeare's play was performed on the eve of the uprising, like Greenblatt and Dollimore, have used this to construct a politically active Shakespeare engaged in resistance to the throne. Others, like Heffner and Worden, have denied that the play was Shakespeare's, and Worden assimilates this to a portrait of Shakespeare as apolitical, either not interested in contemporary power struggles or maintaining a self-protective silence in relation to them: "Other dramatists—Jonson, Marston, Chapman, Daniel—alluded daringly to contemporary political preoccupations, and got into trouble for it. Shakespeare, as far as we know, never got into trouble."[71] Thus alternative versions of events give us either Shakespeare as subversive or Shakespeare as silent and apolitical. Either way, he is not the author of admiring compliments to the Queen that we have encountered in many eighteenth- and nineteenth-century versions of their relationship. Indeed, regardless of whether it was his play performed on February 7, 1601, other aspects of the case strongly suggest Shakespeare's association with the tide of critique of Elizabeth in the 1590s and, on the Queen's part, a position not as Shakespeare's serenely approving and applauding patron but as a wary, shrewd, and suspicious critic of drama and its uses. The episode connects Elizabeth and Shakespeare in a way but also suggests social distance between them, and perhaps indifference or even ignorance on Elizabeth's part concerning the identities of the writers of the playing companies. She does not mention Shakespeare by name here and gives no sign that she is aware that he is the author of a play about Richard II. And she left no other recorded remarks about him whatsoever.

The Enduring Mystery of "The Phoenix and Turtle"

If Elizabeth's possible connections with *A Midsummer Night's Dream* and *Richard II* remain tantalizingly mysterious, they are exceeded in this by the enigmas surrounding the poem "The Phoenix and Turtle." The Queen was often associated with the phoenix: among numerous examples are the "Phoenix" portrait by Nicholas Hilliard[72] and panegyrical verses by such authors as John Lyly, Thomas Churchyard, and Nicholas Breton.[73] The symbol of the unique bird which reproduced itself magically and asexually both expressed Elizabeth's singularity and virginity and enabled subtle negotiation of anxieties surrounding her childlessness and the succession. It is understandable, then, that a particularly baffling poem by Shakespeare in which he uses the figure of a phoenix has inspired interpretation as some kind of allegory about Elizabeth.

This poem, titled by later editors "The Phoenix and Turtle," appeared in 1601, untitled but with Shakespeare's name attached, as one of fourteen short poems appended to *Love's Martyr*, a long, meandering, and somewhat clumsy narrative poem by Robert Chester. Chester's story concerns the love between a female phoenix and a male turtledove, which ends in self-immolation. Other contributors of appended poems included John Marston, George Chapman, and Ben Jonson—all far more illustrious than Chester. Their section of the work was headed "Diverse Poeticall Essaies on the former Subject; viz: the *Turtle* and *Phoenix*. Done by the best and chiefest of our moderne writers." Shakespeare's poem is lapidary and elegiac, expressing high mysteries of love in a series of riddling paradoxes:

> So they loved as love in twain
> Had the essence but in one,

Two distincts, division none.
Number there in love was slain.

It celebrates the love between the two birds in lofty, abstract terms: this was "married chastity," and with their death "Truth and beauty buried be." At the same time, it has a profound funereal solemnity and, unlike Chester's poem and others in the volume, extinguishes any hope of progeny or renewal. The "dead birds," we are flatly told, leave "no posterity."[74]

The Scottish scholar Alexander Grosart, a prolific editor of Elizabethan and Jacobean texts, was in 1878 the first to identify the phoenix of *Love's Martyr* and its appended poems as Elizabeth. The bird's beauty and gifts, combined with its conventional use in panegyric of the Queen, "all inevitably make us think of Elizabeth, and none other possible."[75] The turtledove, meanwhile, must be the "one pre-eminent man in the Court of Elizabeth . . . the illustrious but unhappy Robert Devereux, second earl of Essex" (xxxiv–xxxv). Grosart reverts to the key metaphor used nearly a century earlier by Chalmers: "Let the reader take with him the golden key that by 'Phoenix' Shakespeare intended Elizabeth, and by the 'Dove' Essex, and the 'Phoenix and Turtle,' hitherto regarded as a mere enigmatical epicedial lay . . . will be recognised as of rarest interest" (lx–lxi). According to Grosart, both Chester's and Shakespeare's purpose was to lament the recent execution of Essex and, specifically, the tragic end to Elizabeth's love for him. He brushed aside objections that Elizabeth, unlike the phoenix of the poem, was not dead in 1601; this, he explained, was a tactful poeticism, since Elizabeth was effectively reduced by Essex's beheading to a state of living death, though "still living in her great anguish" (lx). Any further objections that marriage between Elizabeth and Essex was out of the question, since Essex was already married and Elizabeth was many years his senior and well beyond child-bearing age, were equally swept aside by Grosart's romantic and melodramatic vision of their relationship.

> I do not see how any one can study the *Life and Letters* of Robert Devereux, Earl of Essex, as told by Captain Devereux,[76] without having it immovably established to him, that to the close Elizabeth had a deep passion of love for him—thwarted earlier by her sense that it would not do for "Queen" to marry "Subject," and later by his capricious marriage to the widow of Sidney, but never extirpated and destined to a weary "martyrdom" of resurrection when the decollated body lay in its bloody grave. Except the love-tragedy of Stella and Sidney,[77] I know nothing more heart-shatteringly tragic—for pathetic is too weak a word—than the "great Queen's" death-cushion moanings and mutterings over her dead Essex. (xlvii–xvliii)

Essex had "burst upon" Elizabeth "in her still susceptible and passionate mid-age in all the brilliance and fascination of his young prime . . . I know nothing more truly a 'Love martyrdom' than that of Elizabeth and Essex." It culminated, Grosart wrote, in "the great Queen's closing melancholy and bursts of weeping with the name of Essex on her lips, and slow-drawn-out dying" (239).

This mythology of Elizabeth and Essex as tragic lovers, with Elizabeth dying of grief, guilt, and a broken heart, reached back to the popular seventeenth-century secret history of the Queen and the Earl (1678) and was perpetuated by its many redactions and by nineteenth-century histories, biographies, and pictures;[78] it would eventuate in the performances of Bette Davis and Errol Flynn in the Hollywood film *The Private Lives of Elizabeth and Essex* (1939). As with Boaden and Halpin on *A Midsummer Night's Dream*, though Grosart displayed impressive scholarship, the manner in which he reached and expressed his conclusions was not far removed from the "secret history" school of fiction. His use of the term "golden key" revealed that he was approaching "The Phoenix and Turtle" and the *Love's Martyr* volume as a kind of roman à clef. His reading, however, found only limited acceptance. F. J. Furnivall, a distinguished textual scholar, accepted that the phoenix might be Elizabeth, but suggested that the turtle was not Essex, but "a mythic man," invented by the authors of the poems "to live and die with her."[79] Sidney Lee in 1898 simply threw up his hands in exasperation: the poem "may be a mere play of fancy without recondite intention, or it may be of allegorical import; but whether it bear relation to pending ecclesiastical, political, or metaphysical controversy, or whether it interpret popular grief for the death of some leaders of contemporary society, is not easily determined." Apparently utterly confounded, he concluded with an astonishingly philistine comment on this beautiful, mournful, intricately crafted poem: "Happily Shakespeare wrote nothing else of like character."[80] Through the twentieth century, various alternative decodings were proposed: *Love's Martyr* is an allegory of the marriage of its dedicatee, Sir John Salusbury, but Shakespeare chose to interpret the figures of the phoenix and turtle in his own way in his poem;[81] or the phoenix is Lucy Russell, Countess of Bedford, the notable literary patron;[82] or the poem is an elegy for the Catholic widow and martyr Ann Line and celebrates the faith and love she shared with her husband Roger.[83]

Identification of Elizabeth as the phoenix and Essex as the turtle was revived by William H. Matchett in 1965, though with a different, more twentieth-century approach than Grosart's. For Matchett, this was emphatically a political poem: "Shakespeare's subject is not, I suggest, the supposed personal love of Elizabeth and Essex, but the mutual understanding which, it had been hoped, would make

Essex the Queen's copartner in governing the country and determining the succession." The "married chastity" celebrated and mourned in the poem is not a romance but a political alliance whose potential has been extinguished, "leaving no posterity."

> The understanding of Essex and the Queen, from which England had reason to expect such benefit—or so some, apparently including Shakespeare, had thought—has come to a fruitless conclusion. The union of the Phoenix and the Turtle, however excellent it seemed at the time, has been childless; for all its promise, nothing has come of it . . . Shakespeare is not lamenting that the aging Queen and the young Earl have failed to produce a physical offspring; he is lamenting the fact that their mutual understanding has failed without having done England any good. Nothing has been accomplished and the succession remains in doubt.[84]

Matchett overcomes the objection that Elizabeth was still alive slightly more convincingly than Grosart, maintaining that Essex may still have been alive when the poem was composed too; the poem is not about their physical deaths but about the death of the nation's hope for their political union (191–93).

Some of those who have written most eloquently about this reticent and haunting poem have eschewed the quest for a key. Colin Burrow writes that it "feels as though it is coming from another world, and as though it grows from thinking, and thinking gravely, about sacrifice in love, and about where Elizabethan poetry might move next." We should consider it, he suggests, as an effort at this particular stage in Shakespeare's poetic career both to innovate and to address posterity: "to think of the poem as a work which *needs* to be abstract in order to mean the most to the greatest number of readers at least enables us to understand why it is so elusive, so like music pitched just beyond the reach of hearing."[85] Implicit in this musical comparison is another metaphorical sense of the word 'key': this is music pitched in an unknown and inaudible register. Barbara Everett has similarly opined that there is "not much to be gained" from historical readings but still feels that its very elusiveness incites us to seek its key: "the reader halts, never quite sure what it is, to *read* this poem. We seem, even while finding it exquisite, to lack some expertise, some password." It may be, she acknowledges, that this inexplicitness was produced by particular circumstances: "perhaps Shakespeare's obscurity left many aristocratic readers safely uncertain as to what the poet actually meant."[86]

Topical readings always risk being reductive. Yet the poem itself tantalizes us with the feeling that there is, as Everett puts it, some "password" beyond the text, that the author assumes our tacit understanding of something now lost by the passage of time. Other scholars have persisted in the historical quest by developing Matchett's reading into persuasive hypotheses that "the Phoenix, sad and ageing, is Elizabeth I; the Turtle is the devotion of her subjects," and the poem is about the loving union needed between monarch and people.[87] The most recent and detailed contribution to this line of inquiry is the 2007 Arden edition of Shakespeare's poems by Katherine Duncan-Jones and H. R. Woudhuysen, which investigates the dedicatee of the 1601 *Love's Martyr* volume in which "The Phoenix and Turtle" first appeared.[88] Sir John Salusbury (1566?–1612) of Lleweni, Denbighshire, has often been dismissed in earlier discussions of the poem as merely an obscure and uninteresting Welsh knight. In fact he was a close relative to Elizabeth: his mother was Katheryn Tudor of Berain, granddaughter to an illegitimate son of Henry VII. He was vulnerable to royal suspicion and displeasure because of this potential claim to the succession and because of his Catholic connections (his elder brother was executed in 1586 for his part in the Babington Plot). In reaction, Salusbury's persistent concern was to assert his loyalty to the Crown and to seek court preferment. He celebrated in lavish style when he was appointed an Esquire of the Queen's Body in 1595; and in the turbulent year 1601, whereas his cousin Owen Salusbury joined the Essex conspiracy and was shot dead during the uprising, in June Sir John was knighted for his part in suppressing it.

Previous scholars have connected The *Love's Martyr* volume with this occasion of elevation to the knighthood, as an expression of Salusbury's gratitude for royal favor and hope of its continuance.[89] The Arden editors foreground also Sir John's significantly less successful efforts to be elected a Member of Parliament in the autumn of 1601, which were frustrated by local violence in Denbighshire between his supporters and those of a rival candidate. He was therefore unwillingly absent from the parliament to whose representatives Elizabeth made her renowned "Golden Speech," celebrating the love between herself and her people and their symbolic union in the body politic. Duncan-Jones and Woudhuysen show how closely the mystical metaphors of "The Phoenix and Turtle" resemble the striking rhetoric of the "Golden Speech" and of court poetry from the same era. According to their hypothesis, then, the Queen is the phoenix, and the devoted turtledove is both her loyal subjects as a body and Sir John Salusbury as "love's martyr: a man who suffered much for his unshakeable determination to serve his close kinswoman Elizabeth."[90]

The problem remains that the phoenix and turtle in the poem are decidedly dead, whereas the phoenix motif was generally used in Elizabethan poetry and art to express the Queen's miraculous triumph over time and death, either expressing a loyal wish for her to go on forever or mythologizing the fact that the succession must proceed by some nonbiological means. As early as 1582, around the time when it became certain that Elizabeth would never bear a child, Thomas Blenerhasset wrote that

> The *Brittain* Queene shalbe that Phoenix rare,
> Whom death to touch with dart shall never dare:
> Thou shalt on earth eternally remain.[91]

Later, much panegyric of Elizabeth's closing years expressed a wish for her to go on forever, as in a song of 1599:

> Seas, yeares, and beawties ever ebb and flow
> But shee still fixt doth shine
> When all things dyed; her Raigne begins to growe
> To prove shee is devyne.
> Soe those in whose chast harts virtue survives
> Finish their fading yeares, but not their lives.[92]

Predictably, elegies for Elizabeth in 1603 made great use of the phoenix image to poeticize the passing of the crown to James: "Phoenix is dead, / And so a Phoenix follows in her stead"; "See how our *Phoenix* mounts above the skies, / And from the neast another *Phoenix* flies."[93] But in Shakespeare's poem "Love and constancy is dead, / Phoenix and the turtle fled"; they are "enclosed in cinders . . . death is now the phoenix nest . . . leaving no posterity." In the bluntly emphatic closing line, they are simply "these dead birds."[94] This insistence upon extinction is out of keeping not only with other late Elizabethan uses of the phoenix image but also with the *Love's Martyr* volume as a whole, and might lead us back to Matchett's hypothesis that Shakespeare is lamenting the failure of the political hopes invested in Elizabeth's relationship with Essex.

Duncan-Jones and Woudhuysen acknowledge the unquestionable obscurity of "The Phoenix and Turtle," and are therefore judiciously cautious in proposing the connection with Salusbury as something which might assist with understanding the poem, rather than a key which will unlock its riddle. This consummately enigmatic poem particularly incites deciphering, but at the same time firmly rebuffs it. In this case there is much justification in turning to Elizabeth for clues, because of the phoenix motif, but we will probably never know for certain whether this mesmerizing poem is really about her, let alone what it means to say about her.

Seeking Elizabeth in the Sonnets

One of the greatest Shakespearean mysteries to preoccupy scholars is the identity of the addressee, or addressees, of the Sonnets. Here too, though rather less plausibly than in the case of "The Phoenix and Turtle," literary detectives have looked to Elizabeth. An early example was an unpredictable by-product of the Ireland controversy, *An Apology for the Believers in the Shakspeare-Papers,* by George Chalmers, a Scottish-born antiquarian and political writer. By the time this was published in 1797 it was impossible, in the light of William-Henry Ireland's confession, to profess belief in the forged documents, but Chalmers contended that it was reasonable to have done so and that Malone's comprehensive demolition job was objectionable. He averred that it was entirely possible for Elizabeth to have addressed a personal letter to a commoner, given her coarse and promiscuous private character.[95] Ignoring the fact that the letter was now known to be a forgery, Chalmers took its reference to "prettye Verses" as evidence that "*the* SONNETS of Shakspeare were addressed, by him, to Elizabeth" (42). He was untroubled by the fact that most of the Sonnets clearly address a male, since "Elizabeth was often considered as a man" (51). He believed that Shakespeare's goal was marriage to the Queen and was equally untroubled by their age difference: "Lord Orford has proved, that Elizabeth *dawnced,* when she was *sixty-eight*; and from this circumstance, he reasonably inferred, that it was equally natural for her to be in love, as to *dawnce,* at so advanced an age" (55). Chalmers pointed out that his theories were far less outrageous than the suggestion that Shakespeare wrote love poems to a man: "When the admirers of Shakspeare come to perceive, that his sonnets were addressed to Elizabeth, they will be happy to find, that the poet was incapable of such grossness" (61). Shakespeare's supposed love for Elizabeth, then, solves an embarrassing problem and saves the Bard from charges of unspeakable moral turpitude.

In a sequel of 1799 Chalmers developed his theory that Spenser was the rival poet referred to in many of Shakespeare's Sonnets, and that Shakespeare was provoked to write the Sonnets in emulation of him and in competition for the Queen's attention. "Queen Elizabeth is so plainly described in many of the Sonnets," he declares, and adds, "They were not printed, during the reign of Elizabeth; because, probably the poet did not obtain permission from that fairest prude."[96] Elizabeth was again used to save Shakespeare from homosexuality. Sonnet 20, "A woman's face with nature's own hand painted," is a poem addressed to an androgynous "master-mistress" which puns on the word "prick" and continues to be at the center of the debate about Shakespeare's sexuality. Chalmers explains: "The *master mistress,* which has given such offence, and raised such prejudices, only means, *Chiefest* . . . It is for impure minds only, to be continually finding something obscene in objects, that convey nothing obscene, or offensive, to the chastest hearts" (59, n. y; 63). We learn that "*His*, and *her*, and *him*, were frequently confounded" in Shakespeare's time (66). Again and again, reading sonnet after sonnet, Chalmers insists that "every fair construction ought to be made, rather than consider Shakspeare as a miscreant, who could address amatory Verses to a man" (73). By developing the hint of flirtatiousness in Ireland's forged letter, and by seeking desperately to distance the Bard from homosexuality, Chalmers becomes one of the first writers to produce Shakespeare and Elizabeth in love. As we have seen in chapter 2, this scenario would feature extensively in nineteenth-century fictions; its earlier treatment by Chalmers exposes its foundations in anxieties about Shakespeare's sexuality.

For Chalmers, Elizabeth is a "loadstone" to guide the reader through Shakespeare's baffling writings: "The key, which I have thus put into evry hand, will be found sufficient to open the darkest passages of Shakespeare's Sonnets, if the enquirer will, constantly, bear in mind, that he has *Cynthia* [i.e., Elizabeth] for his guide" (68). Yet Chalmers's shortcomings as a reader and interpreter mean that his deployment of this loadstone or key often renders the Sonnets even more perplexing; sadly, in his hands they make less sense, not more. Sonnet 3, with its lines "For where is she so fair whose uneared womb / Disdains the tillage of thy husbandry?," requires a good deal of twisting to make it apply to Elizabeth, but Chalmers doggedly locates the fault in the sonnet, not in his interpretation: "Over the *illation* of Shakspeare, there certainly hangs a thick cloud: Yet, I think, I can, with *spectacles on nose*, see into this *darkness visible*, and discover some glimmerings of sense" (73). He is not merely puzzled by the Sonnets; he does not even like them very much: "As a whole poem, which is often tied together by a very slight ligature, they have two of the worst faults, that can degrade any writing; they are obscure; and they are tedious . . . in affecting the sublime, he sunk, by a natural cadence, into the unintelligible" (82).

The weaknesses of Chalmers's readings were recognized: Boaden's *On the Sonnets of Shakespeare*, so important for connecting *A Midsummer Night's Dream* with Kenilworth, began as a refutation of Chalmers. "Common sense stood aghast," wrote Boaden, "at the monstrous absurdity of the critic's speculation; and respectfully enquired how he could reconcile it to the everlasting allusions to the *male* sex, which are found throughout these poems?" He marveled at "the matchless absurdity of such an hypothesis, as that Shakespeare could have addressed them to Queen Elizabeth . . . Mr Chalmers . . . asserted that in the 64th [*sic*] year of her age, the 'Renowned Empress Queen of England' is addressed by William Shakespeare, a player, as 'His sweet *Boy*.'"[97] Samuel Neil in the 1860s likewise dismissed Chalmers's reading of the Sonnets as love poems to Elizabeth as "absurd" and "*outré*."[98] Elizabeth still lingered, however, in interpretation of the Sonnets. Neil suggested that she might have been one among several addressees and connected Sonnets 82–85, the "rival poet" sonnets, with the incident in which the Queen was alleged to have dropped a glove on stage to catch Shakespeare's attention, and with the composition of the *Merry Wives*; they were, he suggested, apologies to Elizabeth for his reticence in praising her.[99] Neil also used the supposed presence of Elizabeth in the Sonnets to refute suggestions that Shakespeare might have been a Catholic, just as Chalmers had used her to fend off the charge of homosexuality: "We cannot suppose impiety in Shakespere . . . 'Eliza and our James' could scarcely publicly have favoured a recusant."[100] Both Chalmers and Neil thus invoked Elizabeth to produce a Shakespeare that reflected their own conventional attitudes.

The sonnet which has been most extensively and convincingly associated with Elizabeth is 107:

> Not mine own fears nor the prophetic soul
> Of the wide world dreaming on things to come
> Can yet the lease of my true love control,
> Supposed as forfeit to a confined doom.
> The mortal moon hath her eclipse endured,
> And the sad augurs mock their own presage;
> Incertainties now crown themselves assured,
> And peace proclaims olives of endless age.
> Now with the drops of this most balmy time
> My love looks fresh, and death to me subscribes,
> Since spite of him I'll live in this poor rhyme
> While he insults o'er dull and speechless tribes,
> And thou in this shalt find thy monument
> When tyrants'crests and tombs of brass are spent.[101]

In 1848 one "J. R." proposed that the eclipse of the "mortal moon" was the death of Elizabeth, and that the Sonnet "certainly might have been with great propriety" addressed to the Earl of Southampton on his release from the Tower of London on April 10, 1603.[102] Southampton was not only the dedicatee of Shakespeare's early poems but also a candidate for the beloved youth of the Sonnets; he was incarcerated in the Tower by Elizabeth for his part in the Essex Rebellion, but was released by James I following his accession. All of this fits very plausibly with the link made in the poem between regime change and renewed personal freedom and happiness; and the epithet "mortal moon" invokes the conventional poetical identification of Elizabeth with Cynthia or Diana, the moon goddess. Much of the poetry of the last decade of the reign had asserted that Elizabeth was self-renewing like the moon, triumphing over time and death. A song by John Dowland ran:

> See the moon
> That ever in one change doth grow
> Yet still the same; and she is so;
> So, so, so, and only so.[103]

In Shakespeare's sonnet, however, time and death finally prove unconquerable after all. Identifying the "mortal moon" as Elizabeth also implies that she is one of the "tyrants" referred to in line 14, and therefore runs counter to attempts to show Shakespeare and Elizabeth in relations of cosy intimacy or at least mutual regard.

This interpretation was reiterated in 1859,[104] and by Gerald Massey in 1866, who thought the poem criticized Elizabeth's dislike of marriage in general, and of Southampton's marriage in particular: "he speaks bitterly of the Queen as a 'heretic' to love, does not express one word of sorrow when the 'mortal moon' suffers final eclipse, and lets fly his last arrow in the air over the Abbey where the royal tyrants lie low, with a twang on the bow-string unmistakably vengeful."[105] Other scholars, including Sidney Lee in 1898, accepted that Sonnet 107 was about Elizabeth's death, and it began to look like the nearest thing to Shakespeare's missing elegy for the Queen.[106] Some disagreed, however: Thomas Tyler in 1890 accepted that the "mortal moon" was Elizabeth but thought that an eclipse, especially one which had been "endured" or survived, was not an appropriate metaphor for death and proposed instead the Essex Rebellion as the poem's occasion;[107] others suggested the Armada victory. In fact, H. E. Rollins's 1944 Variorum edition lists topical readings which assign the poem to no fewer than thirteen different dates between 1579 and 1609.[108] Many of these readers accepted the identification of Elizabeth as the "mortal moon," although some were reluctant to do so because it entailed that Shakespeare thought her a "tyrant."

Among modern editors, John Kerrigan considered five possible topical referents: the Armada victory; the actual eclipse of the moon in 1595; Elizabeth's survival of her sixty-third year, the "grand climacteric," thought to be a critical turning point in life; her survival of the serious illness that she was rumored to be suffering in 1599–1600; and her death. After detailed discussion and inquiry, he concluded that the case for 1603 was clear.[109] Duncan-Jones agreed that the "mortal moon" was the recently dead Elizabeth, though she pointed out that James's entry into London and coronation were postponed because of plague; the "balmy time" of the poem, then, she thought, was most likely summer 1604.[110] Burrow also found 1603–4 "most likely."[111] These distinguished editors are unanimous that the poem is a topical response to the Queen's demise, and it seems that for once Elizabeth is indeed the key to a work by Shakespeare. We should note, though, that even in this unusually clear case the poem still has an inherent and teasing unspecificity, producing diverse decodings and debate. Once again, a work by Shakespeare both invites and resists topical reading.

Many Elizabeths

The critical interpretations which have found Elizabeth in Shakespeare's works are far too numerous to discuss in full here, but a few more may be mentioned. The idea that Hamlet's resentful attachment to his mother might reflect upon Essex's relationship with Elizabeth was in circulation by 1869.[112] Since at least 1879 scholars have attempted to relate *The Merchant of Venice* to the case of Dr Roderigo Lopez, Elizabeth's physician, who was of Portuguese Jewish descent and was executed in 1594 on charges of spying and plotting to poison the Queen.[113] Various critics have seen resemblances to Elizabeth in Cleopatra.[114] Others have looked beyond direct personal identification to find Elizabeth in Shakespeare's works in more pervasive and ideological ways. In the mid twentieth century the ideas of the "Tudor myth" and the "Elizabethan World Picture" proposed an Elizabeth who presided over and personified Shakespeare's supposed ideal of social order and was the supreme being (below God) in his cosmos. According to John Dover Wilson, Elizabethans regarded their government as "a monarchy divinely ordained, strong, absolute, unchallenged, and entirely popular. To them the blessings of the Tudor government were so patent, so unquestionable that their only fear was lest something should arise to threaten its permanence or supremacy."[115]

By the 1980s this was rejected as a reactionary and simplistic view, as a new generation of critics asserted that Shakespeare's works engaged with politics in complex ways which might be resistant or even radical. New historicists in the United States like Greenblatt and Montrose wrote about the circulation of power in culture and the dynamic relations between subversion and containment,[116] while cultural materialists in the United Kingdom such as Dollimore and Sinfield explored how complex and competing political views—"residual, dominant and emergent" ideologies—could coexist in a culture in the same historical moment.[117] New historicists were especially interested in Elizabethan England as a "theatre state," a term borrowed from the anthropologist Clifford Geertz, meaning "a state that manifests its power and meaning in exemplary public performances."[118] Not only did Shakespeare and his company represent kings and queens on the stage, but the Queen's own power resided in public representations of that power, in ritual and display. There were resonant likenesses between the stage and the court: at the playhouse, a prop known as the chair of state, a large raised and ornamented seat, was frequently center stage for royal scenes or scenes of judgment, just as was the royal "state" or throne at court; and the players' costumes were often cast-offs from the court or from aristocratic households, sumptuous in their colors and materials.[119] Stephen Orgel asserted that "theatrical pageantry, the miming of greatness, is highly charged because it employs precisely the same methods the crown was using to assert and validate its authority."[120] In 1977 Roy Strong had dubbed the body of literature inspired by the Virgin Queen "the cult of Elizabeth."[121] However, Montrose's "Shaping Fantasies" essay, combined with his other influential articles on Elizabethan court authors and with work by other new historicists, rapidly combined to make the so-called "cult" look more like sophisticated critique.[122] It is difficult to go back to a reading of Oberon's vision in *A Midsummer Night's Dream* as merely elegant compliment to Elizabeth or to a notion of Shakespeare as Elizabeth's tame poet.[123] In addition, as new-historicist critics applied themselves to identifying subtexts in Shakespeare's works which expressed the political and cultural tensions of his time, they began to find Elizabeth in less obvious places.

Leonard Tennenhouse wrote in 1986 that Shakespeare's writing "is largely topical and allegorical as he comments on the figures and policies of his time."[124] He applied this approach to *Titus Andronicus*, Shakespeare's early, gory, revenge tragedy. In the play, Lavinia, daughter of the virtuous Roman nobleman Titus, is raped, then has her tongue and hands amputated, and appears on stage, for substantial portions of the play, in this appallingly bloody and mutilated state. Tennenhouse pointed out that Elizabeth's intact female body was often set forward as an emblem of the English nation. His examples of this include the Ditchley portrait, in which we might almost imagine that the map of England has reared up from the globe and become the person of Elizabeth (fig. 4.1); and reports that traitors attempted to harm the Queen by stabbing, burning, or otherwise destroying her image.[125] The monarch represented the body politic; the body politic, therefore, in Elizabeth's reign, was female. "In such an environment as this," Tennenhouse argues, "a drama was never more political than when it turned on the body of an aristocratic woman." Lavinia's horrifically dismembered body, then, is an emblem of disorder in the state.[126] Tennenhouse urged readers to be newly alert to political resonances in victimized Shakespearean heroines, resonances which were grounded in the fact that a woman, Elizabeth, was on the throne.

FIGURE 4.1
Marcus Gheeraerts the Younger, the "Ditchley" portrait of Elizabeth I, 1592. Reproduced by permission of the National Portrait Gallery, London.

Leah Marcus, in her 1988 reading of another early Shakespeare play, *Henry VI Part I,* found intriguing reverberations between Joan la Pucelle (Joan of Arc) and the public image of Elizabeth. Joan, argued Marcus, resembled representations of Elizabeth as a female warrior and as a figure variously viewed as a holy virgin or a sexually suspect and resented woman of power; even the fact that Joan led the French, England's enemies, might be a reflection upon Elizabeth's supposed mismanagement of recent French campaigns.[127] Marcus also suggested that Shakespeare's cross-dressing heroines had something to do with the Queen, who reportedly described herself at Tilbury as a King in the body of a woman: "As they watched Shakespeare's heroines move in and out of their manhood, members of the Elizabethan audience witnessed the creation of sexual composites which resembled the 'man and woman both' that Queen Elizabeth claimed to be."[128] For Marcus the characterizations of Isabella in *Measure for Measure* and of Lady Macbeth also included posthumous reflections upon aspects of Elizabeth.[129]

Meanwhile, a number of critics, including Tennenhouse, Bruce Thomas Boehrer, Steven Mullaney, and Lisa Hopkins, returned to Samuel Neil's 1869 hunch that "the puzzle of history called 'Essex' was well calculated to become the problem of the Critics, called 'Hamlet'" and read the role of Gertrude as a reflection of anxieties about Elizabeth in the closing years of her reign, especially about political power being invested in the body of an aging woman.[130] Karin S. Coddon saw the play's emphasis upon madness as a reflection of political and cultural disorder in Elizabeth's declining years.[131] Peter Erickson also regarded Gertrude's relationship with Hamlet as inflected by the tension between Elizabeth and Essex:

> Gertrude represents the convergence of three issues—sexuality, ageing, and succession—that produced a sense of contradiction, even breakdown, in the cult of Elizabeth in the final years of her reign and that were brought into particular focus by her association with the much younger Essex . . . The latent cultural fantasy in *Hamlet* is that Queen Gertrude functions as a degraded figure of Queen Elizabeth.[132]

He went further and found Elizabeth's domination of her male subjects in the Venus of *Venus and Adonis* and her chastity in the Lucrece of *The Rape of Lucrece* (41). Erickson did not stop there: "The legacy of Venus, cancelled by *The Rape of Lucrece,* is continued in such dominant female characters as the Princess in *Love's Labour's Lost,* Portia in *The Merchant of Venice,* Helena in *All's Well That Ends Well,* and the title characters in *The Merry Wives of Windsor*" (54). In short, "The presence of strong women in Shakespeare's work from the Elizabethan period can be read as oblique glances at the cultural presence of Queen Elizabeth I" (24).

None of these critics regarded the Shakespearean characters under their scrutiny as exact allegorical personae of Elizabeth. Rather, they argued that these prominent female representations could tell us about how aspects of Elizabeth and her presence as an iconic figure in Elizabethan culture were regarded by Shakespeare and his contemporaries. This was described as a "cultural" rather than "characterological" approach;[133] it depended upon the idea of a whole society as having what Montrose has called a "cultural unconscious" or "political imaginary."[134] This newly broad and flexible definition of allegory and allusion opened up possibilities for many fresh readings of Elizabethan texts. Yet as new historicists sought to locate inscriptions of and resistance to forces of political power in Elizabethan texts, they inevitably produced many readings which looked to Elizabeth, the supreme presiding source of that power. To put this crudely, finding Elizabeth in Shakespeare was a convenient and accessible way of making Shakespeare political. Just as in David Hockney's poster for the Folger exhibition, *Shakespeare: The Globe and the World* (fig. 3.1), Elizabeth could be made to personify "the world" in relation to Shakespeare. At the same time, such new-historicist readings were invigorated by the fascination and charisma which the figure of Elizabeth consistently generates, as much for academics as for popular audiences. This led to a point where Elizabeth began to seem almost bewilderingly omnipresent in readings of Shakespeare, and where we might begin to question whether he was really so monomaniacally obsessed with his monarch. The recent Arden editors of *Hamlet* have judiciously commented on new-historicist interpretations that "while these readings have their interest, one would not want to reduce *Hamlet* to a play about the forthcoming demise of Elizabeth."[135]

One of the most valuable legacies of new historicism has been to introduce a sense of the possibilities for tension between Shakespeare and Elizabeth. Many new-historicist readings positioned Shakespeare as a critic of Elizabeth and found antipathy to her even in apparent panegyric. Yet at the same time, because new historicism developed new tools for analyzing Elizabeth as a symbolic figure and her place in the psyche of the nation, it also explored sophisticated ideas of how hostility and panegyric could coexist: how Elizabeth's subjects, including Shakespeare, might have found her simultaneously inspiring and oppressive, desirable and repellent.

Theories about Shakespeare's Plays at Court

Besides the debate about *A Midsummer Night's Dream* as a court wedding play performed in Elizabeth's presence, various scholars have also linked other Shakespearean works with performances for the Queen. Leslie Hotson, for instance, contended that *Twelfth Night* was written for a court performance on January 6, 1601. This was, of course, the actual feast of Twelfth Night; moreover, the Queen's guest was Don Virginio Orsini, Duke of Bracciano, and there is documentary evidence that a play was staged to entertain him.[136] Hotson's theory has been accepted in some quarters but dismissed by most editors of the play.[137] They point out that Hotson's documents refer to dances in the play in question, but *Twelfth Night* has no opportunities for dances; that the use of Orsini's name in the play might have displeased both him and Elizabeth as his host; and that it is unlikely that the play could have been written and rehearsed between December 25, 1600 (when the date of Orsini's visit became known) and January 6, 1601.[138] Even so, the documents presented by Hotson give insight into the processes leading up to a court performance and the practical arrangements made to accommodate a play in the Great Hall of a royal palace. The Lord Chamberlain wrote a memorandum: "To Confer with my Lord Admirall and the Master of the Revells for takeing order generally with the players to make choyse of [a] play that shalbe best furnished with rich apparrell, have greate variety and change of Musicke and daunces, and of a Subject that may be most pleasing to her Majestie." After the event, he noted: "In the Hall, which was richly hanged and degrees [tiers of seats] placed rownd about it, was the play after supper."[139]

In 1972 the highly respected textual scholars William A. Ringler, Jr., and Steven W. May published their discovery of a manuscript poem which evidently concluded a court performance, and which might have been an epilogue to a Shakespeare play. It is headed "to the *Queen* by the players 1598" (probably 1599 new-style), and it runs as follows:

As the diall hand tells ore
the same howers yt had before
still beginning in the ending
circuler account still lending
So most mightie Queen we pray
like the diall day by day
you may lead the seasons on
making new when old are gon.
that the babe which now is yong
& hathe yet no use of tongue
many a shrovetyde here may bow
to that empresse I doe now

that the children of these lordes
sitting at your counsell bourdes
maye be grave & aeged seene
of her that was ther father Quene
once I wishe this wishe again
heaven subscribe yt with amen.[140]

The provenance of this epilogue suggests that it belonged to a performance by the Lord Chamberlain's Men, and Ringler's and May's analysis of its style, including grammar, diction, and versification, finds it similar to writings by Shakespeare. Since the poem refers to Shrovetide, it presumably belongs to a performance on Shrove Tuesday, February 20, 1599.

James Shapiro concurs in the identification of this epilogue as Shakespeare's and notes that the trochaic meter and rhymed couplets not only occur a number of times in Shakespeare's works but appear specifically at the end of *A Midsummer Night's Dream,* in both Oberon's closing speech and the epilogue spoken thereafter by Puck. Shapiro therefore believes that this "dial hand" epilogue would have replaced Puck's epilogue at the court performance of the play.[141] Juliet Dusinberre, however, in her Arden edition of *As You Like It,* claims the epilogue for a court staging of that play. She points out that the motif of beginnings and endings in the opening lines of the epilogue picks up the last lines of dialogue in the play—the Duke's declaration that "We'll so begin these rites / As we do trust they'll end, in true delights" (5.4.186–87)—and that the outer court at Richmond Palace, where the Shrove Tuesday play in 1599 was performed, was noted for its large and magnificent sundial, newly refurbished for the Queen's visit.[142] However, the Arden editors of Shakespeare's poems have examined the evidence and conclude that "we are not convinced that this poem is by Shakespeare."[143]

Shapiro, accepting the poem as Shakespeare's, averred that it was "brave" of him "to broach the touchy subject of Elizabeth's age."[144] In fact, however, the "dial hand" epilogue sounds like much of the court panegyric of the closing years of Elizabeth's reign, a body of poetry which was incessantly and anxiously preoccupied with her age, even if it often expressed this preoccupation by means of hyperbolic denial, just as we have here. It was repeatedly asserted that by conquering fleshly desires, the Queen had also conquered fleshly decay, achieving perpetual youth and perhaps even immortality.[145] John Lyly's *Endymion* (published in 1591) celebrated this idea, and Thomas Dekker's *Old Fortunatus* (1599) included a prologue performed at court which asserted that Elizabeth was "still bright, still one, still divine." The same play's court epilogue prayed for her to remain so until "these yong boyes change their curld lockes to white" and "their children may supply their Steads."[146] An "Ode, of Cynthia," sung before the Queen on May Day 1600, asserted that,

> Landes and Seas shee rules below,
> Where things change, and ebbe, and flowe,
> Spring, waxe olde, and perish;
> Only Time which all doth mowe,
> Her alone doth cherish.
>
> Times yong howres attend her still,
> And her Eyes and Cheekes do fill,
> With fresh youth and beautie;
> All her lovers olde do grow,
> But their hartes, they do not so
> In their Love and duty.[147]

If, as Ringler and May suggest, the "dial hand" epilogue can be dated to Shrove Tuesday 1599, then Elizabeth was sixty-five when she heard its wish for babies and children to see her live on into their own old age. Unlike many of his contemporaries, Shakespeare did not write about the Queen anywhere else in this hyperbolic vein; the nearest he gets to it is in Oberon's vision of the "fair vestal," a passage which, as we have seen, has provoked widely varying interpretations. However, both Dusinberre and Shapiro find tensions below the surface of the poem which make it a little more like Shakespeare's scant other writings about Elizabeth, and therefore a little more likely to be his. Dusinberre accounts for the epilogue's theme of "promises of loyalty from an audience of lords and their families" as befitting a play, *As You Like It,* which she regards as "a festive celebration with its own undertones of political admonition." She imagines the court performance of Shrovetide 1599 as already shadowed by premonitions of the Essex Rebellion of 1601, such that "a discreet point about loyalty" was timely.[148] Shapiro too finds dark notes in the epilogue: "there's a slight undertow to the conceit, the claustrophobic sense of being trapped in time, the uncomfortable thought that Elizabeth will still be around in a half-century."[149]

Shapiro believes that another surviving text also gives us an epilogue not only written by Shakespeare but spoken by him before the Queen to close a court performance. The epilogue for *Henry IV Part 2,* as it is given in both the Quarto and the Folio texts and in modern editions, is regarded by Shapiro as a conflation based on two originally distinct epilogues, one for the playhouse and one for the court.[150] Shapiro maintains that the passage beginning "If my tongue cannot entreat you to acquit me," and ending with "My tongue is weary; when my legs are too, I will bid you good night," is an epilogue intended to be spoken to the playhouse audience by Will Kemp, who would have played the role of Falstaff. This passage makes sustained reference to Kemp's skill at dancing and promises a jig of the kind that customarily concluded playhouse performances at this time. The rest of the epilogue in the printed editions (its opening paragraph and the prayer for the Queen) Shapiro takes to be the epilogue spoken at court, by Shakespeare in his own person as author: "Taking center stage, Shakespeare delivers his own lines ('what I have to say is of my own making'). It's the only time in his plays we hear him speak for and as himself."[151] The speech, then, as reconstructed by Shapiro from the separated sections of text in the printed editions, reads as follows:

> First, my fear; then, my curtsy; last my speech. My fear is your displeasure; my curtsy, my duty; and my speech, to beg your pardons. If you look for a good speech now, you undo me, for what I have to say is of my own making, and what indeed I should say will, I doubt, prove my own marring. But to the purpose, and so to the venture. Be it known to you, as it is very well, I was lately here in the end of a displeasing play, to pray your patience for it, and to promise a better. I meant indeed to pay you with this, which if like an ill venture it come unluckily home, I break, and you, my gentle creditors, lose. Here I promised you I would be, and here I commit my body to your mercies. Bate me some and I will pay you some and, as most debtors do, promise you infinitely. And so I kneel down before you; but indeed, to pray for the Queen. (ibid., 39)

If Shapiro is right, then this might at last be that rare moment that biographers and mythmakers have sought and imagined for centuries: Shakespeare speaking directly to his Queen. Yet even here there is a sense of the barrier between humble playwright and monarch which deflects direct address. The "you" addressed here is clearly plural—"to beg your pardons." This includes the Queen, and her presence perhaps dictated the self-abasement of the opening lines of the speech, yet the audience addressed is also a collective one. Shapiro reads the passage as an artistic manifesto: "It's the closest we get in his work to Shakespeare revealing his determination to move in a new direction, one in which he will demand more of his audience, his fellow players, and himself." For Shapiro there is an abrupt turn at the end of the speech, from deference to the audience to deference to the Queen, as the playwright's sudden falling to his knees compels everyone else in the hall to follow suit (41). Here again, though, the monarch is so elevated, so sublime, that she cannot be directly addressed. "And so I kneel down before you"—this "you" sounds as if it might finally be a singular direct address to the Queen, but again the speaker averts his address and his gaze and turns the "you" into his audience and fellow subjects, who are injoined to pray with him for the third-person Queen. If this is, then, a speech given by Shakespeare before the Queen, it is marked by indirections and evasions; indeed, it is permeated by a sense of the impossibility of addressing her directly. It is strikingly unlike the kind of witty repartee and mutual recognition of one another's qualities which mythmakers have liked to imagine in encounters between Shakespeare and Elizabeth.

Thus scholars continue to scour Shakespeare's oeuvre and surrounding documents for evidence of his contact with the Queen. As we have seen, critics with widely differing backgrounds and methodologies have sought Elizabeth in Shakespeare's works, and their interpretations have varied widely in persuasiveness. Some readings of Elizabeth into Shakespeare's works have constructed narratives which veered close to historical fiction. In a number of cases, however, attempts to find Elizabeth in Shakespeare have produced advances in knowledge of Elizabethan culture and in understanding of Shakespeare's works. Persistent inquiries into possible allusions to Elizabeth, and into Shakespeare's attitude toward her, have at various times moved Shakespeare scholarship forward and encouraged analytical thought about interpretative methodologies. At the same time, the idea of Shakespeare's works as a code to be unlocked has also produced a plethora of theories about the authorship of his plays, most of which are rather far removed from the usual conventions and principles of scholarship. In these too Elizabeth has figured prominently, as we shall discover in the next chapter.

5

New Intimacies: Elizabeth in the Shakespeare Authorship Controversy

The "decoding" approach to literary criticism explored in the last chapter originated in the nineteenth century's institutionalization and professionalization of scholarship. Ambitious publications sought to codify knowledge in monumental and authoritative tomes, such as the *Oxford English Dictionary* and the *Dictionary of National Biography*. Editions of Shakespeare's works began to emanate from the universities of Cambridge and Oxford.[1] Chairs of English Literature were established, and professional academics lectured on Shakespeare and debated his works in print. As syllabi in English Literature began to be constructed, Shakespeare featured prominently, and candidates could apply their knowledge of him to gain examination success, official accreditation, and cultural capital.[2] History, too, became professionalized: Roy Strong has found that historical painting declined in the second half of the century because history became "the province of professors and dons and no longer that of men of letters, artists and poets."[3] However, this institutionalization of knowledge provoked reaction and resistance, especially in the case of Shakespeare, since so many readers felt a personal connection with his works and felt that they had something to say about them. The idea of knowledge as a code to be cracked created opportunities not only for specialists armed with certificates and letters after their names but also for dedicated amateurs who were convinced—often passionately so—that in their independent studies they had found solutions to the intellectual puzzles offered by Shakespeare and must share these with the world.

In the 1850s one such figure, Delia Bacon, published her theories that the works attributed to Shakespeare were in fact by her namesake Sir Francis Bacon, working in collaboration with a clique of Elizabethan intellectuals, and that he had scattered clues to his identity throughout his writings.[4] She assumed that William Shakespeare, a glover's son of Stratford-upon-Avon, was too lowly, provincial, and ill-educated to have produced the celebrated works attributed to him. She also assumed that his works, in common with all Elizabethan culture, were full of concealed meanings: "It was a time when puns, and charades, and engines, and anagrams, and monograms, and ciphers, and puzzles, were not good for sport and child's play merely; when they had need to be close; when they had need to be solvable, at least, only to those who *should* solve them."[5] There is some truth in the contention that the Elizabethans loved allegory and allusion, but Bacon exaggerated this to claim that only a specially gifted elite—not mere university professors but readers like herself, endowed with an unusual natural intelligence and insight—could see into its true meaning. In apportioning such power to the self-convinced interpreter she inevitably blurred the line between discovering meaning and inventing it.

The full and extraordinary story of the Shakespeare authorship controversy has been told elsewhere;[6] our concern here is with its importance for development of the double myth of Shakespeare and Elizabeth. Candidates proposed as the true author of Shakespeare's works have generally been more aristocratic than the man from Stratford, and as members of the Elizabethan court they have been closer to the Queen. In the process, authorship theorists have often sought to solve not only the perceived mystery of the genesis of Shakespeare's works but also the historical riddles surrounding Elizabeth's private life. Why did she not marry? Was she really a virgin? Both Shakespeare and Elizabeth look tantalizingly like conundrums to be solved by the assiduous and resourceful researcher, and these conundrums become even more exciting if they can be found to intersect, or perhaps even to meet in one solution. Consequently, since the late nineteenth century new and scandalous intimacies have been imagined between the poet and the Queen in authorship theories, and the established ideas of Elizabeth as a mother figure to Shakespeare, or a flirtatious admirer, have taken on boldly literal forms.

Baconian Theories: Elizabeth as Shakespeare's Mother

The theory that Shakespeare's plays were written by Francis Bacon originates in the eighteenth century, but through the contributions of Delia Bacon and others it took hold and flourished in the late nineteenth century. By the end of that century, Bacon was supposed to have written not only the works published in his own name and Shakespeare's but also, with extraordinary industry and time-management skills, most of the canon of English Renaissance literature, including the plays of Greene, Peele, and Marlowe, all of Spenser's works, and Burton's *Anatomy of Melancholy*. Bacon was said to have used Masonic and Rosicrucian symbolism in these works to divulge his profound philosophy in encoded form.

Some leading early Baconians, such as William Henry Smith and Constance Mary Pott, were British, but a number of others, including Delia Bacon and Ignatius Donnelly, were American. The authorship controversy offered particular opportunities for the Americanization of Shakespeare. Delia Bacon believed that the secret society, headed by Sir Francis Bacon, that wrote under the name of "Shakespeare" were progressive thinkers: prophets of modernity, and prophets of its political realization in the American republic. She sought to liberate the plays from the folk tradition of rural England, from the oppressive feudalism of the Tudor court, and even from "the sordid playhouse" of Elizabethan London with its "mercenary appeals to the passions of their audience."[7] Instead, her "Shakespeare" was "that heroic scholar from whose scientific dream the New World was made to emerge at last, in the face of the mockeries of his time" (ibid., 184). He was a reforming political philosopher, a democratic visionary, a proto-American. The Baconian hypothesis emerged just as the American appropriation of Shakespeare which we traced in chapter 3 was at its height, and this produced a surge of interest, with more than 255 Baconian publications appearing in the United States between 1857 and 1884.[8] The patriotic appeal of the theory attracted interest from prominent figures like Ralph Waldo Emerson and Walt Whitman, who wrote in 1884 that future scholarship might discover in Shakespeare's plays "the scientific (Baconian?) inauguration of modern Democracy."[9]

The controversy also aroused intense interest in Britain, where a letter from a defender of Shakespeare was published in the *Illustrated London News* of January 10, 1857: "I will have my own cherished 'Will' . . . Why not Sir Walter Raleigh? Why not Queen Elizabeth herself? But, as I began, we won't have Bacon!"[10] This jocular nomination of Elizabeth as an alternative candidate was to prove prescient (see below). However, Elizabeth made her entrance into the controversy not as an authorship claimant but as Shakespeare's, or rather Bacon's, true mother. This sensational hypothesis emerged in *Sir Francis Bacon's Cipher Story*, published between 1893 and 1895 by Dr. Orville Ward Owen, a physician from Detroit. It purported to be a decipherment of some of the many writings now attributed to Bacon, in the form of rambling verses, interpolated with recognizable bursts of Shakespeare and Bacon. Although it claims to be Bacon's true life story, it reads more like historical fiction. It presents a torrent of scandalous revelations: not only did Bacon write Shakespeare, not only was Bacon/Shakespeare Elizabeth's secret son, but Essex was Elizabeth's son too, killed at the command of his own heartless mother.[11] From now on, it became an orthodoxy of Baconian writings that Elizabeth was the mother of Bacon/Shakespeare, and this conviction produced some of the most inventive and astounding contributions to the double myth of Shakespeare and Elizabeth.

These include the startling scene in *Sir Francis Bacon's Cipher Story* when Bacon learns of his true parentage. At court, Robert Cecil, Bacon's jealous enemy, gossips with a lady-in-waiting, and theatrically utters a shocked exclamation to attract Elizabeth's attention. He claims that his companion "told me / That thou art an arrant whore and that thou / Bore a son to the noble Leicester" (93). A furious Elizabeth chases the unfortunate lady round the chamber and violently assaults her, tearing off her clothes and dragging her back and forth by her hair. She threatens even worse retribution, quoting Cleopatra's words to the hapless messenger who brings the news of Antony's marriage: "I'll unhair thy head; thou shalt / Be whipt with wire and stewed in brine, / Smarting in lingering pickle" (95; *Antony and Cleopatra* 2.5.64–66). This extreme caricature also draws upon another Shakespeare play: in his introduction, Owen explained that "it is believed that the character Katharine, in the 'Taming of the Shrew,' was drawn from the character of Queen Elizabeth." His selective allusions and exaggerations, presenting Elizabeth as a vindictive sadist, resemble the vilification of her in *The Century of Queens* (1872) as "so imperious of will, so violent in her demonstrations of anger, in all things so true a daughter of Henry VIII."[12] As she draws a knife and grapples with the lady on the slippery floor, Bacon intervenes, and this provokes Elizabeth's maternal confession: "How now, thou cold-blooded slave, / Wilt thou forsake thy mother?" (97). The secret is out, but she will not acknowledge him, "For fear thyself should prove / My competitor and govern England and me" (98). Bacon narrates how he collapsed in shock, only enraging her more:

> "Fool! Unnatural, ingrateful boy!
> Does it curd thy blood to hear me say
> I am thy mother?"
>   And into her eyes fierce, scornful,
> Nimble lightnings dart
> With blinding flame.
> O, mother, mother! (98)

Though melodramatic and improbable, Owen's *Cipher Story* attracted many followers. Elizabeth Wells Gallup, a high-school principal in Michigan, became

Owen's assistant and then herself a leading Baconian with *The Bi-literal Cypher of Sir Francis Bacon* (1899). Her preface asserted with unshakeable confidence that her materials placed the Baconian case beyond all doubt: "Nothing is left to choice, chance, or the imagination."[13] There followed yet more supposed decipherments of works claimed for Bacon, including his own *Advancement of Learning* and *History of Henry VII,* Shakespeare's plays, and Marlowe's *Edward II.* It was revealed that all these works were not about the many diverse and profound subjects which they seemed to be about; instead, they were really about their author's true identity and tragic dispossession. Most of Elizabethan literature, then, was reduced to the repetitious and monomaniacal whingeings of a frustrated princeling:

> I, therfore, being the first borne sonne of this union [of Elizabeth and Leicester] should sit upon the throne, ruling the people over whom the Supreame Soveraigne doth shewe my right (4) . . . Alledg'd oathe, or any unrighteous rule, sho'ld never from the English throne barre the grandsonne to Henry th'Eight, sonne to Elizabeth i' lawfull marriage (31) . . . My true title sheweth in Cypher againe and againe,—Francis First, King of Great Britaine and Ireland,—or in playes of a somewhat earlier date, various stiles: Th' Prince; the true heire to the throne; th' Prince of Wales; th' first-born sonne t' Elizabeth; sonne to th' Queene and heyre-apparent (83) . . . I repeate this oft since I know not what pages have been work'd out. (230)

The other main subject of Bacon's works turned out to be his own cipher: he often interrupts his narrative to give convoluted and baffling instructions to future code breakers. In 1957 two respected cryptographers, William F. and Elizabeth S. Friedman, conclusively discredited Gallup's cipher theories.[14] They did not question her sincerity but demonstrated that, like Delia Bacon, she had merely found in Shakespeare's works what she had wanted to find.

We have seen in earlier chapters how Shakespeare enjoyed during the nineteenth century the status of transcendent genius, whereas Elizabeth was sometimes denigrated for failing to reward him sufficiently. These characterizations were sharply intensified in Baconian writings, where Elizabeth was often vilified as monstrously cruel and callous. In Owen, a description of Elizabeth began as panegyric but then revealed the truth behind her radiant appearance: "beautiful tyrant, fiend angelical . . . O serpent's heart hid with a flowering face!" (see *Henry VI Part 3*: "O tiger's heart wrapped in a woman's hide!").[15] The emotional pitch rose to histrionic grief as Bacon continued to address her: "O, mother of my life that brought'st me forth."[16] Elizabeth was cast as a despicable, cold-hearted mother, rendering Bacon/Shakespeare a tragic figure: not only an unloved and rejected child, but also England's forgotten prince, her lost philosopher-king. In part this was another adaptation of the enduring popular legend of Elizabeth and Essex. The historical novel *The Noble Traytour* (1857) presented Essex as, in Dobson and Watson's words, "the true—if spoiled and undisciplined—child of the age, snuffed out by the tyranny of the old Queen."[17] Bacon/Shakespeare now took over this role of the true child of the age, the personification of the English Renaissance, thwarted from his destiny and appearing all the more glorious by contrast with his withered royal mother.

Owen and Gallup claimed that Elizabeth's marriage to the Earl of Leicester, though secret, was legitimate. Why, then, was Bacon/Shakespeare's true parentage shrouded in mystery? Why did Elizabeth not solve the succession problem by simply naming him as her heir? Gallup offered a number of reasons, all of which reflected badly upon Elizabeth. Her suppression of Bacon's true parentage was simply the result of an impulsive oath, provoked by his defense of the gossiping lady-in-waiting: "You are my owne borne sonne but you, though truly royall, of a fresh, a masterlie spirit, shall rule nor England, or your mother, nor reigne ore subjects yet t' bee" (29). It was also the result of Elizabeth's political and personal insecurity: incited by Robert Cecil, she feared that Bacon would lead a popular rising against her (conflating him again with Essex [4–5]). Above all, Elizabeth was consumed by extreme vanity: she was

> Th' would-be idol of half the great princes of Europe,—concluding it would be lesse pleasing in a fewe yeares to have all the people knowe that she is the wife of th' Earle of Leicester, then suppose her the Virgin Queene she call'd herselfe . . . For such a triviall, unworthie, unrighteous cause was my birthrighte lost, and nought save the strong will of Elizabeth turned men from conspiracie t' place me on th' throne. To winne back their loyalty she assum'd most kingly aires, and, upon occasion harangued the army, riding upon a richly caparison'd horse before the lines, and naming herselfe th' King. (32)

According to Gallup, then, Elizabeth's enduring iconic status as Virgin Queen was a deceit calculatingly practiced upon posterity and achieved by means of the callous sacrifice of her son Bacon/Shakespeare. The Tilbury speech, Elizabeth's most famous and often-quoted utterance—"I know I have the body but of a weak and feeble woman, but I have the heart and stomach of a king"[18]—was not a piece of brilliant and inspiring martial rhetoric but the ruse of a jealous and paranoid woman to suppress popular allegiance to her own son. Elizabethan politics were here entirely privatized by Gallup and reduced to family romance. In essence, her view was that the Queen was "a brain-sick woman" (31).

Lying not far below the surface of this strange version of history was a deepening and intensifying of the nineteenth-century distrust of the Virgin Queen as unfeminine. Elizabeth was castigated as mentally unstable in assuming kingly airs and above all as unnatural in preferring power to marriage and motherhood. Her dedication to her throne led not merely to the dispossession of her two sons but to her judicial murder of the younger one. Elaboration of this view by Gallup's Bacon/Shakespeare descended into bitter misogyny: "Her whole spirit was but one infernall region, a realm o' Pluto" (63–64), words which echo King Lear when he rails that "But to the girdle do the gods inherit. / Beneath is all the fiend's; there's hell, there's darkness, / There's the sulphurous pit."[19] Gallup evidently found the phenomenon of an autonomous female ruler profoundly troubling, and her Bacon story seems largely designed to punish Elizabeth for her presumption in assuming this role.

Also underlying it, of course, was snobbery. Some nineteenth-century Shakespeareans accentuated Shakespeare's humble origins in order to emphasize his miraculous genius, but this could have an opposite effect, encouraging some to find it incredible that a mere provincial, grammar-school–educated glover's son could have penned the immortal works of the great Bard.[20] In many Baconian writings Elizabeth was vituperated as a bad mother, yet at the same time as a *royal* mother she was the means of elevating Bacon/Shakespeare to a more appropriate social station. Gallup's preface was explicit on this point:

> The plays of Shakespeare lose nothing of their dramatic power or wondrous beauty, nor deserve the less admiration of the scholar and the critic, because inconsistencies are removed in the knowledge that they came from the brain of the greatest student and writer of that age, and were not a "flash of genius" descended upon one of peasant birth, less noble history, and of no preparatory literary attainments. (iii)

Her Bacon/Shakespeare declared, "in my veines a royall currant floweth." He traced its progression from William the Conqueror through his descendants, "in bold Henry Fifth coursing like fire," absorbing Shakespeare's histories into his autobiography. Eventually "That bloud inflam'd my grandsire Henry Eight," and

> Surged in the veines of Queen Elizabeth,
> My royall mother; now, to me come downe,
> Entaileth to me, by a law divine,
> This sole inheritance. (229)

Identification of Elizabeth as Bacon/Shakespeare's mother secured for him an impeccable pedigree which was felt to befit this visionary genius.

As well as looking back to the past, Gallup's Bacon/Shakespeare also speaks across the centuries to us, his future readers, claiming us as his subjects:

> my kingdome is in immortall glory among men from generatio' unto comming generations. An unending fame will crowne my browe, and it is farre better worth in any true thinking minde, I am assured, then many a crowne which kings do have set on with shewe and ceremonie. Yet when I have said it, my heart is sad for the great wrong that I must forever endure. (224)

This is the Bard as once-and-future-king, tragic hero, martyr, and even messiah. He may have been thwarted from saving the world by his wisdom and insight in his own time, but he communicates his vision to ages to come.

After Owen and Gallup, vast numbers of followers endorsed and expanded upon the theory that Bacon/Shakespeare was Elizabeth's son.[21] Isabella S. Nicholls, in an Australian publication of 1913, found buried allusions to the family secret in *Romeo and Juliet, The Tempest,* and the Sonnets,[22] and concluded:

> This brief appreciation of the history and the works of this phenomenal man goes to show, as I have endeavoured to set out, that he was not only the offspring of Queen Elizabeth, one of the World's most able, and brilliant Rulers of men, but one in whom the World is not surprised to find, the Author of the most marvellous literary works of all time. END.[23]

To paraphrase, Bacon/Shakespeare's works are so exceptional that he must have been the son of a gifted queen; because he was the son of a gifted queen, his works are exceptional. This circular reasoning relies upon faith and an emotional desire to believe this version of events. Meanwhile J. E. Roe, author of *Sir Francis Bacon's Own Story* (1918), found Bacon's encoded autobiography in the Sonnets. Sonnets 1–18 were designed to persuade Elizabeth to secure the Protestant succession by declaring Bacon her heir, and Sonnet 22 was a subtle declaration that Elizabeth was his mother.[24] Sonnet 143, with its image of a neglected child chasing its mother, was a depiction of Bacon's relationship with the Queen (13). The often-repeated word "Will" in the Sonnets "stands for the royal Will, the will of Queen Elizabeth, and hence capitalized," as the poems narrate Bacon's struggles with that royal Will (22). Roe too employed circular reasoning: he asserted that "Shakespeare's" plays cannot be by William Shakespeare because the scene of Elizabeth's christening in *Henry VIII* could not have been written by a Catholic."[25] According to Roe, this scene is definitely by "Shakespeare" (not Fletcher), and the

Stratfordian Shakespeare was definitely a Catholic; therefore the Stratfordian Shakespeare could not have written this scene or indeed any of his plays. These are not atypical examples of the quality of scholarship and argument in much anti-Stratfordian writing.

"Shakespeare," the People's Prince

Baconians increasingly vilified the "other" Shakespeare, the mere front man, in order to apotheosize by contrast the wondrous Bacon. Ignatius Donnelly wrote in 1888 that the Shakespeare of Stratford was a peasant from a rural "hole"; he was "a poor, dull, ill-spirited, greedy creature."[26] Once Bacon, the "true" Shakespeare, was revealed by Owen as royalty, the polarity of the two Shakespeares became even more extreme. Alfred Mudie's *The Self-Named William Shake=speare* (1929) revered Bacon as "The Prince of Wales born legitimate but unacknowledged ... philosopher, dramatist, poet and arch-martyr."[27] It explained that the lowly, worldly man from Stratford spelled his name "Shaxper," "Shaksper," "Shaxpere," or "Shakspere," whereas Bacon used the name "Shakespeare" or "Shake-speare," thus concealing himself from the world at large while cunningly enabling the discerning to distinguish him from the Warwickshire peasant (21, 24). Henry Wellington Wack, in 1930, deplored the rustic impostor as "a butcher and taphouse tippler ... a Stratford lout ... a vacuous liquor-lushing loafer ... this hill-billy Shaxper" who "was best known for his guzzleosity."[28]

Wack was an American painter, and his energetic diatribe was the preface to a 1930 play by his colleague William R. Leigh, *Clipt Wings,* which developed the theories of Owen and Gallup. Here Robert Cecil, not Essex, was Elizabeth's second secret son, but Cecil, the bastard of Lord Burghley, was still the jealous, Machiavellian villain of the piece. The play opens with a lurid dramatization of Owen's revelation scene, in which Elizabeth violently assaults a lady who she thinks has defamed her, borrowing threats from Shakespeare's Cleopatra:

> ELIZABETH: I was married to Lord Leicester by a holy man of God! ... [*ELIZABETH, stripping back her sleeves, seizes her by the hair with both hands, and drags her along the floor.*] Thou shalt be beaten with whips of red-hot wire and stewed in brine, thou accursed scullery slattern; thou hast lived too long—too long! [*She hurls the limp form from her, and seizing a dagger from the belt of one of the cowering bystanders, puts her foot on the chest of her victim, and brandishes the knife wildly.*] (27–28)

Following Owen, Bacon's intervention provokes Elizabeth's confession: "'Thou pitiest her, damned fool? Wilt thou take sides with her gainst thy mother?' (*BACON rises to one knee, staring at her, as the truth dawns on him.*)" (29). In a later, private interview, Elizabeth explains to Bacon that she will not acknowledge him because he is not courtly enough and would degrade her throne. Again this enables the "discovery" of autobiography in Bacon/Shakespeare's works, as he echoes the sentiments of Prince Hal in *Henry IV Part 1*: "With maturity I will outgrow whatever childish traits thou find'st fault with, dear madam. Believe me, I do but study my companions, of all ranks, that I may know all states and degrees of men, and their speech; for how else may I paint them to the life—or how else rule them?" (40). There are many other self-conscious echoes of Shakespeare's works in the play, again exemplifying the circular reasoning of Baconian writers: they place fragments of Shakespeare's works in their version of Bacon's life, then imply that this proves that Bacon wrote Shakespeare. This scene also exposes a fundamental paradox: underlying the incorporation of Elizabeth into the Baconian hypothesis is a desire to make Shakespeare royal; yet Leigh simultaneously celebrates him as a man of the people, as someone who understands and engages with all ranks of society. Bacon here personifies a kind of liberal humanism, opposed by an Elizabeth who embodies a rigid, unfeeling elitism, a hierarchical *ancien régime* which is well lost and from which Bacon/Shakespeare would presumably have rescued his subjects all the sooner, emancipating them into democratic modernity. In a later scene Elizabeth upbraids him for consorting with "the dregs of society," and when he speaks for the common people, she recoils at these "low disgusting sentiments" (68, 72).

Elizabeth sends Bacon into exile, from which he returns seven years later to find his enemy Cecil telling Elizabeth that *Hamlet* is an allegory of Bacon's dispossession by his "lewd, lascivious, indecent" mother (48–54). Elizabeth interrogates Bacon, who prophesies that his works will immortalize her: "down the aisles of time thy fame shall vibrate through eternity!" Those "in far lands" will "cry, 'God be praised who gave us fair Queen Elizabeth!'" (76). Her posthumous fame is revealed as not a true image of her glory and success but the literary creation of Bacon/Shakespeare, her forgiving and generous son. Unplacated, she furiously tears the manuscript of *Hamlet* into pieces. (Presumably it was not the prudent Bacon's only copy.) Rowe's or Scott's Elizabeth was the leading connoisseur of Shakespeare in his time, but Leigh takes us to an opposite extreme: Elizabeth as snob, virago, heartless mother, paranoid egotist, and philistine, hell-bent on destroying Bacon/Shakespeare, not nurturing him.

In the rest of the play, Bacon's friends Jonson and Marlowe set up the illiterate Shaxper, an "ignorant and grotesque" horse-holder at the playhouse, as the purported author of the plays of "Shakespeare" (92–94). The evil and embittered Cecil murders Elizabeth (125–34). Shaxper blackmails Bacon for years, until at last Drayton and Jonson go to Stratford, get him drunk, and poison him (156–57). Bacon lives on for some years in seclusion, devoting himself to literature and science. Elizabeth and "Shaxper" are deployed as personifications of the worst extremes of archaic feudal England, a rigid hierarchy in which a tyrannical and cruel monarch presides over illiterate and oafish peasants. Bacon/Shakespeare represents a new, classless, modern way forward in his innate princeliness, far-seeing intellect, and sympathy with all humanity.

The Sonnets as the Diary of a Lost Prince

The year after Leigh's *Clipt Wings,* in 1931, an English writer, Alfred Dodd, turned to Shakespeare's Sonnets for corroboration of the Baconian hypothesis. In his unconventional edition, *The Personal Poems of Francis Bacon (Our Shake-speare), the Son of Queen Elizabeth,* he found the Sonnets to be full of Masonic and Rosicrucian symbolism (Dodd was himself a Mason) and rearranged them into new thematic groups or cantos.[29] The poet's royal mother figured prominently: Sonnets 1–17, urging procreation, became Canto I, "Queen Elizabeth and Francis Bacon: A Plea for Recognition as Her Son and Heir to the English Crown," while Canto II was "The Personal Relationship of Queen Elizabeth and Francis Bacon," and so on. Within each sonnet Dodd highlighted words relevant to his cause, those, for example, having to do with royalty, family, or love, but paid little attention to the actual sense or sentiment of the poem. For instance, "The expense of spirit in a waste of shame" (Sonnet 129, renumbered 41 by Dodd) was headed "The Queen's Passionate Pride: Her Remorse. 'In Memory of Essex. To-day his Mother died' " (75). A note explained: "This Sonnet was written in the light of the tragic circumstances relating to his mother's death" and "the Confession of the Countess of Nottingham that she had kept back the Queen's ring." There was an unsubstantiated tradition that Elizabeth gave Essex a ring to send to her if he were ever in trouble, which he tried to send on the eve of his execution but which was intercepted by the Countess of Nottingham.[30] Dodd placed italics in the poem as follows:

> Th'expense of Spirit in a Waste of Shame
> Is Lust in action, and, till action, lust
> Is *perjured, murderous, bloody full of blame,*
> *Savage, extreme, rude, cruel, not to trust,*

> Enjoy'd no sooner but despised straight,
> Past reason hunted, and no sooner had
> Past reason hated as a swallow'd bait
> On purpose laid *to make the taker mad.* (75)

Words about treachery and insanity, then, were arbitrarily extracted from their context to suit Dodd's purpose. A less committed reader may find it difficult to detect here references to Essex, the filicide Queen, and the perfidious Countess, rather than a meditation upon the remorse and emotional turmoil provoked by sexual desire.

Dodd along with other Baconians believed that Bacon/Shakespeare was in love with Marguerite of Navarre, but that this noble passion was thwarted by Elizabeth. As for Chalmers (see chapter 4), a strong motivating force in Dodd's theories was the desire to rescue and distance Shakespeare from homosexuality or, indeed, for Dodd, any sexuality:

> So . . . exit the Dark Lady that has poor Shaksper in thrall: Exit all those other unclean ideas of prurient minds. In their place emerges from the Shadows a story of a real Prince who became a "beggar borne"—a story for all children at their mother's knee; a Prince who loved a woman and immortalised her in those lines: "Shall I compare thee to a summer's day!" (211)

Once more, Bacon/Shakespeare was a tragic figure, deprived of both his birthright and his personal happiness by Elizabeth. Indeed, for all the limitations of his interpretive strategies, Dodd was sensitive to the melancholy of the Sonnets. He quoted Sonnet 73 ("This [*sic*] time of year thou mayst in me behold") and lamented, "And unless we are greatly mistaken, this broken genius, our Francis, our Shake-speare, was entitled to wear the English Crown" (34). How great might England have become, he suggested, if ruled by such a deep-thinking, deep-feeling paragon? His book was an elegy not only for Bacon's unrecognized genius but also for an England who had missed her glorious destiny.

Dodd produced an expanded edition in 1936 which was even bolder in reading the Sonnets as autobiographical confessions: the front cover bore the sub-title "Shakespeare's Sonnet Diary," and the frontispiece announced the book as "This little Poetic Diary of 'William Shake-speare.'" He sought to reinforce his reading of "The expense of spirit" by juxtaposing it with writings about Elizabeth and Essex which are generally accepted as Bacon's. He also added a page headed "The First Canto Was Not Addressed to a Man," disputing the widely accepted reading of the first seventeen sonnets as admonitions to a young man to marry and have children. He picks out from Sonnet 2 the phrase "the treasure of thy lusty days," which he believes "makes clear the SEX of the person addressed. 'Lusty' means 'Full of health and vigour, Lustful,' but its final meaning is 'Pregnant.' The Poet thus asks 'Where is the TREASURE of thy days of Pregnancy' . . . the 'Treasure' being himself."[31] Sonnet 3 is a little more challenging, with its lines "where is she so fair whose uneared womb / Disdains the tillage of thy husbandry?" But here too Dodd is undaunted:

> The very phrase "Uneared Womb" means a womb that has been relieved of something, the grain having fallen out, leaving a sheath, an empty husk. The Poet-Son asks his Queen-Mother, "Where is she FAIR (i.e. Just) whose empty womb now disdains this act of Tillage"—the fruit of thy husbandry with Nature? (ibid.)

Dodd purged Shakespeare of sexuality by casting it all onto Elizabeth, combining her hard-heartedness with sexual indiscretion, guilt, and remorse to produce a monstrous mother.

Dodd followed *The Personal Poems* with numerous sequels, including *The Marriage of Elizabeth Tudor* (1940) and *The Martyrdom of Francis Bacon* (1946). These are just a few among the vast number of Baconian publications.[32] The Francis Bacon Society, founded in England in 1886, continues to thrive and to publish its magazine, *Baconiana*. Its substantial library was deposited in the University of London Library in 1956, where it is still housed.[33] It spawned offshoots in other countries, including the Bacon Society of America (founded 1922).[34] There are at least two websites dedicated to the cause.[35] Here is a sample of the evidence and reasoning offered there:

> There is no denying that the Shakespeare plays are the most regal ever written—regal both in content and style. The kings and queens in these plays number 27, and a recurrent theme is legitimacy. Not only is monarchy the setting and the subject of the plays; the circumstances of their first performances were often regal. A third of all the Shakespeare plays were first performed for a royal occasion. These include *The Winter's Tale, Cymbeline, The Tempest, Macbeth, Measure for Measure, Merry Wives of Windsor, Twelfth Night, Henry VIII, King Lear, Love's Labour's Lost,* and *Othello.* There is no record of William Shakespeare being presented either to Queen Elizabeth or to King James. If you ask people to say which, in their opinion, is Shakespeare's greatest play, the majority will say Hamlet. The central character

> of this play is the heir to the throne—and one of his lines is "but break, my heart, for I must hold my tongue." Great fiction is always autobiographical. Every great novelist and playwright writes about his own life. There is always a close connection between the written works of a great author and his own life. Dickens, Wilde, Byron, Chekov, Tolstoy, Jane Austen, all show this very clearly. One of Jane Austen's friends, Mrs. Barrett, said that Anne Elliott, the heroine of *Persuasion*, was Jane herself.[36]

It hardly needs pointing out that there is yet more circular argument here, along with abrupt leaps from one point to another, slippery logic, and blank assertion, but nothing that amounts to proof. Some of us must remain unconvinced, and indeed bewildered that so-called arguments such as these have attracted any adherents at all.

Oxfordian Theories: Elizabeth as Shakespeare's Mistress

Another candidate for the authorship of Shakespeare's works, proposed in 1920 by J. Thomas Looney, a teacher from northeast England, is Edward de Vere, the seventeenth Earl of Oxford.[37] Some of Looney's followers placed Oxford at the head of a "Shakespeare Group," including Thomas Churchyard, Bacon, the Earl of Derby, Marlowe, Lyly, Munday, and Greene, that produced the plays and poems under Elizabeth's patronage as nationalist and royalist propaganda. This "Shakespeare," then, was not a disenfranchised and mistreated son but a loyal and dutiful supporter of his Queen.[38]

Elizabeth was drawn more closely into the Oxford/Shakespeare scenario in 1934 by Percy Allen, who subscribed to the idea of Elizabethan literature as an elaborate code:

> the cunning skill of Elizabethan writers, in at once concealing and revealing interesting facts and identities beneath an innocent-looking, yet usually penetrable disguise; and the corresponding cleverness of readers—and presumably of the élite among theatrical audiences also—at penetrating such disguises, and perceiving accordingly the inner purport of the text, made the game, though hazardous, an alluring and sometimes a profitable one, to the parties concerned.[39]

Elizabeth once again provided the key: as Allen puzzled over Shakespeare's works, "little by little, it began to dawn upon me that Lord Oxford and Elizabeth, considered as lover and mistress, solved, in conjunction with Anne Cecil [Oxford's neglected wife], almost every remaining difficulty with which we were confronted" (xii). Particular works offered corroboration: "That the Countess, Bertram and Helena in *All's Well* are, topically considered, Elizabeth, Oxford, and Anne Cecil, will be generally agreed" (14). In addition, *Venus and Adonis,* "A Lover's Complaint," *The Comedy of Errors, Troilus and Cressida, A Midsummer Night's Dream,* and *Hamlet* "all proved to be, in the main, concerned with the complex relations between the three above-named individuals" (xii).

Like the Baconians, Allen could not bear to leave Elizabeth childless and was attracted by the idea of a lost Tudor prince. Since his "Shakespeare" was Elizabeth's lover, not her son, this required the discovery of their secret child, whom he identified in "the black changeling boy of *A Midsummer Night's Dream,* the 'purple flower' of *Venus and* Adonis and of *The Dream,* and the Fair Youth of the Sonnets" (22–23). Since Elizabeth and Anne Cecil were Rosalind and Celia in *As You Like It,* Hermia and Helena in the *Dream,* and Helen and Cressida in *Troilus and Cressida,* Lord Oxford, consequently, stood revealed as Lysander-cum-Demetrius, the desirable one over whom the two Athenian ladies quarrel; while the wrangles of Oberon and Titania, for possession of the changeling boy, dramatized a veridical conflict between the pair, for guardianship of, and control over, their son" (xii–xiii). The affair between Elizabeth and Oxford had developed "during the early 1570s," after Oxford's marriage to Anne Cecil turned sour, and "culminated, probably during 1574, in the birth to Lord Oxford and Elizabeth of a son, who, but for the bar sinister of illegitimacy, would have become king of England, and, it may be, the founder of a new line of kings" (22).

By now the reader will probably be unsurprised to learn that the name of this secret son was none other than Will Shakespeare, "an actor at the Globe Theatre" (23). Allen thus ended up with no fewer than three Shakespeares: Oxford disguised as "Shakespeare," who wrote the plays and poems; his son by Elizabeth, Will Shakespeare, a fair young actor with Paul's Boys and then the Lord Chamberlain's Men; and William Shaksper of Stratford-upon-Avon, "a law student in London, and, subsequently, a dishonest provincial dealer in malt and corn—always and everywhere a social clown," whose name was borrowed by Oxford as a cover (xiii–xiv). Allen confessed his excitement at his extraordinary discoveries: "it was, naturally, somewhat of a thrill that the identity of the Dark Lady of the Sonnets, as Lord Oxford's Queen and mistress, and mother of his son, the Fair Youth of the Sonnets, gradually revealed themselves to me" (xii). Once again the Sonnets were purged of homosexuality; the "lovely boy" was merely a much-loved son addressed by his affectionate father. Sexuality, again, was displaced onto Elizabeth, who was revealed as gripped by an illicit passion.

Unlike the Baconians, Allen could provide a simple explanation for why Elizabeth's son was not acknowledged: he was illegitimate. Like them, though, he grieved for England's lost destiny: "If I am right, therefore, 'Shakespeare's' son was King of England, but for the bar sinister of illegitimacy" (74). Elizabeth and "Shakespeare" became the joint parents of a glorious future for England which remained unrealized. Their son would have been "the founder of a new line of kings, to the exclusion of the Stuart dynasty" (22). England, it was implied, would have been spared the ineptitudes and un-English Catholic leanings of the Stuart monarchs, not to mention the Civil War and its aftermath, and instead would have been ruled by a dynasty combining the political acumen of the Tudors with the genius and humanity manifest in the works of "Shakespeare."

Dorothy and Charlton Ogburn developed the Oxfordian thesis in *The Renaissance Man of England* (1947) and *This Star of England* (1952). They asserted that Oxford's authorship solved all the mysteries of Shakespeare's life and works:

> All the "obscure" passages of the plays leap into clear significance . . . The play *Hamlet* is straight autobiography . . . De Vere himself is Hamlet, . . . Elizabeth is Gertrude . . . The dramas of Shakespeare, taken as a whole, present an epic of his life and time, actually an epic of his love for the Queen, as *Antony and Cleopatra* is the epic of another man of distinguished parts who sacrificed his greatness and finally his life and reputation for a "lass unparallel'd." It is a wondrous story, the most dynamic and romantic story of the modern world.[40]

They differed from Allen in their identification of the son of this epic union: "The state secret so powerfully protected was that the Fair Youth [of the Sonnets] was the son of Oxford and the Queen. He was called Henry Wriothesley, third Earl of Southampton" (49). They agreed, however, that the poet's interest in the Fair Youth was not remotely erotic: "Of the sonnets written to the Fair Youth . . . all are paternal; they disclose a deep devotion coupled with a sense of responsibility and of guilt for the irregular relationship, with a profound sorrow for being unable publicly to claim his son: 'I may not evermore acknowledge thee . . . .'"[41] In their readings of the plays, though, their hypothesis produced some rather odd gender bending and father-son intimacy:

> Finally Elizabeth allowed the boy's own father, Lord Oxford, to have charge of him—as Titania at last yielded to the pleas of Oberon to have for his

own "the little changeling boy." The youth spent much time at the theatre with his father, later becoming Rosalind (who is called "fair youth"), Viola, and others, opposite Oxford's Orlando, Duke Orsino, and so on. (51)

The Oxfordians tended not to denigrate Elizabeth as the Baconians did; they represented her affair with Oxford as a passionate romance and were at least as interested in his relationship with his son. Nevertheless, they resembled the Baconians in their use of Elizabeth as a mother to elevate "Shakespeare" or his son to royal blood and in their elegies for the thwarted potential of this lost prince. The Oxfordian cause, like the Baconian one, continues to thrive, as seen at the websites of the De Vere Society (British) and the Shakespeare Oxford Society and Shakespeare Fellowship (both American).[42]

Elizabeth as "Shakespeare"

We have seen how authorship theories tended to bring Shakespeare and Elizabeth into ever more intimate proximity. It became perhaps inevitable that the two figures would converge to produce a hypothesis that Shakespeare simply was Elizabeth. In 1857, as we saw above, a correspondent to the *Illustrated London News* had jested that the true author of Shakespeare's works might as well be Elizabeth as Bacon. Much later, in 1928, by which time the tide of publications on Shakespeare authorship theories had risen to a flood, Ronald Knox parodied them by proposing that *In Memoriam* had in fact been secretly written by Queen Victoria as an elegy for Lord Melbourne. Elaborate decipherings revealed hidden messages in the poem, such as "V.R.I. the poetess. Alf T. has no duties" or "O Mother, I'm H.M.'s shadow-author! TEN."[43] Both these writers proposed royal authorship as an obvious absurdity, but their jokes were symptomatic of the looming prospect of a theory that Elizabeth was indeed the true author of Shakespeare's works.

George Elliott Sweet eventually put this case in *Shake-speare: The Mystery*, published by a respectable university press, Stanford, in 1956. "Who in all history is best described by the word-picture Shake-speare?" he asked,[44] and offered his answer: "You may rest assured that when you spot the Elizabethan with the greatest Negative Capability, you will have discovered Shake-speare," that is, Queen Elizabeth herself (12). The name "Shake-speare" kept her opponents guessing but hinted at her power, as corroborated, thought Sweet, by a speech she made to the House of Commons in 1586 in which she said she had tried to "make better progress in the art of *swaying the scepter*" (74–75, Sweet's emphasis). He pointed to the analogies of George Eliot and the Brontë sisters, proving that women do sometimes write under male pen-names (74). Though we may find this evidence a little thin, to Sweet the identification was obvious:

> We see in Shake-speare Elizabeth's twin. Their myriad intellects neither clashed nor diverged; they always saw eye to eye. The political propaganda in the plays never came in for any act of censorship because it was written exactly as Elizabeth would write it. Their philosophy was the same, their religion was the same, their desire to instruct while amusing was the same. (72)

Sweet, then, found no evidence whatsoever in Shakespeare's works of critical views on Elizabeth's rule and seemed to know nothing of the possible connection of *Richard II* with the Essex Rebellion. Like other authorship theorists, he turned to the Sonnets to find autobiographical revelations that would confirm his views. For him, the poems were an expression by Elizabeth of her love for Essex, her "lovely boy" (70). Yet again, Elizabeth solved the problem of apparent homoeroticism: "Somewhere or somehow there appears to be a *misplaced gender* about the sonnets," and this is explained if their author is, in fact, a woman writing in male guise (66). Of course, this creates another problem when we come to the Dark Lady sonnets, but Sweet was unruffled: these sonnets are merely dramatic, "detailing the volcanic emotional conflict between two individuals, neither to be identified with himself" (62–63).

Sweet was equally untroubled by Shakespeare's silence on Elizabeth's death and indeed took it as further evidence; the deceased author could not, of course, produce an elegy for herself (25). He was not even perturbed by the fact that this death took place in 1603, when many of Shakespeare's—or rather Elizabeth's—works were as yet unperformed and unpublished. He named the six plays usually supposed to be Shakespeare's last as *Timon of Athens, Pericles, Cymbeline, The Winter's Tale, The Tempest,* and *Henry VIII.* Diverging significantly from accepted critical opinion, he asserted that these are all weak, immature plays; they were in fact juvenilia, suppressed by "Shake-speare" herself as inadequate and therefore only published after her death (25–32). He had answers for all the reader's doubts:

> When would a busy queen have time to write plays? We might well ask: When would a busy actor, memorising play after play, have time to write? It is a well-known maxim that you go to a busy person to get things done. The very fact that there are no plays with Elizabeth as authoress creates the suspicion that there must be hidden plays of hers. (71–72)

It hardly needs pointing out how flawed and inadequate these arguments are.

In the early 1990s new methodologies and technologies were applied to the authorship controversy. Lillian F. Schwartz, an expert in computerized graphics analysis, had already used her skills to investigate the true identity of the Mona Lisa, proposing that it was based on Leonardo da Vinci's self-portrait.[45] Now she was intrigued by the Shakespeare authorship question and approached it by comparing the portrait of Shakespeare by Martin Droeshout in the First Folio with portraits of other claimants. Noticing the difference between the Folio portrait and the Stratford monument commissioned by Shakespeare's family, she surmised that Droeshout's engraving had been designed to depict the true author of the plays. She expected to find the Earl of Oxford revealed in the Folio image, but when she compared and overlaid images she could not find a convincing match between Droeshout's engraving and any pictures of Oxford. She then tried an assortment of other individuals associated with Shakespeare's works and found that the "Armada" portrait of Elizabeth attributed to George Gower fitted neatly together with the Folio image of Shakespeare (fig. 5.1). She suggested in conclusion that "the major model for the First Folio edition is a portrait of Queen Elizabeth I," and asked "is the engraving a tribute to a patroness, a muse?" Or even "is it conceivable that the Queen could have been a collaborator? Or possibly the author?"[46]

Schwartz's article on her experiment was judiciously tentative and speculative, but, not surprisingly, her work received wide media attention, headlining the sensational discovery that Elizabeth was Shakespeare, including an article in the journal *New Scientist* and a program on BBC television.[47] The visual aspect of this story was no doubt a significant part of its press appeal, drawing as it did upon the prominence of Shakespeare and Elizabeth in the popular consciousness as familiar visual icons and merging them into one suggestive image. The interest which it attracted illustrates how alluring and intriguing we continue to find theories, stories, and images which bring Shakespeare and Elizabeth together, in this case taking their convergence to the furthest extreme to combine them in one single figure.

Why "Shakespeare," Not Shakespeare?

Anti-Stratfordian theories have thus generated a number of new versions of the double myth of Shakespeare and Elizabeth. The accounts of imagined scenes between the Queen and the poet which they have produced have often been of poor literary quality, as the extracts quoted here have illustrated. The standards of argument and of evidence in anti-Stratfordian interpretations of Shakespeare's works

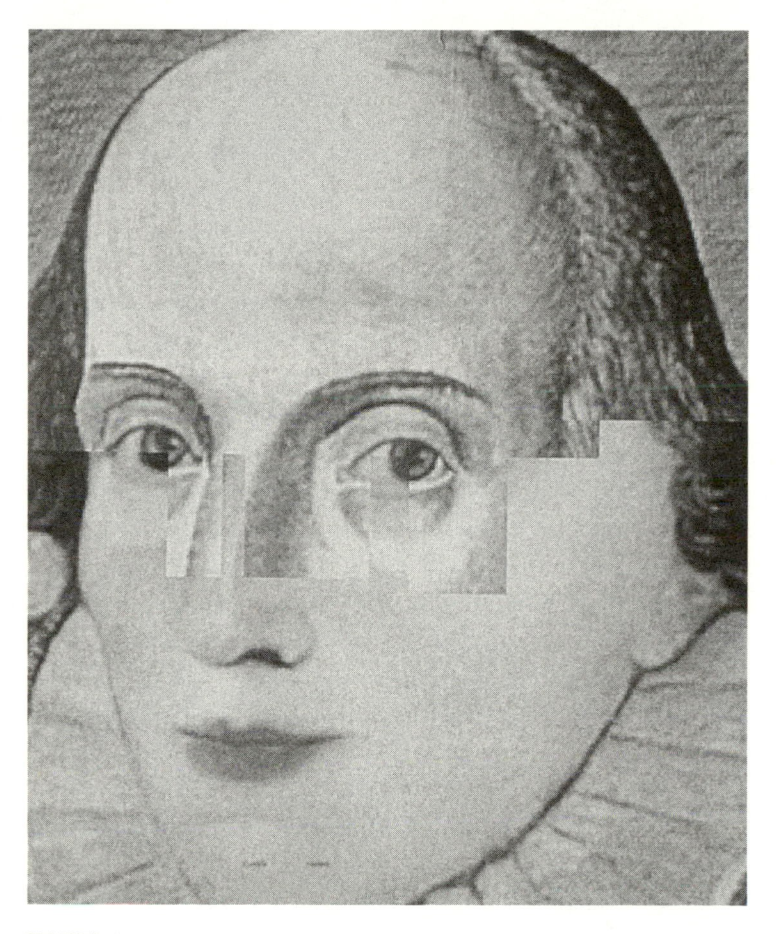

FIGURE 5.1
Lillian F. Schwartz, *The Mask of Shakespeare.* Composite image of Droeshout engraving of Shakespeare and "Armada" Portrait of Elizabeth I.
 Courtesy of the Lillian Feldman Schwartz Collection, Ohio State University Libraries and Foundation.

and of Elizabethan history have also been questionable. Yet these theories have attracted large numbers of adherents from the late nineteenth century until the present day. For some time Mark Rylance, from 1995 to 2005 the first artistic director of Shakespeare's Globe in London, has expressed anti-Stratfordian tendencies: in an interview in 1994 he declared, "I find Francis Bacon the most likely candidate to be the author";[48] and in 2007 he wrote and starred in *I Am Shakespeare,* a touring play which presented the authorship claims of Bacon, Oxford, Christopher Marlowe, and Mary Sidney, all of whom were said to be the secret children of Elizabeth.[49] That autumn, notable British Shakespearean actors, including Sir Derek Jacobi and Jeremy Irons, joined Rylance in signing a "Declaration of Reasonable Doubt about the Identity of William Shakespeare," and Brunel University in London launched an MA degree course in "Shakespeare Authorship Studies."[50] Simply by reason of their popularity and endurance, the authorship theories merit serious analysis as a cultural phenomenon. What is the nature of their appeal? In particular, why have so many anti-Stratfordians found it desirable or necessary to include Elizabeth in their theories and to bring her into unprecedentedly intimate relations with their own candidates for "Shakespeare"?

Going back to the nineteenth-century origins of anti-Stratfordianism, we have seen that authorship theories which elevated "Shakespeare" socially and castigated his "mother," Elizabeth, for cruelly rejecting him accorded with the tendency in this period to venerate the godlike Bard while vilifying the unfeminine Virgin Queen. We have also seen that for some writers authorship theories gave opportunities to find Elizabeth as either mother or lover in the Sonnets, and thereby, after some interpretive maneuvering, to clear Shakespeare of imputations of homosexuality. Considering the movement more broadly, anti-Stratfordian hypotheses may also be seen as early examples of the modern phenomenon of the conspiracy theory. In this case there was supposedly a double conspiracy to suppress the truth: first by Elizabeth and her ministers in her lifetime and then by the academic, literary, and political establishments of later eras. Today, conspiracy theories are often regarded as products of the information age: they boost the sales of popular newspapers with attention-grabbing headlines, and they are spread and elaborated on the internet. Similarly, the rise of Shakespeare authorship theories in the late nineteenth and early twentieth centuries was contemporaneous with the growth of mass-market book publishing and of the popular press. These attention-grabbing claims about the most famous author of all time sold books and newspapers.

The rise of anti-Stratfordianism also coincided with the introduction of mass education. In Britain, the 1870 Education Act set up a national system of Board Schools for all; from 1880 attendance was compulsory, and from 1891 it was free.[51] Universal literacy, or something approaching it, had arrived, although most working-class children still left school as early as possible and with only basic skills. Nevertheless, there were unprecedented numbers of readers who now knew something about Shakespeare from their schooling but would not necessarily wish to follow the sometimes arcane scholarly debates about his texts or passively to accept pronouncements from self-styled academic superiors. The authorship theories offered an accessible reading of Shakespeare and invited readers to join the controversy and the quest. The question "what does Shakespeare mean?" was replaced with the question "who was Shakespeare?" and was answered by means of engaging and dramatic biographical narratives. The fact that these narratives often involved royal scandal and the glamorous figure of Elizabeth added to their appeal.

It is notable that a number of leading anti-Stratfordians from the earliest stages of the movement were women, such as Delia Bacon, Constance Mary Pott, Elizabeth Wells Gallup, and Natalie Rice Clark.[52] In the late nineteenth and early twentieth centuries, women were beginning to gain access to academic institutions but were still some way from enjoying it on the same terms as men: for instance, in Britain they could attend university lectures and take university examinations, but they could not take degrees. Moreover, only a privileged elite achieved even this restricted participation in academia. Among the women listed here, Delia Bacon received only one year of formal school education and later tried and failed to run schools herself, while Clark was the wife of a professor of Greek at Miami University in Ohio.[53] For such women and many others who possessed intellectual aspirations but were positioned either outside or on the fringes of the male academic establishment, the authorship controversy presented an arena of scholarship more open to their endeavors and contributions. This is not to imply that women are less rigorous or reliable scholars than men—far from it—but rather that, in a period when their access to scholarly training and academic status was impeded and frustrating, the anti-Stratfordian cause offered exciting opportunities to engage in research and intellectual debate, and indeed to challenge the male academy which was treating them as second-class citizens.

Gallup presents a slightly different case: she received a more extensive education than most female anti-Stratfordians, at Michigan State Normal College, the Sorbonne, and the University of Marburg, yet she produced one of the most antifeminist characterizations of Elizabeth.[54] Like other nineteenth-century women writers who vilified Elizabeth, her hostility seems to be grounded in an anxiety to establish her own credentials as a respectable subscriber to contemporary conventions of feminine virtues as wifely, maternal, and domestic. This perhaps felt especially necessary to a woman who was pursuing a successful public career in education, as a teacher and high school principal, taking responsibility for raising girls in the way their parents would wish while at the same time daring to publish a work making boldly unconventional claims about two major cultural and historical icons.

The late nineteenth-century movement to decipher Shakespeare also coincided with the rise of spiritualism, and may be seen as one of its many offshoots. As John Michell has written, "Through the apparatus of their cipher systems, Donnelly and the others were 'channelling' Bacon's voice in Shakespeare—or some voice from the world of spirits or imagination . . . As is always the case with automatic writing and the other techniques of spiritism, the quality of the message reflects that of the receiver."[55] Another new cultural development was the rise of detective fiction: in a modern world where meaning and certainty seemed increasingly elusive, popular readerships enjoyed mysteries which solicited interpretation and puzzles which an ingenious mind might solve. Samuel Schoenbaum, who studied the Shakespeare authorship controversy in detail, concluded that "the fundamental appeal . . . of anti-Stratfordian demonstrations generally" must lie in the way that "sober literary history is metamorphosed into a game of detection." This brought about a democratization of scholarship: "To such a game the cultivated amateur can give his leisure hours in hopes of toppling the supreme literary idol and confounding the professionals."[56]

For as long as the Bard has been venerated, efforts to enshrine his works as the property of scholars and connoisseurs of high art have been contested by general readers and popular culture. Anti-Stratfordianism has been strongly connected with the belief that Shakespeare belongs to everyone. Its promoters have usually come from outside the academic and literary establishment and have represented themselves as champions of truth who can read Shakespeare better than that exclusive and self-satisfied establishment. The Ogburns, for instance, wrote, "Oxford expected that his life story—obliterated by Authority from English history—would be understood in his works."[57] More recently, the Francis Bacon Society presents itself on its website as a boldly subversive body which seeks to challenge the institutionalization and elitism of Shakespeare scholarship:

> For over a century now, the general public has been naively manipulated in a subtle way by both the American and British press, and aided by the publishing-industry-machine, that retains the illusion of William Shakespeare's identity with the authorship. Their techniques of *trivializing* the authorship issue, *denying* it exists, *ignoring* it, and with the use of *ridicule,* have woven a powerful spell so strong that it wasn't until the last ten years that more and more people have questioned with a skeptical attitude the Stratford myth, rejecting the party line of the so called scholars, and the so called "experts" . . . Academic professors under the whip of the publish or perish tradition, get contracted once their thesis fits in line with what the publisher dictates to department heads. The socially acceptable William Shakespeare as author routine is the ruling politics of the day. The thought of swaying will leave you out in the cold in this close-knit circle.[58]

This antiauthoritarian stance has created a freedom for anti-Stratfordians to imagine new "Shakespeares" and, in relation to them, new versions of Elizabeth.

In America, authorship theories offered an opportunity to disassemble the icon of British culture and reassemble him in a new, more American form. As one of the curators of the 2007 Folger Shakespeare Library exhibition, *Shakespeare in American Life,* acknowledged, "the greatest boosters of the anti-Stratfordian movement—whether in favor of Sir Francis Bacon or the earl of Oxford—have been Americans."[59] We saw in chapter 3 that the appropriation of Shakespeare by Americans was especially energetic at the end of the nineteenth century and the beginning of the twentieth, a period when anti-Stratfordian publications were also proliferating. According to Peter Rawlings, from Frank Bristol's *Shakespeare and America* in 1898 onward we can trace an "insistence not just on an interaction between America and Shakespeare, but on America's being part of what made Shakespeare possible."[60] Thus Charles William Wallace declared in 1914 that Shakespeare and America were "born together, twinned at a single birth, children of the same ideal."[61] Charles Mills Gayley in *Shakespeare and the Founders of Liberty in America* (1917) asserted that Shakespeare believed in the kind of republican political system later established in the United States, while Alwin Thaler in *Shakespeare and Democracy* (1941) stated categorically that Shakespeare had "democratic sympathies."[62] As Rawlings shows, these numerous nineteenth- and early twentieth-century Americanizers of Shakespeare were not Anglophiles; instead, they were deliberately asserting the difference and distance of Shakespeare from Britishness.[63] For American anti-Stratfordians, then, the inherently antiauthoritarian strain in the movement could be readily aligned with the desire to challenge the ancient cultural predominance of Britain.

In those many Baconian accounts which feature Elizabeth as a cruel mother, we may interpret her as the personification of a heartless and hierarchical old order, against which Bacon/Shakespeare exemplifies humane empathy and a forward-looking interest in people of all ranks. In late nineteenth-century narratives like Owen's and Gallup's, it may not be fanciful to see Elizabeth as associated with Queen Victoria, who in turn is being identified with the autocratic and self-satisfied power of Britannia. Bacon/Shakespeare, as scientist, democrat, and progressive thinker, is a proto-American, unrecognized and suppressed by old mother England, but with an inner confidence that the future will be his. Indeed, the ending of Leigh's *Clipt Wings* explicitly links Bacon with the New World. Elizabeth and Shaxper are dead; Bacon lives on, and gets together with his friends Gosson, Lodge, Burton, Drayton, and Jonson. He tells of Pocahontas, the Native American princess who came to England, whom he has encountered not only at court but also at a performance of *The Tempest,* the play most often invoked as evidence of Shakespeare's interest in the New World. He hands each of his friends a pipe and pushes a pouch of tobacco toward them. When Burton demurs—"I have not acquired this new fashion from the land of Pocahontas"—Bacon, the man ahead of his time, replies, "No? It hath a certain charm."[64]

In Britain, by contrast, identification of the "true," unrecognized author of "Shakespeare's" works has often involved a sense of mourning for a nation which is felt to have missed its destiny. "Shakespeare," or his son, is a lost king and would-be founder of an abandoned dynasty, while Elizabeth features in a variety of roles. For British Baconians, her narcissistic refusal to acknowledge her son deprived the nation of a line of Shakespearean monarchs. For Oxfordians like Allen, she is a less characterful but more romantic figure, consumed by passion and tragically unable to acknowledge her illegitimate son. Either way, Britain has lost the opportunity to be ruled by the true, royal Shakespeare and his heirs. Under such a dynasty, Britain would have escaped the failings of the Stuarts and their consequences in the Civil War and the Glorious Revolution, and might have achieved unimagined greatness.

We have observed a central paradox in the writing of many anti-Stratfordians, who raise their hero to royal blood, rejecting the exaggeratedly boorish "Shaxper" while simultaneously claiming Prince "Shakespeare" as a man of the people. Schoenbaum is persuasive in finding a Freudian "family romance" in such theories, which demonstrate "filial ambivalence" toward the patriarchal figure of the Bard: "on the one hand, denigration of the drunken, illiterate, usurious poacher from the provinces; on the other, ecstatic veneration of the substitute claimant, aristocrat and deity."[65] As a powerful cultural father figure Shakespeare is the object of intense emotions, both love and hate, and those conflicting responses eventuate in splitting him into two. The many anti-Stratfordian narratives that involve Elizabeth also express filial ambivalence toward her as cultural matriarch. She is sometimes celebrated for her beauty, majesty, and exceptional gifts, and she is invoked as a means of conferring royal lineage upon "Shakespeare," but then she is bitterly castigated for her pride and selfishness and her failure to give him maternal affection.

The elevation of "Shakespeare" to royal or aristocratic blood may also be read as a Cinderella-style wish fulfilment fantasy. Anti-Stratfordians frequently found themselves reflected in their candidate for authorship: lawyers discovered that the author of Shakespeare's works must have been a lawyer; Delia Bacon claimed Francis Bacon as an ancestor; and so on. Aggrieved and frustrated outsiders could find common cause with the unrecognized genius and true prince who was excluded from his birthright. Here we may detect other aspects of the Freudian "family romance" being projected onto the anti-Stratfordian's hero, whether Bacon, Oxford, or some other "Shakespeare." Freud writes of a

> familiar day-dreaming which persists far beyond puberty. If these day-dreams are carefully examined, they are found to serve as the fulfilment of wishes and as a correction of actual life . . . the child's imagination becomes engaged in the task of getting free from the parents of whom he now has a low opinion and of replacing them by others, who, as a rule, are of higher social standing.[66]

Chance contact with aristocrats or famous figures "finds expression in a phantasy in which both his parents are replaced by others of better birth." The patriarchal Bard, then, having been found to be disappointingly ordinary, is knocked off his pedestal and replaced with a more illustrious father figure chosen by his "children." The advocates of Bacon or Oxford, identifying with their new paternal hero, thereby elevate themselves too. Elizabeth as mother figure is not safe on her pedestal either. As Freud also writes, "The child, having learnt about sexual processes, tends to picture to himself erotic situations and relations, the motive force behind this being his desire to bring his mother (who is the subject of the most intense sexual curiosity) into situations of secret infidelity and into secret love-affairs" (ibid.). There is undoubtedly a similar iconoclastic pleasure in revealing the national matriarch and Virgin Queen as a participant in furtive and torrid liaisons.

Thus in much anti-Stratfordian writing we may interpret Shakespeare and Elizabeth as a cultural father and mother figure, onto whom are projected mingled adoration, hostility and fantasy. Meanwhile Freud, though offering these theories of the "family romance" which can be fruitfully applied to anti-Stratfordianism, did not make this connection himself. Instead he joined the anti-Stratfordian cause, having been converted to the case for the Earl of Oxford by J. Thomas Looney's book. Perhaps it attracted him as an iconoclast, as an originator of theories which were often at odds with the academic establishment, and as a frequent target himself of skepticism. Whatever his reasons, his case exemplifies the fact that the question "who wrote Shakespeare's works?" is ultimately less intriguing and mysterious than the question "why is this question asked?"

Towards Modernity

Skeptical as we may feel about Shakespeare authorship theories, this controversy was important in opening up discussion of Shakespeare and Elizabeth to new, various, and creative kinds of thinking. Generic boundaries shifted and broke down in anti-Stratfordian writings: the publications of Owen and Gallup were presented as scholarly decipherments and as the authentic autobiographies of Sir Francis Bacon, but were read more like historical novels or dramas. Even more significantly, the boundaries of what could be thought and said about Shakespeare and Elizabeth shifted. It was in anti-Stratfordian writings that Elizabeth was first explicitly imagined as the biological mother or physical lover of "Shakespeare." Conventional protocols governing the representation of the Bard and the Virgin Queen were broken. Depictions of Elizabeth had a new irreverence and sexual frankness, while "Shakespeare" was recreated as a radical and progressive thinker: not a man of his time, not even a man for all time, but a man of *our* time, a modern man, Shakespeare our contemporary. Thus, despite being questionable in their scholarship, authorship theories enabled more adventurous and iconoclastic ways of thinking about Shakespeare and Elizabeth. As the twentieth century began, they were a significant part of the movement toward modern, and indeed modernist, representations of the Queen and the poet.

6

Twentieth-Century Fictions: Shakespeare and Elizabeth Meet Modernism and Postmodernism

We have already considered several trends in the representation of Shakespeare and Elizabeth over the course of the twentieth century. As we have seen, by the beginning of the century Shakespeare was an American national icon as much as a British one, and gradually Elizabeth became a cultural icon in the United States too. Literary criticism moved from modeling a stable and hierarchical Elizabethan world picture, presided over by Elizabeth and promulgated by Shakespeare, to a new-historicist view of Elizabethan culture as formed of multiple and conflicting ideologies and of Shakespeare's works as expressing the anxieties and troubled desires of Elizabeth's male subjects. Meanwhile, through the century the authorship controversy continued unabated and persisted in drawing Elizabeth into theories of Shakespeare's true identity and dynastic connections.

Alongside all these trends, historical fiction and drama flourished, and their authors and audiences continued to be fascinated by Shakespeare and Elizabeth. There was a steady flow of such fictions in the early years of the century: a *Guide to Historical Fiction* published by Ernest A. Baker in 1914 included a subsection entitled "Shakespeare and the Elizabethan Theatre," which listed no fewer than nine novels with this theme and setting published between 1897 and 1911.[1] New technologies brought historical film and television drama, and new fictional meetings between Shakespeare and Elizabeth took place unceasingly both in print and on screen, through midcentury examples like *No Bed for Bacon* (1941) to the 1998 film *Shakespeare in Love*. If anything, the hold of the double myth upon the imaginations of creative artists and their audiences increased, yet its manifestations became more and more diverse, irreverent, and even iconoclastic. The seismic technological, political, and social changes of the century and the rapid pace of innovation meant that history was more important than ever, yet had to be viewed afresh. The modern age produced new ways of looking back, and these included new Shakespeares, new Elizabeths, and new encounters between them.

Some examples of the double myth in the first half of the century simply reiterated Victorian conventions, expressing a nostalgia for old certainties and, in Britain, a desire to cling on to the founding myths of the Empire. In other cases, however, Shakespeare and Elizabeth were reexamined and reconstructed. As we have seen, Elizabeth had received much harsh criticism in the nineteenth century, and toward the end of the century there emerged debate and a fissuring of consensus about the cultural place of Shakespeare too.[2] Adrian Poole has observed that "for the rising generation of writers near the end of the [nineteenth] century the great image of authority was on the wane. [George Bernard] Shaw dared to say what others may have thought, that there was something to be said for Bardicide."[3] This questioning mood continued and intensified in the early decades of the new century. The modernist movement—with its rejection of Victorianism, its dethronement of established figures of cultural authority, and its shattering of traditional artistic conventions—caused the double myth to be viewed from new angles and radically reconfigured. At the same time representations of Shakespeare and Elizabeth were affected in diverse ways by the period's complex combination of class tension and rising social mobility. For some, there was intensified interest in Shakespeare as a common man who was innately superior to his autocratic monarch, but for others he too began to be regarded as a tool of the establishment, far removed from ordinary people and popular culture, and ripe for satire. Meanwhile, the influence of Freud produced more overt discussion of the sexual tensions between the Queen and the poet and of each figure's intriguing sexual ambiguity. They each seemed to offer suitable cases for psychoanalysis: colorful latent material seemed to be lurking behind the manifest content of their biographies, waiting to be probed and revealed by modern intellectual procedures. The homoeroticism of the Sonnets, the frequency of cross-dressing in Shakespeare's plays, and Elizabeth's apparent virginity and androgyny came together to produce two bisexual figures who both desired one another and competed with one another in elaborate combinations and permutations of sexual partners.

We have seen that in the United States Shakespeare was identified with ideas of democracy and freedom and that Elizabeth came to be valued as a charismatic personification of female power. Twentieth-century Britain increasingly felt the influence of American culture, including the reimportation of American versions of the double myth. This gradual deference to America, combined with the two world wars and their aftermaths and the loss of empire, produced in Britain a complex mixture of national pride and national insecurity, and this generated versions of Shakespeare and Elizabeth which hovered between seriousness and irony. The ascent of a second Queen Elizabeth to the throne created some interest in the idea of a new Elizabethan Age, but it was mostly its difference from, rather than its likeness to, the age of the first Queen Elizabeth which was apparent. By the end of the twentieth century, modernism had shaded into postmodernism: after modernism had challenged old certainties and broken them into pieces, postmodernism picked up those pieces and played with them. Myths of the past were now treated primarily as entertaining stories to be embroidered and parodied, with a knowing recognition of the existence of multiple and contradictory versions of history. The question of truthfulness became more or less immaterial: from a postmodern outlook, everything was relative, nothing was absolutely true, and history was something to be viewed askance and ironically, as material for displays of sophisticated and cynical wit rather than displays of national confidence.

Some of the materials treated in this chapter, such as *Between the Acts*, *No Bed for Bacon*, and *Shakespeare in Love*, are well known and have had wide impact. Others are little known and have therefore had little influence, yet are still significant as symptoms of particular cultural and ideological anxieties and desires and as evidence of the imaginative diversity which the double myth of Shakespeare and Elizabeth inspired in the twentieth century.

Reiterations: British Imperialism and Anxiety, 1900–14

The British Empire expanded most rapidly from around 1870 to 1914. This period saw not only the acquisition of new territories but also a British elaboration of the ideology of imperialism, based upon a rousing combination of national pride, opportunities for heroic adventures in far-off lands, and notions of the noble mission of civilizing the uncivilized.[4] In the service of this ideology, Victorian myths of national history were perpetuated and embellished, especially in books for children.[5] J. Edward Parrott presented his *Pageant of British History* (1908) as intended to instil in the youth of Britain "a humble pride in the greatness of their land and a fervent desire so to play their part that Britain may be what she was meant to be—the Viceregent of the Almighty in the uplifting and ennoblement of the world."[6] Such books recounted stories of derring-do by Elizabethan adventurers like Drake and Raleigh, inspired by their Queen; Henrietta E. Marshall's extremely successful *Our Island Story* (1905) rhapsodized, "Oh, the golden days of good Queen Bess!."[7] Elizabeth was also praised for her cultivation of literature, especially the works of Shakespeare. E. Nesbit wrote in 1896, "The reign of Elizabeth was long and prosperous, and England rose then to great glory in arms and art and song. William Shakespeare lived and wrote in her reign . . . the Queen was clever, and loved art and poetry as well as bravery. She rewarded a clever saying with her brightest smile, and showered her favours on men of letters."[8] Supremacy in poetry was an integral part of the imperial project.

A 1911 *History of England* by C.R.L. Fletcher and Rudyard Kipling, intended for use in schools, similarly concluded an account of the exploits of Elizabethan seafarers and the Armada victory with a declaration that Shakespeare was "greater, perhaps, than all the other glories of the reign of Elizabeth." His greatness was precisely located in his assertion of national identity: "Elizabeth used to boast that she was 'mere English'; Shakespeare, whose genius sought the subjects of his plays in all countries and all periods of history, was at heart, and in his art, as mere English as his Queen. His characters may wear the dresses, and bear the names of ancient Romans, of Bohemians, Danes, or Moors, but their language and their thoughts are those of the Englishmen of Shakespeare's own day."[9] Shakespeare was thus claimed to have subsumed national differences into pure Englishness, and accordingly his works were deployed in education to inculcate a unified national identity in the present. In 1901 the British Empire Shakespeare Society was founded, "to promote greater familiarity with Shakespeare's work among all classes throughout the British Empire," and "to form Shakespeare Clubs and Reading Societies . . . in the large provincial towns and in the Colonies." By November 1913 it had some ten thousand members.[10] Shakespeare was a vehicle for the dissemination of English culture and British identity both to the furthest reaches of Britain's global empire and to benighted industrial urban areas within Britain's own shores.

In books which used Shakespeare and Elizabeth to promote Englishness, the line between history and myth was a hazy one. Nesbit assured her young readers that the past was not dull because "really, history is a story."[11] For educative and ideological purposes, history could be told like fiction, and fiction could be used to teach history engagingly. Ernest A. Baker intended his 1914 *Guide to Historical Fiction* for the teacher and student of history, arguing that "Historical fiction is not history, but it is often better than history." The depiction of historical figures as "living personages . . . lifts a veil or furnishes a lens by which we gaze into the depths of character, and see problems and enigmas suddenly grow clear."[12] For Baker the primary purpose of historical fiction was to instil patriotism by bringing the past to life, and this justified adaptations of the historical record and the narrative use of tradition and folklore as much as documentary evidence.

FIGURE 6.1
Anon., *Shakespeare Presenting His Play before Queen Elizabeth.* Jigsaw, c. 1910–20. Reproduced by courtesy of Mr. Bob Armstrong (www.oldpuzzles.com/1501.htm).

Richard Garnett's play *William Shakespeare, Pedagogue and Poacher* (1905) worked along similar lines, retelling well-worn legends. The young Shakespeare in Stratford faces prosecution by Sir Thomas Lucy for deer poaching; he is saved by the sudden arrival of the Earl of Leicester, bearing a summons to court because the Queen has read and enjoyed one of his plays. Elizabeth's special recognition and patronage of the Bard, and Shakespeare's rapid ascent into her favor before he has even left Stratford, are very familiar motifs. The Queen personifies Shakespeare's glorious destiny: "now the sun / Of regal favour rises on my path, / Needs must I follow this to glorious noonday."[13] E. Brandram Jones's novel *In Burleigh's Days* (1916) restages another familiar scene as an aging Elizabeth enjoys a court performance of *Romeo and Juliet.* Shakespeare is presented to her after the play, provoking the usual romantic stirrings: "The player had interested her; his refined, handsome and poetic face appealed to her as a woman, as much as the sonnets had appealed to her mind."[14] The image of Shakespeare performing for Elizabeth at the center of her golden age was firmly embedded in popular culture, as illustrated by a jigsaw puzzle of around 1910–20 (fig. 6.1).[15]

Yet even as British imperialism seemed to be at its most confident, it contained seeds of anxiety. Parrott's *Pageant of British History* declared Britain to be the "Viceregent of the Almighty" in her global civilizing mission but also expressed fears of complacency and backsliding: "we should be false to our sires, false to ourselves, and false to our destiny were we, by selfishness, sloth, or ignorance, to neglect to be great through 'craven fears of being great.'"[16] The British were defensively aware of the rapid political and economic ascent of rival nations, especially Germany and America.[17] The long, relatively stable reign of Victoria was over, and the brutal conduct of the Boer War (1899–1902) had damaged Britain's international reputation and produced a crisis of conscience at home. Governing a global empire was an increasing strain, and imperialism began to be questioned as driven not by noble principles but by the commercial greed of a privileged few.[18] In Europe, international tension was building toward war. Restagings of old encounters between Shakespeare and Elizabeth were perhaps expressions less of continuing confidence in the British Empire than of tenacity to comforting and familiar myths in a time of insecurity and fear. They fit Terence Hawkes's description of "a standard British response to national crisis: the construction of long-past, green, alternative worlds of percipient peasants, organic communities, festivals, folk-art, and absolute monarchy to set against present chaos."[19]

Class Tension: Frank Harris's Shakespeare and Elizabeth

Frank Harris (1856?–1931) was a loud and notorious public figure in the late nineteenth and early twentieth centuries. His career included journalism, literary criticism, authorship, politics, and various enterprises and schemes, and he was infamous for his rampant, self-promoting egotism, the domineering bombast of his conversation, and his priapic sexual appetite. From the early 1880s he was based in London but left for New York on the outbreak of the First World War, which he opposed. A preoccupation with greatness, and thus with Shakespeare, produced *The Man Shakespeare* (1909),[20] *Shakespeare and His Love* (a play of 1910), and *The Women of Shakespeare* (1911). At a society dinner in the 1890s, he famously said: "I know nothing of the joys of homosexuality. You must speak to my friend Oscar about that. And yet, if Shakespeare had asked me, I would have had to submit."[21] For Elizabeth, however, he expressed an antipathy grounded in his self-image as champion of the people against the corruption of inherited power and wealth.

In *The Man Shakespeare,* Harris asserted that Shakespeare came to hate the Queen for her lack of mercy toward the Earls of Essex and Southampton: "he had come to realise the harsh nature of Elizabeth, and he detested her ruthless cruelties."[22] In *Shakespeare and His Love*, when Jonson excitedly tells Shakespeare that his company has been summoned to play at court and the Queen intends to make him Master of the Revels, Shakespeare retorts, "It irks me to ask favours of her: her hands are red with blood." Jonson urges him to seek the post, "For your friends'sake, Will, if not for your own . . . the old cat is breaking fast; she won't last long."[23] The "old cat" duly appears and is evidently well past her prime: she is self-absorbed, callously uninterested in her subjects, and forgetful to the point of senility. After the play, she exclaims, "Ah! there are our players. Well, let that one approach who wrote the piece—I mean—Ach! I forget his name! [*Turns to Lord Burghley.*] Those common names are so hard to remember" (160). Shakespeare is brought forward and bows before her.

THE QUEEN: [*Breathing heavily, as if tired.*] You wrote the piece?

SHAKESPEARE: To please your Majesty!

THE QUEEN: [*Slowly and with difficulty.*] I did say something about it; I've forgotten what—I—Yes—Oh, I wanted to see the fat Knight in love, and you wrote this "Wives of Windsor" to show it: 'tis not ill done, but the Knight was better in the earlier piece, much better; the story better too. (161)

When she offers Shakespeare the post of Master of the Revels, he selflessly asks that instead she should release his friend William Herbert from the Tower; this is especially noble given that Herbert is incarcerated because of his liaison with Mary Fitton, Shakespeare's own unfaithful Dark Lady. The Queen is outraged by such presumption: "Did ever one hear the like? My dog will school me next! You forget your place, man" (162). Shakespeare tries Portia's supplicatory rhetoric, exhorting Elizabeth that mercy

> blesseth him that gives and him that takes;
> 'Tis mightiest in the mightiest . . .[24]

Ah! madam, we learn sympathy from suffering, pity from pain!

THE QUEEN: [*Wearily leaning back in her throne.*] Do we? I don't. (163–64)

She is immune to the beauty of both the poetry and the sentiment.

In Harris's desire to align himself with the common man he extends the nineteenth-century tradition of hostility to Elizabeth to make her snobbish, cantankerous, and hard-hearted; his Shakespeare, by contrast, is magnanimous and principled, a man without rank or title who sees the corruption of those in high office and heroically spurns the public honors which they offer. Though few of his contemporaries saw Harris like this—George Bernard Shaw described him as "neither first-rate, nor second-rate, nor tenth-rate. He is just his horrible unique self"[25]—it is probably how Harris would have liked to see himself. Increasingly, Elizabeth and Shakespeare were mutating from the joint representatives of a socially unified nation to personifications of opposed classes and ideologies. This was a trend which would continue.

"The writing on the wall": *The Dark Lady* (1919)

Harris's *Shakespeare and His Love* appeared in 1910, at the beginning of a decade of tumultuous upheaval. In Britain, some 750,000 lives were lost in the First World War, while many of the 2,500,000 wounded were left permanently disabled.[26] In the aftermath of the conflict, much of it endured in wretched conditions, there was widespread disillusionment and distrust of authority. Meanwhile, the Easter Rising in Ireland in 1916 was followed by a brutal civil war, and challenged Britain's imperial power at uncomfortably close proximity.[27] If Ireland, Britain's neighbor, could not be governed peacefully, how was Britain to sustain her authority over her many more distant colonies? The 1917 Bolshevik Revolution in Russia brought fears of another kind of conflict: class war. Franchise reform in 1918 extended the U.K. electorate from about eight million to over twenty-one million, creating a substantial new body of working-class voters, and socialist politics flourished as the Trades Unions and the Labour Party rose in membership and influence.[28] Opportunities were growing for working people to participate in the government of the nation, yet anxieties about the possible consequences of this caused class barriers to harden and class tensions to become more acute. Although the Great War ended in 1918, conflict and revolution remained in the air, fueled by discontent and disaffection among the thousands of demobilized troops who flooded back into Britain.[29]

Against this troubled background, in 1919 Alfred E. Carey published *The Dark Lady*, a novel in which a young Elizabethan, Kit Champernoun, narrated his progress from court favorite to naval adventurer. Rather than merely offering consoling escapism from the social problems of the present, the novel reflects these in various ways. In an early scene Sir Walter Raleigh visits the Champernoun family at their country house and tells them about Shakespeare. He quotes from *As You Like It*: "I earn that I eat, get that I wear; owe no man hate, envy no man's happiness; glad of other men's good, content with my harm; and the greatest of my pride is to see my ewes graze and my lambs suck" (3.2.64–67). His rural hosts respond with recognition and approval: "'Well spoken,' cried our father, and our mother's eyes sparkled with pleasure. 'Would that England had a million such. In the Court men spend money for that which is not bread.'"[30] Carey takes up the idea, extending back to the seventeenth century, of Shakespeare as a king, royal in his qualities though common in his birth.[31] Raleigh calls Shakespeare "the king of all makers" (21), and when Shakespeare himself appears his demeanor "bore the impress of a king, one to whom homage and reverence were justly due as to the wearer of the crown imperial" (88). Though this elevation of Shakespeare to royal status was a long-established tradition, it has a new force in the turbulent social and political contexts of the modern period. Frederick Gard Fleay in 1881 had applied some verses from 1611 to Shakespeare's supposed practice of playing regal roles on stage:

> Some say, good Will, which I in sport do sing,
> Hadst thou not played some kingly parts in sport,
> Thou hadst been a companion for a king,
> And been a king among the meaner sort.[32]

Throughout Carey's novel, Shakespeare is just such a "king among the meaner sort": he mediates between court and commons, exemplifies sound English values, demonstrates his innate nobility, and generally personifies a new era of democracy and meritocracy.

By contrast Carey's Elizabeth is by no means an idealized personification of monarchy; she is short-sighted, fretful, and demanding (88). She is entertained by a court performance of *A Midsummer Night's Dream,* and Carey repeats the century-old legend of her dropped glove and Shakespeare's impromptu response, as discussed in chapter 2 above. Again Shakespeare plays a monarch:

> Shakespeare, as King Oberon, gave Puck his commands . . . Then, when the traffic of the play permitted, King Oberon lifted Her Majesty's glove and handed it back saying:
>
> > "And now though bent on this high embassy,
> > Yet stoop we to take up our cousin's glove."
>
> The Queen was mightily pleased and cried out aloud, "'Od's pittikins![33] Our magnifico is cousin-german to all regal minds." (89)

The glove anecdote is useful to Carey, despite its staleness, to illustrate again Shakespeare's innate regality and elevate him to equality with the Queen.

Carey's Shakespeare becomes increasingly embroiled in social comment and even political subversion. Elizabeth summons him at the end of *A Midsummer Night's Dream* to thank him "for that device of the ass's head," but this quickly turns into a barbed exchange about ass heads in the church and state. Elizabeth admonishes him, "Meddle not with statecraft, Master Shakespeare, or good sooth the day may dawn when thine own head shall hang loose on its stalk" (91). When rumors circulate of plotting by Essex and Southampton, Shakespeare is implicated: "His genius had set the heather afire. 'Twas a mighty weapon. What if its edge were turned to treason?" (92). A court performance of *Romeo and Juliet* moves its audience not as a celebration of young love but as a portent of doom. Champernoun describes how "the splendour of his poesy filled my blood with riot, his mimic blows of Fate fell inevitable, unerring. Even the Queen looked troubled and scared. 'Od's pittikins,' she cried, 'this beats lawn sleeves and homilies'" (104). But her enthusiasm for drama over sermons is mitigated by her recognition of its disturbing social message: "'Master Shakespeare,'" quoth she, 'you have given us a parable of civic brawl. Would to God we needed not the writing on the wall'" (104).

The Dark Lady offers a distinctively tense and troubled version of the double myth of Shakespeare and Elizabeth. The British nation of 1919 also, arguably, "faced the writing on the wall": it had been decimated and traumatized by an international war of unprecedented horror; it was embroiled in continuing violent civil strife in Ireland; and the years 1919–21 brought national strikes by miners, railwaymen, the police, and many other workers.[34] In April 1919 British troops in India fired on a peaceful meeting in Amritsar, killing hundreds of men, women, and children; the massacre fiercely divided British public opinion and seemed indeed like the writing on the wall for the moral authority of the Empire.[35] Carey's novel is clouded by a national mood of foreboding, in which uncomplicated celebration of the "merrie England" of yore was no longer appropriate.

Shakespeare Exploded: *Old Bill "Through the Ages"* (1924)

Early cinema produced numerous versions of Shakespeare plays, including *King John* (1899), *A Midsummer Night's Dream* (1909), and *Richard III* (1911).[36] Shakespeare attracted filmmakers because his works conferred intellectual respectability upon the new medium and displayed the artistic possibilities of film in their exotic locations and supernatural episodes.[37] Elizabethan history was another frequent subject, combining similar intellectual respectability with the glamor and romance of Elizabeth as tragic heroine. Sarah Bernhardt gave a diva-style performance in

Queen Elizabeth (1912), which retold the doomed love story of Elizabeth and Essex and enjoyed great success in the United States.[38] In one scene Elizabeth and Essex watch *The Merry Wives of Windsor* and Shakespeare is presented to the Queen. *The Life of Shakespeare* (1914) also featured the traditional appearance by Elizabeth.[39] Such films simply reproduced Victorian versions of the Shakespeare-and-Elizabeth myth in a twentieth-century medium.

In 1924, however, the British film *Old Bill "Through the Ages"* took a burlesque approach which reflected its postwar context. The "Old Bill" of the title was not William Shakespeare but a popular cartoon character created by Bruce Bairnsfather, an artist who saw extensive active service as an officer in the First World War. Old Bill was a private in the trenches and a comic Everyman figure, pipe-smoking and bushy-whiskered, who voiced the cynical stoicism of the front-line troops. He first appeared in 1915, most notably in a cartoon of two soldiers in a shell-hole under bombardment, with the caption "Well, if you knows of a better 'ole, go to it." He was enormously popular with the troops but was criticized by some establishment figures as a vulgar and insufficiently heroic representation of the British soldier.[40] Bairnsfather regarded him as the embodiment of a stalwart and commonsensical Britishness, as explained in an introductory caption to *Old Bill "Through the Ages"*:

> There is an heroic figure symbolic of the plain Briton; Symbolic of the everyday man who catches his train and does his job . . . Symbolic too, with his modest heroism and good humoured patience of the real stuff, both warp and weft, of which our History has been woven through the centuries. The Great War was the last proof of his sterling qualities.[41]

Old Bill, then, was a champion of resilience and ordinariness. Though devised during the war, his popularity grew after its end, and he starred in numerous books, plays, and live-action films in the 1920s and '30s. Bairnsfather shared in the embitterment felt by many veterans at their postwar treatment, and Old Bill became a mascot and spokesman for them.[42]

Old Bill "Through the Ages" is a silent live-action film in which the protagonist takes a satirical romp through history. In the trenches, Captain Bairnsfather gives Bill a tin of lobster as a treat, but it is stale and gives Bill hallucinatory dreams. These take him to various historical settings, including the reign of Elizabeth, in which he is a courtier dispatched to bring Shakespeare to court. On his way to Stratford, he is overtaken by a bus and a penny-farthing, and he arrives to find Shakespeare dictating to a typing pool of charming young ladies in above-the-knee farthingales. All this incongruous modernity accentuates the romantic, monumental presentation of Shakespeare: he is first seen with his head resting on his hand, reading a book, in the clothes and posture of his statue in Westminster Abbey (fig. 1.1). When Anne Hathaway tells him of Old Bill's arrival, he complains, "Oh horrors—Bang in the middle of my new sonnet," but he is thrilled to hear of the summons to court: "Ah! This is fame indeed." This is Shakespeare as a vain, pretentious social climber, the polar opposite of the man of the people depicted by Harris and Carey.[43]

The scene shifts to "The Court of the Virgin Queen—A Court of Poets, Lovers, Soldiers, the flower of England's Youth and Chivalry." Shakespeare delivers a recitation in a scene directly based on Eduard Ender's 1860s painting of *Shakespeare Reading "Macbeth" before Queen Elizabeth* (fig. 2.8). Early films often asserted their artistic credentials by modeling scenes upon well-known pictures; Sarah Bernhardt's *Queen Elizabeth* drew upon several nineteenth-century history paintings.[44] *Old Bill* reproduces Ender's composition, with Elizabeth on her throne to the right, flanked by courtiers, other courtiers draped around the room on ornate chairs, and Shakespeare center-stage in Hamlet-like black with a white lace collar. However, in the *Old Bill* version the courtiers, far from being enraptured, are indolent and bored, and Elizabeth is a dotty, cheery old lady. As Shakespeare histrionically declaims fragments of his works so short as to be meaningless—"To be or not to be," "I would I were thy bird," "Romeo, O, Ro-me-o!"—she giggles and nudges the courtier at her side.[45] Old Bill and a friend tap their heads and roll their eyes as Shakespeare rants on, until the line "He jests at scars that never felt a wound" is too much for Bill, who says, "Chuck us over a Mills bomb [a hand grenade], I'll show 'im." This Shakespeare is not a friend and spokesman for the common man but his adversary, the representative of an effete, emasculated, and irrelevant elite culture. Bill lobs his grenade, explodes the Bard from the scene, and takes his place. He begins reciting "The boy stood on the burning deck"—the poem "Casabianca" by Felicia Hemans (1793–1835), beloved of Victorian anthologizers and educators. For Bill, evidently, poetry is all about automatic recall of lines prescribed by those in authority, lines whose original inspiring sentiment has been worn out by overuse.[46]

Bill is hustled from the court, and as Elizabeth looks on, alarmed, bewildered, and amazed, Shakespeare emerges from behind her throne with his hair on end and his clothes scorched and torn, and resumes his recitation. The courtiers, and Old Bill and his two friends sitting outside the chamber, stretch, yawn, and nod off. Bill and his friends are woken by a man offering them pipes and tobacco; Shakespeare, on seeing the smoke, shouts "FIRE! FIRE!" and triggers a mass panic. Elizabeth is curious about the tobacco, upon which Bill pulls out a packet of cigarettes and says "'ere *you* 'ave a fag," as if she were a comrade-in-arms in the trenches. She enjoys her smoke so much that she knights Bill, to which he retorts, "Make it a peerage, and

I'll learn yer to shimmy." Instead of Elizabeth and her court listening in rapt attentiveness to the wondrous Bard, we have Elizabeth and the rough-and-ready Old Bill, a real common man, shimmying away with gusto, as Shakespeare is forgotten. The happy scene is brought to a close by news of the Armada's approach; Elizabeth dispatches her trusted Bill with the command "Bid Drake hold Plymouth."[47]

At the end of his historical dreams Bill wakes to find the First World War over. The film concludes with a vision of the future, long after the Armistice, as Bill and his friends gather for a celebration. Captain Bairnsfather toasts him: "Bill is *always* with us . . . Bill, who has waded through our island history, the old walrus who has won so many wars that he has forgotten how to lose them. Bill . . . the spirit of our Empire!"[48] Shakespeare is very firmly moved from center stage and shoved off into the wings in this rumbustiously carnivalesque work. As Bakhtin writes, carnivalesque rituals "thrust down, turn over, push headfirst, transfer top to bottom, and bottom to top"; they subject the symbolic representative of authority or high culture to "fights, beatings, and blows; they throw the adversary to the ground, trample him into the earth."[49] Shakespeare in *Old Bill "Through the Ages"* may be blown up rather than trampled down, but he is very much the victim of ritual laughter. This is a film which speaks for and to men of the lowest rank, and represents Shakespeare as the personification of a decadent, stale, and incomprehensible high culture. The ordinary British soldiers of the trenches are the heroes here, and the Bard is merely a figure of fun. This participates in a general trend in 1920s film to parody or lampoon Shakespeare, as the medium of film grew in confidence and sought to assert itself as a popular, democratic, modern medium distinct from antiquated high culture.[50]

In some ways, however, *Old Bill "Through the Ages"* recasts rather than overthrows the double myth of Shakespeare and Elizabeth. Previous versions of the meeting of Queen and playwright celebrated and promoted the social cohesion of the nation. This image is not lost in Old Bill's version but reconfigured: now it is Bill who is entitled to enjoy a smoke and a shimmy with Queen Elizabeth, and she in turn thoroughly enjoys sharing them with him. He does not need Shakespeare or any other figure as mediator, such that this scenario creates a new version of the old myth of direct communication and camaraderie between monarch and people.[51]

A Woman's Point of View: *Shake-speare's Sweetheart* (1905)

While Harris, Carey, and the makers of *Old Bill "Through the Ages"* were creating new encounters between Shakespeare and Elizabeth which reflected the shifting

British class politics of the new century, other new versions of the double myth reflected the increasing emancipation of women and increasing frankness about sexual matters. On both sides of the Atlantic, women were campaigning for the right to vote and for greater opportunities in education and the professions. As American writers asserted an affinity between the founding values of their nation and the Elizabethan or Shakespearean spirit of adventure, women too wanted to participate in this freedom and enterprise. The National American Woman Suffrage Association established its national headquarters in New York in 1900; votes for women were granted in some individual states over ensuing years, and in 1920 women's suffrage was ratified across the whole nation. In Britain, Emmeline Pankhurst's Women's Social and Political Union, founded in 1903, gained extensive publicity for its militant actions, but it was mainly in recognition of women's contribution to the war effort that the right to vote for women aged over thirty was granted in 1918.[52] The "new woman"—intellectual, self-willed, androgynous—became a recognizable type in literature.[53]

Sara Hawks Sterling, an American, was one of the first women to write a historical novel about Shakespeare and Elizabeth, *Shake-speare's Sweetheart* (1905). She presented it from a distinctively female point of view, taking Shakespeare's wife, Anne Hathaway, as her first-person narrator. It steered a middle course through the turbulent gender politics of the day: Anne was no stay-at-home wife, but neither was she a man-hating feminist, since she embarked upon travel and adventure in the cause of love and marriage. Sterling borrowed the cross-dressing conventions of Shakespearean comedy: Anne disguised herself as a boy actor named Cesario to follow her husband from Stratford to London. She does this because she suspects that Will is having an affair with a Countess, but the Countess falls in love with her/him, mobilizing a complicated pattern of intersecting and misdirected desires which clearly alludes to *Twelfth Night*. This plot deftly combines homage to Shakespeare with characterization of Anne as a modern girl, full of verve and daring, and with a modern interest in flexible gender identities and unexpected desires.

Anne/Cesario takes the part of Juliet, and a sequence of rehearsal scenes culminates in a triumphant performance before the Queen, after which Shakespeare sets out to write *Twelfth Night* (the uncanny similarities of this plot to that of the 1998 film *Shakespeare in Love* will be discussed further below). The description of the court performance is in many ways conventional: Elizabeth is attended by a "glittering throng" of famous courtiers; she makes an impressive entrance, in dazzling robes and jewels; and she dispenses witty remarks and cuffs on the ear to her retainers.[54] However, the Queen watches the performance with a new kind of close attention. Tradition offered an Elizabeth who discerns more in Shakespeare's plays than other onlookers and has a unique appreciation of his genius, but this time the hidden depth that she discerns is the girl in the boy disguise. "The Queen had been watching me with special intentness from the beginning," says Anne/Cesario/Juliet, "Her steady gaze made me slightly uncomfortable" (256). Elizabeth is pleased with the play, promises Shakespeare her future patronage, and asks to see him and his "Juliet" alone. "The Queen sat there, looking at me as she had done in the play. I trembled, wondering what her steady gaze meant. I never dreamed of the truth. At length she spoke. 'What means this? A maid disguised as a man among players?'" (258). Elizabeth's unique insight here perceives, not Shakespeare's genius, but a desiring female body concealed by male dress. It is implied that she understands these things, as a woman in a masculine role and as a monarch who hides a woman's desires beneath her regal exterior. When she hears the full love story of Will and Anne, she is moved, presumably because of the repression of love in her own story. She gives the couple her blessing and dispatches Anne back to wifely domesticity in Stratford with some sage marital counseling: "Go back to Stratford with thy husband and let thy trust in him henceforth be perfect. Such as he grow not on every bush" (260). Thus she acts as a mouthpiece for proverbial motherly wisdom. Yet at the same time her motives for apparently restoring the sexual status quo seem somewhat mixed: Elizabeth appears to envy Anne her Romeo-husband and "gaz[es] at his noble figure critically" as she commissions further performances from him, ensuring that in practice she will see more of him than will the dutiful Anne back in Stratford (257). Moreover, the Queen's penetrating gaze upon Anne herself, which made her so uncomfortable, is very like a visual undressing, and, following the Countess's attraction to Anne/Cesario, produces a distinct frisson of homoeroticism.

Later, in *A Room of One's Own*, Virginia Woolf would imagine a sister for Shakespeare. Like him, she aspired to be a London playwright but she would have ended up pregnant and dead, a tragic suicide buried at the crossroads, because there was no place or scope for her in Elizabethan England.[55] In Sterling's novel, Shakespeare's wife succeeds in her bold and emancipated behavior because it is contained by the conventions of femininity and heterosexuality: she dresses as a boy, travels, and acts on the stage, but all in the cause of married love. The novel is thus an intriguing mixture, on the one hand celebrating the marital fidelity of Will and Anne, but on the other, by incorporating the cross-dressing of Shakespearean comedy and the sexual enigma of Elizabeth, opening itself to more fluid and flexible representations of gender and sexuality. The wife is both wooed by another woman (the Countess) and romanced by her own husband while she is in the guise of a man; and Elizabeth is an androgynous figure, implied to be harboring turbulent secret desires, who turns a powerful and penetrative gaze on both husband and wife. Sterling's novel carefully avoids radical feminism by maintaining heterosexual love as its narrative goal, but at the same time its use of Shakespeare and Elizabeth for the exploration of alternative sexualities initiates a trend which would flourish in subsequent decades.

Shakespeare and Elizabeth Off Duty: Shaw's *Dark Lady of the Sonnets* (1910)

The Victorian use of Elizabeth to campaign for more concerted royal patronage of the theatre was succeeded in the new century by a campaign for a state-funded National Theatre founded as a memorial to Shakespeare. George Bernard Shaw participated with a Shakespeare-and-Elizabeth playlet, *The Dark Lady of the Sonnets* (1910). Shaw had a complicated relationship with Shakespeare and his reputation, at once critical, admiring, and competitive.[56] In *Plays for Puritans* (1901) he coined the term "Bardolatry," deriding those who worshiped Shakespeare.[57] Accordingly, in the playlet both Shakespeare and Elizabeth are treated irreverently, including unprecedentedly bold and comic depiction of sexual tension between them.

The play begins as Shakespeare arrives at the terrace of Whitehall Palace on Midsummer Night for an assignation with a lady. A cloaked figure, whom the audience quickly identify as Elizabeth, emerges from the palace, sleepwalking and rambling in her speech. She renounces cosmetics: "Out, damned spot . . . All the perfumes of Arabia will not whiten this Tudor hand." Shakespeare, mistaking her for the mistress he intended to meet, addresses her as Mary (presumably Mary Fitton, sometimes considered to be the Dark Lady of the Sonnets). Elizabeth, still sleepwalking, thinks of Mary Queen of Scots, and exclaims guiltily, "Mary! Mary! Who would have thought that woman to have had so much blood in her!"[58] Shakespeare is impressed by her eloquence and makes notes furiously (137–38). This note-taking continues throughout the playlet, to the point that Elizabeth, once awake, becomes annoyed by it (144); Shaw suggests that Shakespeare's ideas come less from divine inspiration than from diligent observation.

Shakespeare calls himself "the king of words," provoking Elizabeth's scorn: "A king, ha!" (138). The Queen's identity is revealed when Shakespeare's mistress, the real Dark Lady, arrives for her assignation with him, finds him mistakenly trying to kiss Elizabeth instead, and strikes them both down. In the aftermath of the scuffle, the Dark Lady recognizes Elizabeth, and falls to her knees "in abject terror," saying, "Will: I am lost: I have struck the Queen." Shakespeare sits up, "as majestically as his ignominious posture allows," and declares affrontedly, "Woman: you have struck WILLIAM SHAKESPEAR!" (139–40). This initiates a verbal duel which descends into class-conscious mudslinging: Elizabeth mocks Shakespeare as a newly made gentleman while he casts aspersions on her legitimacy. Both are exposed as parvenus who stand on their dignity because of their social insecurity. By catching them unawares and in the privacy of night, the playlet reveals their human flaws and thereby burlesques their iconic cultural status, satirizing their self-importance as they vie for supremacy. Rather than mutually enhancing each other's cults, here Shakespeare and Elizabeth posture and squabble as rivals for the status of top national treasure.

Quarreling gradually turns into flirtation. Of course, flirtatious banter between Shakespeare and Elizabeth was nothing new, but there is an iconoclastic edge to the blunt frankness which Shaw gives to Shakespeare, making him speak even more plainly than Henry V in his courtship of Katherine of France. No Victorian Shakespeare would have dared to say to his Queen, "It is no fault of mine that you are a virgin, madam, albeit 'tis my misfortune" (142). The Dark Lady wisely withdraws, leaving Shakespeare to petition Elizabeth to finance a national theatre. Elizabeth has now, in effect, taken over the role of the Dark Lady, Shakespeare's shady and mysterious mistress. She pretends to be affronted by his sauciness but is clearly flattered and pleased. At last she decides it is time to leave:

> ELIZABETH: And now, sir, we are upon the hour when it better beseems a virgin queen to be abed than to converse with the naughtiest of her subjects . . . I shall scarce dare disrobe until the palace gates are between us.
>
> SHAKESPEAR: [*kissing her hand*] My body goes through the gate into the darkness, madam; but my thoughts follow you.
>
> ELIZABETH: How! to my bed!
>
> SHAKESPEAR: No, madam, to your prayers, in which I beg you to remember my theatre . . . Goodnight, great Elizabeth. God save the Queen!
>
> ELIZABETH: Amen. (147)

We are left in uncertainty as the conventional flirtation between Shakespeare and Elizabeth is given a new bawdiness, and also undercut and destabilized. Is Shaw's Shakespeare really entranced by his beauteous Queen? Or is he simply a self-promoting, play-acting opportunist, maneuvering to save his neck and to secure royal patronage for the theatre?

Shakespeare, then, remains enigmatic: behind his public mask seems to lie a succession of other masks, and what we learn of the "real" Shakespeare is that he is a consummate performer. Nevertheless, by catching him and his Queen off guard and by night, Shaw reveals more human figures behind the public images of the godlike Bard and the imperial Gloriana. He plays knowingly with established Shakespeare-and-Elizabeth conventions to discover two characters whose capabilities, vanities, and desires are imagined on a realistic scale.

Shakespeare Lifts Elizabeth's Farthingale

The double myth of Shakespeare and Elizabeth features in two key modernist works of literature, both published in 1922: James Joyce's *Ulysses* and T. S. Eliot's *The Waste Land.* As these authors sought to make a new art and forge a new iconography, they looked back at the great icons of the past, took them apart, and reassembled them. For both of them, sex is the means of bringing Shakespeare and Elizabeth down from their pedestals. In *Ulysses,* a conversation among Stephen Dedalus's companions ranges across *Hamlet,* biographical Shakespeare traditions, and Anne Hathaway. An allegation that Shakespeare had sex with Elizabeth is slyly dropped into a list of his extramarital conquests:

> — The height of fine society. And sir William Davenant of Oxford's mother with her cup of canary for every cockcanary.
>
> Buck Mulligan, his pious eyes upturned, prayed:
>
> — Blessed Margaret Mary Anycock!
>
> — And Harry of six wives' daughter and other lady friends from neighbour seats, as Lawn Tennyson, gentleman poet, sings.[59]

Henry VIII's sexual appetite is projected onto his daughter, who in turn is reduced to merely one among a dream of fair women seduced by Shakespeare, while the whole idea of the great poet as an English institution is deflated to become the absurd figure of "Lawn Tennyson, gentleman poet."

In "The Fire Sermon," the third section of Eliot's *Waste Land,* we encounter "Elizabeth and Leicester / Beating oars" in her barge on the Thames.[60] Eliot's note quotes from the Spanish ambassador's account of the Queen and her favorite flirting, petting, and joking about marriage during a pleasure trip on her barge

(71–72, line 279n). Their superficially playful banter is fraught with political self-interest: Leicester tries to seduce Elizabeth into making him King, while she dangles him in suspended animation. These ghosts of the past are appropriate denizens of Eliot's modern Waste Land, a place of sterile love games. The scene of Elizabeth and Leicester on the royal barge looks back to the lines beginning "The Chair she sat in, like a burnished throne" (54, line 77), which introduce the neurotic modern couple of "A Game of Chess." This passage in turn echoes Shakespeare's description of Cleopatra on her barge, who with Antony forms yet another pair of histrionic and decadent lovers.[61] Then, moving forward through the poem from the scene of Elizabeth and Leicester, we immediately encounter the Thames maidens, bathetically and squalidly seduced on the river: "By Richmond I raised my knees / Supine on the floor of a narrow canoe" (62, lines 294–95). Elizabeth and Leicester, Shakespeare's Antony and Cleopatra, and all the sexually maneuvering couples of the poem merge into a landscape of relationships which are arid, empty, and heartless.

Shaw, Joyce, and Eliot had discovered that Shakespeare and Elizabeth could be made both more human and more modern by exposing their private sexualities. Moreover, because these icons were each sexually ambiguous, they offered rich potential for exploring alternative gender roles and desires. Lytton Strachey, one of the Bloomsbury Group, established by *Eminent Victorians* (1918) as an irreverent biographer of British heroes and heroines, turned to earlier subjects in *Elizabeth and Essex* (1928). He sought to "look below the robes," to find the true, "naked" Elizabeth, and revealed a withered, androgynous creature consumed by a raging lust for beautiful young men.[62] Though Strachey did not include Shakespeare in his story, he strongly influenced a Shakespeare-and-Elizabeth novel of 1933, *The Phoenix and the Dove,* by Cunliffe Owen. The central plot is Harry Wriothesley's affair with Elizabeth Vernon, but this draws Shakespeare and the Queen into a merry-go-round of polymorphous perversity: Harry loves both Shakespeare and Elizabeth Vernon, and Elizabeth Vernon loves (and sleeps with) both Harry and Shakespeare, "proud of the perfect functioning of her body, which gave such pleasure to men."[63] Meanwhile, Owen's Elizabeth I, like Strachey's, is an omnisexual predator, lusting after both Harry and Elizabeth Vernon. The novel clearly reflects the interest in sexual variations created by the Bloomsbury Group and by Freud.

Owen shares and intensifies Strachey's misogynistic disgust at Queen Elizabeth's aging and desiring female body; she is an "old vulture, prinking and coying" (125). Harry is repelled as he sits at her feet and is leeringly fondled by her: "he felt the odour of her ancient breath, and the words hissed out through gaps in the worn-down teeth and shrunken gums" (128). Owen dwells on the elaborate artificial construction of the public Elizabeth:

> With ruffs and farthingales and rails and wheels and hoops and bodices, with wicker work and corded loops and knots of wire, with splendid stuffs and garish wigs, with rings and necklaces and feathered hats, with gleaming stomachers and scarves all mixed and swollen out beyond their usual size, she created the image, and squeezed and pulled and fitted her mysterious frame inside it. (98–99)

Like Strachey, he is interested in what scandalous secrets might lurk beneath these ornate layers, but he imagines a secret even more shocking and substantial. As Harry, sitting at the Queen's feet, leans against her farthingale to submit to her repellent caresses, he feels something beneath the folds of her skirt—something unnamed, but alarmingly solid and tumescent. He rushes from the room, nauseated, to seek out the Earl of Essex and join his rebellion (128). Essex too has discovered her secret: "'So, you too have learnt that,' he said. 'I will ask no more, I will accept your help'" (132). Much later, as Elizabeth lies on her deathbed, she muses that the well-guarded and appalling truth of her hermaphroditism will shortly be revealed: "they would find that she was but half-woman, that necessity, not artifice, had dictated her coquettish but fruitless marriage policies, that she had not sacrificed herself nobly for her country's good so much as been sacrificed ignobly by Nature, cruel to her from the hour of her birth" (319).

As for Shakespeare, he, like the Queen, loves both Harry, for whom he writes "Shall I compare thee to a summer's day?" and Elizabeth Vernon, whom he impregnates (122–23, 208, 237). Elizabeth I is at first enraged by *Venus and Adonis,* which she interprets as a satire upon her unrequited passion for Harry, then won over by Shakespeare's unaristocratic "frankness and sincerity," and he rises to become her most intimate favourite (185, 210, 212). Harry and Elizabeth Vernon, who began the novel looking like the juvenile romantic leads, dwindle into married respectability; their role becomes that of onlookers, who struggle to analyze the strange, fascinating relationship between Queen and poet. Vernon believes that Shakespeare is bewitching the Queen: "She cannot resist him any more than you or I could when we first met him. His charm is a power given him by God, so that he may do his work and be England's greatest artist. One day, when he has done with the Queen, she will come out of her dream" (244). Shakespeare's divine genius is here reconfigured as the power to seduce both his contemporaries and posterity. Vernon goes on more vehemently: "He is the Vampire of Souls. If she yields to him, our sacrifice and hurt will have been vain. For she is what he looks for and cannot find, what made him take both of us. She is two-natured, and can give him the completeness of the two-fold life, which is the least so great a nature as his requires" (244). Thus because each of them possesses a kind of bisexuality, Shakespeare and Elizabeth I are the only fitting and adequate match for one another. This echoes Virginia Woolf's idea of the great creative mind as androgynous and of "Shakespeare's mind as the type of the androgynous, of the man-womanly mind."[64] Vernon continues:

> We ordinary women are content with men, and you common men are content with women; but he is a giant, and so is she. They are gods—I have watched them awe-stricken—and are not bound by the laws which bind us. They can do what seems good to them.
>
> But she is not as great as he, because she will yield,[65] as we have yielded. So we are all three the playthings of the god Shakespear. (244)

Harry, who has felt the phallus beneath the farthingale, retorts with a more bitter and iconoclastic line: "They are not gods, those two, they are monsters. Will is a clever, heartless climber, who has wormed his way up the Court with devilish cruelty and cunning, while the Queen is the horrible, and seemingly everlasting, fruit of her father's debaucheries" (245).

Shakespeare and Elizabeth are united not only in their bisexuality but also in living by pretense. In the end, this is Elizabeth's tragedy and Shakespeare's triumph. As Shakespeare grows older, he tells what he has learned: "Only . . . by feigning can life be real, by becoming a tale that is told, rather than a thing which is done . . . even my little Queen among the apricocks, with few lines to say, in my play *Richard*,[66] will outlive Elizabeth of England. I have found the secret" (274). The dying Elizabeth reflects that "All her politics could not have changed England's destiny one whit. She was but an additional, and more splendid figure in the masque," whereas "Shakespear's poems would be living still when she and all memory of her had vanished" (322–23). Developing the implication present in Shaw's *Dark Lady*, Owen acclaims Shakespeare as the greatest of pretenders. Whereas earlier Bardolaters had praised him for seeing into the eternal verities, for a growing number of twentieth-century writers the essential reality grasped by Shakespeare was that everything is unreal, merely an illusory performance.

Another sexually voracious and repugnant Elizabeth appeared in *My Shakespeare, Rise!* (1935), a novel by the American-born Clara Longworth de Pineton, Comtesse de Chambrun, who also wrote books on the Sonnets and on Shakespeare's life. This was an even more hostile account, driven by the author's Catholicism and belief that Shakespeare too was an adherent to the old faith. As mentioned in chapter 4 above, a rumor that Shakespeare died a Catholic had circulated since the seventeenth century, and in 1794 a "spiritual testament," a declaration of Catholic belief, apparently by the poet's father John Shakespeare, was reported to have been found in the Shakespeare family home.[67] Pineton believed that Shakespeare grew up in a Catholic family and drew literary inspiration from deep-rooted pre-Reformation English folklore.[68] According to her, his youthful fervor to love and serve the Queen was bitterly dispelled when he saw her lewd behavior with the Earl of Leicester at Kenilworth in 1575 and, later, her cruelty to the Earl of Essex. Pineton's Shakespeare is an enthusiastic participant in *Richard II* on the eve of the Essex Rebellion and takes the provocative role of Bolingbroke, displaying his own innate kingliness, his anger at Elizabeth's injustices, and his patriotism (245–49). He is even chosen to impersonate James I in Essex's procession through the City, a fitting role since he "might well have been a fellow to any monarch . . . like a sovereign he moved among his fellows" (253). Unusually, after Elizabeth's death Pineton shows Shakespeare enjoying greater intimacy with King James: "though his plays, as you know, found favour with Queen Elizabeth, I doubt that he ever came to much personal speech with her Majesty" (295).

For Pineton, then, with her Catholic perspective on Shakespeare, there is no close relationship between Queen and poet, only his bitter disillusionment with her lechery and tyranny. This novel illustrates the development of an alternative religious perspective on the double myth of Shakespeare and Elizabeth, one which has recently come to the fore again (see Epilogue below). At the same time it belongs to its own cultural moment in its revelations of the Queen's licentious sexuality and in its positioning of Shakespeare as a potential leader of insurrection. In the early twentieth century, class politics and sexual politics were dominant themes in representations of Shakespeare and Elizabeth, but these concerns shifted and altered as the world plunged into war once more.

The Past as Pageant, the Past in Pieces: *Between the Acts* (1941)

In chapter 3 we encountered some American pageant plays from the early twentieth century which at once looked back to Elizabethan England for the roots of the American nation and promoted an inclusive "people's theatre." In Britain, similar historical pageant plays became popular in the period between the two world wars. Retelling glorious moments from the nation's story gave reassurance and confidence at a time when the connections between past and present seemed increasingly precarious. These community dramas were performed in streets, fields, or village halls; they had large casts of local people, regardless of their lack of performing experience, and they affirmed a collective identity shared by cast and audience. Lionel R. McColvin's *To Kill the Queen,* set in the Elizabethan era and performed in Ipswich in June 1931, carried a prefatory note: "This Pageant Play has been written specially for out-door performance and so as to embrace the maximum opportunity for dancing and music, and to provide as many individual speaking parts as possible. It may, if necessary, be given without any scenery and with very few properties."[69] Such plays offered a kind of people's history and to this extent were democratic and modern; yet in retelling popular history they inevitably restated familiar myths. Pageant plays could also reaffirm old social hierarchies and notions of a world in which the high and the low contentedly knew their places: McColvin's pageant was staged "under the Patronage of the Most Hon. the Marquess of Salisbury, and the Most Hon. the Marquess of Exeter" (ibid.).

E. Hamilton Gruner's *With Golden Quill: A Cavalcade, Depicting Shakespeare's Life and Times* (1936) acclaimed the Bard as "the Empire's hero,"[70] while E. M. Forster attempted the pageant genre in *England's Pleasant Land,* performed at Milton Court in Surrey in 1938.[71] The irony of these plays celebrating a peaceful, harmonious England as portents of war loomed ever more threateningly was profoundly felt by Virginia Woolf, who presented her own fictional version of a village pageant, set in June 1939, in her last novel, *Between the Acts* (1941). This pageant attempts a comprehensive narrative of English history, naturally including Elizabeth I. She is played by Eliza Clark, the brawny village shopkeeper, who "could reach a flitch of bacon or haul a tub of oil with one sweep of her arm" (52). She is at once magnificent and absurd—"Her head, pearl-hung, rose from a vast ruff . . . her cape was made of cloth of silver—in fact swabs used to scour saucepans"—and inspires laughter and applause in equal measure. The laughter, though, is partly that of fond recognition, of both Eliza Clark and Elizabeth I, and the applause is for the impressiveness not only of the monumental Queen but also of the monumental village shopkeeper, a personification of doughty English spirit, soldiering on even when her ruff becomes unpinned and she forgets her lines (53).

Woolf's choice of surname for Eliza Clark may pay homage to Alice Clark (1874–1934), who was a member of the Somerset Clark family shoe company, a campaigner for women's suffrage, and the author of the notable academic study *The Working Life of Women in the Seventeenth Century* (1919). This landmark book, still the most thorough study of its field, argued that before the Industrial Revolution manufacture and commerce took place on a domestic scale, enabling women to play a full and rewarding part in the economic life of the nation.[72] Woolf's Eliza has much in common with the seventeenth-century female craftswomen and tradeswomen idealized by Alice Clark, who presided over shops in their homes for their local communities. At the same time, her depiction may allude to the contemporary Queen Elizabeth, wife of King George the VI, who was renowned for her sense of duty and her common touch. She and the King famously remained in London throughout the Blitz, and made morale-boosting visits to urban areas devastated by bombs.[73] Memorable images of the Queen stepping over rubble and cheering the afflicted were widely publicized in newspaper photographs and cinema newsreels, giving new shape to the old myths of concord between the monarchy and the people.

Reflecting these contexts, Eliza Clark combines in her person regality and ordinariness, impressiveness and incompetence. Woolf's treatment of her oscillates constantly between a sense of how inspiring it is to allow oneself to be caught up in the veneration of icons of national unity and how absurd and inadequate such icons are when viewed with a critical eye. Naturally, Shakespeare is invoked: "For me Shakespeare sang," announces Eliza (52). She is interrupted by the mooing of a cow and the twittering of a bird, which at once undermine her restatement of the old double myth and reinforce it: the song of Shakespeare is ridiculously reduced to a cow's moo but is simultaneously recuperated as the enduring voice of nature, expressing an essential, unchanging Englishness, rooted in the land. A stage set representing a theatre is hastily assembled: "Were they about to act a play in the presence of Queen Elizabeth? Was this, perhaps, the Globe theatre?" (54). It is indeed; Woolf's characters, knowing history only as mediated by myth, assume that Elizabeth watched Shakespeare's plays at the Globe. The play-within-the-pageant is a pastiche of Shakespeare's late romances, in which Eliza is shown another fictionalized and even more grotesque version of herself, a withered crone named Elsbeth, preserver of the past in the fireside tales that she passes on, but also guardian of the future, who saves and brings up the lost babe who is the rightful heir (55–56). The scene ends with all the other performers dancing around Eliza in "a mellay; a medley; an entrancing spectacle . . . It didn't matter what the words were; or who sang what. Round and round they whirled, intoxicated by the music" (57–58). No one is sure what it means, but everyone enjoys it immensely and applauds wildly. The first act of the pageant draws to a close with the gramophone chanting "Dispersed are we" (59).

Woolf at once lovingly celebrates the favorite myths of the English past and disintegrates them into a jumble of meaningless fragments, no longer able to cohere as "the motor bike, the motor bus, and the movies" begin to fracture the village community (47) and airplanes pass forebodingly overhead, drowning out the conventional ritual of the vicar's vote of thanks with their ominous roar (114–15).

The community is poised between old certainties which are sliding out of reach and the terrifying uncertainty of the future: "The horns of cars on the high road were heard. And the swish of trees. They were neither one thing nor the other; neither Victorians nor themselves. They were suspended, without being, in limbo. Tick, tick, tick, went the machine" (106). They need Shakespeare and Elizabeth in their pageant more than ever, yet in Woolf's eyes they can no longer derive sustenance and reassurance from the myth. She recognized a simultaneous resistance to and craving for the tradition personified by Shakespeare and Elizabeth, an ambivalence which would continue through the wartime period and beyond.

Shakespeare and Elizabeth Survive the Blitz: *No Bed for Bacon* (1941)

No Bed for Bacon, by Caryl Brahms and S. J. Simon, although a comic novel, is fraught with anxieties which reflect its publication at the height of the Blitz. In its presentation of the conventional scene of Elizabeth watching a Shakespeare play, the emphasis is upon the fragile unpredictability of drama and of life: the performance takes place in the fraught aftermath of the Essex Rebellion, and the peace and stability of the nation are uncertain. The play is *Twelfth Night,* and Viola is played by Lady Viola Compton, disguised as a boy actor named John Pyk. She is in love with drama and with Shakespeare (as with *Shake-speare's Sweetheart,* this aspect of *No Bed for Bacon* will be echoed later in the film *Shakespeare in Love*). The performance takes place on a knife-edge: will the furious and embittered Queen be placated by the play, or will she punish the players for their complicity in the attempted uprising? Will Viola be exposed as a boy (although Shakespeare and Elizabeth already know her secret)? Will Shakespeare realize that Viola is in love with him? And the most immediate question: Will the play succeed? At first the prospects look doubtful: Viola, intimidated by the illustrious audience in the shadowy, candlelit hall, forgets her first line and has to be shoved on stage by Will; as he watches from the wings, Will anxiously swigs beer and mops his brow.[74] The atmosphere is tense and foreboding.

But theatre works its magic and makes everything all right: "The play went on. Gradually Master Will's words took a hold on the audience. Illyria was the perfect escape from the problems of Elizabethan England. Even the Queen was seen to smile" (253). We did not hear much about "the problems of Elizabethan England" in nineteenth-century versions of this scene, but like Carey's postwar *Dark Lady* of 1919, Brahms and Simon's midwar novel is marked by a dark and unsettled contemporary mood. Success is imagined as a fleeting contingency, snatched from the general difficulty of life; the emphasis is upon muddling through, doing one's best against daunting odds, and coping gamely with the unexpected, all the responses associated with British "wartime spirit." The venue for the play is Temple Hall, a temporary home for the players after the burning down of the Globe playhouse. Like many British people bombed out of their homes, schools, or workplaces, the players are having to make do with the provisional, to cope with whatever is thrown at them, and to exercise an inventive pragmatism.

Alison Light has written of how the traumatic wartime experiences of the twentieth century created a "strongly anti-heroic mood" in Britain, with "a revolt against, embarrassment about, and distaste for the romantic languages of national pride"; and how the rhetoric of "our finest hour," always in any case inherently elegiac, seems to have dwindled away over the course of the twentieth century.[75] *No Bed for Bacon* as a comic novel in some ways participates in this significant shift in national sensibility by debunking the myth of the Elizabethan golden age. Yet at the same time it contributes to a new version of the British heroic spirit—an unheroic heroism and unromantic romanticism—in emphasizing the need for everyone to do what he or she can in difficult conditions; to rise to the occasion but to do so unshowily. As the play proceeds, Shakespeare realizes that Viola has pulled off a successful performance because of her real passion for him: as she speaks the line "My state is desperate for my master's love," her voice falters (253). His reaction is one of stoicism and duty: he sends her away so that he can get on with his writing. His plays emerge from concerted effort, not divine inspiration, nor even inspiration from his own experience of love. The tradition that Elizabeth sacrificed her personal life for her public and national duty is here transposed onto Shakespeare. He must get on, doggedly, with producing Britain's national literature.

Three years later, in 1944, Laurence Olivier's film of *Henry V* drew connections between past and present in a somewhat less stoical manner which demonstrated that the rhetoric of "our finest hour" was not yet exhausted. Made while the war was still taking a severe toll on both the armed forces and civilians, with no end yet in sight, the film was dedicated "to the commandos and airborne troops of Great Britain, the spirit of whose ancestors it has been humbly attempted to recapture in some ensuing scenes."[76] The medieval age in which Henry V won his famous victory at Agincourt was viewed through an Elizabethan lens: the film began as a reconstruction of a performance at the Globe playhouse, with some of *No Bed for Bacon*'s sense of muddling through despite the limitations of theatre, but it then widened out to battle scenes on an epic scale. Audiences were invited to identify with the triumphant heroism of Henry and his troops, riding forth to victory despite massive odds against them. The rousing message was that the national success of Henry's age, and of Shakespeare's, could be achieved again in the present. This idea of recapturing past glories persisted after the war came to an end, but it seemed increasingly difficult to embrace it unequivocally.

The 1950s: A New Elizabethan Age

The close of the Second World War brought hopes of future peace and prosperity and gathering enthusiasm for the idea of a revival of the Elizabethan golden age. Britain was ruled by a Queen Elizabeth, the consort of George VI, and it was certain that their daughter would be Queen Elizabeth II. In 1948, as Princess Elizabeth, she visited University College, Oxford, and was entertained by a *Masque of Hope,* in which Saint George prophesies a golden age under her rule, adapting Cranmer's rapturous lines about the young Elizabeth I from Shakespeare's (and Fletcher's) *Henry VIII.*[77] Inevitably, ideas of a new Elizabethan age were prominent when Elizabeth II acceded to the throne in 1952 and was crowned the following year.[78]

Yet there were significant limits to this idealism and optimism, and the rhetoric of restored Elizabethan glory often seemed like wishful thinking or propaganda. Princess Elizabeth's 1948 visit to Oxford took place in the year when Burma and Ceylon were released from British imperial rule and only a year after India, Britain's most valuable colony, had achieved independence (also creating the new, self-governing nation of Pakistan). Over successive years more imperial territories achieved self-rule, some remaining within the federation of nations designated as the British Commonwealth, others severing ties with Britain. Whereas Victorians had found the origins of, and analogues for, their own imperial expansion in the Elizabethan age, the new Elizabethans seemed to be reversing the process begun by the first Queen Elizabeth and losing everything that she and her successors had gained. The new world order was dominated by two superpowers, the United States and Russia, and by the nuclear bomb, with its attendant terrors of mass annihilation. Britain's sense of her place and identity within this new world was fraught with uncertainty and self-doubt. Meanwhile, within her own borders, although the creation of the "welfare state" by the Labour government of 1945–51 offered hope of a fairer society, economic hardship and the restrictions of class continued to affect many Britons. Any sense of postwar jubilation was muted by the persistence of the rationing of basic commodities until 1954. The nation celebrated at the Festival of Britain in 1951, but behind the fleeting party mood lay social divisions, fears for the future, and much anxious national introspection.[79]

These confusing times were summed up by the fictional 1950s British schoolboy Nigel Molesworth, created by Geoffrey Willans and Ronald Searle. He expressed a mixed mood of fresh-start enthusiasm, wry cynicism, and world-weary resignation in his inimitable style: "No one kno wot to do about anything at the moment so they sa the future is in the hands of YOUTH . . . we are young elizabethans and it can't be altered—i expect drake felt the same way." He imagined himself transported back to the first Elizabethan age:

> Fie fie—the grown ups canot kno what a privilege it is to be YOUTH in this splendid age of Queen Bess—when all are brave proud fearless etc and looking with clear eyes at the future. (Not so clear after some of those evenings at Court, i trow, when all drink BEER.) All the same it is up to us boys because the grownups hav made such a MESS of it all.[80]

The response of some of those grownups was to continue feeding the "tinies," to use Molesworth's term, the old familiar myths. As discussed in the Introduction above, Ladybird books had both authority and popularity with a generation of young British readers. The Ladybird *Story of the First Queen Elizabeth* appeared in 1958, just two years after Molesworth's version of Elizabethanism. It ran through the exciting stories of Elizabeth's incarceration in the Tower of London, Sir Francis Drake's circumnavigation of the globe, and the victory over the Spanish Armada, then related the rise of "William Shakespeare, the greatest of all poets and playwrights."[81] Readers were told that "the Queen liked Shakespeare's plays so much that he was frequently commanded to bring his company to the palace. It is wonderful to think that many of the plays which we see to-day were first acted before the great Queen Elizabeth herself." This coercive instruction to admire the "wonderful" Shakespeare and Elizabeth was illustrated by Elizabeth not in fact watching a play but, as in all those Victorian paintings, leaning forward attentively while a flamboyantly gesturing Shakespeare read to her from a manuscript (fig. 0.1). This was Shakespeare removed from the commerce and populism of the playhouse to be Elizabeth's personal court entertainer. It presented Elizabeth as Shakespeare's primary audience and granted us a glimpse of the meeting of their lofty minds. The picture and text could as easily have been made in 1858 as 1958. They illustrate the remarkable persistence through changing times of celebratory reiterations of the double myth of Shakespeare and Elizabeth; but these increasingly coexisted with versions which were less confident and more experimental.

Shakespeare and Elizabeth Do Not Meet

The Ladybird book continued to circulate through the 1960s and '70s, engrossing children with its restatement of old myths. Yet, at the same time, emerging cultural trends began to keep Shakespeare and Elizabeth apart. Scholars were now well aware that Elizabeth almost certainly did not go to the playhouse and that there was no evidence of her direct patronage of Shakespeare. The respected theatre historian and illustrator C. Walter Hodges sardonically mocked the ill-informed who wanted to bring the Queen and the poet together: "Impossible to imagine that Good Queen Bess never even met the Swan of Avon. After all, they were both famous, and lived in London, and his theatre was only a little way down the river from her home."[82] Moreover, as we saw in discussing criticism of *A Midsummer Night's Dream* in chapter 4, some left-leaning critics were keen to assert Shakespeare's populism and detach him from the court. Others, under the influence of Jan Kott's landmark book *Shakespeare Our Contemporary* (translated into English in 1965), or driven by the exigencies of holding the interest of young people in the classroom, stressed Shakespeare's relevance to modern-day political and social issues, which entailed playing down his Elizabethan context and his court connections. Shakespeare biographies of the last fifty years, in a marked departure from earlier practice, tend to mention Elizabeth only incidentally as part of the general cultural context. Equally, in recent biographies of Elizabeth, Shakespeare tends to be mentioned only briefly as part of the cultural flowering of the later years of her reign.

This tendency is evident in Anthony Burgess's biographical novel *Nothing Like the Sun* (1964), in which Shakespeare does not meet Elizabeth but hears of her from his beloved fair youth, Harry Wriothesly (*sic*), who vilifies her as "a rotting heap of old filth."[83] In the traditional scene of Elizabeth watching a Shakespeare play, the author is not a favorite invited to the royal box but an insignificant onlooker from the sidelines, recording his rushed impressions of the scene in his diary:

> *January 27th*
>
> It was yesterday and I have scarce breath to write. Liveried barges to Greenwich and then the great roaring fires and braziers against the bright thin cold as we deck ourselves, wine too and ale and chines and boarheads and a tumbling profusion of kickshawses, then we gasp in to the Great Hall, the Queen chewing on broken teeth in her magnificence, gold throne, bare diamond-winking bosoms glowing in the heat of logs and seacoal, laughing lords and tittering ladies and the Queen's bead-eyes on my lord

> E, amethysts bloodstones carbuncles flashing fingers jewelled swordhilts the clothofgold bride and silken yawning groom. (147)

The play is *A Midsummer Night's Dream*; as the references here to the bride and groom indicate, Burgess subscribes to the wedding-play theory. He does not, however, imagine that this brought Shakespeare to the notice of the Queen, although Shakespeare observes her closely. He is at once an ingenu, overwhelmed by the glitter and opulence of the court, and a cynic who notes Elizabeth's broken teeth and the bored detachment of the aristocratic bridegroom. The play is a mixed success: "And so, amid coughs, to our play, Will Ostler trembling and forgetting his lines and finger-clicking for bookholder to prompt but all else going well save for Kemp, impromptu king, who got not so much laughter as he thought his due and chided the audience for this" (147–48). Shakespeare is merely an anonymous jobbing writer, helplessly dependent on an inadequate and wayward company of actors, and even less significant than them: when he later comes almost to blows with Kemp, he is reminded that "I am but a poet" (148).

The court performance is a token of worldly success but is experienced by Shakespeare largely as a struggle and a chore. Its main significance for him is that he can deploy it to pursue his courtship of the Dark Lady, here identified as a Moorish prostitute:

> So I go today to her house, clear flashing winter sunlight making a world all of tinkling money, and I am admitted at once, for all must go well for me now. I have a gift for her if she will accept it, it is no more than a dish of candy from the Court, but it is from the Court the Court, mark that, madam. Aye, my play was done before the Queen's majesty at Greenwich. Before the Queen? Aye, that. And what did she wear and what noble lords and ladies were there and tell me all all all. And so I told her all. (148)

Elizabeth here features as a remote figure, a celebrity with trivial glamor who generates inconsequential gossip; she is merely a name to be dropped, a social password. Shakespeare's contact with her is entirely impersonal, no more than that of a tradesman with an elevated client, and is itself a commodity to be traded as he hustles his way through the obstacles and opportunities of Elizabethan London, pursuing his ambitions and desires. Cultural commentators in the 1960s made much of talented and self-promoting young men who rose from humble origins to become iconic figures in swinging London—writers, artists, actors, pop stars, photographers, fashion designers, footballers—and who seemed much more vibrant and charismatic than the increasingly irrelevant royal family. Burgess's Shakespeare similarly uses his wits to chance and charm his way to success.

There was no appearance by Shakespeare in the acclaimed 1971 BBC television series *Elizabeth R*, probably because of its aspiration to authenticity and definitiveness. It continues to be sold on DVD as "meticulously researched" and "considered by many to be the most faithful representation of Elizabeth's life."[84] Elizabeth goes nowhere near any playhouses, and the entertainments which she is seen enjoying at court include sung masques, dancing, and an acrobatic display, but no Shakespearean plays. Shakespeare is present only in a shadowy way on the margins of the action in the final episode: the Earl of Southampton departs for Ireland lamenting that it will be dull because there are no theatres there; and on the eve of their rebellion Essex and his supporters watch a somewhat inept performance of the deposition scene from *Richard II*.[85] Shakespeare never appears in person and is never even named. Meanwhile, however, *Elizabeth R* was propelling the Queen to unprecedented fame and celebrity.

Elizabeth as International Star

There may have been some skepticism about the reign of Elizabeth II as a new Elizabethan age, but from the mid twentieth century Elizabeth I herself certainly enjoyed a new reign in popular history, fiction, film, and television drama. Margaret Irwin's trilogy of novels *Young Bess* (1944), *Elizabeth, Captive Princess* (1948), and *Elizabeth and the Prince of Spain* (1953), reinvented her as a passionate, spirited, clever, and resourceful heroine, an inspiration to modern girls. Bette Davis's performances in *The Private Lives of Elizabeth and Essex* (1939) and *The Virgin Queen* (1955) merged the Queen's identity with that of the Hollywood actress: charismatic, determined, caustically witty but also susceptible to love. Numerous romantic novels such as Jean Plaidy's *Gay Lord Robert* (1955) and *The Young Elizabeth* (1961) offered thrilling narratives of the Queen's tempestuous passions.[86] Elizabeth mostly does not meet Shakespeare in such works, not because of historical accuracy or left-wing ideology, but because she does not need him. The main interest is in her personal challenges and dilemmas as she steers a course between lovers and political crises, and her relations with Shakespeare are superfluous.

In short, Elizabeth became a star, a status conclusively secured by Glenda Jackson's magnificent performance in *Elizabeth R* (first screened in the United Kingdom in 1971). Jackson's Elizabeth reveled in her own wit, independence, and power and offered a compelling feminist characterization which is still widely remembered. Elizabeth's unwomanliness may have troubled the Victorians, but for the later twentieth century her combination of ambition, professional success, and private passion, of brainpower, sex appeal, and self-belief, made her an inspiring heroine. She spoke to urgent concerns about how women could reconcile public roles and private lives and about the rewards and costs of seeking success and fulfilment in both spheres. Following *Elizabeth R*, she continued to be a staple heroine of popular novels like Plaidy's *Queen of This Realm* (1984) and Susan Kay's *Legacy* (1985).

Elizabeth R was produced by the British Broadcasting Corporation, and was a great success in Britain, but it was essentially an export product. The expenses of the lavish costumes and high production values could only be recouped by overseas sales, especially to North America and Europe. Its commercial appeal was enhanced by the BBC brand, which bestowed an aura of authenticity. Elizabeth, like Shakespeare, was now a global commodity. Her new international allure meant that, for the first time since the eighteenth century, Shakespeare needed her, to add glamor and appeal to his image, more than she needed him. While he appeared less in fictions about Elizabeth, and she appeared less in Shakespeare biographies, two Shakespearean-related works of imagination from the 1970s show that the urge to give Elizabeth a starring role was hard to resist.

Elizabeth was central to a production of *A Midsummer Night's Dream* for the annual Shakespeare festival at Stratford, Ontario. The town of Stratford, with its own Avon River, was founded and named by a director of the Canada Company in 1832; it subsequently grew into a city which was a center of the Canadian railway industry and of furniture manufacture. In the early 1950s, with these industries in decline, city authorities and local residents combined to found a theatre festival based around the works of Shakespeare, adroitly turning a city name which had expressed homage to British origins into a cultural and commercial asset and a distinctive civic identity. The Stratford Shakespeare Festival is now the major commercial attraction of the city, boasting the largest classical repertory theatre in North America and drawing annual audiences of some 600,000.[87]

Robin Phillips's production of *A Midsummer Night's Dream* was first presented in the 1976 season starring Jessica Tandy and was then revived in 1977 starring Maggie Smith. Both actresses doubled the roles of Hippolyta and Titania, and both these characters were presented as aspects of Elizabeth. The production opened with Hippolyta, dressed unmistakably as Elizabeth in ruff, farthingale, and red curled wig, alone and illuminated by a shaft of white light, while a distant voice sang a "Dream Madrigal" (fig. 6.2):[88]

I have had a most rare vision
A strange and wondrous dream
Past the wit of man to say what dream it was

FIGURE 6.2
Dame Maggie Smith as Hippolyta in *A Midsummer Night's Dream,* dir. Robin Phillips, Stratford Festival, Ontario, Canada, 1977. Photograph by Robert C. Ragsdale. Reproduced by permission of Dame Maggie Smith and the Stratford Festival of Canada Archives.

Methought I was—
Methought I was—
Methought I loved—
Man is but a fool, a patched fool
If he offer to say what dream it was.[89]

This song was based on Bottom's waking words, transplanted from 4.1.199–200 and redeployed to make the whole play, in effect, something dreamed by Queen Elizabeth.[90] Peter Brook, in his ground-breaking 1970 RSC production, had introduced doubling of Hippolyta and Titania and of Theseus and Oberon in order to make the middle acts of the play in the moonlit wood seem like the dream life of the courtly characters of the enclosing "real-life" acts set in Athens. The wood became a space of the subconscious, where tensions could be released and repressed desires explored. Phillips followed Brook's strategy but introduced and foregrounded Elizabeth, so that it was her personal subconscious which was the space of exploration.

As in *Elizabeth R,* sumptuous and meticulously researched costumes were an important feature of the production, and it attracted large audiences with the visual pleasures of heritage theatre.[91] However, Phillips also hoped to disturb preconceptions about the Elizabethan golden age and about Gloriana, emphasizing the sinister undercurrents of Elizabethan court culture—which he regarded as fraught with "falsehood and greed, callousness and spitefulness"[92]—and exploring the multiple facets of Elizabeth's personality. The tradition that Elizabeth achieved public success at the price of a troubled and unfulfilled personal life was now given a distinctly post-Freudian slant that probed Elizabeth's disturbed psyche, as seen in the 1977 program:

> The Queen was essentially a mystery to her people . . . Standing always in the light, she cast ominous shadows. Her mind travelled to dark, wooded places to which no other mortal had access. She was steadfast and capricious; compassionate and imperious; compounded of flesh and blood and of iron and air. She was a young girl flirting with love and a great Queen commanding it. She was Gloriana and she was a faded, ageing woman, desperately lonely.[93]

Theseus/Oberon was depicted as an Elizabethan courtier like Leicester or Essex, but with emphasis (especially in Jeremy Brett's 1976 performance) on his desire to master and dominate the Queen, so that the first and last acts dramatized Elizabeth's fears and anxieties about marriage.[94] Titania, then, represented the freer, happier sides of Elizabeth's personality, and the moonlit scenes in the wood represented the Virgin Queen's fantasies about the possibilities of love. Indeed, all the female characters wore jeweled gowns and red curled wigs which resembled Elizabeth's, making them all seem to represent different aspects of her erotic life.

Again like *Elizabeth R,* Phillips's *Dream* reflected the contemporary feminist movement. In an early scene a crowd of ladies styled like Elizabeth faced Theseus and his male entourage, dramatizing the antagonism of the sexes. Jeremy Brett's 1976 performance as Theseus and Oberon emphasized both characters' harsh patriarchal oppression of femininity, sensuality, and imagination.[95] It was clear how much Elizabeth would have to sacrifice if she accepted marriage. This was reflected in the young lovers' plot too: one (female) critic, using the vocabulary of the times, noted that "Hermia and Helena take a women's lib approach to their roles."[96]

The production had particular topicality on its second run, in 1977, because it coincided with a modern Elizabethan celebration. It was the opening production of the Twenty-fifth Stratford Shakespeare Festival in Ontario, marking the Silver Jubilee of the Festival. The same summer also marked the Silver Jubilee of Queen Elizabeth II. As a journalist noted, on the very same day that over a hundred theatre critics gathered in Stratford, Ontario, for the gala opening night of the *Dream,* in London "Queen Elizabeth was preparing to ride in her coronation coach to mark her jubilee reign."[97] The reviewer for the London *Evening Standard* surmised that the Elizabethan theme of the production "may have been a nod towards the [Queen's] Silver Jubilee."[98] It is unlikely that Phillips's *Dream,* which not only explored the erotic games and fantasies of the Virgin Queen but also ended with her as a melancholy and sterile figure, was offering a direct parallel with Elizabeth II, but the critic of the *Boston Globe* illuminated these simultaneous events: "in the flowing regality of Philips's concept, the point is dazzling: Shakespeare shining beyond the shadow of his monarch, Stratford shining in the celebration of the current queen, as well as in its own remarkable 25-year history."[99] As members of the British Commonwealth, Canadians acknowledged the Queen of England as their head of state and politely congratulated her on her Jubilee; but Phillips's *Dream* demonstrates that, like their American neighbors, they were increasingly feeling their distance from Britain and making Shakespeare and Elizabeth I their own.

Phillips's *Dream* thus asserted Canada's ownership of the high-cultural heritage of Shakespearean drama and Elizabethan history. One U.S. review bore the headline "The Bard Resides in Stratford, Ontario"; another declared that "Today the Shakespearean festival in Canada is recognized as the finest cultural center for classical dramatic literature on the North American continent."[100] Some critics expressed concern that the production depended upon stars who were British (Smith, Brett) or American (Hume Cronyn, Tandy), but others acclaimed the Festival for achieving a global importance which attracted international stars: "North America's and Britain's finest actors are in residence at Stratford."[101] In short, Stratford, Ontario, was asserting its ability to rival Stratford, England.

Meanwhile, back in Britain, ATV, one of the subsidiary companies of ITV (Independent Television), the BBC's commercially funded rival, aspired to emulate the international commercial and critical success of *Elizabeth R* with a dramatized life of Britain's other great cultural asset, William Shakespeare. Joint funding was secured from the Italian broadcasting corporation RAI, and John Mortimer was commissioned as writer. He published a version in novel form, *Will Shakespeare,* in 1977, and the television series was screened in the United Kingdom in 1978.[102] Despite intentions to sell the series for broadcast in the United States, this never came about, although it was widely shown throughout Europe and has had a long global afterlife on video and DVD.[103]

While the makers of *Elizabeth R* omitted Shakespeare, it is noteworthy that Mortimer, to some extent working in *Elizabeth R*'s shadow, felt the need to include the Queen in his account of Shakespeare's life. In the novel version, Shakespeare is summoned to court to explain his part in the Essex Rebellion and is reduced to confused impressionism by the dazzling, dizzying presence of Elizabeth: "He remembered sunlight, streaming in from a high window, a dead white face in a scarlet wig, and a white satin dress like a bride's dress sparkling with jewels, glittering like the sun . . . And then that voice came at him, now flicking him like a fire, now cold as ice, now gentle as a lover's voice, now terrible as the rebuke of a Prince."[104] According to this account, an appointment with Elizabeth was like something between the Last Judgment and an audience with the Wizard of Oz. Shakespeare is resoundingly humiliated by Elizabeth: "Lost for words, little poet? Tell me, what is the great crime for which you seek my mercy? A halting verse? A limp rhyme to end a scene, as I have heard many times in your comedies?" (203). She yawns at his prepared speech of apology and dismisses *Richard II* as "A poor play! Journeyman's work. Sorely botched." Shakespeare is utterly disarmed and defeated, while Elizabeth, on her personal stage in her presence chamber, triumphs as the greater performer and greater intellect of the two.

The usual scene of the Queen watching a Shakespeare play is set, as in *No Bed for Bacon,* in the aftermath of the Essex Rebellion, investing it with tension and anxiety. The play is *Henry IV Part 2,* staged in the Great Hall at Nonesuch Palace, "where the firelight and candles shone on polished marble and fine brocade, where the women's bosoms and the gentlemen's fine silks and velvets would send the senses swooning, and where only the dogs of the finest breeds pissed against the great hunting tapestry under the ladies' footstools" (205). The glittering court props are much the same as ever, but the addition of the pissing dogs at once alludes to Shakespeare[105] and seems modern in its wry scatological humor. The Queen is stiff and expressionless as she watches the play. When Cecil enters with a writing desk, all eyes turn to her as she signs Essex's death warrant, and Shakespeare's play is interrupted and upstaged by her performance of power (207).

Later, Shakespeare comes to court once more to plead for clemency for Southampton. Now Mortimer dwells upon Elizabeth's grotesque decrepitude in her declining years, a conventional depiction of the Queen deriving largely from Strachey which has exercised enduring and often misogynistic fascination; even in *Elizabeth R,* in the final episode Jackson played a gothic Elizabeth who looked like a hideously adorned living corpse. In Mortimer's version, "her skin was drawn so tight and her pale face had the appearance of a skull, rouged and decked out with a red wig. She moved slowly, her legs were tired and she was worn out by cares of State" (218). Yet her inner vigor is not defeated: "her old eye was still bright and restless as a sparrow hawk's, and she still spoke clear and commanding" (ibid.). Shakespeare cannot interest her in Southampton's cause; she is preoccupied and disquieted by the fashion for young men to dress in black, in emulation of Hamlet, and urges Shakespeare to "Give us old fat Falstaff again. Is there to be no more laughter in England?" (220). Though old and tired, she remains the guardian of "merrie England." She has an eye on posterity too, telling Shakespeare, "You and I, a woman and a poet, why, we are giants, sir!" (219).

Mortimer's Elizabeth (played on screen by Patience Collier) was closely related to Jackson's as an imposing figure who combined shrewd wit with the wisdom of experience. Mortimer could not help being influenced by this recent acclaimed and forceful performance, and his Shakespeare could not help being overwhelmed and emasculated by his encounters with this Elizabeth. It was a version of the double myth which was marked by contemporary feminist politics, and which appeared on the eve of the 1979 election in which Britain submitted to the government of another indomitable and intimidating woman, Margaret Thatcher.

The 1980s and '90s: Shakespeare and Elizabeth Turn Postmodern

By the 1980s the widespread fascination with Elizabeth extended into literary criticism, where, as we have seen, new-historicist interest in the circulation of power gave her a renewed prominence in readings of Shakespeare. Critics investigated what Elizabeth meant, as a dominant figure of female power, in the psyche of the nation and the playwright. More generally, new historicism encouraged an analytical self-consciousness about the role of myth-making in history, about the impossibility of a wholly impartial or factual history, and indeed about myth-making and representation as having their own history.

Meanwhile historical fiction, drama, and film became ever more playful in their relation to historical truth. Arguably, many intrinsic characteristics of these genres have always anticipated the postmodern, such as their transgression of boundaries between reality and fiction and between academic and popular culture, their voracious absorption and inventive redisposition of diverse source materials, and their concern with what works as a good read or a good show rather than factual accuracy.[106] These inherently postmodern qualities became even more pronounced in fictional versions of Shakespeare and Elizabeth as the twentieth-century fin de siècle approached.

In 1984 Dario Fo, the Italian playwright, satirist, socialist, and political activist, visited Britain (he came to the Edinburgh Festival) and wrote his play *Elizabeth: Almost by Chance a Woman.*[107] Margaret Thatcher had just won a landslide victory in her second general election, following Britain's victory over Argentina in the Falklands War. Thatcherism was in the ascendant, and the Prime Minister was embarking upon a new domestic conflict, her ferocious battle with the striking National Union of Mineworkers. This context undoubtedly colored Fo's portrait of Elizabeth as a Machiavellian and paranoid autocrat, and anti-Thatcherite resonances were especially apparent when the play was staged in London in 1986, translated by and starring Gillian Hanna. Elizabeth was imperious, androgynous, solipsistic, manipulative, sexually insatiable, foul-mouthed, and barely sane—an extreme version, in short, of all the negative traits attributed to her since the nineteenth century and a damning portrait of an iconic female predecessor who was often compared with Mrs. Thatcher by journalists and by the Iron Lady herself.[108]

Fo's Elizabeth is dependent upon a seedy and garrulous old bawd, Dame Grosslady, who applies dubious cosmetics and potions to plaster over the Queen's physical decrepitude and fashion her imposing public image. There are highly comic scenes as Fo gives the tradition of misogynistic disgust at Elizabeth's aging female body a more vibrant carnivalesque treatment.[109] The Queen's physique is misshapen, desiring, collapsing, uncontainable, and increasingly resistant to the cosmetics and corsets which Dame Grosslady struggles to apply while rambling in a peculiar idiolect full of scatology and profanity. The grotesque body is constantly thrust before us and seems to figure a kind of base, ribald, popular vigor which the Virgin Queen may seek to suppress in her desire to present a flawless public image, but which in fact she can neither contain nor control, nor do without.

Fo invokes Shakespeare's plays to depict Elizabeth's political insecurity. Elizabeth distractedly paces her chamber and thrusts her sword into the tapestries to expose imagined eavesdroppers and assassins,[110] an uncannily Hamlet-like gesture which the real Elizabeth's godson, Sir John Harington, reported that she habitually performed after the Essex Rebellion.[111] She holds a bundle of papers and rants, "Who is this bastard? Does he write these slanders all on his own? Or maybe he's just an imbecile? I haven't slept a wink all night, trying to work it out . . . Shakespeare. Who is this Shakespeare?" (4). She recognizes herself in the playwright's Henry IV and Richard III, and also especially in Hamlet: "are you trying to tell me it's not an exact portrait of me? [. . .] You'll find my expressions in it . . . my cries of despair . . . my curses . . . things I've shouted here, in this room. How did Shakespeare know all this?" (5).[112] She believes that *Hamlet* is the story of her private life, but with the genders reversed: Ophelia is the Earl of Essex, and Hamlet's ghostly father, seeking revenge, is Anne Boleyn (28). What especially troubles and incenses her are the political implications: "But the thing that really gets up my nose is the way this bastard slanders me, saying I'm bringing the country to ruination. His: 'Something rotten in the State of Denmark' . . . What he means is my sewer, here, in England" (33, authorial ellipses). To illustrate her point, she speaks passages of *Hamlet* with the genders reversed, and Dame Grosslady agrees with her that it is an incitement to revolution. As a dramatist who since the 1950s had faced censorship by the Italian government and the Catholic Church, Fo seems to be satirizing the paranoia of those in authority and at the same time celebrating the power of literature to unnerve and destabilize them. It is notable that he draws most upon *Hamlet,* a revenge tragedy whose depiction of a claustrophobic court full of whisperings, conspiracies, and deceptions lends itself readily to parallels with the devious factional politics many saw as prevalent in centers of government in the 1980s.

Elizabeth finds more and more of herself in Shakespeare and begins to speak spontaneously in Shakespearean or quasi-Shakespearean lines. "In our country," she says, "the quality of justice is now strained, it hangeth balanced from a butcher's hook." Dame Grosslady admires the quotation from Shakespeare, but Elizabeth replies irritably, "It's not Shakespeare's, it's mine [. . .] I dare say it will turn up in one of his pot boilers sooner or later" (43). Again, when Elizabeth uses the phrase "hoist with his own petard," Dame Grosslady applauds it as Shakespeare, but Elizabeth snaps, "It's mine" (43). Shakespeare may have purposefully plagiarized and parodied her, or he may have invaded her mind; either way, he eventually drives her mad, and she descends into a rambling monologue of Shakespearean fragments: "What do I fear? Myself? There's none else by. Elizabeth loves Elizabeth. That is I am I. Is there a murderess here? No. Yes. I am," and so on (91).[113]

This compelling dramatic finale is in part an echo of Benjamin Britten's *Gloriana* (1953), another work which shows an aging Elizabeth at the time of the Essex Rebellion, and which ends with the Queen uttering disjointed quotations from her own famous speeches.[114] In Britten's case, writing amid the disintegration of the British Empire and the postwar uncertainties of the new Elizabethan age, Elizabeth's climactic cadenza of broken quotations may be seen as voicing the sense of fragmentation and loss now evoked by this former icon of national and imperial glory. Fo, however, suggests that he has given Elizabeth Shakespearean quotations just for fun, so that audiences can play spot-the-quote: "The final monologue is constructed like a mosaic, borrowing various phrases from Shakespeare's most famous plays [. . .] so you can amuse yourselves by recognising them . . . I have put in some phrases of my own to link them up . . . just for the pleasure of masking the sources and to fabricate a genuine forgery" (Preface, xvii). His fast-and-loose attitude to quotation and to authenticity is distinctively postmodern, treating history and canonical literature as a lucky dip of good lines to be rummaged through at random, repatterned, and enjoyed. At the same time, however, this may be a strategic disclaimer concealing and facilitating political comment. Elizabeth's monologue may be just a jumble of snatched and broken lines, so often repeated by now as to be comfortably familiar and emptied of meaning. Or, it may be a dramatization of how powerful imaginative writing can haunt and undermine those who assume tyrannical power. Fo's play as a whole may be enjoyed as just an entertainment, a scabrous caricature of Elizabeth and a game of Shakespearean allusion; but at the same time that lightness of touch enables an exploration—potently topical in the 1980s, especially in Britain—of the innate insecurity of those who lay claim to absolute power.

A critic of late twentieth-century historical fiction has found in the genre "a resistance to old certainties about what happened and why; a recognition of the subjectivity, the uncertainty, the multiplicity of 'truths' inherent in any account of past events; and a disjunctive, self-conscious narrative, frequently produced by eccentric and/or multiple narrating voices."[115] This works as a description of the surface of Fo's play but does not accommodate its political content and topicality. A more completely postmodern work, in its avoidance of any kind of message, relevance, or truth, is Robert Nye's novel *The Late Mr Shakespeare* (1998). Pickleherring, the narrator, warns us at an early stage not to trust him: "I only tell you stories about Shakespeare. I only tell you tales which I have heard. You are not required to believe any particular one of them."[116] He is an old man who was once a boy actor and knew Shakespeare, therefore himself personifying a venerable tradition: William Beeston, a source for Aubrey and Rowe, was just such a figure, and so were narrators of many Shakespearean fictions, including Mortimer's *Will Shakespeare*. Pickleherring might look like a direct and authoritative source, as an eyewitness, but he only claims to be a preserver and embellisher of unreliable stories:

> What matters is that it's told tales I am telling you. Tales told me. Twice-told tales. Tales, tales, tales, tales. Here there are Canterbury tales, and old wives' tales. Here there are tales of tubs and of roasted horses. One tale is

good until another's told. All are the tales of every common tongue. Tales, idle tales, fictions.

And if some of my told tales are tall, that's because in the minds of the tellers the late Mr William Shakespeare was a giant. (68)

Pickleherring's multiple tales include several different accounts of Shakespeare's conception, among which we can choose as we please. His parents may have been John and Mary Shakespeare, or Mary Shakespeare and the vicar of Holy Trinity Church, or even John Shakespeare and Elizabeth I. The novel plays games with the reader based on the things we think we know or would like to believe about Shakespeare, including our desire to link him with Elizabeth. Pickleherring lists resemblances between Shakespeare and Elizabeth, then puts to us tantalizingly, "So then, now then, what if Queen Elizabeth was Shakespeare's mother?" (73) He narrates how in 1563 Elizabeth went to Kenilworth to escape from the plague, and at the age of thirty was "a lively piece." She met John Shakespeare in the Forest of Arden, and they bathed together in the warm springs by Tiddington Mill (74–77). Bathing quickly turns into something more energetic:

John Shakespeare has her. The father of William Shakespeare is up her.

"O Mr Spermspear!" cries Queen Elizabeth. "O Mr Shakespunk! Mr Shakespunk! Mr Shakespunk! O Mr Fuckster, O make your donkey go in deeper, my gentleman!"

So John Shakespeare does.

He does what the Queen tells him.

He does Queen Elizabeth thoroughly. (80)

While imagining this scene more explicitly than any predecessor, Nye adroitly works in a joke about the many different versions and spellings of Shakespeare's name in documents, as well as an allusion to Bottom's encounter with Titania. When Pickleherring suggests to a reminiscing John Shakespeare, however, that he encountered the Faerie Queen, he meets with a blankly uncomprehending, endearingly robust, and rather Bottom-like response: "'Elizabeth was no fairy,' he said shortly. 'She was warm as toast'" (83). We are warned that John Shakespeare, the only source for the story, was drunk when he told it and was a habitual fantasist (84). Ultimately, then, Nye proposes that we should simply allow ourselves to be entertained by the multiplicity of stories about Shakespeare's conception and the rest of his life, and that there is no purpose in caring about whether or not they are true. Puzzling over Shakespeare mysteries is understood as an inconclusive and idle pastime, but in Nye's terms that is a reason not to dismiss it but to relish it.

Conservative Postmodernism? *Shakespeare in Love* (1998)

If, as suggested above, historical novels and dramas have always anticipated postmodernism in their self-consciously creative use of the past, this may be even truer of historical films, produced under even greater pressure to achieve commercial success with broad modern audiences. Recent decades have seen much analysis of the freedom and flexibility with which film has used history. Leger Grindon has argued that "history in the cinema is seldom disinterested, but rather constitutes an address to the present."[117] Claire Monk and Amy Sargeant have reminded us that "historical films *are films*—indeed, are an important part of popular cinema—rather than an errant and inevitably flawed species of historical documentation . . . a 'historical' film will often be a work of pure entertainment and pure fiction."[118] Consequently, according to Deborah Cartmell and I. Q. Hunter, recent historical films and fictions are not only "postmodern as academics understand the term—allusive, ironic, knowingly intertextual," but also "firmly in the line of popular culture's playful and opportunistic treatment of history. Films, to the despair of historians, have always taken a 'postmodern' approach to the past, viewing it not as a dull chronicle but as a dynamic resource for exciting stories and poetic, morally uplifting untruths."[119] The relation of historical films to authenticity, then, has always been complex. Representation of a particular period setting must be accurate enough to receive the audience's recognition, but this may rely upon reference to popular and mythologized notions of that period rather than to scholarly historical research. Indeed, the visual appeal of historical films means that they have a special affinity with the postmodern tendency to treat the past as a huge dressing-up box.

Historical film therefore flourished in the late twentieth century and became even more self-conscious about its own story-telling and refashioning of the past. According to Pam Cook, period films of the 1990s, such as Derek Jarman's *Edward II* (1991), Sally Potter's *Orlando* (1993), Jane Campion's *The Piano* (1993), and Shekhar Kapur's *Elizabeth* (1998), were characterized by "travesty, masquerade and pastiche" and "adventures in hybridity."[120] Julianne Pidduck and Andrew Higson have coined the term "post-heritage" for costume films which flaunt their ludic wit, knowingness, and irreverence.[121] Apparent superficiality and triviality, if handled in a self-consciously stylized way, can paradoxically imply intellectual sophistication. Higson elaborates:

> pastiche may to some audiences seem depthless and superficial. But it can also be fun, it can be playful, in the way it both implies a sense of

authenticity yet at the same time acknowledges the conventionality and hybrid quality of the representation: "it's only a story—enjoy it!"[122]

This was the context for the 1998 film *Shakespeare in Love,* in which the filmmakers found a particularly fortunate fit between the hybridity and inauthenticity of historical film and the same qualities in Shakespeare's own works. Pam Cook has argued that "costume drama, with its emphasis on masquerade, is a prime vehicle for exploration of identity, encouraging cross-dressing not only between characters, but metaphorically between characters and spectators, in the sense that the latter can be seen as trying on a variety of roles in the course of the film."[123] Transvestism and transexuality were preoccupations of 1990s films such as *The Crying Game* (1992), *Orlando* (1994) and *Priscilla, Queen of the Desert* (1994).[124] Since cross-dressing and related themes of masquerade and confused identity are also preoccupations of Shakespearean comedy, *Shakespeare in Love* seemed at once historically authentic and modishly of the moment. Cook continues: "costume drama is also notoriously inauthentic, as any costume historian will testify . . . Despite extensive and meticulous period research, anachronisms and geographical transgressions abound—indeed, they are endemic to the genre."[125] Higson has developed her point to describe how postheritage film "enables the anomalous and the perverse to be inserted into the apparently authentic historical location, it enables the past to be mixed with the present, it enables the fantastic to mingle with the realist."[126] All of this, again, sounds strikingly like Shakespeare's own very flexible refashioning of historical source materials. Thus the very inauthenticities of *Shakespeare in Love* imply an impudent but affectionate authenticity to Shakespeare.

The massive success of the film—it had worldwide box-office takings of over $100 million, unprecedented for a British-made costume drama, and was garlanded with awards[127]—may be attributed to this especially shrewd and knowing hybridity. It combined the conventions and cachet of the postmodern British art-house historical film with the funding and gloss of a Hollywood blockbuster. Correspondingly, the casting mingled respected British thespians with big-name U.S. stars. Gwyneth Paltrow, who played the heroine, Viola, especially personified this crossover quality: she had already displayed her accomplished English accent in *Emma* (1996) and *Sliding Doors* (1998), enabling her "to 'pass' in British drama, while remaining Pure Hollywood."[128] The screenplay was a collaboration between Los Angeles–born Marc Norman, whose previous credits included *Cutthroat Island, Waterworld,* and *Oklahoma Crude,* and Tom Stoppard, known for his witty philosophical plays for the London stage, including his archly absurdist supplementation of Shakespeare in *Rosencrantz and Guildenstern Are Dead* (1967).

Norman consulted the scholar Stephen Greenblatt, whom he selected, he said, because he called universities around the United States for names of "the major dudes in Shakespeare studies, and everyone kept mentioning Stephen Greenblatt."[129] He seems to have approached Greenblatt in the hope that he would fill out and verify for him the details of Shakespeare's life, an ironic aim given that Greenblatt was the leading figure of new historicism, a school of criticism which foregrounded representations rather than facts and argued that historical documents were rhetorical artefacts rather than repositories of truth. Adding a further level of irony, however, his discussions with Norman inspired Greenblatt to write a biography of Shakespeare, although biography is a genre dealing in real-life facts and therefore in the 1980s would have seemed inimical to new historicism.[130] Moreover, Greenblatt aimed this biography, *Will in the World* (2004), at a popular audience, and achieved a best-seller. His academic status and scholarly knowledge became commodities to be traded in his encounter with Hollywood, and in return his association with *Shakespeare in Love*, frequently mentioned in interviews promoting *Will in the World*, added a populist sheen to his work which no doubt assisted its commercial success. While Norman as a maker of popular film turned to Greenblatt for academic respectability, Greenblatt emerged from their contact as a "major dude" with a hit book which extended his fame far beyond the academy.

This convergence of high culture with commercial populism was a hallmark of *Shakespeare in Love* itself and formed another kind of homage to Shakespeare. One reviewer described it as "that rare thing, a literate crowd pleaser," which, as Douglas Brode has noted, "puts this film in the same league as [Shakespeare's] own literate, crowd-pleasing plays."[131] The director, John Madden, remarked, "I always felt that it had the power to reach an extraordinarily wide demographic—everyone from groundlings to royalty."[132] His precise use here of the class coordinates of Elizabethan theatre audiences—groundlings at the lowest end, the Queen at the highest—points to the importance of the scene in the film when Shakespeare and Elizabeth finally, after much anticipation, meet and speak face to face, a scene which encapsulates this transgression of class boundaries. They have nearly met twice before. Shakespeare is backstage when *The Two Gentlemen of Verona* is successfully performed at court for Elizabeth, but he is preoccupied with private concerns: writer's block and kissing the alluring Rosaline (Burbage's mistress).[133] Later, he disguises himself as Viola's female chaperone to accompany her to court, where Lord Wessex will present her to the Queen and seek royal consent to their marriage. During her audience Viola enthuses to Elizabeth about Shakespeare's plays: she enjoys having "stories acted for me by a company of fellows," but the Queen retorts, "They are not acted for you, they are acted for me" (93). The two women are rivals in claiming ownership of Shakespeare's plays but are allied in the personal connection which they feel with them. The disguised Will observes Elizabeth from the shadows: "He is watching and listening. He has never seen the Queen so close. He is fascinated" (stage direction, 94). The scene initiates an intuitive bond linking Will, Viola, and Elizabeth and separating them from the oafish Wessex and the crowd of anonymous courtiers. When Elizabeth pushes Wessex into a wager that a play cannot show nature and truth, it is Will, still in drag and apparently unseen in the crowd, who calls out and takes it up, and "Queen Elizabeth is the only person amused" (95). She is also, with her traditional penetrating gaze, the only one to discern the truth that Viola is no virgin bride but "has been plucked" (95)—in fact, of course, by Will. There is a kind of affinity, collusion, and mutual understanding among the three of them. Moreover, in 1998 cinema audiences also saw "Will," the actor Joseph Fiennes, making passionate love to a younger and rather Viola-like version of the Queen in Shekhar Kapur's *Elizabeth,* where he played Robert Dudley.

Will, then, lurks in the shadows of Elizabeth's court disguised as a woman, and, in a neat symmetry, their climactic face-to-face encounter ensues from the androgynous Queen's self-concealment in the shadows of the playhouse. At the end of *Romeo and Juliet,* she emerges to defend the players from arrest for including a real woman in their cast, and once again she is complicit with Viola and Will, benignly condoning the fiction that Viola is a boy pretending to be a girl, since "I do know something of a woman in a man's profession, yes, by God, I do know about that" (148). She judges Will to have won the wager that "a play can show the very truth and nature of love." Fixing him "with a beady eye," she invites him to court at Greenwich to talk with her some more, and to come as himself this time, referring back to his female disguise. Once again her penetrating gaze has seen through an imposture (148–49).

When *Shakespeare in Love* was released some critics remarked upon its echoes of *No Bed for Bacon,* especially the use of a heroine who is in love with Shakespeare and disguises herself as a boy actor. Both works also position Shakespeare for much of the time as an anxious observer and use the conventional scene of Elizabeth watching a Shakespeare play as a front for backstage dramas, tensions, and subterfuges. Even more striking, however, are the resemblances between *Shakespeare in Love* and Sara Hawks Sterling's *Shake-speare's Sweetheart*: not only the infatuated boy-actor heroine, but also the scenes of *Romeo and Juliet* in rehearsal and then in a climactic performance before the Queen, and Elizabeth's astute but discreet penetration of the boy/girl actor's disguise.[134] Perhaps Norman and Stoppard consulted Sterling's novel, or perhaps some standard pieces of general knowledge about Shakespeare and Elizabeth—the prevalence of cross-dressing in Shakespearean comedy, boys playing women on the Elizabethan stage, Elizabeth's exceptional intelligence—produced these coincidentally similar outcomes. Either way, Norman and Stoppard drew upon long-established conventions of Shakespeare-and-Elizabeth mythology, and assumed their audience's amused familiarity with this mythology too.

Indeed, *Shakespeare in Love* is largely a compendium of conventional ingredients. We have witnessed Elizabeth's witty banter with Shakespeare innumerable times before. The film also emulates *No Bed for Bacon* and Shaw's *The Dark Lady of the Sonnets* in showing Shakespeare hastily jotting down the well-turned phrases of others that he overhears, thereby jokily deflating the idea of divine inspiration. Joseph Fiennes seems to have thought that he had a fresh take on Shakespeare in stressing his ordinariness: "I never felt like it was Shakespeare but a guy called Will, and he was a hustler."[135] Yet this view of Shakespeare as chancer and opportunist on the make in Elizabethan England had already been developed by Shaw, Burgess, and Mortimer, as we have seen.

Elizabeth R was based upon painstaking historical research, but *Shakespeare in Love* takes a different approach: despite Norman's hopeful solicitation of Greenblatt's scholarly expertise, it looks less to academia than to myths and previous fictions, and thereby spins fiction upon fiction, airily and playfully. This feels fresh and postmodern, yet to some extent it is a return to the principles of nineteenth-century historical fiction, when a novelist or painter was as likely to be influenced by *Kenilworth* as by historical scholarship. In fact, the film has generated much debate as to its postmodernism or conservatism, and how far it refashions cultural myths ironically or merely reproduces them. Judi Dench's brief award-winning performance as Elizabeth may be seen as postmodern in its allusive qualities, combining elements of Glenda Jackson, Margaret Thatcher, Dench's Queen Victoria in *Mrs Brown* (1997), and Elizabeth II, who is likewise reputed to prefer slapstick to poetry (which makes Dench's Elizabeth I nod off [18]). Higson and others place it in the genre of innovative postheritage films of the 1990s. Renée Pigeon finds it less conservative than Kapur's *Elizabeth* because the Queen's unmarried state is implied to be not a "bitter sacrifice" but a source of autonomy and pleasure preferable to the enforced marriage imposed upon Viola.[136] It is certainly refreshing to see an older Elizabeth who looks her age without being physically repellent. Julianne Pidduck made enthusiastic claims for the radical qualities of both *Shakespeare in Love* and Kapur's *Elizabeth*, as part of a reaction against British heritage films based on works by Jane Austen or E. M. Forster:

> Kapur's and Madden's versions of the English Renaissance bristle with sinister plots and poisonings, religious, political and artistic rivalries,

> audaciously improvised plays and histories not yet written. These two films re-imagine the British past not through mannered conversation and polite realism, but rather through unformed identities, energetic craftsmanship and raw potential . . . they embody the spirit, if not the reality, of Tony Blair's wished-for "Cool Britannia."[137]

She celebrated the liberated sexuality enabled by the Elizabethan setting: "Sex, intrigue, raw physicality and violence distinguish these Elizabethan films from a largely demure British tradition . . . Finally and crucially, in an affront to costume drama's tender sensibilities, the costumes *come off*" (135).

For other critics, however, *Shakespeare in Love* was as disappointing and shallow as Blair's Cool Britannia. Jonathan Romney in *The Guardian* found it merely another conventional exercise in period cinema: "*Shakespeare in Love* is determined to play it safe and please everyone . . . despite all the efforts to puncture the bubble of historical accuracy, this is absolutely mainstream costume romance. Every last codpiece is given the painstaking period look; the muddy streets feel researched to the last wisp of straw . . . What we get is an all-out attempt to dazzle us with English Heritage prestige."[138] Its playful and festive mood may be seen as reductive and trivializing: as Richard Burt has noted, "the most difficult conflicts Elizabeth resolves in *Shakespeare in Love* are whether Viola can go to Virginia and who won a wager over whether a play can truly represent romantic love."[139] There are no decisions to be made here "about sending men to war or executing princes and rebellious aristocrats"; this is the Elizabethan period evacuated of Elizabethan political history and packaged as sheer entertainment, not so very far from the old idea of "merrie England."

As for the Shakespearean and postmodern motif of cross-dressing, the film flirts with transgressive gender relations and sexualities but quickly and emphatically reasserts a conservative heterosexuality. Over the years since the release of the film, there has been much speculation about Joseph Fiennes's sexuality, and he has become something of a gay icon.[140] *Shakespeare in Love* has contributed to this sexually ambiguous reputation: in one scene Viola, still dressed as a boy in doublet, hose, and moustache, reads and is ravished by Will's love sonnet "Shall I compare thee to a summer's day?"; and in another, Will, still believing Viola to be "Thomas Kent," is passionately kissed by her/him.[141] In both cases, however, her (rather unconvincing) disguise is swiftly removed, and her femininity is immediately reinstated and reaffirmed. Will addresses the sonnet to Viola, not Thomas; he is decidedly troubled to be kissed by a boy and is immensely relieved to learn that she is a woman. For Elizabeth Klett, in providing unequivocal answers to questions about Shakespeare's authorship and sexuality, the film reinstates Shakespeare as an "authentic and heteronormative" cultural authority.[142] His triumph is to write a play which is endorsed by the Queen because it shows "the very truth and nature of love"; and this truth-to-life is achieved because it is inspired by Will's real love for a real woman, and because Juliet is played by that real woman herself, acting out her real doomed passion for Romeo/Shakespeare. All of this constitutes a decidedly Romantic and conservative view of the relation between art and life as direct and simple, and of art as good only if it is realist and representational.[143]

Above all, the climactic encounter between Shakespeare and Elizabeth simply plays out once again the myth of their mutual appreciation. "Come to Greenwich," says the Queen, "and we will speak some more" (149). It looks very much as if she will go on to give the poet "many gracious Marks of her Favour," just as she did in Rowe's biography of 1709.[144] This comes at the end of a century which had produced many diverse and sometimes bizarre versions of the double myth of Shakespeare and Elizabeth. They had been bitter antagonists, they had been mother and son, and they had been lovers. Elizabeth had given Shakespeare some of his best lines, or her mind had been disturbingly filled with lines he had written, or she had merged with him to become the secret author of his works. Yet this most widely known and widely enjoyed recent version of their encounter rounded off the century by reverting to the ancient folklore of a meeting of minds between the mighty Queen and the gifted commoner-poet. There was a sense that they were trapped in cliché; Elizabeth might wish to "speak some more" to Shakespeare, but perhaps they were merely going on and on saying much the same things. Yet as their conversation has continued into the twenty-first century, it has taken some unpredictable turns, suggesting that they do indeed have more to say to each other.

EPILOGUE

Shakespeare and Elizabeth in the Twenty-first Century

As they accompany one another into a new millennium, Shakespeare and Elizabeth are as prominent as ever in western culture. The twentieth century ended with the traditions of their double myth reviewed and restated, albeit playfully, in *Shakespeare in Love*, but the opening of the twenty-first century has provided unexpected catalysts to adaptation, mutation, and creative departures from tradition.

Fin de siècle: *Elizabeth Rex* (2000)

Timothy Findley's play *Elizabeth Rex* was produced for the Stratford Shakespeare Festival in Ontario in the millennium year. This dark and self-consciously fin-de-siècle drama reacts against the "heteronormative" version of Shakespeare and Elizabeth in *Shakespeare in Love*. On the eve of Essex's execution, Elizabeth passes the night in a barn with Shakespeare's playing company, who have just performed for her. Fierce debate ensues between the Queen and Ned Lowenscroft, an adult actor of women's parts who is dying of syphilis contracted from a soldier. He is a kind of counterpart to Elizabeth: he enters in makeup and a half-unlaced gown, with syphilitic sores and shedding hair, at once a travesty of the Queen and a true image of her morally and emotionally cankered state.[1] Ned and Will urge Elizabeth to find the woman in herself and pardon Essex; she retorts to Ned, "If you will teach me to be a woman . . . I will teach you how to be a man" (act 1, scene 8, p. 50). They act out parts of *Antony and Cleopatra*, a work-in-progress by Will inspired by Elizabeth and Essex; Cleopatra is played first by Elizabeth, then, more movingly, by Ned (act 2, scene 4, pp. 59–61). In the course of this, Will is drawn to confess his love for the Earl of Southampton (quoting Sonnet 20, about the "master-mistress of my passion"), Ned for his Captain, and Elizabeth for her Robin (act 2, scene 4, pp. 57, 61–62; scene 7, p. 69). Ned and Elizabeth swap clothes and roles, and he redoes her makeup to look more natural: "Too much white, Madam. Too much red. An actor would know better" (act 2, scene 6, pp. 66–67). There is both opposition and affinity between this effeminate man and masculine woman, while Will mediates between them, observing and combining qualities of each.

While Robin Phillips's 1976–77 production of *A Midsummer Night's Dream* for the Stratford Festival had explored Elizabeth's private erotic life in a feminist but entirely heterosexual fashion, now Findley took the excavation of her personal life in a different direction by emphasizing queerness. Shakespeare and Ned as men loving men are mirrored by Elizabeth as a masculine lover of young men. Ned's syphilis has clear topical implications: as a fatal disease contracted by a homosexual man through an act of love, it stands for HIV/AIDS. The interest in same-sex desire, the sense that gender identities may fluctuate, and the exploration of how desire may be inflamed by unpredictable or inappropriate objects, all make the play feel distinctively of its time. As we have seen, in the early twentieth century such themes had emerged in works like Sterling's *Shake-speare's Sweetheart*, Strachey's *Elizabeth and Essex*, and Owen's *The Phoenix and the Dove*, yet these works tended to use implication, metaphor, and other oblique forms of expression. A new explicitness about sexuality was evident in the later twentieth century, in works such as Faye Kellerman's *The Quality of Mercy* (1989), which gave graphic descriptions of how its cross-dressing heroine was bedded by both Elizabeth and Shakespeare. However, Kellerman depicted the lesbian Queen as rapacious and repellent. *Elizabeth Rex* treated the queer desires of its protagonists as neither horrific nor sensational but matter for sympathy and tragedy (though of course it would have been more radical still to represent homosexual characters as not even tragic). It was symptomatic of significant cultural progress in attitudes to homosexuality that the prestigious Stratford Festival chose for its flagship millennium production this play about the queerness of Shakespeare and Elizabeth. *Elizabeth Rex* was a smash hit and won the Governor General's Literary Award for Drama; indeed, Findley himself, who died in 2002, was one of Canada's most respected and garlanded authors.[2]

In an introduction to the play, Findley reveals that behind all this topical, millennial treatment of sexuality may lie a rather traditional and Romantic idea of selfhood: "What emerged, for me, from this barn filled with contradictions and emotional conflicts, was a sense that neither gender nor sexuality, politics nor ambition, are as important as integrity . . . This echoes Polonius's advice in *Hamlet*: 'This above all: to thine own self be true'" (10).[3] It would be disappointing if the central message of this seemingly radical play turned out to be merely a reiteration of the trite proverbial wisdom of Polonius. Yet Findley's comment is in keeping with turn-of-the-century identity politics in that the play explores identity as something that is not fixed and innate but has to be acquired and invented. Being true to oneself may mean casting off origins and discarding an identity imposed by social convention. Integrity in this play is not something to be preserved but something to be discovered, perhaps in surprising places; something to be imagined and created. Thus the sexual ambiguity of Shakespeare and Elizabeth, combined with their shared skill in constructing personae, enabled the double myth to be inventively reshaped to speak to fin-de-siècle concerns.

Elizabeth the Enemy: A Catholic Shakespeare?

Late-twentieth-century works like *Shakespeare in Love* and Nye's *The Late Mr Shakespeare* made it appear that the double myth of Shakespeare and Elizabeth had been taken over by fluidity, plurality, relativism, textual play, and knowing, tongue-in-cheek reiterations of old myths, and that this was the last word on the subject. Yet the new century brought some reaction against postmodernism, with a turn back toward a quest for truth and a renewed interest in religious faith. Scholarship produced a fresh version of Elizabethan history in which Catholicism was a significant part of the landscape, and this in turn produced Shakespeare as Catholic rebel and Elizabeth as the head of a cruel and oppressive regime.

As we have seen, rumors that Shakespeare "died a papist" were in circulation since the late seventeenth century, and his putative Catholicism has been periodically investigated ever since.[4] A new contribution was Ernst Honigmann's *Shakespeare: The "Lost Years"* (1985). Scholars have always been baffled and intrigued by the lack of biographical evidence for Shakespeare between the birth of his twins Hamnet and Judith in Stratford in February 1585 and Robert Greene's attack on him as a young rival playwright, an "upstart crow," in London in 1592.[5] Both Oliver Baker in 1937 and E. K. Chambers in 1944 suggested that Shakespeare might have spent part of the 1580s in Lancashire, still a largely Catholic county, serving in various Catholic households, including Hoghton Tower, where a player named William Shakeshafte was mentioned in a family will of 1581.[6] Honigmann found support for identification of Shakespeare with Shakeshafte in the fact that John Cottam, the schoolmaster in Stratford-upon-Avon from 1579 to 1581, came from a Lancashire recusant family who were connected with the Hoghtons.

Meanwhile, for the past few decades historians such as Christopher Haigh, J. J. Scarisbrick, and Eamon Duffy have reshaped our understanding of the English

Reformation by compiling convincing evidence that Catholicism was deeply rooted in many parts of the English populace and was an enduring cultural presence long after the establishment of the Protestant Church of England in 1559.[7] This has gradually filtered through to Shakespearean studies to encourage the idea of a Catholic Shakespeare, or at least a Shakespeare who came from a strongly Catholic family and community and whose worldview was shaped by the religious persecutions and tensions of the Elizabethan age. Versions of this account of Shakespeare were taken up by Stephen Greenblatt in *Hamlet in Purgatory* (2001) and *Will in the World* (2004) and by the popular historian Michael Wood in his 2003 BBC television series and book *In Search of Shakespeare*. Also in 2003, in Germany, Hildegard Hammerschmidt-Hummel published *William Shakespeare: Seine Zeit, Sein Leben, Sein Werk*, asserting more vehemently "that Shakespeare was a Catholic and that his religion is the key to understanding his life and work."[8] According to Hammerschmidt-Hummel, Shakespeare's adherence to the old faith and his opposition to Elizabeth's Protestant regime explain why half of his plays had to be "suppressed" until the First Folio of 1623, seven years after his death, and why he resisted writing in praise of Elizabeth.[9]

The idea of a Catholic Shakespeare was also forcefully promoted by Richard Wilson in *Secret Shakespeare* (2004), who put forward more evidence of links between Shakespeare's community in Stratford and Lancashire Catholicism and between Shakespeare and notable recusants such as Robert Southwell and John Somerville, a Warwickshire man who in 1583 set out to shoot the Queen.[10] Wilson used selective close reading to find what he claimed were hitherto unnoticed allusions to the Jesuit missions and Catholic martyrdoms of Elizabeth's reign woven throughout the fabric of Shakespeare's works. His principal argument was that Shakespeare's Catholic heritage in a Protestant state accounts for his apparent ability, acclaimed down the centuries, to see issues from several different points of view and to remain essentially enigmatic and unknown behind his texts. For Wilson this was not a Keatsian "negative capability" or a timeless and godlike universality but the product of specific historical and ideological circumstances: he argued that Shakespeare at once adhered to and reacted against a Catholic upbringing, eschewing the evangelical martyrdom of the Jesuits for "a project of freedom of conscience and mutual toleration" and a "*politique* respect for the secrecy of the human heart" (ix). Thus Wilson's reading developed out of new historicism to find a topical historical explanation for Shakespeare's mysterious self-effacement and lack of polemicism.

In particular, Wilson found in Shakespeare's reticence about Elizabeth not the silence of a seer whose timeless wisdom raises him above worldly concerns but the self-protective silence of a shrewd judge of political expediency. Increasingly, indeed, as Wilson's discussion proceeded, he read this as a speaking silence, the critical gesture of a resentful enemy, and ultimately not silence at all but a cover for layers of dissident religious and political meaning. Wilson noted the recurrent themes in Shakespeare's works, from *Titus Andronicus* to *Julius Caesar* to *King Lear*, of tests of loyalty and linked this to the Elizabethan state's "theatre of allegiance," in which Catholics were constantly enforced to make displays of obedience to the Crown or face dire consequences (21). He found encoded and invariably hostile allegorical references to Elizabeth: *Venus and Adonis*, for instance, is a cautionary tale of the futility of martyrdom, where "the whorishness of the 'love-sick Queen' (line 175) towards the helpless victim analogises Elizabeth's exploitation of loyal papists" (126–43). In short, according to Wilson, Shakespeare regarded Elizabeth as "the Queen of torturers" (99), and his feelings toward her rendered him "Shakespeare in hate."[11]

Wilson's book stirred animated debate among fellow academics, but Clare Asquith's *Shadowplay* (2005) brought the idea of Shakespeare as a Catholic dissident to a wider public. Asquith returned to the view of nineteenth-century scholars and authorship theorists that Shakespeare wrote in a code only decipherable by cognoscenti. She believed that such decoding reveals hidden allegorical and topical narratives which declare Shakespeare to have been a leader of the English Catholic resistance. She constructed an extensive glossary of code words, central to which were two antitheses: "the terms 'high' and 'fair,' which always indicate Catholicism, and 'low' and 'dark,' which always suggest Protestantism."[12] Thus, in *A Midsummer Night's Dream* Hermia represents "prudish, fractious" Protestant characteristics, whereas Helena represents Catholic values (33). For Asquith too, then, Shakespeare as a fervent Catholic was inevitably a critic of Elizabeth (though in the middle of his career she believed he reluctantly accepted royal patronage in an attempt to influence Elizabeth). She reproduced the traditional model of Elizabeth as Shakespeare's most perceptive audience and the underlying folklore of direct communication between monarch and commoner, bypassing self-interested politicians: "the Queen took pride in deciphering codes and allegories that defeated her advisers," which created "a pleasing sense of complicity between the canny Queen and the calculating dramatist" (114, 118).

Consequently Asquith found Elizabeth in many of Shakespeare's female characters. Portia in *The Merchant of Venice* is Elizabeth, and her suitors represent Catholic Spain (the Prince of Aragon), European Protestantism (the Prince of Morocco—because of his darkness), and loyal England (Bassanio) (115–16). Olivia in *Twelfth Night* is also Elizabeth, criticized for her resistance to marriage, and suspended "in a quandary" between "the religion formulated by her father and brother" and the pressures of contemporary Catholic and Protestant factions (166–68). However, according to Asquith, as Shakespeare's career went on and his hopes that Elizabeth might be persuaded to alleviate the persecution of Catholics were quashed, he grew in bitterness against her, and this intensified after her death. Thus the evil Queen in *Cymbeline* is a "venomous portrait" of her: "She maintains her power through schemes, potions and herbs; in an image of Elizabeth's paralysing hold on the country, her ultimate plan is to bring about Cymbeline's slow death through poison . . . She is the image of duplicity" (254). Sycorax in *The Tempest* is "another angry caricature of Elizabeth and the blight she inflicted on England," recognizable as such because she is "connected with the moon, with wicked charms and with Algiers, a country just as notorious as sixteenth-century England for piracy" (267).

This last claim, about Algiers as England, exemplifies one of the chief weaknesses of Asquith's book: her "decodings" often rely upon supposed connections which seem either forced or coincidental or both. They also produce readings which are often far removed from, or even opposed to, most experiences of watching or reading each work. Thus, bizarrely, the vivacious and witty Maria in *Twelfth Night,* consort and accomplice of the *bon viveur* Sir Toby Belch, is supposed to be Mary Tudor (169); and even more bizarrely, in *Romeo and Juliet* the nurse's long rambling speech about Juliet's toddlerhood (1.3.1–59), full of bawdy jokes, is there not to establish her character as an affectionate, earthy purveyor of old wives' tales but, through various scattered details, to remind listeners of the martyrdom of the Jesuit Edmund Campion some fifteen years earlier (75–76). Such strained and unpersuasive interpretations are further undermined by Asquith's lack of knowledge of Shakespeare's sources and of Elizabethan Catholic literature and her poor understanding of Elizabethan literature in general, most of which she assumes is dull, arcane, and unreadable unless decoded by her scheme. She is right that Elizabethans loved puns, devices, and riddles, but her extension of this to read all texts as code makes her sound uncannily like Delia Bacon and her anti-Stratfordian disciples, and, as in their cases, enables Asquith to find whatever meanings she wants to find.

Many of Wilson's local readings also seem overstrained, as when he suggests that the flower in *A Midsummer Night's Dream* on which Cupid's arrow falls, marking it with "love's wound" (2.1.167), "could well signify the stigmata of England's recusant community, penalised for acquiescing in a deluded international conspiracy" (145); or that in *As You Like It,* "the lioness, 'couching, head on ground, with catlike watch' to wake the wretch lying beneath an 'old oak, whose boughs were mossed with age / And high top bald with dry antiquity' [4.3.103–17], looks very like a symbol of Elizabeth, hungrily waiting for the Jesuit "guild" to sting Catholics out of their torpor beneath a senile and unprotecting Rome" (119). Shakespeare's supposed Catholicism remains unproven, and the evidence is fragmentary: the Catholic spiritual testament supposedly by Shakespeare's father is lost and may have been a forgery anyway; the William Shakeshafte named in the Lancashire Catholic will may well have been an entirely different person from William Shakespeare. In an authoritative article of 2007, Peter Davidson and Thomas McCoog, S. J., both highly respected scholars of Elizabethan recusant culture, declared that "In essence, Wilson deftly transformed antiquarian speculation into uncontested fact without offering any new evidence whatsoever. Historical conjectures progressed from 'it is possible that' or 'may have' through 'could have' to 'must have.'"[13] Yet it is true that the Catholic culture of Elizabethan England, and its significance as a context for Shakespeare's works, has not until recently received due attention. It is also the case, despite centuries of mythology in which Shakespeare and Elizabeth are mutual admirers, that his works do display an unusual reticence about Elizabeth, and that the few passages of apparent panegyric which they contain, as in *A Midsummer Night's Dream*, can be read as veiled criticism.[14] Much work remains to be done, and will no doubt appear. (As I write, a book on Shakespeare and religion by Alison Shell, another notable scholar of Catholic culture in the English Renaissance, is eagerly awaited.)

Asquith's book received damning reviews from eminent academics such as Anne Barton and David Womersley.[15] They justly criticized the standards of her scholarship and argument, yet in her indignant replies, Asquith accused Womersley of being antireligious and Barton of a lack of interest "in what was once meant by English Catholicism."[16] Less academic reviewers gave the book favorable notices in a number of newspapers in both the United States (where it was first published) and the United Kingdom, and Asquith's "discovery" of Shakespeare's Catholic code was even reported as a news item.[17] It seems to have struck a chord with general readers: on Amazon's U.S. and U.K. webpages enthusiastic customer responses were posted, such as "This is less a book than a revelation. It hardly seems possible that Shakespeare's plays could be even more brilliant and more penetrating then they are already revealed to be. But that is exactly the case," and "This book all but obsoletes almost all that has ever been written on Shakespeare. Buy, read, enjoy!."[18] On the website which published Womersley's negative review, admirers of Asquith sprang to her defense.[19]

Why has the idea of a Catholic, dissident Shakespeare attracted such interest? For Wilson, it is a necessary corrective to a combined "media myth" and "academic illusion . . . of the playwright as Anglican spokesman." He asserts that "the construction of a Shakespeare in love with Protestant empire serves the ideological function of annexing the plays to the dominant Anglo-Saxon discourses of populism and individualism, and so to globalisation and American hegemony" (3). As we have seen in the present book, it is true that Shakespeare and Elizabeth and the supposed bond between them were extensively used to promote the British imperial project. Now that Britain feels uncomfortable with its imperial past and wishes to distance itself from it, a dissident Shakespeare and a tyrannical Elizabeth serve a current desire to deconstruct old national certainties and expose them as ideological constructs. A Catholic Shakespeare also appeals because he looks excitingly fresh and radical, not a pillar of the establishment but an Elizabethan subversive. At the same time he has an aura of integrity, as a believer who stayed loyal to an old faith, and this has appeal as an antidote to the relativism, playfulness, and irresponsibility of postmodernism.

Wilson further suggests that Shakespeare as a member of a nation violently divided by religious conflict particularly speaks to us in the light of recent events: "We know so much more about religious violence than critics before 11 September 2001" (7). His assertion that we are living through a "return of fundamentalism" (ibid.) must command assent as we observe the influence of conservative Christianity in the United States and Muslim extremism worldwide. As we have seen, for the nineteenth and twentieth centuries, social class was a prominent issue in representations of Shakespeare and Elizabeth: their encounter either affirmed social unity across classes or, later, dramatized class tension. Now that we live in an increasingly classless society, religion may be taking the place of class as a charged and emotive issue in versions of their double myth. Some of the most visible social divisions today are not between those of different class but between those with religious conviction and those without, and between those of different faiths. Interest in a Catholic Shakespeare (and anti-Catholic Elizabeth) reflects the complex and evolving resurgence of religion in the modern world.

At a time when, once again, some believers are willing to die and kill in the name of their faith, the religious persecutions and martyrdoms of the sixteenth century, and the difficult coexistence of different faith communities in England, seem freshly relevant. The interest in a Catholic Shakespeare may also bespeak a general revival of interest in spirituality, if not, on the whole, in institutional Christianity (although the size and vitality of the Catholic community in modern Britain, of which I am myself a member, should not be underestimated). Asquith, in an interview with the U.S.-based Catholic website *Godspy,* said her book is about England's identity. At a time when England is redefining itself in relation to a devolved Scotland and an expanded European Union, a revisionist account of the place of Catholicism in England's history and culture "*must* produce a change in the way we look at our past, and the way we look at ourselves, in England." She spoke of Shakespeare as expressing a message for England about this identity in his hidden code, "and, indeed, for America; which is, what do you do with spirituality? How does it relate to politics?."[20] For Asquith, then, her own Catholic faith apparently leads her to hope that rediscovering spirituality in Shakespeare, an iconic and internationally revered author, might be a way of reviving spirituality in the modern world.

Religion seems to be coming to the fore, then, as a contentious issue, as class difference becomes less important. The pursuit of a classless society has also involved a democratization of culture in which the authority of self-styled intellectuals and academic experts is open to challenge. Part of the appeal of *Shadowplay* undoubtedly lay in the popular fascination with conspiracies and secret codes, which has been given added fuel in recent years by the success of Dan Brown's novel *The Da Vinci Code* (2003). Like anti-Stratfordian hypotheses, *Shadowplay* has a strong anti-establishment appeal. Not only does it posit a Shakespeare who was resistant to the establishment of his time but its author is herself not a professional academic but an independent scholar who, according to the blurb on her book jacket, "lives in Somerset with her husband and five children."[21] The more scholars like David Womersley, an Oxford professor, criticized her book, the more nonacademic readers, attracted by a code which made Shakespeare's plays newly comprehensible to them, leapt to her defense and accused him and his like of pomposity and narrow-mindedness.

Some responses from the weblog of the American novelist and critic Jane Smiley may help to account for the success of *Shadowplay*. Smiley described how she had gone through life without questioning the traditional view of Shakespeare as a godlike genius "not locatable in any particular place or time." She was startled, therefore, by Asquith's account of the horrors of Elizabethan persecution of Catholics and by the conclusion that "the specific circumstances of the reigns of Elizabeth I and James I were too dramatic and dangerous, too fraught with meaning, for Shakespeare or any writer to have been able to detach himself from them." This, she said, had a profound effect upon her: "I thought for days about *Shadowplay* after I read it. Something about the construction I had made of art itself (and therefore of my own life) was smashed. Not only could you not transcend your circumstances, your very deepest views and feelings could be misrepresented for centuries."[22] Academics since the rise of new historicism in the 1980s have been familiar with the ideas that Shakespeare was shaped by his times, that his works are full of political resonances, that these are not always evident on the surface of his works, and that he was a critic rather than a loyal flatterer of Queen Elizabeth; indeed, these have become critical orthodoxies. Yet to a well-read and respected novelist, in 2006, these were new and revelatory concepts. Asquith's claims for a Catholic Shakespeare are debatable, and her assertion of a hidden code in his plays is highly dubious, but the attention she gained by means of such sensationalism succeeded in communicating to a general readership an idea of Shakespeare as historicized and political which had not, by the end of the twentieth century, fully broken through from the academy to wider cultural consciousness—as we can see from the reiteration in *Shakespeare in Love* of the old myth of Shakespeare and Elizabeth as mutual admirers.

Thus the idea has taken hold of Shakespeare and Elizabeth not as gracious patron and loyal poet but as antagonists: she the presiding figure of a repressive and brutal regime, relying upon a sinister network of informants and torturers; he a resentful and discreetly critical subject, or perhaps even a leading and ardent figure in the Catholic resistance. It is an idea which seems likely to provoke further debate and to have further impact in popular culture.

Historical Fiction Meets Science Fiction: Shakespeare and Elizabeth Meet Doctor Who (2007)

The appeal of Wilson's and Asquith's books seems to lie in their claims to tell the hidden truth about Shakespeare and to offer a Shakespeare who was true to a cause. This assertion of truth is a reaction against postmodernism, but postmodernism is not over, and continues to create a climate congenial to historical fiction. As the genre flourishes and evolves, its preoccupation with Shakespeare and Elizabeth is, if anything, increasing. In 2005 Sarah L. Johnson surveyed historical novels published recently or available in U.S. public libraries and found some forty or more based on Elizabeth or Shakespeare or both. The genre has widened far beyond the model established by Scott: traditional historical novels form just one among thirteen subgenres listed by Johnson, alongside romantic historical novels and historical romances, historical mysteries, time-slip novels, "alternate history," historical fantasy, and more.[23] Johnson notes a tendency toward "genre blending" as boundaries are increasingly crossed between historical fiction and other types of "genre fiction," such as detective fiction, science fiction, and fantasy (xviii). Hybridity is the current trend and is producing a surge of creativity.

As early as 1954 the leading science-fiction author Isaac Asimov wrote a short story called "The Immortal Bard," in which Shakespeare traveled in time to the present, only to be humiliated by failing a university course on his own works. More recent authors have been interested less in bringing Shakespeare to the present than in transporting different kinds of genre fiction to the Elizabethan past. Patricia Finney's 1992 spy thriller *Firedrake's Eye,* set in 1583, featured a plot against the Queen and a Shakespearean wise madman named Tom O'Bedlam; it had two sequels, *Unicorn's Blood* (1998) and *Gloriana's Torch* (2003). Another hybrid genre is Elizabethan detective fiction: Shakespeare turns amateur sleuth in the *Shakespeare and Smythe* series by Simon Hawke, beginning with *A Mystery of Errors* (2000), and Elizabeth solves crimes in the Queen Elizabeth Mysteries by Karen Harper. At time of writing the latter series runs to eight volumes, beginning with *The Poyson Garden* (1999), in which Princess Elizabeth cross-dresses like a Shakespearean boy heroine to investigate a series of poisonings. A currently thriving sub-subgenre is Elizabethan detective fiction for children, including the Lady Grace Mysteries—which began in 2004, with the titles *Assassin, Betrayal, Conspiracy,* and so on, heading on through the alphabet and written by a team of authors—and Mary Hooper's excellent *At the House of the Magician* (2007).

Fantasy authors for adults have imagined alternative versions of history. Harry Turtledove's *Ruled Britannia* (2002) proposes an England conquered by the Spanish Armada. Elizabeth is a prisoner in the Tower of London, but her supporters plot rebellion, to be fomented by a patriotic new play about Boudica by—who else?—Shakespeare. Even more inventive is Sarah A. Hoyt's *Shakespearean Fantasy Trilogy,* commencing with *All Night Awake* (2002), in which a hermaphroditic elf called Quicksilver is Shakespeare's lover and helps him when the treacherous Marlowe implicates him in a conspiracy against the Queen. To sum up, in current popular fiction the Elizabethan period is hot. The mingling of genres and creative approach to history are producing original and surprising versions of Shakespeare and Elizabeth and keeping them very much alive in popular culture.

While this rule-breaking and innovation have been going on in printed fiction, in 2005 the BBC revived its much-loved science fiction television series *Doctor Who,* which originally ran from 1963 to 1989. The show is a national institution in Britain and on its return could rely upon nostalgic affection among its original viewers while seeking to secure a new young audience. In the hands of executive producer Russell T. Davies and his team of writers, the new *Doctor Who* has many postmodern qualities, including self-aware jokes about the program's own history and devoted fan base, the planting of coded puzzles running between episodes, references to popular culture, and a general wit, panache, and lightness of touch. As most readers will be aware, the Doctor travels in space and time, not only to the future, but also to the past: in the 2005 season he encountered Charles Dickens and went back to the Second World War; in 2006 he met Queen Victoria and Madame de Pompadour and saved the world during the coronation of Elizabeth II. In the 2007 season it was surprising not that he met Shakespeare and Elizabeth I but that it had apparently taken him so long.

In fact, the series' archives reveal that this was not their first encounter. In the 1965 six-episode story "The Chase," the Doctor had a "time television" on which he saw Elizabeth giving Shakespeare the idea for *Hamlet.* Moreover, the cultured Doctor has often quoted Shakespeare over the years, especially *Hamlet,* and has even claimed to have helped him write it.[24] However, in 2007 "The Shakespeare Code," written by Gareth Roberts, was the first whole episode with this setting and theme. The title, an obvious reference to *The Da Vinci Code,* implied a promise to solve a historical mystery. It was filmed on location at the rebuilt Globe Theatre on the south bank of the Thames, itself a commercial artefact aspiring to a kind of time travel as it aims to recreate the experience of watching a Shakespeare play in its original setting. The Doctor takes his new traveling companion, Martha Jones, on a tourist trip through time to London in 1599, to see "popular entertainment for the masses" at the playhouse, a description by the Doctor which aligns Shakespeare's works in their period with *Doctor Who* in the present.

The excitement of the Doctor and Martha at meeting Shakespeare in person is dissipated by first appearances—he is unprepossessingly vulgar, arrogant, and libidinous—but on further acquaintance his intelligence and his skill with words become apparent. It is because of his literary genius that he has been chosen by three witches, in fact aliens called Carrionites, to be their tool in a plan to conquer the universe. They have temporarily taken over his mind to insert an incantation into the script of his latest play which, when performed, will turn the Globe into an "energy converter" and bring hordes of fellow Carrionites flocking to conquer the Earth. It is with his gift of words, again, that he defeats them, uttering an improvised counterincantation, urged on by the Doctor and completed by a timely quotation from *Harry Potter* by Martha. Along the way, several mysteries of Shakespeare's career are solved: the play taken over by the Carrionites and then destroyed in their defeat is *Love's Labours Won,* which explains why this play is referred to in a 1598 list of Shakespeare's works but has never come to light; and Martha, who is black, is the Dark Lady who inspires the Sonnets.

This cheerfully preposterous plot is constructed upon a framework of fairly thorough knowledge of both Shakespearean biography and Shakespearean myth. *Shakespeare in Love* addressed an adult audience with knowing jokes about traditional representations of Shakespeare and Elizabethan England. "The Shakespeare Code" does some of this too, but is also mindful of the large proportion of its audience who are young and still in the process of encountering Shakespeare in education. It aims to entertain them with similarly knowing jokes but plays less fast and loose with documented historical facts than *Shakespeare in Love* does: Shakespeare's works are placed in roughly the right sequence, for instance, and there is reference to the death of his son in 1596. Indeed, one of the main qualities of the episode is the way in which it plays wittily with the different levels of knowledge in its audience. The Doctor is an expert, citing quotations, dates, and facts to reassure Shakespeare nerds that scholarship is being respected, and to reassure grown-ups watching with their children that the program is complementing, not contradicting, information about Shakespeare disseminated at school. Martha's knowledge, meanwhile, is more shaky, giving her the opportunity to ask lots of questions on behalf of the viewer. She is the on-screen representative of both the adult who only vaguely remembers their contact with Shakespeare at school and the child who is still in the midst of that classroom contact. Overall, the program takes a line toward its younger viewers which is responsible but never solemn or didactic, presenting Shakespeare as important but fun.

The time-travel conceit enables particular play with the fact that the Doctor, Martha, and viewers of all ages all know more about Shakespeare's career than he does, since he is only part-way into it. Martha tells him, "You've written about witches," but Shakespeare looks baffled, and the Doctor cautions her under his breath "Not quite yet." The script recycles the joke from Shaw's *Dark Lady, No Bed for Bacon,* and *Shakespeare in Love* that Shakespeare gets his best lines from others: the Doctor feeds him "All the world's a stage," "The play's the thing," and more, with Shakespeare repeatedly musing, "I might use that." However, the significant difference here, of course, is that these are not spontaneous remarks, but quotations by the Doctor from Shakespeare's works; it is Shakespeare's own published and famous lines that he is being fed from the future. Time loops vertiginously and collapses inward: while in these moments it fleetingly seems as if Shakespeare is stealing ideas from the Doctor, in fact he is stealing only from his future self (a point underlined when he takes a fancy to a Dylan Thomas line quoted by the Doctor, and the Doctor warns him off). Meanwhile the viewer's position of hindsight from the present gives a pleasurable feeling of advantage over the great Shakespeare himself.

As part of this game with history, the episode also teases us with the possibility of a visit to the playhouse by Elizabeth, recognizing that some viewers will expect this as part of the Shakespearean package, while others who have done their homework will not. Near the beginning of the episode we see a regal lady sitting alone in a box watching the play, but this turns out to be one of the Carrionites.

Later, Shakespeare gives directions to an actor for a rehearsal, telling him, "You never know, the Queen might turn up," but muttering resentfully to himself, "As if. She never does." Finally, after the spectacular appearance of the Carrionite hordes as a whirling and blazing spiral of witches rising from the playhouse, followed by their equally spectacular mass expulsion, Elizabeth turns up, having heard all the talk of the amazing pyrotechnics and commanding a repeat performance. She is Elizabeth in her aged, hard-faced, stiffly-costumed mode. Shakespeare and the Doctor are both equally delighted to see her, but this quickly turns to dismay and alarm on the Doctor's part when she exclaims, "The Doctor! My sworn enemy! Off with his head!," blurring clichéd caricature of Elizabeth's lethal temper with Lewis Carroll's Red Queen. As they run for their lives, Martha asks the Doctor what he has done to upset her, but he has no idea: "Can't wait to find out! That's something to look forward to!"—something, of course, for audiences to look forward to as well.

"The Shakespeare Code" was clearly influenced by *Shakespeare in Love,* a film which many adult viewers, though few children, would have seen and remembered. At the same time, it is a descendant of the books for children discussed in chapter 6, like the Edwardian histories of England and the Ladybird *Story of the First Queen Elizabeth,* in its effort to convey to a young audience that Shakespeare and Elizabethan England matter, and that they are engaging and exciting. It is relatively traditional in its assertion of Shakespeare's genius, its deference to historical fact, and its continuation of the long-standing compulsion to fill in the gaps in Shakespeare's biography. However, it adds to this a populist, postmodern vivacity, and a witty exploitation of the particular opportunities of time travel to play games with what we know, or think we know, or ought to know, about Shakespeare and Elizabeth. It was also a distinctively new treatment of the double myth in that for the first time the Globe playhouse became a portal in time and space through which psychic energy surged and extraterrestrial beings swarmed. It was a new experience for Shakespeare and Elizabeth to encounter not just each other but time travelers, hostile aliens, and the pseudotechnical jargon of science fiction.

What Next? Imagining New Meetings for Shakespeare and Elizabeth

I began this book by suggesting that the principal ingredients in the enduring myth of Shakespeare and Elizabeth were gender and sexuality, class, and national identity. These issues look rather different now than they did in earlier periods. As women have assumed a more public role, Elizabeth I has seemed increasingly relevant and heroic rather than disturbingly unfeminine, and this has shifted the balance in her iconographic pairing with Shakespeare; she is no longer just an admiring accessory to the Bard but a domineering presence. Moreover, as alternative sexualities become more widely accepted, Shakespeare and Elizabeth have been coupled not in order to regularize their sexual reputations, as in the eighteenth and nineteenth centuries, but in order to exploit and explore their queerness. Meanwhile class has been overtaken as a socially divisive issue by religion, as seen in the controversial idea of a Catholic Shakespeare. Finally, as the British seek to question and leave behind much of the iconography of their imperial past, America has assumed a global position of cultural imperialism and has disseminated the double myth of Shakespeare and Elizabeth as a commodity in the entertainment industry. Some trends in the ongoing development of the double myth are contradictory: postmodernism has subjected the past to an irreverent and ironic gaze and does not yet seem to be exhausted, yet at the same time a desire for authenticity in depictions of the past has never disappeared and may even be undergoing a resurgence. It is unpredictable how, or whether, this tension will resolve itself.

Interest in Elizabeth as a woman in a man's world shows no sign of abating, as shown by the recent screen biographies starring Cate Blanchett, Helen Mirren, and Anne-Marie Duff.[25] These have emphasized Elizabeth's womanly passions for Leicester and Essex and the question of her virginity; consequently, they have not had room for Shakespeare. Nevertheless, interest in Elizabeth's sexual ambiguity seems likely to continue, as does interest in Shakespeare's homosexuality or bisexuality, and this may well continue to bring them together: when combined, as in Findley's *Elizabeth Rex*, there are opportunities for comparisons and contrasts which accentuate their different forms of sexual subversiveness. More gender bending seems likely then, and also more genre bending. We can expect further creative fusions of popular genres, and the fictional treatment of history with increasing freedom and inventiveness. In scholarship, religion will almost certainly continue to be an issue: much work is being done on the significant presence of Catholicism in English Renaissance culture, a presence suppressed until recently in most accounts of the period, and though Shakespeare's Catholicism will probably never be proved or disproved, this shifting understanding of his cultural context is bound to reflect upon both him and Elizabeth. At time of writing, Hammerschmidt-Hummel's biography of a Catholic Shakespeare has been recently published in English,[26] and it seems likely that the combined impetus of this book with Wilson's and Asquith's will cause the intriguing figure of Shakespeare as Catholic rebel to break through into popular fiction; after all, he offers rich opportunities for plots involving secret conspiracies, sinister enmities, and heroic dedication to an oppressed cause.

As well as continuing generic hybridity, cultural fusions are likely to play a part in future representations of Shakespeare and Elizabeth. This book has emphasized the importance of the double myth for Anglophone culture, and this culture extends, of course, in differing degree to many of the nations which were formerly part of the British Empire, where Shakespeare's works and Elizabethan history were part of the colonial educational syllabus. We have considered two recent examples of the Shakespeare-and-Elizabeth myth in Canada (Phillips's *Midsummer Night's Dream* and Findley's *Elizabeth Rex*). I also indicated in chapter 2 that Shakespeare study, performance, and adaptation have a long and rich history in India. Recent years have brought a two-part film biography of Elizabeth I directed by an Indian, Shekhar Kapur (1998, 2007) and the performance in Indian and British towns and cities (including Stratford-upon-Avon) of an extremely successful and exciting production of *A Midsummer Night's Dream* which featured a South Asian cast speaking a number of different languages of the Indian subcontinent (including English).[27] Just as we have seen a Bollywood *Pride and Prejudice* (*Bride and Prejudice*, dir. Gurinder Chada, 2004), there are surely abundant possibilities to reimagine Shakespeare and Elizabeth from postcolonial angles and cast a different light upon their double myth.

While much changes, some things remain the same. The National Curriculum for British schools has engendered fierce debate since it was introduced by Margaret Thatcher's government in 1988, with periodic attempts to make it reflect the multiculturalism of modern Britain countered by opposing efforts to make it induct students of all ethnic backgrounds into a British cultural identity. Through all of this, Shakespeare and Elizabeth have remained secure on the syllabus; in fact, if anything, children are doing more Shakespeare at earlier ages than ever before. Such teaching tends not to emphasize gender bending or the Bard's secret Catholicism; instead, it mostly asserts the idea that Shakespeare speaks to us across the centuries and expresses timeless truths, while also drawing upon the period color of the Elizabethan age and Elizabeth's personal glamor in her lavishly ornamented costumes. Carolyn Steedman has written eloquently of the appeal of conservative versions of history for schoolchildren and of the difficulty of replacing history as a narrative of great rulers and conquests with the history of ordinary people. An eight-year-old child will always, she suggests, choose to trace a picture of a sixteenth-century queen rather than, say, a handloom weaver because of "the desire for pretty things—clothes and power." Traditional heroic history offers the pleasures of fairytale, psychodrama, and the family romance: "the bravery of kings, great queens weeping, the world narrowed to an island, the figures on the stage moved by incomprehensible yet easily labelled motives—greed, wickedness, folly"—much the same pleasures, in fact, as are offered by a Shakespeare play.[28] For these reasons and more, Elizabeth I appears to remain securely installed in the classroom, and Shakespeare even more so, not only in Britain but also in other English-speaking nations, as the accepted pinnacle of literary achievement in English. Arguably, we are obliged to continue to offer Shakespeare and Elizabeth to our children, in order to make them fluent in our shared cultural language and equip them with what we call "general knowledge." While we do so, while everyone recognizes Shakespeare and Elizabeth and shares at least a little knowledge about them, they will continue to be prominent figures in popular culture as well as the heritage industry and the academy. No doubt our children will fashion their own versions of them which we cannot yet imagine, but it seems certain that they will want to continue inventing meetings between them.

This book has been mainly about the indeterminacy and mobility of the past. The future, of course, is even harder to determine. But all the evidence suggests that Shakespeare and Elizabeth will continue to be useful to us, enabling us to articulate our relationships with history, heritage, and culture. They have proved themselves able to evolve with the times and adapt to shifting concerns. We can be confident that Shakespeare and Elizabeth will continue to meet, sometimes repeating old conversations, sometimes starting new and unexpected ones, for some time to come.

NOTES

INTRODUCTION

1 Peach, *First Queen Elizabeth*, 44–45. I am grateful to Gwynneth Knowles for the generous gift of this book.
2 See ch. 4 below for a full account of these divergent readings.
3 Rowe, "Life of Shakespear," viii.
4 Ryan, *Dramatic Table Talk*, 2:156–57.
5 Jones, *In Burleigh's Days*, 230.
6 See Jan Kott's enormously influential *Shakespeare Our Contemporary* (1965).
7 Norman and Stoppard, *Shakespeare in Love*, 149.
8 Schoenbaum, *Shakespeare's Lives*; Taylor, *Reinventing Shakespeare*; Dobson and Watson, *England's Elizabeth*; Walker, *The Elizabeth Icon*. On Shakespeare, see also Hawkes, *That Shakespeherian Rag*; Dobson, *Making of the National Poet*; O'Sullivan, *Shakespeare's Other Lives*; Hodgdon, *The Shakespeare Trade*; Gross, *After Shakespeare*; and Orgel, *Imagining Shakespeare*. For more examples see Taylor, *Reinventing Shakespeare*, 372. On Elizabeth, see also Ziegler, *Elizabeth I Then and Now*.
9 Hackett, *Virgin Mother, Maiden Queen*; Hackett, "Historiographical Review"; Montrose, "Spenser and the Elizabethan Political Imaginary."
10 See Levin, "All the Queen's Children."
11 Nietzsche, *Use and Abuse of History*, quoted in Rozett, *Constructing a World*, 16.
12 Schoenbaum, *Compact Documentary Life*, 183.
13 His mother was Mary Boleyn, who was Henry VIII's mistress before his liaison with her sister Anne.
14 Chambers, *The Elizabethan Stage*, 4:75–130.
15 Gurr, *Shakespeare Company, 1594–1642*, 167–68.
16 Gurr, *Shakespearean Stage*, 23–24, 71.
17 Gurr, *Shakespearean Stage*, 164; Chambers, *Elizabethan Stage*, 1:216.
18 Chambers, *Elizabethan Stage*, 1:226–28. See Hotson, *First Night of "Twelfth Night,"* illustration facing 136, for a reconstruction of the Great Hall of Whitehall Palace as it might have looked for a performance before the Queen.

19 Schoenbaum, *Compact Documentary Life*, 249; Kernan, *Shakespeare, the King's Playwright*, 203; Kay, *Shakespeare: His Life, Work, and Era*, 241; Chambers, *Elizabethan Stage*, 4:75–130.

20 Gurr, *Shakespeare Company*, 302–4; Kernan, *King's Playwright*, 203–9; Cunningham, *Accounts of the Revels at Court*, 203–5, 210; Duncan-Jones, *Ungentle Shakespeare*, 170–71.

21 Greg, *Bibliography of the English Printed Drama*, 245, no. 150; 298, no. 187; Shakespeare, *Love's Labour's Lost*, ed. Woudhuysen, 74–75, 303–4. On *The Merry Wives of Windsor* and Elizabeth, see ch.1 below.

22 Lyly, *Complete Works*, ed. Bond, 1:25, 31, 35, 64–65, 70–71.

23 Spenser, *Poetical Works*, xxviii–xxix.

24 Duncan-Jones, *Ungentle Shakespeare*, 119.

25 *Norton Shakespeare*, 3356.

26 Jonson, *Every Man in his Humour*, xv; Duncan-Jones, *Ungentle Shakespeare*, 119, 177–78.

27 Gurr, *Playgoing in Shakespeare's London*, 61, 203.

28 *Calendar of State Papers Domestic 1601–1603*, 136. See also Chambers, *Elizabethan Stage*, 2:48 n. 5; Chambers, *William Shakespeare*, 2:327. Contractions have been expanded.

29 Compare, for instance, John Chamberlain to Dudley Carleton, June 24, 1600: the Queen was present at a wedding at Lady Russell's house after which "there was a masque of eight maids of honour and other gentlewomen, in the name of the Muses who came to seek one of their fellows." *Calendar of State Papers Domestic 1598–1601*, 445.

30 Compare John Chamberlain to Sir Ralph Winwood, Jan. 17, 1603: "The Court has flourished more than ordinary this Christmas . . . there has been golden play, and Mr. Secretary lost 600*l*. in one night, chiefly to Edw. Stanley and Sir John Lee." *Calendar of State Papers Domestic 1601–1603*, 283.

31 Picard, *Elizabeth's London*, xxii.

32 Ibid., 219.

33 Hentzner, *Journey into England*, 41–42.

34 Neale, *Queen Elizabeth*, 216.

35 Schoenbaum, *Compact Documentary Life*, 106; Eagle and Carnell, *Oxford Literary Guide*, 56.

36 Hotson, *First Night of "Twelfth Night*;" Shapiro, *1599*, 39–41, 85–87. See ch.4 below.

37 Rowse, *William Shakespeare*, 442.

38 Shakespeare and Fletcher, *King Henry VIII*, ed. McMullan.

39 Chettle, *Englandes Mourning Garment*, B3r.

40 Meres, *Palladis Tamia*, quoted in *Norton Shakespeare*, 3324.

41 E.g., Halliwell in ch. 2 below.

42 E.g., R. Wilson, *Secret Shakespeare*, 294–95.

43 Jonson, "To the memory of my beloved, the Author, Mr. William Shakespeare: and what he hath left us," in *Norton Shakespeare*, 3351–52.

44 Barroll, "A New History," 441–64. I am grateful to Kate McLuskie, Director of the Shakespeare Institute, Stratford-upon-Avon, for discussing this with me.

45 Jonson, "Conversations with Drummond," 470; Neale, *Queen Elizabeth*, 393.

46 E.g., Mosse, *Nationalism and Sexuality*; Parker et al., *Nationalisms and Sexualities*; Meyer, *Gender Ironies of Nationalism.*

47 Dobson, "Bowdler and Britannia," 141–43.

48 Schoenbaum, *Shakespeare: Globe and World*, 95.

49 Elizabeth I, *Collected Works,* 170, speech of Mar. 15, 1576; 188, speech of Nov. 12, 1586; 97, speech of Nov. 5, 1566.

50 Barton, "King Disguised," 97.

51 Renan, "Qu'est-ce qu'une nation?" quoted in Hobsbawm, *Nations and Nationalism since 1780,* 12. See also Hastings, *Construction of Nationhood,* 7.

52 Hastings, *Construction of Nationhood,* 2–3.

53 See Sturgess, *Shakespeare and the American Nation,* esp. 197.

54 Jenkins, *Heroines of History,* 322, quoted in Dobson and Watson, *England's Elizabeth,* 272.

55 Markoe, "The Tragic Genius of Shakspeare; an Ode," in *Miscellaneous Poems* (Philadelphia, 1787), quoted in Dobson, *Making of the National Poet,* 230.

56 Wallace, "Shakespeare and America: The Perpetual Ambassador of the English-Speaking World," in Rawlings, *Americans on Shakespeare,* 502.

57 Lewis, *Mary Queen of Scots,* 87.

58 See ibid., passim.

CHAPTER ONE

1 Watkins, *Representing Elizabeth.*

2 *Le Comte d'Essex* (1678), English trans. *Secret History of Elizabeth and Essex* (1680); La Mothe, *Nouvelles d'Elisabeth Reyne d'Angleterre,* English trans. *Novels of Elizabeth* (1680, 1681); *Secret History of Alancon and Elizabeth* (1691).

3 Dobson and Watson, *England's Elizabeth,* 89–102; Watkins, *Representing Elizabeth,* ch. 7.

4 He reputedly jested that "William the Conqueror was before Richard the Third." Schoenbaum, *Shakespeare's Lives,* 17.

5 Schoenbaum, *Shakespeare's Lives,* 59–66; Mary Edmond, "Sir William Davenant," in *ODNB.*

6 Duncan-Jones, *Ungentle Shakespeare,* 15.

7 See Dobson, *Making of the National Poet;* Taylor, *Reinventing Shakespeare,* ch. 1.

8 Dobson, *Making of the National Poet,* 14.

9 Dryden, Prologue to *The Tempest,* A4r.

10 Dobson, *Making of the National Poet,* 74–75.

11 F. E. Halliday, *Cult of Shakespeare,* 43.

12 Jonson, "To the memory of . . . Shakespeare," in *Norton Shakespeare,* 3351–52.

13 Otway, *Caius Marius,* A3r–v.

14 V.E., "Advertisement," in Shakespeare, *Collection of Poems,* A2r–v. Rowe's life of Shakespeare is referred to as having recently appeared but as having omitted this incident.

15 Dennis, *Comical Gallant,* A2r.

16 Shakespeare, *Merry Wives,* ed. Craik, 4.

17 See, for instance, Shakespeare, *Merry Wives,* ed. Craik, 1–13; Schoenbaum, *Compact Documentary Life,* 196–98; Kay, *Shakespeare,* 180–83; Duncan-Jones, *Ungentle Shakespeare,* 97–98.

18 Excepting a brief interval of eight months when the office was held by William Brooke, Baron Cobham.

19 See ch. 4 below.

20 On Dec. 26 and 27, 1596, Jan. 6, 1597, and Feb. 6 and 8, 1597. Shakespeare, *Merry Wives,* ed. Craik, 11–13, 5 n. 3.

21 Wood, *In Search of Shakespeare,* 208–9.

22 John Dennis, "The Person of Quality's Answer to Mr. Collier's Letter: Containing a Defence of a Regulated Stage" (1704), in *Original Letters,* 1:232.

23 Rowe, "Life of Shakespear," viii–ix.

24 Otway, *Caius Marius,* A3r–v.

25 Rowe, "Life of Shakespear," viii.

26 Taylor, *Reinventing Shakespeare,* 78.

27 Gildon, "Remarks on the Plays of Shakespear," 291.

28 Flloyd, *Bibliotheca Biographica,* 3:O2v; *Biographia Britannica,* 6:3632–34 (this entry on Shakespeare may have been written by either William Warburton or Philip Nichols); Chambers, *William Shakespeare,* 287; Berkenhout, *Biographia Literaria,* 1:399.

29 Marcus, *Unediting the Renaissance,* 70–71.

30 Rowe, "Life of Shakespear," v.

31 Schoenbaum, *Shakespeare's Lives,* 72.

32 Rowe, "Life of Shakespear," xviii.

33 Lanier, *Shakespeare and Popular Culture,* 113–14.

34 *Biographia Britannica,* 6:3628 n. D; 6:3632–33 n. O.

35 [Stafford], *Compendious or Briefe Examination* (1751), A1r–v.

36 Stafford, *Compendious or Briefe Examination* (1876), viii–ix.

37 *Biographia Britannica,* 6:3628 n. D; 6:3633.

38 F. E. Halliday, *Cult of Shakespeare,* 42–45.

39 de Grazia, *Shakespeare Verbatim,* 76.

40 Rowe, "Life of Shakespear," x.

41 de Grazia, *Shakespeare Verbatim,* 75–77.

42 Rowe, "Life of Shakespear," x.

43 de Grazia, *Shakespeare Verbatim,* 76.

44 Dennis, *Comical Gallant,* A2r.

45 Rowe, "Life of Shakespear," viii.

46 Dobson, "Bowdler and Britannia," passim.

47 Dennis, "Prologue to the Subscribers for *Julius Caesar.*"

48 See Dobson, *Making of the National Poet,* 146–58, 161.

49 Lillo, Epilogue to *Marina,* 59–60.

50 *Ode to Shakespeare,* in Bodleian Library MS Mus d 14, quoted in Dobson, *Making of the National Poet,* 227.

51 Bate, "Shakespeare Phenomenon," 11; Taylor, *Reinventing Shakespeare,* 114.

52 Brewer, *Pleasures of the Imagination,* 366, 369, 392, 478.

53 Dobson, *Making of the National Poet,* 2.

54 Marsden, Introduction to *Appropriation of Shakespeare,* 4.

55 Cibber, First Dissertation, in *Dissertations on Theatrical Subjects,* 36–37.

56 Colley, *Britons,* 85–86.

57 *Shakespeare, Comedies, Histories, and Tragedies,* ed. Capell, 1:A3r–v.

58 *Works of Shakespear,* ed. Warburton, 1:115.

59 *Biographia Britannica*, 6:3633.
60 Dobson, *Making of the National Poet*, 135–36.
61 Ibid., 141–43.
62 Ellis, *That Man Shakespeare*, 86, 76.
63 F. E. Halliday, *Cult of Shakespeare*, 67–68.
64 Spenser, *Poetical Works*, *Faerie Queene* III, proem 5.
65 See Phillips, *Images of a Queen*; Hackett, *Virgin Mother, Maiden Queen*, esp. 105–12, 130–32, 139–44.
66 Watkins, *Representing Elizabeth*, passim.
67 Dobson and Watson, *England's Elizabeth*, 80, 119.
68 Lillo, Epilogue to *Marina*, 59–60.
69 Watkins, *Representing Elizabeth*, 11.
70 Colley, *Britons*, 201.
71 Dobson and Watson, *England's Elizabeth*, 90.
72 Lewis, *Mary Queen of* Scots, 136–46; Dobson and Watson, *England's Elizabeth*, 103–7.
73 Davies, "Life of Lillo," xxxviii–xxxix.
74 Ibid., xxxvii, quoting John Milton, "L'Allegro," line 133.
75 *Bell's Edition of Shakespeare's Plays*, 6:H2r.
76 Berkenhout, *Biographia Literaria*, 399.
77 Bate, *Shakespearean Constitutions*, 19.
78 Malone, *Inquiry into the Authenticity*.
79 For a full account of the Ireland forgeries, see Pierce, *Great Shakespeare Fraud*, and Schoenbaum, *Shakespeare's Lives*, 132–67.
80 "Queen Elizabeth's Letter," in Samuel Ireland, *Miscellaneous Papers by Shakspeare*.
81 Boaden, *Letter to Steevens*, 36.
82 [Waldron], *Free Reflections*, 8.
83 Boaden, *Letter to Steevens*, 35–39.
84 *The Oracle*, Jan. 23, 1796, quoted in Schoenbaum, *Shakespeare's Lives*, 159.
85 W.-H. Ireland, *Authentic Account*, 17.
86 Woudhuysen, "Queen's Own Hand."
87 Waldron, *Free Reflections*, 21.
88 W.-H. Ireland, *Authentic Account*, 25.
89 Waldron, *Free Reflections*, 22.
90 Waldron, Dedication to *The Virgin Queen*.
91 Trevor R. Griffiths, "Francis Godolphin Waldron," in *ODNB*.
92 Ibid.
93 de Grazia, *Shakespeare Verbatim*, 5.

CHAPTER TWO

1 Deverell, Prologue to *Mary, Queen of Scots*.
2 Austen, *Mansfield Park*, 335.
3 Dibdin, *Metrical History of England*, 2:86.

4 Symmons, "Life of W. Shakspeare," x. This biography was first printed in Samuel Weller Singer's edition of Shakespeare in 1826; see Nigel Aston, "Charles Symmons," in *ODNB.*

5 Malone, *Life of William Shakspeare,* 11.

6 Rowe, "Life of Shakespear," xxix–xxx.

7 Malone, "Historical Account of the English Stage," 166–67.

8 Schoenbaum, *Shakespeare's Lives,* 225.

9 Ryan, *Dramatic Table Talk,* 2:156–57.

10 Dryden, Prologue to *The Tempest,* A4r; Schoenbaum, *Shakespeare's Lives,* 159; see ch. 1 above.

11 Harvey, "Biographical Memoir of Shakspeare," ix, vii.

12 See Ellis, *That Man Shakespeare,* 127.

13 Halliwell, *The Life of William Shakespeare,* 151.

14 Chettle, *Englandes Mourning Garment,* B3r; see Introduction above.

15 Otway, *Caius Marius,* A3r–v.

16 Neil, *Shakespere: A Critical Biography,* 46–48.

17 Neil, *Shakespeare for the Worthies,* 31.

18 Schoenbaum, *Shakespeare's Lives,* 225.

19 For a full account of Collier's forgeries, see Freeman and Freeman, *John Payne Collier.*

20 Collier, *New Facts Regarding the Life,* 33.

21 Collier, *New Particulars Regarding the Works,* 56–58.

22 Ibid. 58–59.

23 Collier, "Life of William Shakespeare," xcv, cii–iii, cxci–iii.

24 Schoenbaum, *Shakespeare's Lives,* 256.

25 Dyce, Preface to *Remarks on Collier's and Knight's Editions,* vi.

26 Halliwell, *Life of Shakespeare,* 190. On Halliwell's collusive silence about Collier's other error, see McCue, "John Payne Collier."

27 Halliwell, *Observations on the Shaksperian Forgeries.*

28 Schoenbaum, *Shakespeare's Lives,* 259–63.

29 Ingleby, *Complete View of the Shakspere Controversy,* 12.

30 F. E. Halliday, *Cult of Shakespeare,* 145–46.

31 Neil, *Shakespere: A Critical Biography,* 46.

32 Neil, *Shakespeare for the Worthies,* 30.

33 For other errors in scholarship arising from Collier's forgeries and persisting into the twentieth century, see McCue, "John Payne Collier."

34 Dobson, *Making of the National Poet,* 211–13; Ellis, *That Man Shakespeare,* 67–70.

35 See Lukács, *Historical Novel,* esp. 19, 25, 31; Kelley and Sacks, *Historical Imagination in Early Modern Britain,* esp. ix–x, 1; Strong, *Painting the Past,* 38.

36 Scott's publisher wanted him to set his next novel at the time of the Armada victory, but he refused. See Henderson, "Othello Redux?" 15.

37 See Scott, *Kenilworth,* 397–402.

38 Ibid., 398.

39 Ibid., 291n, 397, 401, 407.

40 Strong, *Painting the Past,* 38.

41 Scott, *Kenilworth*, xxxii.
42 Percy, "Origins of the English Stage," 143; and see Schoenbaum, *Shakespeare's Lives*, 93–94.
43 Scott, *Kenilworth*, xxii.
44 Ibid., 399.
45 Austen, *Mansfield Park*, 335.
46 Scott, *Kenilworth*, 163.
47 Probably 1601–2; see *Norton Shakespeare*, 1832.
48 Cornwell, *Open Book*, Oct. 10, 2004.
49 Shaw, *Forms of Historical Fiction*, 21–22.
50 Watson, "Kemble, Scott, and the Bard," 73.
51 Poole, *Shakespeare and the Victorians*, 7.
52 Scott, *Kenilworth*, 174; Sutherland, *Life of Scott*, 12; Ellis, *That Man Shakespeare*, 111; Rozett, *Constructing a World*, 104.
53 Sutherland, *Life of Scott*, 227–28, 234, 247–48.
54 Ibid., 247.
55 See Henderson, "Othello Redux?" 17; Dobson and Watson, *England's Elizabeth*, 306 n. 54; Jung and Plachta, "Queen Sings Coloratura," 202.
56 Chorley, Introduction to *Kenilworth: A Masque*; *Merchant of Venice*, 5.1.1–110.
57 Deverell, Prologue to *Mary, Queen of Scots.*
58 Malone, *Life of Shakspeare*, 392.
59 Harvey, "Biographical Memoir of Shakspeare," vii.
60 Symmons "Life of Shakspeare," x.
61 Cornwall, Introduction to *Complete Works of Shakespeare*, ed. White (1857), 1:xi.
62 *Complete Works of Shakespeare*, ed. White (1857), 1:72.
63 Jameson, *Memoirs of Female Sovereigns*, 1:306–7.
64 Costello, *Memoirs of Eminent Englishwomen*, 1:iii–iv. See Ziegler, "Re-Imagining a Renaissance Queen," 205–6.
65 "Elizabeth and Victoria. From a woman's point of view," *Victoria Magazine* 3 (June 1864): 99, quoted in Ziegler, "Re-imagining a Renaissance Queen," 206.
66 Jameson, *Memoirs of Female Sovereigns*, 282.
67 Kingsley, "Raleigh and His Time," 122.
68 [Martin], *Peter Parley's Tales about Kings and Queens*, 188. The British Library catalogue attributes this work to the originator of the Peter Parley pseudonym, the American Samuel Griswold Goodrich. However, the pseudonym was adopted by a number of other authors and seems most likely in this case to stand for the English children's writer William Martin. See Margaret Kinnell Evans, "Martin, William [*pseud.* Peter Parley] (1801–1867)," in *ODNB*.
69 Richmond, "Elizabeth I in Imperial Britain," 226.
70 Franssen, "Bard and Ireland," 73.
71 Carlyle, "Hero as Poet," 167.
72 See Singh, *Colonial Narratives / Cultural Dialogues*, 120–52; Trivedi, Introduction to *India's Shakespeare*, ed. Trivedi and Bartholomeusz, 15, 30, 36; Majumdar, "That Sublime 'Old Gentleman,'" 264–65.

73 Schoch, *Victoria and Theatre,* 128–29, ch.11 passim.
74 Ibid., 148–50.
75 Ibid., 151–52, 129–30, xiv; Foulkes, Introduction to *Shakespeare and the Victorian Stage,* 8; Poole, *Shakespeare and the Victorians,* 203, Fowler, "Scott's *Elizabeth,*" 25.
76 Chapman, *History of Theatrical Entertainments at Court,* 38.
77 Briggs, *Age of Improvement,* 312, 368–76; Heyck, *History of British Isles 1688 to 1914,* 277–78.
78 Heyck, *History of British Isles 1688–1914,* 293–95.
79 Briggs, *Age of Improvement,* 368–76; Heyck, *History of British Isles 1688–1914,* 294.
80 Quoted in Briggs, *Age of Improvement,* 344.
81 Briggs, *Age of Improvement,* 299–300.
82 *Times,* Jan. 26, 1849, quoted in Dobson and Watson, *England's Elizabeth,* 150.
83 Chapman, *History of Theatrical Entertainments at Court,* 2.
84 Schoch, *Victoria and Theatre,* 134.
85 See Introduction above.
86 Schoch, *Victoria and Theatre,* xiv–xv.
87 Ibid., 191–92.
88 Foulkes, *Performing Shakespeare in the Age of Empire,* 46–47; Schoch, *Victoria and Theatre,* 186–89.
89 Christopher Ricks, "Tennyson, Alfred, First Baron Tennyson," in *ODNB.*
90 Drake, *Shakspeare and His Times,* 1:39–40.
91 Drake, *Noontide Leisure,* 1:77–9.
92 Somerset, *Shakspeare's Early Days,* 45.
93 See Holland, "Dramatizing the Dramatist," 144.
94 See Strong, *And When Did You Last?*
95 Strong, *Painting the Past,* 8–9, 16, 37.
96 Taylor, *Reinventing Shakespeare,* 124–25. The Gallery was the subject of an exhibition at the Folger Shakespeare Library, *Marketing Shakespeare: The Boydell Gallery (1789–1805) and Beyond,* Sept. 20, 2007–Jan. 5, 2008.
97 Oakley, "Words into Pictures," 11. For a useful catalogue of Shakespeare paintings and for other associated materials, see Rusche's *Shakespeare Illustrated* website.
98 Walker, *Elizabeth Icon,* 140.
99 Other early paintings on the theme of Shakespeare reading to Elizabeth included John James Chalon's *Shakespeare Reading to Queen Elizabeth* (undated) and John Wood's *Shakespeare Reading One of His Plays to Queen Elizabeth* (1835). See Dobson and Watson, *England's Elizabeth,* 130.
100 R. F. Williams, *Youth of Shakspeare,* 121.
101 R. F. Williams, *Secret Passion,* 1:99.
102 R. F. Williams, *Shakspeare and His Friends,* 1:103.
103 See Fowler, "Scott's *Elizabeth*"; Ashton, *Catalogue of Paintings at the Theatre Museum, London,* 49–51; Dobson and Watson, *England's Elizabeth,* plate 5, 129–30. Although not altogether well received at the Royal Academy in 1840, the painting went on to be exhibited at the Royal Scottish Academy in 1841, again there in 1880, and at the inaugural exhibition of the Shakespeare Memorial Theatre Picture Gallery in 1881; it also circulated as

an etching of the painting by the artist's brother, William Bell Scott, published in 1866–67.

104 Dobson and Watson, *England's Elizabeth,* 150.

105 Fowler, "Scott's *Elizabeth,*" 30.

106 John Morrison, "Scott, David (1806–1849)," in *ODNB.*

107 Fowler, "Scott's *Elizabeth,*" 26.

108 Morrison, "Scott, David," in *ODNB.*

109 See Strong, *And When Did You Last?* 63; Dobson and Watson, *England's Elizabeth,* fig. 20, 161–64.

110 Jonson, "Conversations with Drummond," 470.

111 *Norton Shakespeare,* 3333–34; see ch. 4 below.

112 Hilaric Faberman, "Augustus Leopold Egg," in *ODNB.*

113 See preceding discussion of Halliwell, *Life of Shakespeare;* [Martin], *Peter Parley's Tales about Kings and Queens;* the Christmas Shakespeare performances at Windsor and associated publications; and Egg's *Queen Elizabeth Discovers.*

114 Curling, *Shakspere; Poet, Lover, Actor, Man* (1848), 2:6–7, republished as *The Forest Youth* (1853). All references here are to the 1848 edition.

115 Elizabeth I, *Collected Works,* 325–26.

116 Given as "Sudley" in the printed text; my correction.

117 *The Life of Shakespeare,* dir. Frank R. Growcott and J. B. McDowell (1914); see *IMDb,* http://www.imdb.com/title/tt0221347/.

118 Curling, *Geraldine Maynard,* 1:137–49.

119 Royal Shakespeare Theatre, *Catalogue of Royal Shakespeare Theatre Picture Gallery,* 16, catalogue nos. 27–39.

120 See Rusche, "The Artists: Charles Cattermole, *Scenes from the Life of Shakespeare,*" *Shakespeare Illustrated* website.

121 Dobson and Watson, *England's Elizabeth,* 130–32, plate 6.

122 These include its Scottish theme, its praise of the Stuart dynasty thought to originate with Banquo, and its motif of witchcraft, a theme on which James had himself published. *Norton Shakespeare,* 2555–56.

123 Walker, *Elizabeth Icon,* 140.

124 Museum of History of Science, Oxford, "Rudolf II and Tycho."

125 McIntosh, "New York's Favorite Pictures," 6.

126 Other recorded examples of paintings of Shakespeare and Elizabeth include George Pycroft (1819–94), *Elizabeth Watching Falstaff in "Henry IV Part 1" at the Globe* (c. 1840–60): John Laslett Potts, *Shakespeare Reading before Queen Elizabeth* (1875); Henry Nelson O'Neil, *Shakespeare Reading "A Midsummer Night's Dream" to Queen Elizabeth* (1877); W. R. Beverley, *Queen Elizabeth in Her Carriage, Going to the Globe Theatre, to Witness a New Play of Shakespeare* (1879), a drop-scene for a theatre in Stratford-upon-Avon; Joseph Haier, *Shakespeare and Queen Elizabeth* (1886); Sir John Gilbert, *A Christmas Play by Shakespeare before Queen Elizabeth* (undated); and a large painting of Shakespeare at the court of Elizabeth by Heinrich Schlimartzki. See Fowler, "Scott's *Elizabeth,*" 27, 36; Dobson and Watson, *England's Elizabeth,* 130; Strong, *And When Did You Last?* 161–62; Oakley, "Words into Pictures," 11–12; Walker, *Elizabeth Icon,* 140–42; Hartmann, *Shakespeare in Art,* 22.

127 Gregg, *Elizabeth; or, The Origin of Shakespeare,* 108–9.
128 Franssen, "Bard and Ireland," 76.
129 See Holland, "Dramatizing the Dramatist," 138.
130 See ch. 1 above.
131 See, for instance, Taylor, "Incredible Shrinking Bard," 197: "Shakespeare's reputation peaked in the reign of Queen Victoria."
132 F. E. Halliday, *Cult of Shakespeare,* 149–50.
133 Roznovits, *Shakespeare in Late Victorian England,* 12–28.
134 See Roznovits, *Shakespeare in Late Victorian England,* 20; Sawyer, *Victorian Appropriations of Shakespeare.*
135 Poole, *Shakespeare and the Victorians,* 1.
136 Schoch, *Victoria and Theatre,* 70.
137 Taylor, *Reinventing Shakespeare,* 248.
138 On Candlemas (Feb. 2) 1602 (1601 old style), in the diary of the young law student John Manningham. See Introduction to *Twelfth Night,* ed. Warren and Wells, 1.
139 Although nearly sixty years later Leslie Hotson would argue from some suggestive but inconclusive documents that the play was first performed before Elizabeth at court on Twelfth Night 1601. Hotson, *First Night of "Twelfth Night."*
140 Taylor, *Reinventing Shakespeare,* 248–49.
141 A. Halliday and Lawrence, *Kenilworth, A Comic Operatic Extravaganza,* 3.
142 Schoch, *Not Shakespeare,* 28.
143 See Walker, *Elizabeth Icon,* 144, fig. 14.
144 See Hall, *Max Beerbohm Caricatures,* 207, plate 196.
145 Schmidgall, *Shakespeare and Opera,* 331; Jung and Plachta, "Queen Sings Coloratura," 202.

CHAPTER THREE

1 See Vaughan and Vaughan, *Shakespeare in American Life,* esp. A. T. Vaughan, "Shakespeare Discovers America."
2 See Teague, *Shakespeare and the American Popular Stage,* ch.1.
3 Sturgess, *Shakespeare and the American Nation,* appendix 1; V. M. Vaughan, "Shakespeare's Dissemination," 27.
4 Quoted in Teague, *Shakespeare and the American Popular Stage,* 38.
5 V. M. Vaughan, "Shakespeare's Dissemination," 29.
6 Markoe, "The Tragic Genius of Shakspeare; an Ode," in *Miscellaneous Poems* (Philadelphia, 1787), quoted in Dobson, *Making of the National Poet,* 230.
7 Quoted in Sturgess, *Shakespeare and the American Nation,* 67.
8 James Fenimore Cooper, *Notions of the American; Picked up by a Travelling Bachelor* (London, 1828; Philadelphia, 1833), quoted in Rawlings, *Americans on Shakespeare,* 59.
9 White, *Memoirs of the Life of Shakespeare,* x.
10 Sturgess, *Shakespeare and the American Nation,* chs 1–2; V. M. Vaughan, "Shakespeare's Dissemination," 23–33.

11 Bristol, *Shakespeare's America, America's Shakespeare,* 53–54; Sturgess, *Shakespeare and the American Nation,* 59, 129.
12 Sturgess, *Shakespeare and the American Nation,* 182–86; Teague, *Shakespeare and the American Popular Stage,* ch.3.
13 White, *Memoirs of the Life of Shakespeare,* x–xi; White, "Essay toward Shakespeare's Genius," cxcv, cxcviii, ccl; Sturgess, *Shakespeare and the American Nation,* ch.5.
14 White, *Shakespeare's Scholar,* 343–44.
15 Henry Cabot Lodge, "Shakespeare's Americanisms," *Harper's Monthly Magazine* 29 (1895), in Rawlings, *Americans on Shakespeare,* 395–96.
16 William Cullen Bryant, "Two Speeches" (1870–71), in Rawlings, *Americans on Shakespeare,* 278.
17 Ashley Thorndike, "Shakespeare in America," lecture delivered in 1927, published in *Aspects of Shakespeare,* ed. L. Abercrombie (Oxford, 1933), repr. in Rawlings, *Americans on Shakespeare,* 525.
18 As in Henry Clay Folger's annotations in his edition of Carlyle's *On Heroes.* See Ziegler, "Duty and Enjoyment," 109.
19 As summed up by his widow. Ibid., 109.
20 Hopkinson, *Plays and Poems of Shakespeare,* 1:xvi–xvii.
21 Jenkins, *Heroines of History,* 279, 290, 309.
22 White, *Memoirs of the Life of Shakespeare,* 141.
23 Ibid., 104, 126; White, Introduction to *Merry Wives,* in *Works of Shakespeare,* ed. White (1865), 2:202, 207.
24 White, "Essay toward Shakespeare's Genius," cxcviii–cxix.
25 McIntosh, "New York's Favorite Pictures."
26 *Century of Queens,* facing 168. I am grateful to Steve Hackett for the gift of this book.
27 C. E. Hughes, rev. Betty T. Bennett, "Clarke, Mary Victoria Cowden," in *ODNB.*
28 Schoch, *Not Shakespeare,* 3 n. 3; Teague, *Shakespeare and the American Popular Stage,* 82–83.
29 See Vaughan and Vaughan, *Shakespeare in American Life,* 35–48, 127–30.
30 Twain, epigraph to *1601,* in *"1601," and "Is Shakespeare Dead?"*
31 I have retained most of Twain's archaic spellings to illustrate the fun that he has with them, but I have expanded most of the archaic contractions for ease of reading.
32 Leslie A. Fiedler, Afterword, 1–2, in Twain, *"1601," and "Is Shakespeare Dead?"*
33 Twain, *Is Shakespeare Dead?* 30, in *"1601," and "Is Shakespeare Dead?"*
34 This is attested to by press cuttings pasted into the British Library's copy of Koch, *Shakespeare, the Playmaker.*
35 Koch, *Shakespeare, the Playmaker,* 28.
36 Also pasted into the British Library's copy.
37 On the importance of *The Tempest* as the first Shakespeare play to be inspired by American materials, see A. T. Vaughan, "Shakespeare Discovers America," 11–12.
38 Sturgess, *Shakespeare and the American Nation,* 123.
39 Koch, *Raleigh, the Shepherd of the Ocean,* 53.
40 Compare Curling, *Shakspere; Poet, Lover, Actor, Man* (1848), 2:6–7; see ch. 2 above.
41 Hotspur, *1 Henry IV,* 1.3.200.

42 Green, *The Lost Colony* (1937), act 1, scene 3, p. 34.
43 Green, *The Lost Colony* (1946), act 1, scene 4, p. 43.
44 Green, *Lost Colony* (1937), 34.
45 Ibid., 35.
46 Ibid., 41–42.
47 Ibid., 100.
48 Green, *Lost Colony* (1946), xiv–xv.
49 Green, *Lost Colony* (1937), 6.
50 Green, *Paul Green Reader*, 12.
51 Green, *Lost Colony* (1937), 33.
52 See *Lost Colony* website.
53 See Hodgdon, *Shakespeare Trade*, 130–46, and Dobson and Watson, *England's Elizabeth*, 275–83.
54 See Hodgdon, *Shakespeare Trade*, 147–60, and Dobson and Watson, *England's Elizabeth*, 246–49.
55 See Schoenbaum, *Shakespeare: Globe and World*, 10.
56 Hodgdon, *Shakespeare Trade*, ch. 4.
57 National Maritime Museum, "Last Chance to View Elizabeth Exhibition."
58 Ziegler, Acknowledgements, in *Elizabeth I Then and Now*, 12.
59 Vaughan and Vaughan, *Shakespeare in American Life*, 48–61, 63–76, 167–69.
60 Ko, "Shakespeare Festivals," 89.
61 Gail Kern Paster, Foreword, in Vaughan and Vaughan, *Shakespeare in American Life*, 7.

CHAPTER FOUR

1 Taylor, *Reinventing Shakespeare*, 222.
2 Schoenbaum, *Shakespeare's Lives*, 79–81.
3 See Tillyard, *Elizabethan World Picture*, and *Shakespeare's History Plays*.
4 *Midsommer Nights Dreame*, ed. Furness, 75.
5 *Works of Shakespear*, ed. Warburton, 1:113.
6 See Joseph Hunter in 1845, in *Midsommer Nights Dreame*, ed. Furness, 76–78, 89; R. Wilson, *Secret Shakespeare*, 144–45.
7 Walter Whiter, *Specimen of a Commentary on Shakespeare* (1794), 186; James Plumptre, *Appendix to Observations on "Hamlet"* (1797), 61; see *Midsommer Nights Dreame*, ed. Furness, 78–79.
8 Boaden, *Sonnets of Shakespeare*, 8. This essay first appeared in the *Gentleman's Magazine*, Sept. and Nov. 1832; see Halpin, *Oberon's Vision*, 16.
9 Boaden is quoting Gascoigne; see Gascoigne, *Princely Pleasures*, 102. A few years ago Martin Wiggins of the Shakespeare Institute, Stratford-upon-Avon, used the surviving texts to direct a reconstruction of the Princely Pleasures at Kenilworth. This led him to conclude that, had Shakespeare been present among the common people admitted to the pageants, he would not have been able to see the pageants which Boaden thinks were referred to in Oberon's vision. Martin Wiggins, personal communication, Jan. 17 2008.

10 One account describes a "blaz^e of burning darts, flying too & fro, leamz [i.e., gleams] of starz coruscant, streamz and hail of firie sparkes, lightninges of wildfier a water and lond." Laneham, *A Letter*, 16, 24; and see Gascoigne, *Princely Pleasures*, 95.

11 Boaden thought seventeen years had elapsed, dating *MSND* to 1592, but 1595 is a more likely date, making the interval twenty years.

12 Halpin, *Oberon's Vision*, 16, 28.

13 Curling, *Shakspere: Poet, Lover, Actor, Man*, 2:279.

14 Rowe, "Life of Shakespear," viii.

15 Boaden, *Sonnets of Shakespeare*, 14–15; Chambers, *William Shakespeare*, 1:358; *Midsummer Night's Dream*, ed. Brooks, lv.

16 See, for instance, Montrose, "Renaissance Literary Studies;" Greenblatt, *Shakespearean Negotiations*.

17 Montrose's essay was first published in 1983 in *Representations*, the flagship journal of new historicism; this version is reprinted in Dutton, *New Casebook: Midsummer Night's Dream*. It was subsequently republished several times, sometimes in slightly revised forms, e.g., in Ferguson et al., *Rewriting the Renaissance*.

18 Montrose, "Shaping Fantasies," in Dutton, *New Casebook: Midsummer Night's Dream*, 102–3. All further references are to this edition.

19 Hodgdon, *Shakespeare Trade*, 216–21. I am grateful to an audience at the Shakespeare Institute in Stratford-upon-Avon for additional information about this.

20 Duncan-Jones, *Ungentle Shakespeare*, 9–12.

21 Greenblatt, *Will in the World*, 47.

22 Barroll, "New History," 461.

23 Tieck, commentary on *Der Sommernachtstraum*, 353.

24 I am grateful to Rosemary Ashton and Annette Schäffler for their kind assistance in translating Tieck.

25 Tieck, commentary on *Der Sommernachtstraum*, 353.

26 Dowden, *Shakspere: A Critical Study*, 67; Sachs, Introduction to *A Midsummernight's Dream*, in *Works of Shakespeare: Parallel Edition*, trans. Schlegel and Tieck, 7: C–D; G. J. Williams, *Our Moonlight Revels*, 4.

27 *Midsommer Nights Dreame*, ed. Furness, 266.

28 Massey, *Shakspeare's Sonnets*, 481.

29 *Midsommer Nights Dreame*, ed. Furness, 264; Fleay, *Chronicle History of Shakespeare*, 181; S. Lee, *Life of Shakespeare*, 161–62.

30 *Midsommer Nights Dreame*, ed. Furness, 80.

31 Chambers, *Elizabethan Stage*, 1:124, 2:194, 2:358–59, 4:109.

32 *Midsummer Night's Dream*, ed. Brooks, liii–lvi.

33 *Midsummer Night's Dream*, ed. and intro. Wells (Penguin, 1967), 12–14.

34 Wells, "*Midsummer Night's Dream* Revisited," esp. 15–17.

35 *Midsummer Night's Dream*, ed. Holland, 112.

36 G. J. Williams, *Our Moonlight Revels*, 263–65.

37 For Tieck's celebration of Friedrich Wilhelm IV as patron of the *Dream* and art-loving ruler, see Feodor Wehl, *Didaskalia* (Leipzig, 1867), 2, quoted in *Midsommer Nights Dreame*, ed. Furness, 329–30.

38 Dollimore and Sinfield, *Political Shakespeare*; Dollimore, *Radical Tragedy*; Hawkes, *Shakespeherian Rag.*

39 Wells, "*A Midsummer Night's Dream* Revisited," 16–17.

40 See ch. 1 above.

41 Wiles, *Shakespeare's Almanac*, 170.

42 See Duncan-Jones, "*Christs Teares*"; Duncan-Jones, "Bess Carey's Petrarch"; Hackett, "*Midsummer Night's Dream*," in Howard and Dutton.

43 *Norton Shakespeare*, 3333.

44 Ibid., 3333–34.

45 *Richard II*, ed. Black, 565, 582.

46 Ibid., 567.

47 Albright, "Shakespeare's *Richard II*."

48 Ibid., 699–701.

49 *Richard II*, ed. Black, 584.

50 Ibid., 579–82.

51 Greenblatt, *Power of Forms*, 3–4.

52 Jonathan Dollimore, "Shakespeare, Cultural Materialism and the New Historicism," in Dollimore and Sinfield, *Political Shakespeare*, 8.

53 Barroll, "New History," 441–64, esp. 443.

54 Worden, "Which Play?"; letters by Frank Kermode, Peter Womack, and Blair Worden, *London Review of Books*, Sept. 25, Oct. 9 and 23, Nov. 6 and 20, 2003.

55 *Norton Shakespeare*, 641.

56 Shapiro, *1599*, 103.

57 *Norton Shakespeare*, 3379; Shakespeare, *Richard* II, ed. Forker, 111–20.

58 *Richard II*, ed. Black, 577; Worden, "Which Play?" 22–24.

59 Sir John Harington, *Tract on Succession*, quoted in Healy, *Richard II*, 21.

60 Quoted in P. Williams, "Court and Polity," 270.

61 Chambers, *William Shakespeare*, 1:65; *Norton Shakespeare*, 950.

62 *Richard II*, ed. Forker, 515–16. See also Albright, "Shakespeare's *Richard II*," 688; Clare, "Censorship of Deposition Scene."

63 *Norton Shakespeare*, 3333; Albright, "Shakespeare's *Richard II*," 690.

64 Albright, "Shakespeare's *Richard II*," 706, 712.

65 Barroll, "New History," 447–48.

66 *Calendar of State Papers Domestic 1598–1601*, vol. 278, art. 78.

67 Duncan-Jones, "Globe Theatre," 125.

68 Chambers, *William Shakespeare*, 1:65.

69 See Schoenbaum, *Compact Documentary Life*, 218–19.

70 See Chambers, *William Shakespeare*, 1:66.

71 Worden, "Which Play?" 24.

72 Nicholas Hilliard (attrib.), *Queen Elizabeth I* (c. 1575), Tate Britain.

73 See E. C. Wilson, *England's Eliza*, 21, 23, 27, 33, 79, 137, 148, 208, 244, 248n, 259n, 279, 290, 322n, 365n, 367n, 376, 380, 382n, 384.

74 *Norton Shakespeare*, 2004–6.

75 *Poems of Robert Chester*, ed. Grosart, xxiii.

76 Devereux, *Lives and Letters of the Devereux.*

77 I.e., Penelope Rich and Sir Philip Sidney, as fictionalized in Sidney's sonnet sequence *Astrophel and Stella.*

78 Dobson and Watson, *England's Elizabeth,* 14, 21–23.

79 F. J. Furnivall, "On Chester's Love's Martyr" (1880) and *The Royal Shakspere* (1898), quoted in Matchett, *Phoenix and the Turtle,* 111–12. See also Underwood, *Phoenix and Turtle,* 34.

80 S. Lee, *Life of Shakespeare,* 183–84.

81 Carleton F. Brown, *Poems by Salusbury and Chester* (1913); see Underwood, *Phoenix and Turtle,* 35–38.

82 Underwood, *Phoenix and Turtle,* 42–51.

83 Pineton, *My Shakespeare, Rise!* 275–76, 360–64; Finnis and Martin, "Another Turn for the Turtle"; letters by Clare Asquith and Gerard Kilroy, *Times Literary Supplement,* no. 5222 (May 2, 2003), 17; Asquith, *Shadowplay,* 182.

84 Matchett, *Phoenix and the Turtle,* 194–95.

85 Shakespeare, *Complete Sonnets and Poems,* ed. Burrow, 89–90.

86 Everett, "Set upon a golden bough," 13–14.

87 Shakespeare, *Complete Sonnets and Poems,* ed. Burrow, 85, and see the discussions by Marie Axton and Anthea Hume to which he refers (n. 4).

88 *Shakespeare's Poems,* ed. Duncan-Jones and Woudhuysen, 91–123.

89 See Max Wolff (1932), Thomas P. Harrison (1951), and William Empson (1966) as cited in Underwood, *Phoenix and Turtle,* 42, 55–62, 72–73.

90 *Shakespeare's Poems,* ed. Duncan-Jones and Woudhuysen, 108.

91 Blenerhasset, *Revelation of the True Minerva,* E4v.

92 Gorges, *Poems,* 131–32.

93 *Sorrowes Joy,* 21–22; Hazlitt, *Fugitive Tracts,* 2nd series, no. 2.

94 *Norton Shakespeare,* 2004–6.

95 Chalmers, *Apology for the Believers,* 35–36.

96 Chalmers, *Supplemental Apology,* 101, 90.

97 Boaden, *Sonnets of Shakespeare,* 4–5.

98 Neil, *Shakespere: A Critical Biography,* 104–8.

99 Ibid., 46–48; Neil, *Shakespeare for the Worthies,* 31. See chs. 1 and 2 above.

100 Neil, *Shakespere: A Critical Biography,* 70.

101 *Norton Shakespeare,* 1959.

102 J.R., *Athenaeum,* Jan. 15, 1848, 66; see *Sonnets,* ed. Rollins, 1:266.

103 John Dowland, *Third Book of Songs* (1603), no. 7, in Fellowes, *English Madrigal Verse,* 481. See Hackett, *Virgin Mother, Maiden Queen,* ch. 6.

104 J.G.R. [probably the same person as "J.R."], "Shakespeare's Sonnets."

105 Massey, *Shakspeare's Sonnets,* 316.

106 Minto, *Characteristics of English Poets,* 287; S. Lee, *Life of Shakespeare,* 147–49.

107 *Shakespeare's Sonnets,* ed. Tyler, 22–25, 266.

108 *Sonnets,* ed. Rollins, 1:263–67.

109 Shakespeare, *Sonnets and Lover's Complaint,* ed. Kerrigan, 313–20.

110 *Shakespeare's Sonnets,* ed. Duncan-Jones, 21–24, 324.

111 Shakespeare, *Complete Sonnets and Poems*, ed. Burrow, 594.

112 Neil, *Shakespeare for the Worthies*, 30.

113 This association was made by Frederick Hawkins in 1879 and by Sidney Lee in 1880; by 1909 it was taken for granted by Edward Calisch. See S.A., review of *Jew in Early English Literature*, 324. It has recently received extensive attention, e.g., in Greenblatt, *Will in the World*, 273–81.

114 See for instance Morris, "Elizabeth 'Shadowed' in Cleopatra"; Rinehart, "Shakespeare's Cleopatra and England's Elizabeth."

115 J. D. Wilson, "Political Background of *Richard II* and *Henry IV*," 40.

116 E.g., Greenblatt, *Shakespearean Negotiations.*

117 Dollimore, *Radical Tragedy*, 7, quoting Raymond Williams, *Marxism and Literature.*

118 *Norton Shakespeare*, 49.

119 Gurr, *Shakespearean Stage*, 194.

120 Orgel, "Making Greatness Familiar," 45. See also Tennenhouse, *Power on Display*, 102–12.

121 Strong, *Cult of Elizabeth.*

122 Montrose, "Celebration and Insinuation"; "'Perfecte paterne of a Poete'"; "'Eliza, Queene of Shepheardes'"; "Gifts and Reasons"; "Of Gentlemen and Shepherds"; "Elizabethan Subject and Spenserian Text."

123 See, for instance, G. J. Williams, *Our Moonlight Revels*, 3; Hackett, Introduction to Shakespeare, *A Midsummer Night's Dream*, ed. Wells (Penguin, 2005), xl–xlvii. See also Shakespeare, *Hamlet*, ed. Thompson and Taylor, 38–39.

124 Tennenhouse, *Power on Display*, 1.

125 Strong, *Portraits of Elizabeth I*, 40.

126 Tennenhouse, *Power on Display*, 102–9.

127 Marcus, *Puzzling Shakespeare*, ch. 2, passim; 80. See also Jackson, "Topical Ideology."

128 Marcus, *Puzzling Shakespeare*, 101.

129 Ibid., 183–84, 104–5.

130 Tennenhouse, "Violence Done to Women"; Boehrer, *Monarchy and Incest*; Mullaney, "Mourning and Misogyny"; Hopkins, "'Ripeness is all.'"

131 Coddon, "'Such strange desyns.'"

132 Erickson, *Rewriting Shakespeare*, 83, 86.

133 Patterson, *Shakespeare and the Popular Voice*, 178 n. 7; and see Erickson, *Rewriting Shakespeare*, 75.

134 Montrose, "Spenser and the Elizabethan Political Imaginary."

135 Shakespeare, *Hamlet*, ed. Thompson and Taylor, 41.

136 Hotson, *First Night of "Twelfth Night".*

137 The theory is referred to as probable in Kernan, *King's Playwright*, 17, and as fact in Weir, *Elizabeth the Queen*, 249. It is rejected in the introductions to editions of *Twelfth Night* by Mahood, 4–5; Lothian and Craik, xxviii–xxix; and Warren and Wells, 4–5. Gay is noncommittal in her introduction to Donno's edition, 1–3.

138 Shakespeare, *Twelfth Night*, ed. Lothian and Craik, xxviii–xxix.

139 Hotson, *First Night of "Twelfth Night,"* 15–16.

140 Ringler and May, "Epilogue Possibly by Shakespeare," 138–39; *Riverside Shakespeare*, ed. Evans (1974), 1851–52; *Riverside Shakespeare*, 2nd ed., ed. Evans and Tobin, 1978.

141 Shapiro, *1599*, 85–86.
142 Shakespeare, *As You Like It*, ed. Dusinberre, 6–7, 37–42, 349–54.
143 *Shakespeare's Poems*, ed. Duncan-Jones and Woudhuysen, 467.
144 Shapiro, *1599*, 87.
145 See Hackett, *Virgin Mother, Maiden Queen*, ch. 6.
146 E. C. Wilson, *England's Eliza*, 114–17.
147 Francis Davison, *A Poetical Rhapsody* (1602), quoted in E. C. Wilson, *England's Eliza*, 318.
148 Shakespeare, *As You Like It*, ed. Dusinberre, 353–54.
149 Shapiro, *1599*, 86.
150 See, for instance, *Norton Shakespeare*, 1375–76.
151 Shapiro, *1599*, 39.

CHAPTER FIVE

1 See Taylor, *Reinventing Shakespeare*, 182–204.
2 Hawkes, *Shakespeherian Rag*, 55.
3 Strong, *Painting the Past*, 107.
4 Bacon, "Shakespeare and His plays"; Bacon, *Philosophy of Shakspere Unfolded*.
5 Unpublished MS quoted by Nathaniel Hawthorne in preface to Bacon, *Philosophy of Shakspere Unfolded*, x.
6 See, for instance, Schoenbaum, *Shakespeare's Lives*, 383–451; the mildly anti-Stratfordian Michell, *Who Wrote Shakespeare?* and the forthcoming book on the Shakespeare authorship controversy by James Shapiro.
7 Bacon, "Shakespeare and His Plays," 191.
8 Sturgess, *Shakespeare and the American Nation*, 176.
9 Ibid., 177.
10 Schoenbaum, *Shakespeare's Lives*, 403.
11 O. W. Owen, *Bacon's Cipher Story*, 63–64.
12 *Century of Queens*, 98–99.
13 Gallup, *Bi-literal Cypher*, iv.
14 Friedman and Friedman, *Shakespearean Ciphers Examined*.
15 1.4.138. In the *Norton Shakespeare* this play is entitled *Richard Duke of York*.
16 O. W. Owen, *Bacon's Cipher Story*, 58, 61.
17 Dobson and Watson, *England's Elizabeth*, 164.
18 Elizabeth I, *Collected Works*, 325–26.
19 Conflated text, 4.6.123–25.
20 F. E. Halliday, *Cult of Shakespeare*, 170.
21 E.g., Parker Woodward, *The Strange Case of Francis Tidir* (1901); Comyns Beaumont, *The Private Life of the Virgin Queen* (1947). See Michell, *Who Wrote Shakespeare?* 150.
22 Nicholls, *Eldest Son of Queen Elizabeth*, 12–13, 33, 38.
23 Ibid., 73.
24 Roe, *Bacon's Own Story*, 12, 13, 20–21.
25 See Introduction above for discussion of the authorship of this passage.

26 Schoenbaum, *Shakespeare's Lives*, 406–7.

27 Mudie, *Self-Named Shake=speare*, title page.

28 Henry Wellington Wack, "'Shakespeare': Man—Mask—Myth?" preface to Leigh, *Clipt Wings*, v–ix.

29 Dodd, *Personal Poems of Bacon* (1931), 50.

30 Dobson and Watson, *England's Elizabeth*, 92–94.

31 Alfred Dodd, *Personal Poems of Bacon*, 2nd ed. (1936), 78.

32 For an overview, see Bokenham, *Brief History of Bacon-Shakespeare Controversy*.

33 See *MASC* 25, http://www.ucl.ac.uk/ls/masc25/full.php?CollectionID=218.

34 *American Baconiana* 1.1 (Feb. 1923) records the first meeting of the Bacon Society of America.

35 *The Francis Bacon Society Incorporated*, http://www.baconsocietyinc.org/, and *Sir Francis Bacon's New Advancement of Learning*, http://www.sirbacon.org/.

36 Carr and Gerald, "Bacon's Royal Parentage."

37 Looney, *"Shakespeare" Identified*. Another claimant is the cousin of William Shakespeare of Stratford, also named William, son of Richard Shakespeare of Warwick, as proposed in Alexander, *Autobiography of Shakespeare*, which includes some encounters between this Shakespeare and Elizabeth.

38 See, for instance, Douglas, *Oxford as "Shakespeare,"* 31–33, 57.

39 Allen, *Anne Cecil, Elizabeth and Oxford*, 2.

40 Ogburn and Ogburn, *Renaissance Man*, 46–47.

41 Sonnet 36; Ogburn and Ogburn, *Renaissance Man*, 50.

42 De Vere Society, http://www.deveresociety.co.uk/; Shakespeare Oxford Society, http://www.shakespeare-oxford.com; Shakespeare Fellowship, http://www.shakespearefellowship.org/.

43 Knox, "Authorship of *In Memoriam*." I am indebted to Lady Sally Vinelott for this reference.

44 Sweet, *Shake-speare: The Mystery*, 44.

45 Schwartz, "It Is I (Mona-Leo)"; and see Schwartz's website, http://www.lillian.com.

46 Schwartz, "The Mask of Shakespeare." I am grateful to Lillian F. Schwartz, Professor Geoff Smith, and Laurens R. Schwartz for providing me with copies of this article and of the associated composite images.

47 Lewin, "Did Queen Bess?"; *War of the Wills*, produced and directed by Samira Osman, BBC TV, 1994. See Schwartz, "Film and Television."

48 Gerald, interview with Rylance, 1994.

49 See Edmonds, review of Rylance, *I Am Shakespeare*.

50 I am grateful to Kate Rumbold of the Shakespeare Institute for alerting me to the events mentioned in this paragraph.

51 Morgan, *History of Britain*, 550.

52 See Schoenbaum, *Shakespeare's Lives*, 385–94, 401–5, 415–25.

53 Ibid., 386, 419.

54 Ibid., 415.

55 Michell, *Who Wrote Shakespeare?* 152.

56 Schoenbaum, *Shakespeare's Lives,* 434. See also Lanier, *Shakespeare and Modern Popular Culture,* 139–40.

57 Ogburn and Ogburn, *Renaissance Man,* 56.

58 Gerald, "Who We Are."

59 V. M. Vaughan, "Shakespeare's Dissemination," 32.

60 Rawlings, *Americans on Shakespeare,* 2.

61 Charles William Wallace, "Shakespeare and America: The Perpetual Ambassador of the English-Speaking World" (1914), in Rawlings, *Americans on Shakespeare,* 501.

62 Sturgess, *Shakespeare and the American Nation,* 4, 6.

63 Rawlings, *Americans on Shakespeare,* 23.

64 Leigh, *Clipt Wings,* 150–51.

65 Schoenbaum, *Shakespeare's Lives,* 444.

66 Freud, "Family Romances," 222–23.

CHAPTER SIX

1 Baker, *Historical Fiction,* 56–57.

2 Poole, *Shakespeare and Victorians,* 3–5.

3 Ibid., 230.

4 Heyck, *History of the British Isles 1688–1914,* 371–74; Morgan, *History of Britain,* 593.

5 See Richmond, "Elizabeth I in Imperial Britain."

6 Parrott, *Pageant of British History,* vi.

7 Marshall, *Our Island Story,* 330.

8 Nesbit, *Royal Children,* 84–85.

9 Fletcher and Kipling, *History of England,* 138.

10 Foulkes, *Performing Shakespeare,* 130–31.

11 Nesbit, *Royal Children,* 5.

12 Baker, *Historical Fiction,* viii.

13 Garnett, *Shakespeare, Pedagogue and Poacher,* 104–5.

14 Jones, *In Burleigh's Days,* 230.

15 I am grateful to Mr. Bob Armstrong and Dr. Ginger Vaughan for their kind assistance in supplying me with this image.

16 Parrott, *Pageant of British History,* vi.

17 Heyck, *History of the British Isles 1688–1914,* 372; Morgan, *History of Britain,* 566, 572, 593–94.

18 Heyck, *History of the British Isles 1688–1914,* 432–35; Morgan, *History of Britain,* 559–65.

19 Hawkes, *Shakespeherian Rag,* 109.

20 Based on a series of articles written ten to fourteen years previously for the *Saturday Review.*

21 Richard Davenport-Hines, "Harris, James Thomas [Frank] (1856?–1931)," in *ODNB.*

22 Harris, *Man Shakespeare,* 397–98.

23 Harris, *Shakespeare and His Love,* 148–49.

24 *Merchant of Venice,* 4.1.182–83.

25 Davenport-Hines, "Harris [Frank]," in *ODNB.*

26 Morgan, *History of Britain,* 586.

27 Heyck, *History of British Isles 1870–present,* 141–43; Morgan, *History of Britain,* 597.

28 Morgan, *History of Britain,* 592.

29 See Graves, *Goodbye to All That,* 234–35; Hawkes, *Shakespeherian Rag,* 104.

30 Carey, *Dark Lady,* 21.

31 Dryden, Prologue to *The Tempest,* A4r, and see chs 1 and 2 above.

32 *Richard II,* ed. Black, 567.

33 An oath borrowed from Imogen in *Cymbeline,* 4.2.295.

34 Morgan, *History of Britain,* 597.

35 Heyck, *History of British Isles 1870–present,* 185.

36 See *Silent Shakespeare.*

37 Lanier, *Shakespeare and Popular Culture,* 43–44.

38 Based on a French play, *Les Amours de la Reine Elisabeth* (1911), by Emile Moreau, the film was made in London but premiered in New York then toured the U.S. See *Les Amours de la Reine Elisabeth*; Hodgdon, *Shakespeare Trade,* 112.

39 U.S. title *Loves and Adventures in the Life of Shakespeare,* dir. J. B. McDonell and Frank R. Growcott (1914); see Gifford, *British Film Catalogue,* no. 04426.

40 Mark Bryant, "Bairnsfather, (Charles) Bruce (1887–1959)," in *ODNB.*

41 *Old Bill,* reel 1, 79 ft. References to this film are to the copy owned by the British Film Institute and are given by reel and by foot as measured from the beginning. I am grateful to the staff of the BFI for arranging a research viewing for me. Sadly, they were unable to provide me with stills from the film. For further information about the film, see Gifford, *British Film Catalogue,* no. 07234, and *Old Bill "Through the Ages,"* BFI National Archive.

42 See "Prose and Poetry: Bruce Bairnsfather" and "Memorable Order of Tin Hats."

43 *Old Bill,* reel 2, 3590 ft; reel 3, 3670–4100 ft.

44 Hodgdon, *Shakespeare Trade,* 225 n. 8.

45 *Old Bill,* reel 3, 4140–4310 ft.

46 Ibid., reel 3, 4360–4400 ft.

47 Ibid., reel 3, 4425–4800 ft.

48 *Old Bill,* reel 4, closing captions.

49 Bakhtin, *Rabelais,* 370. See also Stallybrass and White, *Politics and Poetics of Transgression.*

50 Lanier, *Shakespeare and Popular Culture,* 44.

51 See Introduction above.

52 Heyck, *History of British Isles 1870–present,* 15, 120.

53 Morgan, *History of Britain,* 577; Heyck, *History of British Isles 1688–1914,* 350.

54 Sterling, *Shake-speare's Sweetheart,* 251–54.

55 Woolf, *Room of One's Own,* 46–47.

56 Taylor, *Reinventing Shakespeare,* 234–40.

57 Shaw, Preface to *Three Plays for Puritans,* 33.

58 Shaw, "Dark Lady," 136.

59 Joyce, *Ulysses,* ch. 9, 202. I am grateful to John Morton for pointing out this quotation to me.

60 Eliot, "Waste Land," p. 61, lines 279–80. All further references are to this edition.

61 *Antony and Cleopatra*, 2.2.197ff.
62 Strachey, *Elizabeth and Essex*, 9.
63 C. Owen, *Phoenix and Dove*, 197.
64 Woolf, *Room of One's Own*, 94.
65 The text gives "will not yield," but this may be a typographical error; "will yield" makes better sense.
66 *Richard II*, 3.4.
67 Schoenbaum, *Shakespeare's Lives*, 79–81.
68 Pineton, *My Shakespeare, Rise!* x–xi, 13.
69 McColvin, *To Kill the Queen*, vii.
70 Quoted in Ellis, *That Man Shakespeare*, 232.
71 Gillian Beer, Introduction to Woolf, *Between the Acts*, xxxi.
72 Sandra Stanley Holton, "Clark, Alice (1874–1934)," in *ODNB*.
73 Lawrence Goldman, "Elizabeth [*née* Lady Elizabeth Angela Marguerite Bowes-Lyon] (1900–2002), queen of Great Britain," in *ODNB*.
74 Brahms and Simon, *No Bed for Bacon*, 250–51.
75 Light, *Forever England*, 8, 19.
76 On-screen caption at beginning of *Henry V*, dir. Olivier. The film was released in the U.K. in November 1944 but not in the U.S. until June 1946; see http://www.imdb.com/title/tt0036910/releaseinfo.
77 Dobson and Watson, *England's Elizabeth*, 77–78; *Henry VIII*, 5.4.14–62; and see Introduction above.
78 Dobson and Watson, *England's Elizabeth*, 234.
79 Morgan, *History of Britain*, 634–49.
80 Willans and Searle, "Young Elizabethan," 214.
81 Peach, *First Queen Elizabeth*, 44–45.
82 Hodges, letter of May 27, 1984, quoted in Fowler, "Scott's *Elizabeth*," 25.
83 Burgess, *Nothing like the Sun*, 109, 197.
84 *Elizabeth R*, dir. Graham et al., DVD sleevenotes.
85 "Sweet England's Pride," written by Ian Rodger, dir. Roderick Graham, episode 6 of *Elizabeth R*.
86 See Dobson and Watson, *England's Elizabeth*, 243–46, for many more examples of popular historical novels about Elizabeth.
87 Stratford, Ont., "Know Your City—History"; Stratford Festival of Canada, "Our History."
88 I am indebted to Jane Edmonds, Archivist of the Stratford Festival, for help in obtaining this picture and other materials relating to this production.
89 Knowles, "Phillips' Dream," 39.
90 Warren, *Text and Performance*, 62.
91 See, for instance, Fraser, "Phillips Brings Special Vision," and Nelson, "Stratford Festival Opens New Production."
92 "Gloriana and her Court," in Stratford Festival Canada Programme 1976.
93 "Background to the play," in Stratford Festival Canada Programme 1977. Also published as "August Opening for Shakespeare's *Dream*".

94 Knowles, "Phillips' Dream," 42.
95 Knowles, "Phillips' Dream," 41, 45; Warren, *Text and Performance*, 62–63.
96 Duke, "Phillips' Version of *Dream*."
97 Syse, "Bard Resides in Stratford, Ontario."
98 Edwards, "Bewitching Double."
99 Kelly, "Regal Opening."
100 Syse, "Bard Resides in Stratford, Ontario"; Bowden, "Bard's Fest in 25th Year."
101 Cushman, "Flying the Flag"; Hadley, "*Dream* Is Top Quality."
102 *Will Shakespeare*, dir. Wood, Cullingham, and Knights.
103 Also known as *William Shakespeare, His Life and Times*, and available in North American format VHS as *The Life of Shakespeare*. See Vahimagi, *British Television*, 246; *IMDb*, http://www.imdb.com/title/tt0075526/; *Screen Online*, http://screenonline.org.uk/tv/id/1140675.
104 Mortimer, *Will Shakespeare*, 203.
105 Crab urinating against a lady's farthingale under the dining table in *Two Gentlemen of Verona*, 4.4.1–33.
106 See Kearns, "Dubious Pleasures."
107 Italian title *Quasi per Caso una Donna: Elisabetta*. "Dario Fo: Nobel Prize 1997."
108 See, for instance, Harris, "Prima Donna inter Pares"; "Women's Warrior Maggie."
109 On the grotesque body in the carnivalesque, see Bakhtin, *Rabelais*, 18–28, 315–18; Stallybrass and White, *Politics and Poetics*, 8–9, 20–25.
110 Fo, *Elizabeth: Almost by Chance*, 2.
111 Neale, *Queen Elizabeth*, 385.
112 Authorial ellipses except where indicated by square brackets.
113 Cf. *Richard III*, 5.5.136–39.
114 See Dobson and Watson, *England's Elizabeth*, 30, 228.
115 Rozett, *Constructing a World*, 2.
116 Nye, *Late Mr Shakespeare*, 38.
117 Grindon, *Shadows on the Past*, 1.
118 Monk and Sargeant, *British Historical Cinema*, 4.
119 Cartmell and Hunter, Introduction to Cartmell, Hunter, and Whelehan, *Retrovisions*, 2.
120 Cook, *Fashioning the Nation*, 6–7.
121 Pidduck, "Screening the Elizabethans," 69. I am indebted to Rosalyn Alexander for guidance on criticism of "heritage" films.
122 Higson, *English Heritage*, 66.
123 Cook, *Fashioning the Nation*, 6–7.
124 Pidduck, "Screening the Elizabethans," 133.
125 Cook, *Fashioning the Nation*, 6–7.
126 Higson, *English Heritage*, 67.
127 Higson, *English Heritage*, 99, 106; "Business Information for *Shakespeare in Love*," *IMDb*, http://www.imdb.com/title/tt0138097/business.
128 Pidduck, "Screening the Elizabethans," 133.
129 Lacher, "He's got Will Power."
130 See May, "Interview with Greenblatt"; Silverblatt, "*Will in the World*: An Interview"; and Gewertz, "Greenblatt Teases Out."

131 Brode, *Shakespeare in the Movies*, 240.
132 Quoted in Klett, "*Shakespeare in Love*," 26.
133 Norman and Stoppard, *Shakespeare in Love*, 17.
134 These resemblances have also been noticed by Burt in "No Holes Bard."
135 Quoted in Klett, "*Shakespeare in Love*," 28.
136 Pigeon, "'No Man's Elizabeth,'" 20–22.
137 Pidduck, "Screening the Elizabethans," 130.
138 Romney, "Comedy, Love."
139 Burt, "End of the Shakespearean," 211.
140 Triggers for this have included his kiss with Jeremy Irons in the film of *The Merchant of Venice* (2004), gay roles in *Edward II* on stage (2001) and *Running with Scissors* on screen (2006), and enigmatic statements about his private life in interviews. See, for instance, Rebello, "Running from Stardom"; Applebaum, interview with Fiennes; images of Joseph Fiennes at http://www.bentblog.com/art26207184.htm; "Fiennes Open about Gay Kiss."
141 Norman and Stoppard, *Shakespeare in Love*, 58, 61, 67.
142 Klett, "*Shakespeare in Love*," 26.
143 Norman and Stoppard, *Shakespeare in Love*, 148; Klett, "*Shakespeare in Love*," 36.
144 Rowe, "Life of Shakespear," viii. See ch. 1 above.

EPILOGUE

1 Findley, *Elizabeth Rex*, act 1, scene 1, p. 16, s.d.
2 "Timothy Findley" obituary.
3 *Hamlet*, 1.3.78.
4 R. Wilson, *Secret Shakespeare*, 64.
5 Schoenbaum, *Shakespeare's Lives*, 12, 22–24, 65, 74–75, 331–33, 506, 516–17, 532–38.
6 R. Wilson, *Secret Shakespeare*, 48–49.
7 Haigh, *Reformation and Resistance*; Scarisbrick, *Reformation and English People*; Haigh, *English Reformation Revised*; Duffy, *Stripping of Altars*.
8 Hammerschmidt-Hummel, "'Most Important Subject.'"
9 Hammerschmidt-Hummel, *Life and Times of Shakespeare*.
10 R. Wilson, *Secret Shakespeare*, 105.
11 R. Wilson, "Shakespeare in Hate."
12 Asquith, *Shadowplay*, 32.
13 Davidson and McCoog, "Unreconciled."
14 See Introduction and ch. 4 above.
15 Barton, "The One and Only"; Womersley, "*Da Vinci Code* of Shakespeare."
16 Asquith, reply to Womersley; Asquith, reply to Barton.
17 For a favorable review, see Haven for *Washington Post*; for a news report, see Thorpe, "Shakespeare Was a Political Rebel." The paperback edition of *Shadowplay* is bedecked with glowing commendations.
18 Comments from http://www.amazon.com.

19 *The Social Affairs Unit,* Dec. 5, 2005, and Feb. 20, 2006.

20 Murphy, "Cracking Shakespeare's Catholic Code."

21 She is also a Viscountess, but this is not mentioned. For a description of Asquith writing the book on the kitchen table in intervals of domestic life, see R. M. Lee, "Shakespeare, the Secret Rebel."

22 Smiley, weblog, Jan. 4, 2006.

23 Johnson, *Historical Fiction,* v–xiii.

24 In "City of Death" (1979). "*Doctor Who* Fact File: The Shakespeare Code."

25 *Elizabeth* and *Elizabeth: The Golden Age,* both dir. Shekhar Kapur; *Elizabeth I,* dir. Tom Hooper; *The Virgin Queen,* dir. Coky Giedroyc.

26 Hammerschmidt-Hummel, *Life and Times of Shakespeare.*

27 Shakespeare, *Midsummer Night's Dream,* dir. Supple.

28 Steedman, "True Romances," 28, 31.

BIBLIOGRAPHY

COMPLETE WORKS OF SHAKESPEARE (IN CHRONOLOGICAL ORDER)

The Works of Mr. William Shakespear. Edited by Nicholas Rowe. 6 vols. London, 1709.

The Works of Shakespear. Edited by William Warburton. 8 vols. London, 1747.

Mr William Shakespeare, His Comedies, Histories, and Tragedies. Edited by Edward Capell. 10 vols. London, 1767–68.

Bell's Edition of Shakespeare's Plays. 9 vols. London, 1774.

The Plays and Poems of William Shakespeare . . . First American Edition. Edited by Joseph Hopkinson. 6 vols. Philadelphia, 1795.

Shakspeare's Dramatische Werke. Translated by August Wilhelm von Schlegel, with commentary and notes by Ludwig Tieck. Berlin, 1825–33.

The Complete Works of William Shakspeare. Leipzig, 1837.

The Works of William Shakespeare. Edited by J. Payne Collier. 8 vols. London, 1844.

The Complete Works of Shakespeare. Introduced by Barry Cornwall [Bryan Waller Procter]. Edited by Richard Grant White. 3 vols. London and New York, 1857.

The Works of William Shakespeare. Edited by Richard Grant White. 12 vols. Boston, 1865.

The Riverside Shakespeare. Edited by G. Blakemore Evans. Boston: Houghton Mifflin, 1974.

The Riverside Shakespeare. 2nd ed. Edited by G. Blakemore Evans and J.J.M. Tobin. Boston and New York: Houghton Mifflin, 1997.

The Norton Shakespeare. General editor Stephen Greenblatt. New York and London: Norton, 1997.

EDITIONS OF SINGLE WORKS BY SHAKESPEARE (ALPHABETICALLY BY TITLE AS PUBLISHED)

As You Like It. Edited by Juliet Dusinberre. Arden Shakespeare, 3rd series. London: Thomson, 2006.

A Collection of Poems. London: B. Lintott, [1709?].

Complete Sonnets and Poems. Edited by Colin Burrow. Oxford: Oxford University Press, 2002.

Hamlet. Edited by Ann Thompson and Neil Taylor. Arden Shakespeare, 3rd ser. London: Thomson, 2006.

King Henry VIII. With John Fletcher. Edited by Gordon McMullan. Arden Shakespeare, 3rd ser. London: Thomson, 2000.

King Richard II. Edited by Charles R. Forker. Arden Shakespeare, 3rd ser. London: Thomson, 2002.

The Life and Death of King Richard the Second. Edited by Matthew W. Black. In a *New Variorum Edition of Shakespeare*. Philadelphia and London: J. B. Lippincott, 1955.

Love's Labour's Lost. Edited by H. R. Woudhuysen. Arden Shakespeare, 3rd series. London: Thomas Nelson, 1998.

The Merry Wives of Windsor. Edited by T. W. Craik. World's Classics. Oxford: Oxford University Press, 1994.

A Midsommer Nights Dreame. Edited by Horace Howard Furness. In a *New Variorum Edition of Shakespeare*. 8th ed. 1895; repr. Philadelphia and London: J. B. Lippincott, 1923.

A Midsummernight's Dream. In *The Works of William Shakespeare, parallel ed.: English and German*, translated by A.W. von Schlegel and Ludwig Tieck, Preface and Introductions by Charles Sachs, vol. 7. Leipzig and Philadelphia, 1884–87.

A Midsummer Night's Dream. Edited by Stanley Wells. 1967; repr. Harmondsworth, U.K.: Penguin, 1995.

A Midsummer Night's Dream. Edited by Harold F. Brooks. Arden Shakespeare, 2nd ser. London: Methuen, 1979.

A Midsummer Night's Dream. Edited by Peter Holland. World's Classics. 1994; repr. Oxford: Oxford University Press, 1995.

A Midsummer Night's Dream. Edited by Stanley Wells. Introduction by Helen Hackett. London: Penguin, 2005.

Shakespeare's Poems. Edited by Katherine Duncan-Jones and H. R. Woudhuysen. Arden Shakespeare, 3rd ser. London: Thomson, 2007.

Shakespeare's Sonnets. Edited by Thomas Tyler. London, 1890.

Shakespeare's Sonnets. Edited by Katherine Duncan-Jones. Arden Shakespeare, 3rd ser. London: Thomas Nelson, 1997.

The Sonnets. Edited by Hyder Edward Rollins. 2 vols. In a *New Variorum Edition of Shakespeare*. Philadelphia and London: J. B. Lippincott, 1944.

The Sonnets and A Lover's Complaint. Edited by John Kerrigan. Harmondsworth: Penguin, 1986.

Twelfth Night. Edited by M. M. Mahood. Harmondsworth: Penguin, 1968.

Twelfth Night. Edited by J. M. Lothian and T. W. Craik. Arden Shakespeare, 2nd ser. London: Methuen, 1975.

Twelfth Night. Edited by Roger Warren and Stanley Wells. Oxford: Oxford University Press, 1994.

Twelfth Night. Edited by Elizabeth Story Donno. Introduction by Penny Gay. Rev. ed. New Cambridge Shakespeare. 1985; repr. Cambridge: Cambridge University Press, 2004.

OTHER WORKS

Albright, Evelyn May. "Shakespeare's *Richard II* and the Essex Conspiracy." *PMLA* 42.3 (Sept. 1927): 686–720.

Alexander, Louis C. *The Autobiography of Shakespeare: A Fragment.* London: Headley Brothers, 1911.

Allen, Percy. *Anne Cecil, Elizabeth and Oxford.* London: Denis Archer, 1934.

American Baconiana 1.1 (Feb. 1923). http://www.sirbacon.org/links/abacon11.htm.

Les Amours de la Reine Elisabeth (1912). Directed by Louis Mercanton. http://ftvdb.bfi.org.uk/sift/title/59771.

Applebaum, Stephen. Interview with Joseph Fiennes. http://www.bbc.co.uk/films/2004/11/30/joseph_fiennes_the_merchant_of_venice_interview.shtml.

Armstrong, Bob. Collection of antique jigsaw puzzles. http://www.oldpuzzles.com/ (accessed June 17, 2008).

Ashton, Geoffrey. *Catalogue of Paintings at the Theatre Museum, London.* Edited by James Fowler. London: Victoria and Albert Museum, 1992.

Asimov, Isaac. "The Immortal Bard." (1954). In *Earth Is Room Enough.* London: Panther, 1957.

Asquith, Clare. *Shadowplay: The Hidden Beliefs and Coded Politics of William Shakespeare.* New York: Public Affairs, 2005.

———. Reply to David Womersley. *Social Affairs Unit,* Jan. 12 2006. http://www.socialaffairsunit.org.uk/blog/archives/000685.php.

———. Reply to Anne Barton. *New York Review of Books* 53.11 (June 22, 2006). http://www.nybooks.com/articles/19110.

Assassin. The Lady Grace Mysteries. London: Doubleday Children's, 2004.

"August Opening for Shakespeare's *Dream.*" *Fanfares* (Stratford Festival, Ontario) 10.2 (Aug. 1976): 1, 4.

Austen, Jane. *Mansfield Park.* Edited by Tony Tanner. 1814; repr. Harmondsworth: Penguin, 1966.

Bacon, Delia. "William Shakespeare and His Plays: An Enquiry Concerning Them." *Putnam's Monthly* 7 (1856). In *Americans on Shakespeare 1776–1914,* edited by Peter Rawlings, 169–99. Aldershot, U.K.: Ashgate, 1999.

———. *The Philosophy of the Plays of Shakspere Unfolded.* London, 1857.

Baker, Ernest A. *A Guide to Historical Fiction.* 1914; repr. New York: Argosy-Antiquarian, 1968.

Bakhtin, Mikhail. *Rabelais and His World.* Translated by Hélène Iswolsky. 1965; repr. Cambridge, Mass.: MIT Press, 1968.

Barroll, Leeds. "A New History for Shakespeare and His Time." *Shakespeare Quarterly* 39.4 (Winter 1988): 441–64.

Barton, Anne. "The King Disguised: Shakespeare's *Henry V* and the Comical History." In *The Triple Bond: Plays, Mainly Shakespearean, in Performance,* edited by Joseph G. Price, 92–117. University Park, Pa.: Pennsylvania State University Press, 1975.

———. "The One and Only." *New York Review of Books* 53.8 (May 11, 2006). http://www.nybooks.com/articles/18972.

Bate, Jonathan. *Shakespearean Constitutions: Politics, Theatre, Criticism 1730–1830.* Oxford: Clarendon, 1989.

———. "The Shakespeare Phenomenon." In *Shakespeare in Art,* by Jane Martineau et al., 9–19. London and New York: Merrell, 2003.

Berkenhout, John. *Biographia Literaria; or, A Biographical History of Literature.* Vol. 1, *From the Beginning of the Fifth to the End of the Sixteenth Century.* London, 1777.

Biographia Britannica; or, The Lives of the Most Eminent Persons who have Flourished in Great Britain and Ireland. 6 vols. London, 1747–66.

Blenerhasset, Thomas. *A Revelation of the True Minerva.* Introduced by Josephine Waters Bennett. 1582; repr. New York: Scholar's Facsimile, 1941.

Boaden, James. *A Letter to George Steevens, Esq., Containing a Critical Examination of the Papers of Shakspeare; Published by Mr. Samuel Ireland.* London, 1796.

———. *On the Sonnets of Shakespeare.* London, 1837.

Boehrer, Bruce Thomas. *Monarchy and Incest in Renaissance England: Literature, Culture, Kinship, and Kingship.* Philadelphia: University of Pennsylvania Press, 1992.

Bokenham, T. D. *A Brief History of the Bacon-Shakespeare Controversy.* Northampton, U.K.: Francis Bacon Research Trust, 1982.

Bowden, Ramona B. "Bard's Fest in 25th year." *Post-Standard* (Syracuse, N. Y.), June 10, 1977.

Brahms, Caryl, and S. J. Simon. *No Bed for Bacon.* 1941; repr. London: Transworld/Black Swan, 1999.

Brewer, John. *The Pleasures of the Imagination: English Culture in the Eighteenth Century.* London: HarperCollins, 1997.

Briggs, Asa. *The Age of Improvement, 1783–1867.* London and Harlow: Longman, 1959.

Bristol, Michael D. *Shakespeare's America, America's Shakespeare.* London and New York: Routledge, 1990.

Brode, Douglas. *Shakespeare in the Movies: From the Silent Era to "Shakespeare in Love."* Oxford: Oxford University Press, 2000.

Burgess, Anthony. *Nothing like the Sun: A Story of Shakespeare's Love Life.* London: Heinemann, 1964.

Burt, Richard. "No Holes Bard: Homonormativity and the Gay and Lesbian Romance with *Romeo and Juliet.*" In *Shakespeare without Class: Misappropriations of Cultural Capital,* edited by Donald Hedrick and Bryan Reynolds, 153–86. Basingstoke and New York: Palgrave, 2000.

———. "*Shakespeare in Love* and the End of the Shakespearean: Academic and Mass Culture Constructions of Literary Authorship." In *Shakespeare, Film, Fin de Siècle,* edited by Mark Thornton Burnett and Ramona Wray, 203–31. Basingstoke: Macmillan, 2000.

Calendar of State Papers, Domestic Series, Elizabeth 1598–1601. Edited by Mary Anne Everett Green. London, 1869.

Calendar of State Papers, Domestic Series, Elizabeth 1601–1603. Edited by Mary Anne Everett Green. London, 1870.

Carey, Alfred E. *The Dark Lady.* London: John Long, 1919.

Carlyle, Thomas. "Lecture III: The Hero as Poet. Dante; Shakespeare." May 12, 1840. In *On Heroes, Hero-Worship, and the Heroic in History: Six Lectures,* 126–85. London, 1841.

Carr, Francis, and Lawrence Gerald. "Bacon's Royal Parentage." http://www.sirbacon.org/links/parentage.htm.

Cartmell, Deborah, I. Q. Hunter, and Imelda Whelehan, eds. *Retrovisions: Reinventing the Past in Film and Fiction.* London and Sterling, V.: Pluto, 2001.

The Century of Queens: With Sketches of Some Princes of Literature and Art. New York, 1872.

Chalmers, George. *An Apology for the Believers in the Shakspeare-Papers.* London, 1797.

———. *A Supplemental Apology for the Believers in the Shakspeare-Papers.* London, 1799.

Chambers, E. K. *The Elizabethan Stage.* 4 vols. Oxford: Clarendon, 1923.

———. *William Shakespeare: A Study of Facts and Problems.* 2 vols. Oxford: Clarendon, 1930.

Chapman, J[ohn] K[emble], ed. *A Complete History of Theatrical Entertainments, Dramas, Masques, and Triumphs, at the English Court, from the Time of King Henry the Eighth to the Present Day, Including the Series of Plays Performed before Her Majesty, at Windsor Castle, Christmas, 1848–9.* London, 1849.

Chester, Robert. *The Poems of Robert Chester 1601–1611.* Edited by Alexander B. Grosart. Manchester, 1878.

Chettle, Henry. *Englandes Mourning Garment. The English Experience,* no. 579. 1603; Repr. Amsterdam and New York: Da Capo / Theatrum Orbis Terrarum, 1973.

Chorley, Henry F. Introduction to *Kenilworth: A Masque of the Days of Queen Elizabeth: As Performed at the Birmingham Festival.* Music by Arthur S. Sullivan. Words by Henry F. Chorley. London, 1865.

Cibber, Theophilus. *Dissertations on Theatrical Subjects.* London, 1756.

Clare, Janet. "The Censorship of the Deposition Scene in *Richard II.*" *Review of English Studies,* n.s., 41.161 (Feb. 1990): 89–94.

Coddon, Karin. "'Such strange desyns': Madness, Subjectivity and Treason in *Hamlet* and Elizabethan Culture." *Renaissance Drama* 20 (1989): 51–75.

Colley, Linda. *Britons: Forging the Nation 1707–1837.* 1992; repr. London: Pimlico, 1994.

Collier, J. Payne. *New Facts Regarding the Life of Shakespeare.* London, 1835.

———. *New Particulars Regarding the Works of Shakespeare.* London, 1836.

———. "The Life of William Shakespeare." In *The Works of William Shakespeare,* edited by J. Payne Collier, 1:lix–cclxvi. London, 1844.

Le Comte d'Essex. Histoire Angloise. 2 vols. Paris, 1678.

Cook, Pam. *Fashioning the Nation: Costume and Identity in British Cinema.* London: British Film Institute, 1996.

Cornwall, Barry [Bryan Waller Procter]. Introduction to *The Complete Works of Shakespeare.* Edited by Richard Grant White. London and New York, 1857.

Cornwell, Bernard. Special on historical fiction. *Open Book,* BBC Radio 4, Oct. 10, 2004.

Costello, Louisa Stuart. *Memoirs of Eminent Englishwomen.* 4 vols. London, 1844.

Cunningham, Peter, ed. *Extracts from the Accounts of the Revels at Court, in the Reigns of Queen Elizabeth and King James I.* London, 1842.

Curling, Captain Henry. *Shakspere: The Poet, the Lover, the Actor, the Man: A Romance.* 3 vols. London, 1848. Republished as *The Forest Youth, or, Shakspere as He Lived: An Historical Tale.* London, 1853.

———. *Geraldine Maynard; or, The Abduction: A Tale of the Days of Shakspeare.* 3 vols. London, 1864.

Cushman, Robert. "Flying the Flag." *Observer Review* (London), June 19, 1977.

"Dario Fo: The Nobel Prize in Literature 1997." In *Les Prix Nobel: The Nobel Prizes 1997*, edited by Tore Frängsmyr, translated by Paul Claesson. Stockholm: Nobel Foundation, 1998. http://nobelprize.org/nobel_prizes/literature/laureates/1997/fo-bio.html.

Davidson, Peter, and Thomas McCoog, S. J. "Unreconciled: What Evidence Links Shakespeare and the Jesuits?" *Times Literary Supplement*, Mar. 16, 2007, 12–13.

Davies, Thomas. "Some Account of the Life of Mr. George Lillo." In *The Works of Mr George Lillo, With Some Account of his Life*, 1:ix–xlviii. London, 1775.

de Grazia, Margreta. *Shakespeare Verbatim: The Reproduction of Authenticity and the 1790 Apparatus.* Oxford: Clarendon, 1991.

Dennis, John. *The Comical Gallant: or, The Amours of Sir John Falstaffe.* London, 1702.

———. "Prologue to the Subscribers for *Julius Caesar*" (1707). In *A Collection and Selection of English Prologues and Epilogues*, edited by Acton Frederick Griffiths, 3:1–3. London, 1779.

———. *Original Letters, Familiar, Moral and Critical.* 2 vols. London, 1721.

de Vere Society. http://www.deveresociety.co.uk/.

Deverell, Mary. *Mary, Queen of Scots: An Historical Tragedy, or Dramatic Poem.* London, 1792.

Devereux, Hon. Walter Bourchier, ed. *Lives and Letters of the Devereux, Earls of Essex, in the Reigns of Elizabeth, James I, and Charles I, 1540–1646.* 2 vols. London, 1853.

Dibdin, Thomas. *A Metrical History of England.* 2 vols. London, 1813.

Dobson, Michael. *The Making of the National Poet: Shakespeare, Adaptation and Authorship, 1660–1769.* Oxford: Clarendon, 1992.

———. "Bowdler and Britannia: Shakespeare and the National Libido." *Shakespeare Survey* 46 (1994): 137–44.

Dobson, Michael, and Nicola J. Watson. *England's Elizabeth: An Afterlife in Fame and Fantasy.* Oxford: Oxford University Press, 2002.

"*Doctor Who* Fact File: The Shakespeare Code." http://www.bbc.co.uk/doctorwho/episodes/2007/302.shtml.

Doctor Who. "The Shakespeare Code." Written by Gareth Roberts. Series 3, episode 2. First broadcast in the U.K. on BBC1 TV, Apr. 7, 2007.

Dodd, Alfred. *The Personal Poems of Francis Bacon (Our Shake-speare), the Son of Queen Elizabeth.* Liverpool: Daily Post, 1931.

———. *The Personal Poems of Francis Bacon (Our Shake-speare), the Son of Queen Elizabeth.* 2nd ed. Liverpool: Daily Post, 1936.

Dollimore, Jonathan. *Radical Tragedy: Religion, Ideology and Power in the Drama of Shakespeare and His Contemporaries.* 2nd ed. 1984; repr. Hemel Hempstead: Harvester Wheatsheaf, 1989.

Dollimore, Jonathan, and Alan Sinfield, eds. *Political Shakespeare: New Essays in Cultural Materialism.* Manchester and New York: Manchester University Press, 1985.

Douglas, Montagu W. *The Earl of Oxford as "Shakespeare": An Outline of the Case.* London: Cecil Palmer, 1931.

Dowden, Edward. *Shakspere: A Critical Study of His Mind and Art.* London, 1875.

Drake, Nathan. *Shakspeare and His Times.* 2 vols. London, 1817.

———. *Noontide Leisure; or, Sketches in Summer.* 2 vols. London, 1824.

Dryden, John. Prologue to *The Tempest, or the Enchanted Island*, by Sir William Davenant and John Dryden. London, 1670.

Duffy, Eamon. *The Stripping of the Altars: Traditional Religion in England, 1400–1580*. New Haven: Yale University Press, 1992.

Duke, Marion I. "Phillips' Version of *Dream* a Jewel of Intellect, Vision." *Listowel Banner* (Ontario), Aug. 26, 1976.

Duncan-Jones, Katherine. "*Christs Teares,* Nashe's 'forsaken extremities.'" *Review of English Studies,* n.s., 49.194 (1998): 167–80.

———. "Bess Carey's Petrarch: Newly Discovered Elizabethan Sonnets." *Review of English Studies,* n.s., 50.199 (1999): 304–19.

———. *Ungentle Shakespeare: Scenes from His Life.* London: Thomson Learning /Arden Shakespeare, 2001.

———. "The Globe Theatre, February 7, 1601." In *I Wish I'd Been There: Twenty Historians Revisit Key Moments in History,* edited by Byron Hollinshead and Theodore K. Rabb, 120–33. London: Macmillan, 2008.

Dyce, Alexander. *Remarks on Mr. J. P. Collier's and Mr. C. Knight's Editions of Shakespeare.* London, 1844.

Eagle, Dorothy, and Hilary Carnell, eds. *The Oxford Literary Guide to the British Isles.* Oxford: Oxford University Press, 1977.

Edmonds, Richard. Review of Mark Rylance, *I Am Shakespeare. Stage,* Sept. 11, 2007. http://www.thestage.co.uk/reviews/review.php/18183/i-am-shakespeare.

Edwards, Sydney. "A Bewitching Double by Exile Maggie." *Evening Standard* (London), June 8, 1977.

Eliot, T. S. "The Waste Land" (1922). In *Selected Poems.* London: Faber, 1954.

Elizabeth. Directed by Shekhar Kapur. Written by Michael Hirst. Starring Cate Blanchett. Polygram Filmed Entertainment et al., 1998. Universal Pictures UK DVD, 2006.

Elizabeth I. *Collected Works.* Edited by Leah S. Marcus, Janel Mueller, and Mary Beth Rose. Chicago and London: University of Chicago Press, 2000.

Elizabeth I. Directed by Tom Hooper. Written by Nigel Williams. Starring Helen Mirren. Channel 4 U.K. TV series, 2005.

Elizabeth: The Golden Age. Directed by Shekhar Kapur. Written by William Nicholson and Michael Hirst. Starring Cate Blanchett. Motion Picture ZETA, 2007. Universal Pictures UK DVD, 2008.

Elizabeth R. Directed by Roderick Graham et al. Written by John Prebble et al. Starring Glenda Jackson. BBC TV series, 1971. BBC Worldwide DVD, 2006.

Ellis, David. *That Man Shakespeare: Icon of Modern Culture.* Robertsbridge, E. Sussex: Helm Information, 2005.

Erickson, Peter. *Rewriting Shakespeare, Rewriting Ourselves.* Berkeley: University of California Press, 1991.

Everett, Barbara. "Set upon a Golden Bough to Sing: Shakespeare's Debt to Sidney in 'The Phoenix and Turtle.'" *Times Literary Supplement* 5107 (Feb. 16, 2001): 13–14.

Fellowes, E. H., ed. *English Madrigal Verse 1588–1632.* 3rd ed. Revised and enlarged by F. W. Sternfeld and D. Greer. Oxford: Oxford University Press, 1967.

Fiennes, Joseph. "Fiennes Open about Gay Kiss." *Contactmusic,* Jan. 20, 2005. http://www.contactmusic.com.

———. Images on *bentblog.* http://www.bentblog.com/art26207184.htm.

Findley, Timothy. *Elizabeth Rex.* Winnipeg: Blizzard Publishing, 2000.

Finney, Patricia. *Firedrake's Eye.* London: Sinclair-Stevenson, 1992.

———. Personal website. http://www.patricia-finney.co.uk/.

Finnis, John, and Patrick Martin. "Another Turn for the Turtle: Shakespeare's Intercession for Love's Martyr." *Times Literary Supplement* 5220 (Apr. 18, 2003): 12–13.

Fleay, Frederick Gard. *A Biographical Chronicle of the English Drama, 1559–1642.* London, 1891.

———. *A Chronicle History of the Life and Work of William Shakespeare, Player, Poet, and Playmaker.* London, 1886.

Fletcher, C.R.L., and Rudyard Kipling. *A History of England.* Rev. ed. Oxford: Clarendon, 1911.

Flloyd, Thomas. *Bibliotheca Biographica: A Synopsis of Universal Biography, Ancient and Modern.* 3 vols. London, 1760.

Fo, Dario. *Elizabeth: Almost by Chance a Woman [Quasi per Caso una Donna: Elisabetta].* Translated by Gillian Hanna. Introduced by Stuart Hood. 1984; repr. London: Methuen, 1987.

Foulkes, Richard. *Performing Shakespeare in the Age of Empire.* Cambridge: Cambridge University Press, 2002.

———, ed. *Shakespeare and the Victorian Stage.* Cambridge: Cambridge University Press, 1986.

Fowler, James. "David Scott's *Queen Elizabeth Viewing the Performance of 'The Merry Wives of Windsor' in the Globe Theatre* (1840)." In *Shakespeare and the Victorian Stage,* edited by Richard Foulkes, 23–38. Cambridge: Cambridge University Press, 1986.

The Francis Bacon Society Incorporated. http://www.baconsocietyinc.org/.

Franssen, Paul. "The Bard and Ireland: Shakespeare's Protestantism as Politics in Disguise." In *Shakespeare Survey 54: Shakespeare and Religions,* edited by Peter Holland, 71–79. Cambridge: Cambridge University Press, 2001.

Fraser, John. "Phillips Brings Special Vision to Regal *Dream.*" *Toronto Globe and Mail,* Aug. 19/20, 1976.

Freeman, Arthur, and Janet Ing Freeman. *John Payne Collier: Scholarship and Forgery in the Nineteenth Century.* 2 vols. Yale: Yale University Press, 2004.

Freud, Sigmund. "Family Romances" (1909). In *On Sexuality,* Penguin Freud Library, vol.7, translated by James Strachey, edited by Angela Richards, 217–25. 1977; repr. Harmondsworth, U.K.: Penguin, 1991.

Friedman, William F., and Elizabeth S. Friedman. *The Shakespearean Ciphers Examined.* Cambridge: Cambridge University Press, 1957.

Gallup, Elizabeth Wells. *The Bi-literal Cypher of Sir Francis Bacon.* Detroit and London, 1899.

Garnett, Richard. *William Shakespeare, Pedagogue and Poacher: A Drama.* London and New York: John Lane, 1905.

Gascoigne, George. *The Princely Pleasures at Kenelworth Castle.* In *Complete Works,* edited by John W. Cunliffe, 2:91–131. Cambridge: Cambridge University Press, 1910.

Gerald, Lawrence. Interview with Mark Rylance, 1994. *Sir Francis Bacon's New Advancement of Learning.* http://www.sirbacon.org/markrylance.htm (accessed June 17, 2008).

———. "Who We Are." *Sir Francis Bacon's New Advancement of Learning.* http://www.sirbacon.org/credits.html (accessed June 17, 2008).

Gewertz, Ken. "Greenblatt Teases Out a Knowable Shakespeare." *Harvard University Gazette,* Sept. 30, 2004. http://www.news.harvard.edu/gazette/2004/09.30/01-shakespeare.html.

Gifford, Dennis. *The British Film Catalogue.* 3rd ed. Vol. 1, *Fiction Film 1895–1994.* London and Chicago: Fitzroy Dearborn, 2000.

Gildon, Charles. "Remarks on the Plays of Shakespear." In *The Works of Mr. William Shakespear,* edited by Nicholas Rowe, 7:257–444. London, 1710.

Gorges, Sir Arthur. *Poems.* Edited by Helen Estabrook Sandison. Oxford: Oxford University Press, 1953.

Graves, Robert. *Goodbye to All That.* 1929; repr. Harmondsworth, U.K.: Penguin, 1960.

Green, Paul. *The Lost Colony: A Symphonic Drama in Two Acts.* Chapel Hill: University of North Carolina Press, 1937.

———. *The Lost Colony: A Symphonic Drama in Two Acts.* Revised ed. Chapel Hill: University of North Carolina Press, 1946.

———. *A Paul Green Reader.* Edited by Laurence G. Avery. Chapel Hill and London: University of North Carolina Press, 1998.

Greenblatt, Stephen. *Shakespearean Negotiations: The Circulation of Social Energy in Renaissance England.* Berkeley: University of California Press, 1988.

———. *Hamlet in Purgatory.* Princeton: Princeton University Press, 2001.

———. *Will in the World: How Shakespeare Became Shakespeare.* London: Jonathan Cape, 2004.

———, ed. *The Power of Forms in the English Renaissance.* Norman, Okla.: Pilgrim Books, 1982.

Greg, W. W. *A Bibliography of the English Printed Drama to the Restoration.* London: Bibliographical Society, 1970.

Gregg, Tresham D. *Queen Elizabeth; or the Origin of Shakespeare. A Drama in Five Acts.* London, 1872.

Grindon, Leger. *Shadows on the Past: Studies in the Historical Fiction Film.* Philadelphia: Temple University Press, 1994.

Gross, John, ed. *After Shakespeare: An Anthology.* Oxford: Oxford University Press, 2002.

Gurr, Andrew. *The Shakespearean Stage 1574–1642.* 3rd ed. Cambridge: Cambridge University Press, 1992.

———. *Playgoing in Shakespeare's London.* 2nd ed. Cambridge: Cambridge University Press, 1996.

———. *The Shakespeare Company, 1594–1642.* Cambridge: Cambridge University Press, 2004.

Hackett, Helen. *Virgin Mother, Maiden Queen: Elizabeth I and the Cult of the Virgin Mary.* Basingstoke: Macmillan, 1995.

———. "Historiographical Review: Dreams or Designs, Cults or Constructions? The Study of Images of Monarchs." *Historical Journal* 44.3 (Cambridge University Press, 2001): 811–23.

———. "*A Midsummer Night's Dream.*" In *A Companion to Shakespeare's Works,* Vol. 3, *The Comedies,* edited by Jean Howard and Richard Dutton, 338–57. Oxford: Blackwell, 2003.

———. Introduction to *A Midsummer Night's Dream,* by William Shakespeare, edited by Stanley Wells, xxi–lxxi. London: Penguin, 2005.

Hadley, Ted R. "*Dream* Is Top Quality." *Union-Sun and Journal* (Lockport, N.Y.), July 11, 1977.

Haigh, Christopher. *Reformation and Resistance in Tudor Lancashire.* Cambridge: Cambridge University Press, 1975.

Haigh, Christopher, ed. *The English Reformation Revised.* Cambridge: Cambridge University Press, 1987.

Hall, N. John. *Max Beerbohm Caricatures.* New Haven and London: Yale University Press, 1997.

Halliday, Andrew, and Frederic Lawrence. *Kenilworth or Ye Queene, Ye Earle, and Ye Maydenne. A Comic Operatic Extravaganza.* [London, 1859].

Halliday, F. E. *The Cult of Shakespeare.* London: Gerald Duckworth, 1957.

Halliwell, James Orchard. *The Life of William Shakespeare.* London, 1848.

———. *Observations on the Shaksperian Forgeries at Bridgewater House.* London, 1853.

Halpin, Rev. N. J. *Oberon's Vision in the Midsummer-Night's Dream, Illustrated by a Comparison with Lyllie's Endymion.* London, 1843.

Hammerschmidt-Hummel, Hildegard. "'The Most Important Subject That Can Possibly Be': A Reply to E.A.J. Honigmann." *Connotations* 12.2–3 (2002/2003): 155–66. http://www.uni-tuebingen.de/uni/nec/ham-hu1223.htm.

———. *The Life and Times of William Shakespeare 1564–1616.* London: Chaucer Press, 2007. Translation of Hildegard Hammerschmidt-Hummel, *William Shakespeare: Seine Zeit, Sein Leben, Sein Werk.* Mainz: von Zabern, 2003.

Harper, Karen. *The Poyson Garden.* New York: Delacorte, 1999.

Harris, Frank. *The Man Shakespeare and His Tragic Life-Story.* London: Frank Palmer, 1909.

———. *Shakespeare and His Love.* London: Frank Palmer, 1910.

Harris, Robert. "Prima Donna inter Pares." *Observer Review* (London), Jan. 3, 1988, 17.

Hartmann, Sadakichi. *Shakespeare in Art.* Boston: L. C. Page, 1901.

Harvey, W. "Biographical Memoir of Shakspeare." In *The Works of Shakspeare,* iii–xii. London, 1825.

Hastings, Adrian. *The Construction of Nationhood: Ethnicity, Religion and Nationalism.* Cambridge: Cambridge University Press, 1997.

Haven, Cynthia L. "Papist Plots." Review of Clare Asquith, *Shadowplay. Washington Post,* Book World sec., Aug. 14, 2005.

Hawke, Simon. *A Mystery of Errors.* New York: Forge, 2000.

Hawkes, Terence. *That Shakespeherian Rag: Essays on a Critical Process.* London and New York: Methuen, 1986.

Hazlitt, W. C., ed. *Fugitive Tracts.* 2 vols. London, 1875.

Healy, Margaret. *Writers and Their Work: William Shakespeare, "Richard II."* Plymouth, U.K.: Northcote House, 1998.

Henderson, Diana E. "Othello Redux? Scott's *Kenilworth* and the Trickiness of "Race" on the Nineteenth-Century Stage." In *Victorian Shakespeare,* vol. 2, *Literature and Culture,* edited by Gail Marshall and Adrian Poole, 14–29. Basingstoke: Palgrave, 2003.

Henry V. Directed by Laurence Olivier. Written by William Shakespeare. Two Cities Films, 1944. ITV DVD, 2003.

Hentzner, Paul. *A Journey into England in the Year 1598.* Translated by Richard Bentley. Edited by Horace Walpole. Strawberry Hill, 1757.

Heyck, Thomas William. *A History of the Peoples of the British Isles from 1688 to 1914.* London: Routledge, 2002.

———. *A History of the Peoples of the British Isles from 1870 to the Present.* London: Routledge, 2002.

Higson, Andrew. *English Heritage, English Cinema: Costume Drama since 1980*. Oxford: Oxford University Press, 2003.

Hobsbawm, E. J. *Nations and Nationalism since 1780: Programme, Myth, Reality*. Cambridge: Cambridge University Press, 1990.

Hodgdon, Barbara. *The Shakespeare Trade: Performances and Appropriations*. Philadelphia: University of Pennsylvania Press, 1998.

Holland, Peter. "Dramatizing the Dramatist." In *Shakespeare Survey 58: Writing about Shakespeare*, edited by Peter Holland, 137–47. Cambridge: Cambridge University Press, 2005.

Hooper, Mary. *At the House of the Magician*. London: Bloomsbury, 2007.

Hopkins, Lisa. "'Ripeness is all': The Death of Elizabeth in Drama." *Renaissance Forum: An Electronic Journal of Early Modern Literary and Historical Studies* 4.2 (2000). http://www.hull.ac.uk/renforum/.

Hopkinson, Joseph. "The Life of Shakspeare." In *The Plays and Poems of William Shakespeare . . . First American Edition*, edited by Joseph Hopkinson, vol. 1. Philadelphia, 1795.

Hotson, Leslie. *The First Night of "Twelfth Night."* London: Rupert Hart-Davis, 1954.

Hoyt, Sarah A. *All Night Awake*. New York: Ace, 2002.

In Search of Shakespeare. Written and presented by Michael Wood. BBC TV series, 2003.

Ingleby, C. M. *A Complete View of the Shakspere Controversy*. London, 1861.

Internet Movie Database (IMDb). http://imdb.com/.

Ireland, Samuel, ed. *Miscellaneous Papers and Legal Instruments under the Hand and Seal of William Shakspeare*. London, 1796.

Ireland, W[illiam]-H[enry]. *An Authentic Account of the Shaksperian Manuscripts, &c.* London, 1796.

J.G.R. "Shakespeare's Sonnets." *Notes and Queries*, 2nd ser., 7 (Feb. 12, 1859): 125.

Jackson, Gabriele Bernhard. "Topical Ideology: Witches, Amazons, and Shakespeare's Joan of Arc." *English Literary Renaissance* 18 (1988): 40–65.

Jameson, Anna. *Memoirs of Celebrated Female Sovereigns*. 2 vols. London, 1831.

Jansohn, Christa, ed. *Queen Elizabeth I: Past and Present*. Münster: Lit Verlag, 2004.

Jenkins, John S. *Heroines of History*. New York, 1851. *Internet Archive*. www.archive.org/details/heroinesofhistoroojenkiala.

Johnson, Sarah L. *Historical Fiction: A Guide to the Genre*. Westport, Conn., and London: Greenwood, 2005.

Jones, E. Brandram. *In Burleigh's Days*. London: John Long, 1916.

Jonson, Ben. *Every Man in His Humour*. Edited by Martin Seymour-Smith. London: Ernest Benn, 1966.

———. "Conversations with William Drummond." In *The Complete Poems*, edited by George Parfitt, rev. ed., 459–80. Harmondsworth: Penguin, 1988.

Joyce, James. *Ulysses*. 1922; repr. Harmondsworth: Penguin, 1971.

Jung, Winfried, and Bodo Plachta. "The Queen Sings Coloratura: Elizabeth I and Belcanto Opera." In *Queen Elizabeth I: Past and Present*, edited by Christa Jansohn, 195–209. Münster: Lit Verlag, 2004.

Kay, Dennis. *Shakespeare: His Life, Work, and Era*. London: Sidgwick and Jackson, 1992.

Kearns, Cleo McNelly. "Dubious Pleasures: Dorothy Dunnett and the Historical Novel." *Critical Quarterly* 32.1 (Spring 1990): 36–48.

Kellerman, Faye. *The Quality of Mercy.* London: W. H. Allen, 1989.

Kelley, Donald R., and David Harris Sacks, eds. *The Historical Imagination in Early Modern Britain: History, Rhetoric and Fiction, 1500–1800.* Cambridge: Cambridge University Press, 1997.

Kelly, Kevin. "A Regal Opening for *Dream.*" *Boston Globe,* June 8, 1977.

Kernan, Alvin. *Shakespeare, the King's Playwright: Theater in the Stuart Court 1603–1613.* New Haven and London: Yale University Press, 1995.

Kingsley, Charles. "Sir Walter Raleigh and His Time." In *Plays and Puritans and Other Historical Essays,* 83–207. London, 1873.

Klett, Elizabeth. "*Shakespeare in Love* and the End(s) of History." In *Retrovisions: Reinventing the Past in Film and Fiction,* edited by Deborah Cartmell, I. Q. Hunter, and Imelda Whelehan, 25–40. London and Sterling, V.: Pluto, 2001.

Knowles, Richard Paul. "Robin Phillips' Strange and Wondrous Dream." *Theatre History in Canada* 9.1 (Spring 1988): 38–58.

Knox, Ronald A. "The Authorship of *In Memoriam.*" In *Essays in Satire,* 223–35. London: Sheed and Ward, 1928.

Ko, Yu Jin. "Shakespeare Festivals." In *Shakespeare in American Life,* edited by Virginia Mason Vaughan and Alden T. Vaughan, 88–99. Washington, D.C.: Folger Shakespeare Library, 2007.

Koch, Frederick Henry. *Raleigh, the Shepherd of the Ocean: A Pageant-Drama.* Raleigh, N.C.: Edwards and Broughton, 1920.

Koch, Frederick H., et al. *Shakespeare, the Playmaker.* Grand Forks: University of North Dakota, 1916.

Kott, Jan. *Shakespeare Our Contemporary.* Translated by Boleslaw Taborski. 1965; repr. London: Routledge, 1988.

La Mothe, Marie Catherine, Comtesse d'Aulnoy. *Nouvelles d'Elisabeth Reyne d'Angleterre.* Translated by Spencer Hickman as *The Novels of Elizabeth, Queen of England.* 2 vols. London, 1680, 1681.

Lacher, Irene. "He's Got Will Power: The Literati Are Abuzz over Stephen Greenblatt's Take on Shakespeare." *Los Angeles Times,* Nov. 21, 2004, E6.

Laneham, Robert. *A Letter.* 1575; repr. Menston: Scolar, 1968.

Lanier, Douglas. *Shakespeare and Modern Popular Culture.* Oxford: Oxford University Press, 2002.

Lee, Robert Mason. "Shakespeare, the Secret Rebel." *Macleans.ca,* Aug. 5, 2005. http://www.macleans.ca/culture/books/article.jsp?content=20050801_110172_110172.

Lee, Sidney. *A Life of William Shakespeare.* London, 1898.

Leigh, William R. *Clipt Wings: A Drama in Five Acts.* New York: Thornton W. Allen, 1930.

Levin, Carole. "All the Queen's Children: Elizabeth I and the Meanings of Motherhood." *Explorations in Renaissance Culture* 30.1 (Summer 2004): 57–76.

Lewin, Roger. "Did Queen Bess Have a Head for Shakespeare?" *New Scientist,* no. 1795 (Nov. 16, 1991): 15.

Lewis, Jayne Elizabeth. *Mary Queen of Scots: Romance and Nation.* London and New York: Routledge, 1998.

Light, Alison. *Forever England: Femininity, Literature and Conservatism between the Wars.* London and New York: Routledge, 1991.

Lillo, George. *Marina.* London, 1738.

Looney, J. Thomas. *"Shakespeare" Identified in Edward de Vere, the Seventeenth Earl of Oxford.* London: Cecil Palmer, 1920.

The Lost Colony. http://www.thelostcolony.org.

Lukács, Georg. *The Historical Novel* (1938). Translated by Hannah and Stanley Mitchell. London: Merlin Press, 1962.

Lyly, John. *Complete Works.* Edited by R. Warwick Bond. Vol. 1. Oxford: Clarendon, 1902.

McColvin, Lionel R. *To Kill the Queen: A Pageant Play.* London: Noel Douglas, 1931.

McCue, Jim. "John Payne Collier, the Scholar Forger." *Essays in Criticism* 57.4 (2007): 287–300.

McIntosh, DeCourcy E. "New York's Favorite Pictures in the 1870s." *Magazine Antiques,* Apr. 2004. Available at *LookSmart Find Articles.* http://findarticles.com.

Majumdar, Sarottama. "That Sublime 'Old Gentleman': Shakespeare's Plays in Calcutta, 1775–1930." In *India's Shakespeare: Translation, Interpretation, and Performance,* edited by Poonam Trivedi and Dennis Bartholomeusz, 260–67. Newark: University of Delaware Press, 2005.

Malone, Edmond. *An Inquiry into the Authenticity of Certain Miscellaneous Papers and Legal Instruments Published Dec. 24 1795.* London, 1796.

———. "An Historical Account of the English Stage" (1790). In *The Plays and Poems of William Shakspeare,* edited by James Boswell the younger, vol. 3. London, 1821.

———. *The Life of William Shakspeare,* with *An Essay on Phraseology and Metre* by James Boswell. Limited ed. London, 1821.

Marcus, Leah. *Puzzling Shakespeare: Local Reading and Its Discontents.* Berkeley: University of California Press, 1988.

———. *Unediting the Renaissance: Shakespeare, Marlowe, Milton.* London and New York: Routledge, 1996.

Marsden, Jean I., ed. *The Appropriation of Shakespeare: Post-Renaissance Reconstructions of the Works and the Myth.* Hemel Hempstead: Harvester Wheatsheaf, 1991.

Marshall, Henrietta E. *Our Island Story: A Child's History of England.* London: T. C. and E. C. Jack, 1905.

[Martin, William]. *Peter Parley's Tales about Kings and Queens.* London, 1848.

MASC 25: Mapping Access to Special Collections in the London Region. http://www.ucl.ac.uk/ls/masc25/.

Massey, Gerald. *Shakspeare's Sonnets Never Before Interpreted: His Private Friends Identified.* London, 1866.

Matchett, William H. *The Phoenix and the Turtle: Shakespeare's Poem and Chester's "Loues Martyr."* The Hague: Mouton, 1965.

May, Thomas, "A Will and a Way: An Interview with Stephen Greenblatt." *Amazon.com.* http://www.amazon.com/gp/feature.html/103–1398685–9279825?docId=551085 (accessed June 18, 2008).

"The Memorable Order of Tin Hats." *FirstWorldWar.com.* http://www.firstworldwar.com/features/moth.htm.

Meyer, Tamar, ed. *Gender Ironies of Nationalism: Sexing the Nation.* London and New York: Routledge, 2000.

Michell, John. *Who Wrote Shakespeare?* London: Thames and Hudson, 1996.

Minto, William, *Characteristics of English Poets from Chaucer to Shelley.* Edinburgh and London, 1874.

Monk, Claire, and Amy Sargeant, eds. *British Historical Cinema: The History, Heritage and Costume Film.* London and New York: Routledge, 2002.

Montrose, Louis. "Celebration and Insinuation: Sir Philip Sidney and the Motives of Elizabethan Courtship." *Renaissance Drama,* n.s., 8 (1977): 3–35.

———. "'The Perfecte Paterne of a Poete': The Poetics of Courtship in *The Shepheardes Calender.*" *Texas Studies in Literature and Language* 21 (1979): 34–67.

———. "'Eliza, Queene of Shepheardes' and the Pastoral of Power." *English Literary Renaissance* 10 (1980): 153–82.

———. "Gifts and Reasons: The Contexts of Peele's *Araygnement of Paris.*" *English Literary History* 47 (1980): 433–61.

———."Of Gentlemen and Shepherds: The Politics of Elizabethan Pastoral Form." *English Literary History* 50 (1983): 415–59.

———. "'Shaping Fantasies': Figurations of Gender and Power in Elizabethan Culture." *Representations* 2 (Spring 1983): 61–94.

———. "The Elizabethan Subject and the Spenserian Text." In *Literary Theory/Renaissance Texts,* edited by Patricia Parker and David Quint, 303–40. Baltimore: Johns Hopkins University Press, 1986.

———. "*A Midsummer Night's Dream* and the Shaping Fantasies of Elizabethan Culture: Gender, Power, Form," In *Rewriting the Renaissance: The Discourses of Sexual Difference in Early Modern Europe,* edited by Margaret W. Ferguson et al., 65–87. Chicago: University of Chicago Press, 1986.

———. "Renaissance Literary Studies and the Subject of History." *English Literary Renaissance* 16 (1986): 5–12.

———. "'Shaping Fantasies': Figurations of Gender and Power in Elizabethan Culture." In *New Casebook: A Midsummer Night's Dream,* edited by Richard Dutton, 101–38. Basingstoke: Macmillan, 1996.

———. "Spenser and the Elizabethan Political Imaginary." *English Literary History* 69 (2002): 907–46.

Morgan, Kenneth O., ed. *The Oxford History of Britain.* Rev. ed. Oxford: Oxford University Press, 2001.

Morris, Helen. "Queen Elizabeth 'Shadowed' in Cleopatra." *Huntington Library Quarterly* 32 (1968–69): 271–78.

Mortimer, John. *Will Shakespeare.* Sevenoaks: Coronet/Hodder and Stoughton, 1977.

Mosse, George L. *Nationalism and Sexuality: Respectability and Abnormal Sexuality in Modern Europe.* New York: Howard Fertig, 1985.

Mudie, Alfred. *The Self-Named William Shake=speare.* London: Cecil Palmer, 1929.

Mullaney, Steven. "Mourning and Misogyny: *Hamlet* and the Final Progress of *Elizabeth I.*" *Shakespeare Quarterly* 45.2 (Summer 1994): 139–58.

Murphy, Debra. "Cracking Shakespeare's Catholic Code: An interview with Clare Asquith." *Godspy,* Nov. 22, 2005. http://ddarchive.godspy.com/reviews/Cracking-Shakespeares-Code-An-interview-with-Claire-Asquith-author-of-Shadowplay.cfm.html.

Museum of the History of Science, University of Oxford. "Rudolf II and Tycho." http://www.mhs.ox.ac.uk/tycho/rudolph.htm.

National Maritime Museum. "Last Chance to View Elizabeth Exhibition." Press release, Sept. 1, 2003. http://www.nmm.ac.uk/server/show/conWebDoc.9416.

Neale, J. E. *Queen Elizabeth I.* 1934; repr. Harmondsworth: Penguin, 1960.

Neil, Samuel. *Shakespere: A Critical Biography.* London, 1861.

———. *A Biography of Shakespeare Written for the Worthies of Warwickshire.* Warwick, 1869.

Nelson, James. "Stratford Festival Opens New Production: *Midsummer Night's Dream.*" *Star Phoenix* (Saskatoon, Sask.), Aug. 20, 1976.

Nesbit, E. *Royal Children of English History.* London, 1896.

Nicholls, Isabella S. *The Eldest Son of Queen Elizabeth.* Sydney: William Brooks, 1913.

Norman, Marc, and Tom Stoppard. *Shakespeare in Love.* London: Faber and Faber, 1999.

Nye, Robert. *The Late Mr Shakespeare.* London: Chatto and Windus, 1998.

Oakley, Lucy. "Words into Pictures: Shakespeare in British Art, 1760–1900." In *A Brush with Shakespeare: The Bard in Painting, 1780–1910*, edited by Ross Anderson, 3–22. Montgomery, Ala.: Montgomery Museum of Fine Arts, 1985.

Ogburn, Dorothy, and Charlton Ogburn. *The Renaissance Man of England.* 3rd ed. 1947; repr. New York: Coward-McCann, 1955.

Old Bill "Through the Ages." Directed by Thomas Bentley. Starring Syd Walker. Ideal film co., 1924.

Old Bill "Through the Ages." British Film Institute National Archive. http:www.bfi.org.uk/nftva/catalogues/film/2409.

Orgel, Stephen. "Making Greatness Familiar." In *The Power of Forms in the English Renaissance,* edited by Stephen Greenblatt, 41–46. Norman, Okla.: Pilgrim, 1982.

———. *Imagining Shakespeare: A History of Texts and Visions.* Basingstoke: Palgrave Macmillan, 2003.

O'Sullivan, Maurice J., ed. *Shakespeare's Other Lives: An Anthology of Fictional Depictions of the Bard.* Jefferson, N.C., and London: McFarland, 1997.

Otway, Thomas. *The History and Fall of Caius Marius: A Tragedy.* London, 1680.

Owen, Cunliffe. *The Phoenix and the Dove: A Novel.* London: Rich and Cowan, 1933.

Owen, Orville W. *Sir Francis Bacon's Cipher Story.* Books 1–2. London, 1894.

The Oxford Dictionary of National Biography (ODNB). Oxford: Oxford University Press. http://www.oxforddnb.com.

Parker, Andrew, et al., eds. *Nationalisms and Sexualities.* New York and London: Routledge, 1992.

Parrott, J. Edward. *The Pageant of British History.* London: Thomas Nelson, 1908.

Patterson, Annabel. *Shakespeare and the Popular Voice.* Oxford: Blackwell, 1989.

Peach, L. du Garde. *The Story of the First Queen Elizabeth.* Ladybird Adventures from History. Loughborough: Wills and Hepworth, 1958.

Percy, Thomas. "On the Origins of the English Stage." In *Reliques of Ancient English Poetry,* 4th ed, vol. 1, bk. 2, 128–53. London, 1794.

Phillips, James Emerson. *Images of a Queen: Mary Stuart in Sixteenth-Century Literature.* Berkeley: University of California Press, 1964.

Picard, Liza. *Elizabeth's London: Everyday Life in Elizabethan London.* London: Weidenfeld and Nicolson, 2003.

Pidduck, Julianne. "*Elizabeth* and *Shakespeare in Love*: Screening the Elizabethans." In *Film/Literature/Heritage: A Sight and Sound Reader,* edited by Ginette Vincendeau, 130–35. London: British Film Institute, 2001.

Pierce, Patricia. *The Great Shakespeare Fraud.* Stroud: Sutton, 2004.

Pigeon, Renée. "'No Man's Elizabeth': The Virgin Queen in Recent Films." In *Retrovisions: Reinventing the Past in Film and Fiction,* edited by Deborah Cartmell, I. Q. Hunter, and Imelda Whelehan, 8–24. London and Sterling, V.: Pluto, 2001.

Pineton, Clara Longworth de, Comtesse de Chambrun. *My Shakespeare, Rise!* Stratford-upon-Avon and London: Shakespeare Press / J. B. Lippincott, 1935.

Poole, Adrian. *Shakespeare and the Victorians.* Arden Critical Companions. London: Thomson Learning, 2004.

"Prose and Poetry: Bruce Bairnsfather." *FirstWorldWar.com.* http://www.firstworldwar.com/poetsandprose/bairnsfather.htm.

Rawlings, Peter, ed. *Americans on Shakespeare 1776–1914.* Aldershot: Ashgate, 1999.

Rebello, Stephen. "Running from Stardom." *Advocate: The National Gay and Lesbian Newsmagazine,* Sept. 12, 2006. Available at http://www.thefreelibrary.com.

Richmond, Velma Bourgeois. "Elizabeth I in Imperial Britain: A Myth for Children." In *Queen Elizabeth I: Past and Present,* edited by Christa Jansohn, 211–31. Münster: Lit Verlag, 2004.

Rinehart, Keith. "Shakespeare's Cleopatra and England's Elizabeth." *Shakespeare Quarterly* 23 (1972): 81–86.

Ringler, William A., Jr., and Steven W. May. "An Epilogue Possibly by Shakespeare." *Modern Philology* 70 (Nov. 1972): 138–39.

Roe, J. E. *Sir Francis Bacon's Own Story.* Rochester, N.Y.: DuBois, 1918.

Romney, Jonathan. "Comedy, Love, and a Bit with a Dog." *Guardian* (London), Jan. 29, 1999. http://film.guardian.co.uk/News_Story/Critic_Review/Guardian/0,,36510,00.html.

Rowe, Nicholas. "Some Account of the Life, &c. of Mr. William Shakespear." In *The Works of Mr. William Shakespear,* edited by Nicholas Rowe, 1: i–xl. London, 1709.

Rowse, A. L. *William Shakespeare: A Biography.* London: Macmillan, 1963.

Royal Shakespeare Theatre. *Catalogue of Pictures and Sculptures: Royal Shakespeare Theatre Picture Gallery.* 6th ed. Stratford-upon-Avon: Royal Shakespeare Theatre, 1970.

Rozett, Martha Tuck. *Constructing a World: Shakespeare's England and the New Historical Fiction.* Albany: State University of New York Press, 2003.

Roznovits, Linda. *Shakespeare and the Politics of Culture in Late Victorian England.* Baltimore and London: Johns Hopkins University Press, 1998.

Rusche, Harry. *Shakespeare Illustrated.* http://shakespeare.emory.edu/illustrated_index.cfm.

Ryan, Richard. *Dramatic Table Talk.* Vol. 2. London, 1825.

S. A. Review of *The Jew in Early English Literature,* by H. Michelson, and other books. *Jewish Quarterly Review,* n.s., 19.3 (Jan. 1929): 321–25.

Sawyer, Robert. *Victorian Appropriations of Shakespeare.* London: Associated University Presses, 2003.

Scarisbrick, J. J. *The Reformation and the English People.* Oxford: Blackwell, 1984.

Schmidgall, Gary. *Shakespeare and Opera.* Oxford: Oxford University Press, 1990.

Schoch, Richard W. *Not Shakespeare: Bardolatry and Burlesque in the Nineteenth Century.* Cambridge: Cambridge University Press, 2002.

———. *Queen Victoria and the Theatre of Her Age.* Basingstoke and New York: Palgrave Macmillan, 2004.

Schoenbaum, S. *Shakespeare: The Globe and the World.* New York and Oxford: Folger Shakespeare Library and Oxford University Press, 1979.

———. *William Shakespeare: A Compact Documentary Life.* Rev. ed. 1977; repr. New York and Oxford: Oxford University Press, 1987.

———. *Shakespeare's Lives.* Rev. ed. 1970; repr. Oxford: Oxford University Press, 1993.

Schwartz, Lillian F. "It Is I (Mona-Leo)." In *Digital Visions: Computers and Art,* edited by Cynthia Goodman, 82–83, fig. 51. New York: Abrams, 1987.

———. "Lillian F. Schwartz: Film and Television." http://lillian.com/reviews/tv.html.

———. "The Mask of Shakespeare." *Pixel: Journal of Scientific Visualization* 3.3 (March/April 1992): 12–19.

———. Personal website. http://www.lillian.com.

Scott, Walter. *Kenilworth: A Romance.* Edited by J. H. Alexander. 1821; repr. Harmondsworth: Penguin, 1999.

Screen Online. http://www.screenonline.org.uk.

The Secret History of the Duke of Alancon and Queen Elizabeth. London,1691.

The Secret History of the Most Renowned Q. Elizabeth, and the E. of Essex. English trans. of *Le Comte d'Essex. Histoire Angloise* (1678). Cologne [London], 1680.

Shakespeare Fellowship. http://www.shakespearefellowship.org.

Shakespeare in Love. Directed by John Madden. Written by Marc Norman and Tom Stoppard. Starring Gwyneth Paltrow and Joseph Fiennes. Miramax Film, 1998. Universal Studios VHS, 1999.

Shakespeare Oxford Society. http://www.shakespeare-oxford.com.

Shakespeare, William. *A Midsummer Night's Dream.* Directed by Tim Supple. Dash Arts Theatre Co., 2006.

Shapiro, James. *1599: A Year in the Life of William Shakespeare.* London: Faber, 2005.

Shaw, George Bernard. Preface to *Three Plays for Puritans,* edited by Dan H. Laurence, introduced by Michael Billington, 7–39. 1901; repr. London: Penguin, 2000.

———. "The Dark Lady of the Sonnets" (1910). In *Misalliance, The Dark Lady of the Sonnets, and Fanny's First Play.* London: Constable, 1914.

Shaw, Harry E. *The Forms of Historical Fiction: Sir Walter Scott and His Successors.* Ithaca and London: Cornell University Press, 1983.

Silent Shakespeare. British Film Institute. http://www.bfi.org.uk/booksvideo/video/details/shakespeare/more.html.

Silverblatt, Michael. "*Will in the World*: An Interview with Stephen Greenblatt." W. W. Norton & Co. http://www.wwnorton.com/rgguides/willintheinterview.htm (accessed June 18, 2008).

Singh, Jyotsna G. *Colonial Narratives / Cultural Dialogues: "Discoveries" of India in the Language of Colonialism.* London and New York: Routledge, 1996.

Smiley, Jane. Weblog, Jan. 4, 2006. http://www.huffingtonpost.com/jane-smiley/try-this_b_13289.html.

Somerset, Charles A. *Shakspeare's Early Days: An Historical Play.* London, 1829.

Sorrowes Joy. Or, a Lamentation for our late deceased Soveraigne Elizabeth, with a triumph for the prosperous succession of our gratious king, James. Cambridge, 1603.

Spenser, Edmund. *Poetical Works.* Edited by J. C. Smith and E. de Selincourt. 1912; repr. Oxford: Oxford University Press, 1970.

[Stafford, William.] Attrib. William Shakespeare. *A Compendious or Briefe Examination of Certayne Ordinary Complaints of Divers of our Countrymen in These our Days.* 1581; repr. London, 1751.

———. *W. Stafford's Compendious or Briefe Examination of Certayne Ordinary Complaints.* Introduced by Frederic D. Matthew. Edited by Frederick J. Furnivall. 1581; repr. London, 1876.

Stallybrass, Peter, and Allon White. *The Politics and Poetics of Transgression.* London: Methuen, 1986.

Steedman, Carolyn. "True Romances." In *Patriotism: The Making and Unmaking of British National Identity,* edited by Raphael Samuel, vol. 1, *History and Politics,* 26–35. London and New York: Routledge, 1989.

Sterling, Sara Hawks. *Shake-speare's Sweetheart.* Philadelphia: George W. Jacobs, 1905.

Strachey, Lytton. *Elizabeth and Essex: A Tragic History.* 1928; repr. Oxford: Oxford University Press, 1981.

Stratford Festival Canada Programme 1976. Stratford, Ont.: Stratford Shakespearean Festival Foundation of Canada, 1976.

Stratford Festival Canada Programme 1977. Stratford, Ont.: Stratford Shakespearean Festival Foundation of Canada, 1977.

Stratford Festival of Canada. "Our History." http://www.stratfordfestival.ca/about/history.cfm.

Stratford, Ontario. "Know Your City—History." *Our City Life in Stratford, Ontario, Canada.* http://www.city.stratford.on.ca/site_ourcitylife/know_your_city_history.asp.

Strong, Roy. *Portraits of Queen Elizabeth I.* Oxford: Clarendon, 1963.

———. *The Cult of Elizabeth: Elizabethan Portraiture and Pageantry.* London: Thames and Hudson, 1977.

———. *And When Did You Last See Your Father? The Victorian Painter and British History.* London: Thames and Hudson, 1978.

———. *Painting the Past: The Victorian Painter and British History.* London: Pimlico, 2004.

Sturgess, Kim C. *Shakespeare and the American Nation.* Cambridge: Cambridge University Press, 2004.

Sutherland, John. *The Life of Sir Walter Scott: A Critical Biography.* Oxford: Blackwell, 1995.

Sweet, George Elliott. *Shake-speare: The Mystery.* Stanford: Stanford University Press, 1956.

Symmons, Charles. "The Life of W. Shakspeare." In *The Complete Works of William Shakspeare,* i–xvi. Leipzig, 1837.

Syse, Glenna. "The Bard Resides in Stratford, Ontario." *Chicago Sun-Times,* June 9, 1977.

Taylor, Gary. *Reinventing Shakespeare: A Cultural History from the Restoration to the Present.* London: Hogarth, 1989.

———. "Afterword: The Incredible Shrinking Bard." In *Shakespeare and Appropriation,* edited by Christy Desmet and Robert Sawyer, 197–205. London and New York: Routledge, 1999.

Teague, Frances. *Shakespeare and the American Popular Stage.* Cambridge: Cambridge University Press, 2006.

Tennenhouse, Leonard. *Power on Display: The Politics of Shakespeare's Genres.* New York and London: Methuen, 1986.

———. "Violence Done to Women on the Renaissance Stage." In *The Violence of Representation: Literature and the History of Violence,* edited by Nancy Armstrong and Leonard Tennenhouse, 77–97. London: Routledge, 1989.

Thorpe, Vanessa. "Shakespeare Was a Political Rebel Who Wrote in Code, Claims Author." *Observer* (London), Aug. 28, 2005. http://observer.guardian.co.uk/uk_news/story/0,6903,1557964,00.html.

Tieck, Ludwig. Commentary on *Der Sommernachtstraum.* In *Shakspeare's Dramatische Werke,* translated by August Wilhelm von Schlegel, with commentary and notes by Ludwig Tieck, 3:352–55. Berlin, 1830.

Tillyard, E.M.W. *The Elizabethan World Picture.* London: Chatto and Windus, 1943.

———. *Shakespeare's History Plays.* London: Chatto and Windus, 1944.

"Timothy Findley 1930–2002." Obituary. *CBC News.* http://www.cbc.ca/news/obit/findley/ (accessed June 18, 2008).

Trivedi, Poonam, and Dennis Bartholomeusz, eds. *India's Shakespeare: Translation, Interpretation, and Performance.* Newark: University of Delaware Press, 2005.

Turtledove, Harry. *Ruled Britannia.* New York: NAL, 2002.

Twain, Mark. *"1601," and "Is Shakespeare Dead?"* Edited by Shelley Fisher Fishkin. New York and Oxford: Oxford University Press, 1996.

Underwood, Richard Allan. *Shakespeare's "The Phoenix and Turtle": A Survey of Scholarship.* Salzburg: Universität Salzburg, 1974.

Vahimagi, Tise. *British Television: An Illustrated Guide.* 2nd ed. Oxford: Oxford University Press, 1996.

Vaughan, Alden T. "Shakespeare Discovers America: America Discovers Shakespeare." In *Shakespeare in American Life,* edited by Virginia Mason Vaughan and Alden T. Vaughan, 11–21. Washington, D.C.: Folger Shakespeare Library, 2007.

Vaughan, Virginia Mason. "Shakespeare's Dissemeninination in Nineteenth-Century America." In *Shakespeare in American Life,* edited by Virginia Mason Vaughan and Alden T. Vaughan, 23–33. Washington, D.C.: Folger Shakespeare Library, 2007.

Vaughan, Virginia Mason, and Alden T. Vaughan, eds. *Shakespeare in American Life.* Washington, D.C.: Folger Shakespeare Library, 2007.

The Virgin Queen. Directed by Coky Giedroyc. Written by Paula Milne. Starring Anne-Marie Duff. BBC TV, 2006.

[Waldron, Francis Godolphin] *Free Reflections on Miscellaneous Papers and Legal Instruments Under the Hand and Seal of William Shakespeare, in the Possession of Samuel Ireland.* London, 1796.

———. *The Virgin Queen, A Drama in Five Acts; Attempted as a Sequel to Shakespeare's Tempest.* London, 1797.

Walker, Julia M. *The Elizabeth Icon: 1603–2003.* Basingstoke: Palgrave Macmillan, 2003.

Warren, Roger. *Text and Performance: "A Midsummer Night's Dream."* Basingstoke: Macmillan, 1983.

Watkins, John. *Representing Elizabeth in Stuart England: Literature, History, Sovereignty.* Cambridge: Cambridge University Press, 2002.

Watson, Nicola J. "Kemble, Scott, and the Mantle of the Bard." In *The Appropriation of Shakespeare: Post-Renaissance Reconstructions of the Works and the Myth,* edited by Jean I. Marsden, 73–92. Hemel Hempstead: Harvester Wheatsheaf, 1991.

Weir, Alison. *Elizabeth the Queen.* London: Jonathan Cape, 1998.

Wells, Stanley. "*A Midsummer Night's Dream* Revisited." *Critical Survey* 3.1 (1991): 14–29.

White, Richard Grant. "An Essay toward the Expression of Shakespeare's Genius." In *The Works of William Shakespeare,* edited by Richard Grant White, 1:clxxxix–cclii. Boston, 1865.

———. *Shakespeare's Scholar.* New York, 1854.

———. *Memoirs of the Life of William Shakespeare.* Boston, 1865.

Wiles, David. *Shakespeare's Almanac: A Midsummer Night's Dream, Marriage and the Elizabethan Calendar.* Cambridge: D. S. Brewer, 1993.

Will Shakespeare. Written by John Mortimer. Directed by Peter Wood, Mark Cullingham, and Robert Knights. Starring Tim Curry. Associated Television, first broadcast June, 13 1978–July 18, 1978.

Willans, Geoffrey, and Ronald Searle. "How to Be a Young Elizabethan." In *Whizz for Atoms* (1956), repr. in *Molesworth,* by Geoffrey Willans and Ronald Searle, 214–28. London: Penguin, 1999.

Williams, Gary Jay. *Our Moonlight Revels: "A Midsummer Night's Dream" in the Theatre.* Iowa City: University of Iowa Press, 1997.

Williams, Penry. "Court and Polity under Elizabeth I." *Bulletin of the John Rylands Library of Manchester* 65.2 (Spring 1983): 259–86.

Williams, Robert Folkestone. *Shakspeare and His Friends.* 3 vols. London, 1838.

———. *The Youth of Shakspeare.* Paris, 1839.

———. *The Secret Passion.* 3 vols. London, 1844.

Wilson, Elkin Calhoun. *England's Eliza.* Harvard Studies in English, vol. 20. 1939; New York: Octagon, 1966.

Wilson, John Dover. "The Political Background of Shakespeare's *Richard II* and *Henry IV.*" *Shakespeare Jahrbuch* 75 (1939): 36–51.

Wilson, Richard. *Secret Shakespeare: Studies in Theatre, Religion and Resistance.* Manchester: Manchester University Press, 2004.

———. "Shakespeare in Hate: Performing the Virgin Queen." *Poetica* 36 (2004): 149–67.

"Women's Warrior Maggie." *Daily Mail,* Oct. 2, 1990, 2.

Womersley, David. "The *Da Vinci Code* of Shakespeare Scholarship." *Social Affairs Unit,* Dec. 5, 2005. http://www.socialaffairsunit.org.uk/blog/archives/000685.php.

Wood, Michael. *In Search of Shakespeare.* London: BBC Worldwide, 2003.

Woolf, Virginia. *A Room of One's Own.* 1929; repr. London: Granada, 1977.

———. *Between the Acts.* Edited by Stella McNichol. Introduction and notes by Gillian Beer. 1941; London: Penguin, 1992.

Worden, Blair. "Which Play Was Performed at the Globe Theatre on 7 February 1601?" *London Review of Books* 25.13 (July 10, 2003): 22–24.

Woudhuysen, H. R. "The Queen's Own Hand: A Preliminary Account." In *Elizabeth I and the Culture of Writing,* edited by Peter Beal and Grace Ioppolo, 1–27. London: British Library, 2007.

Ziegler, Georgianna. "Re-imagining a Renaissance Queen: Catherine of Aragon among the Victorians." In *"High and Mighty Queens" of Early Modern England: Realities and Representations,* edited by Carole Levin, Jo Elldridge Carney, and Debra Barrett-Graves, 203–22. New York and Basingstoke: Palgrave Macmillan, 2003.

———. "Duty and Enjoyment: The Folgers as Shakespeare Collectors in the Gilded Age." In *Shakespeare in American Life,* edited by Virginia Mason Vaughan and Alden T. Vaughan, 100–111. Washington, D.C.: Folger Shakespeare Library, 2007.

———, ed. *Elizabeth I Then and Now.* Washington D.C.: Folger Shakespeare Library, 2003.

INDEX